DO YOU KNOW HOW TO BREAK A WITCH'S CURSE?

METHOD 1:
A LOVING KISS FROM A PRINCE ON A WHITE HORSE.

NEVER MET ONE.

METHOD 2:
HOPE THE WRATHFUL WITCH HAS A CHANGE OF HEART.

I'M IN THIS MESS 'CAUSE I CAN'T FIND THAT BITCH!

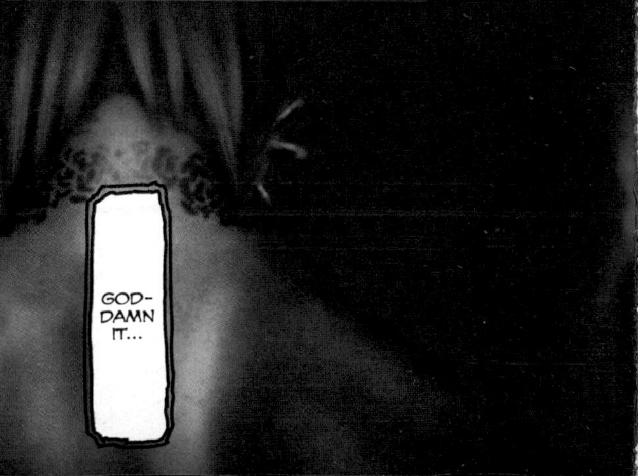
GOD-DAMN IT...

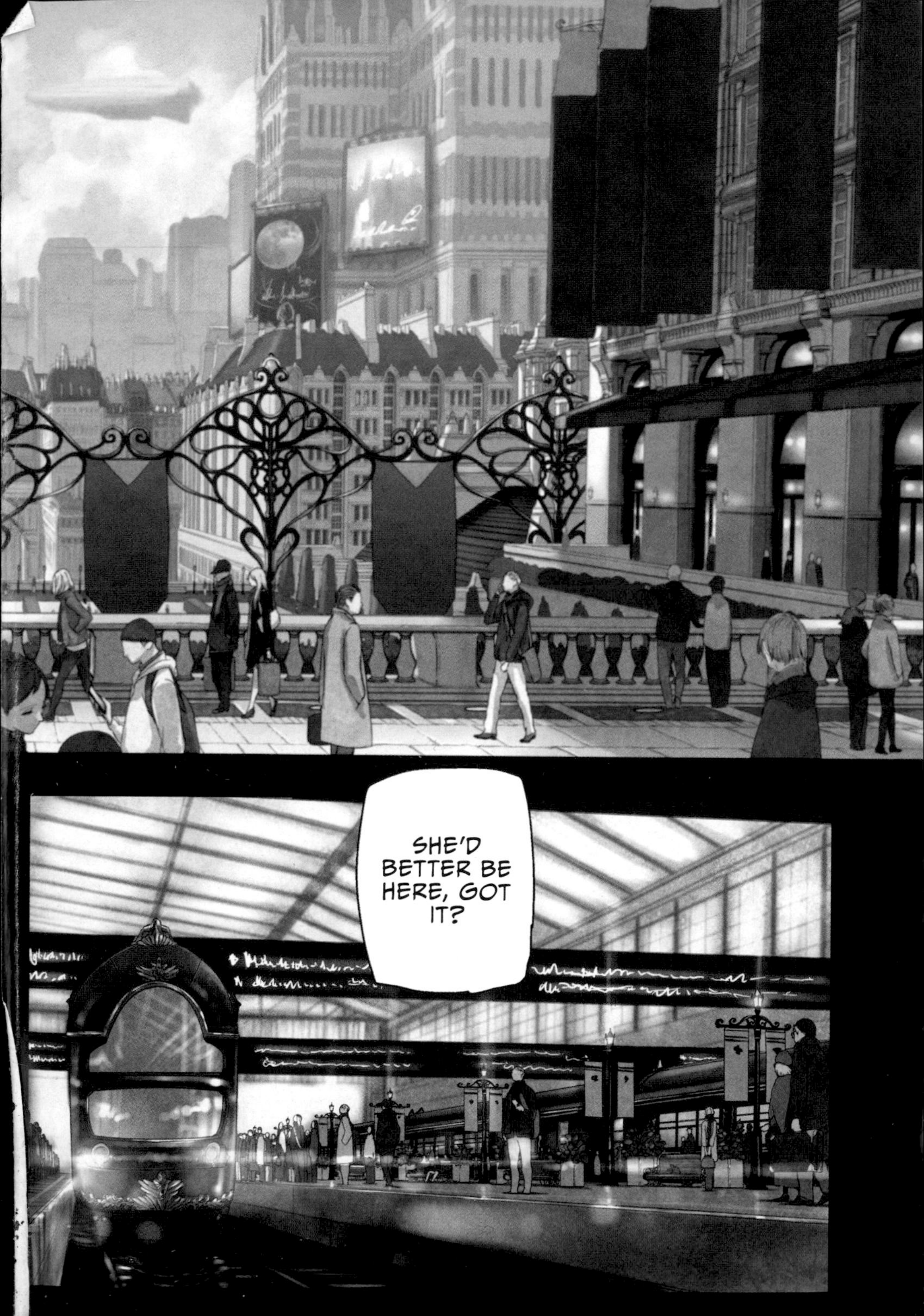
SHE'D BETTER BE HERE, GOT IT?

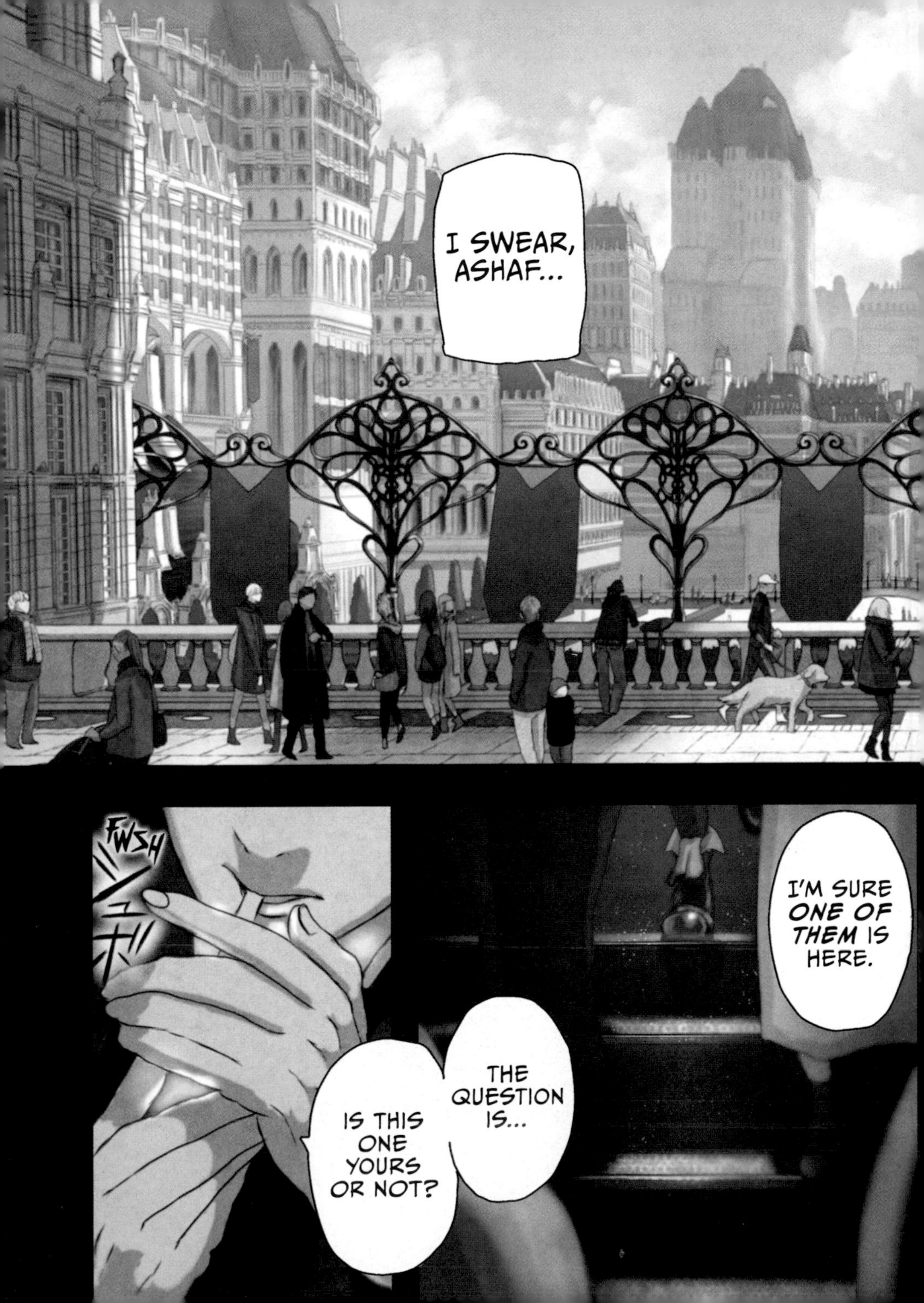
I SWEAR, ASHAF...
I'M SURE *ONE OF THEM* IS HERE.
THE QUESTION IS...
IS THIS ONE YOURS OR NOT?
FWSH

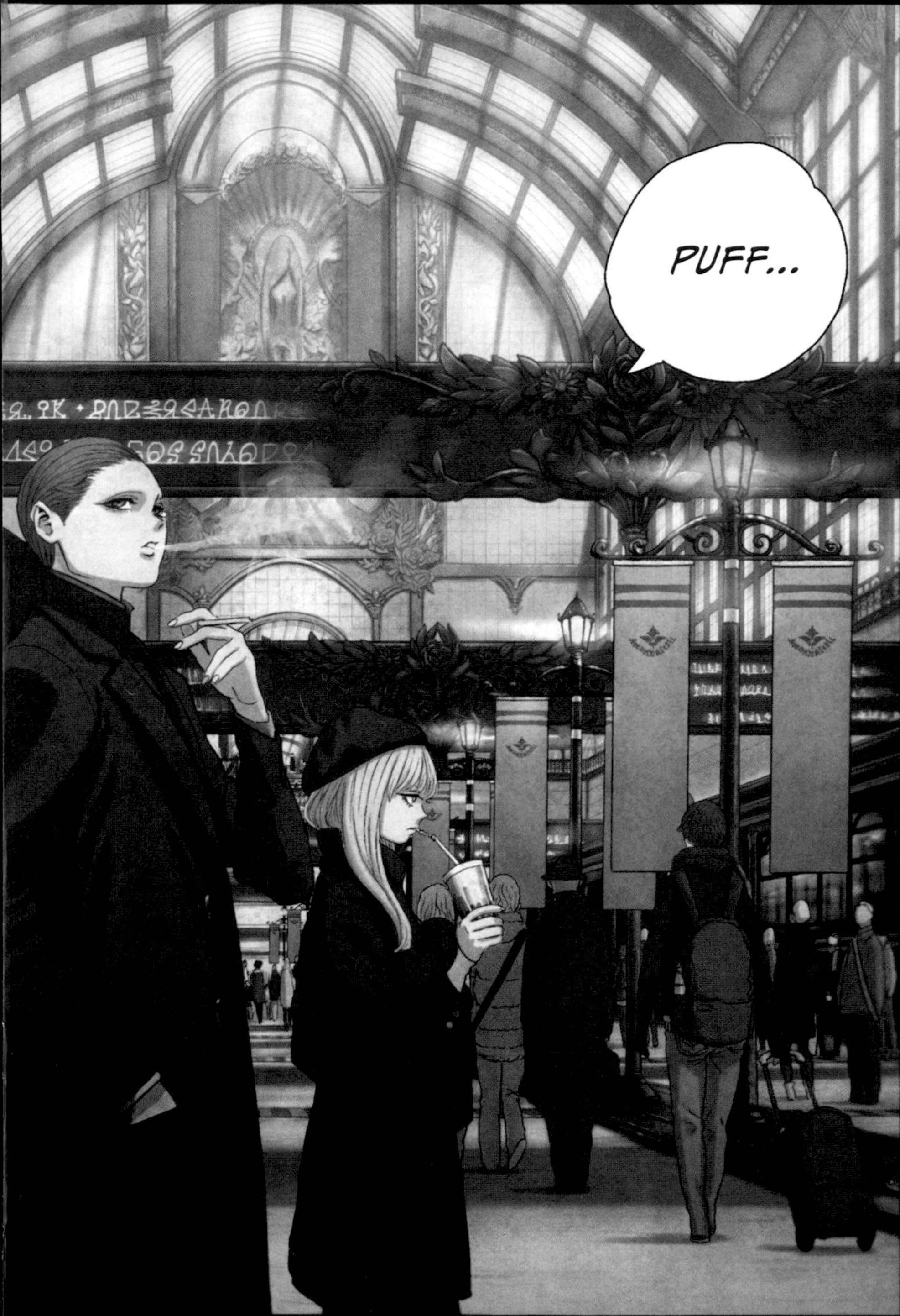
PUFF...

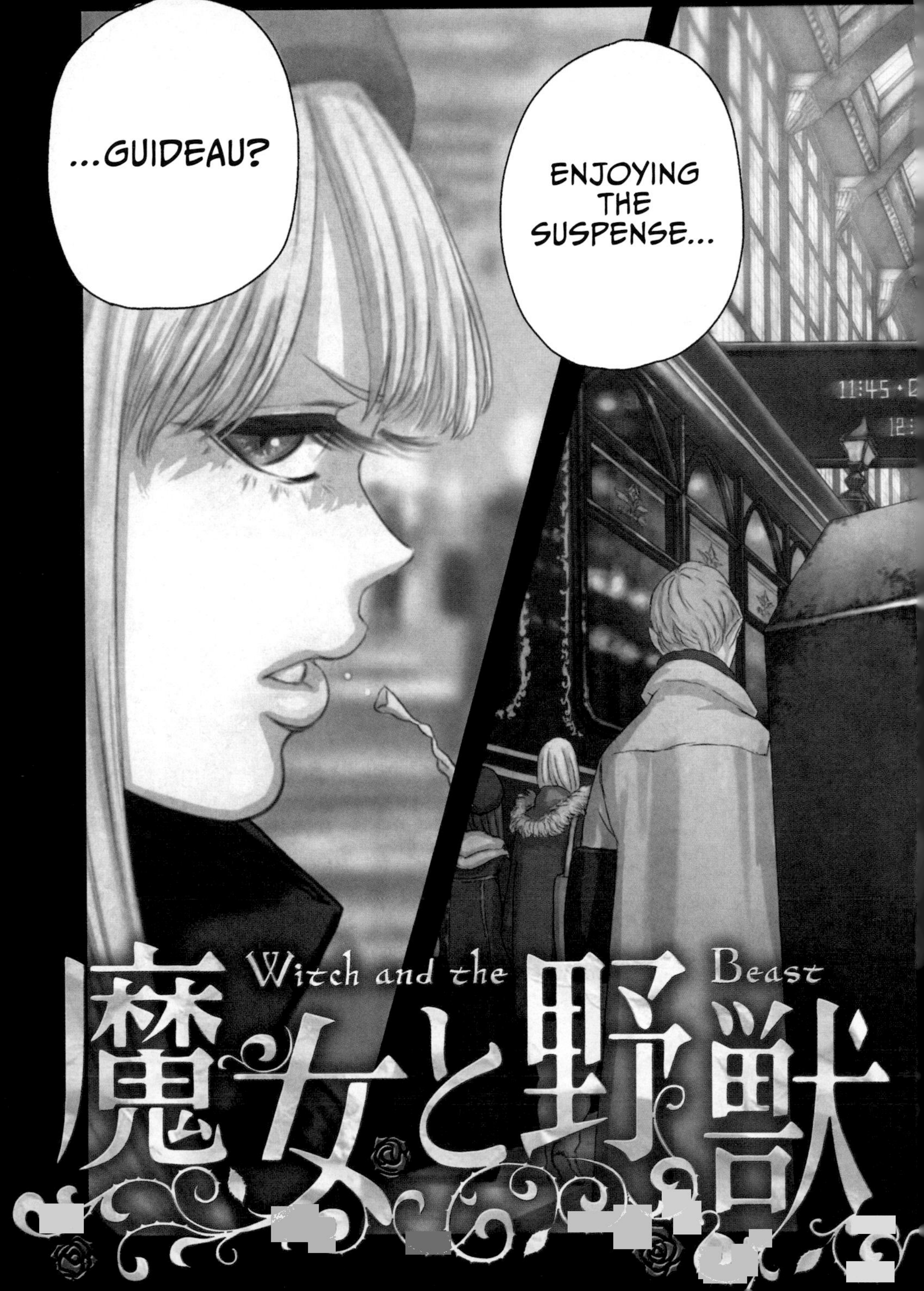
ENJOYING THE SUSPENSE...
...GUIDEAU?
11:45
Witch and the Beast
魔女と野獣

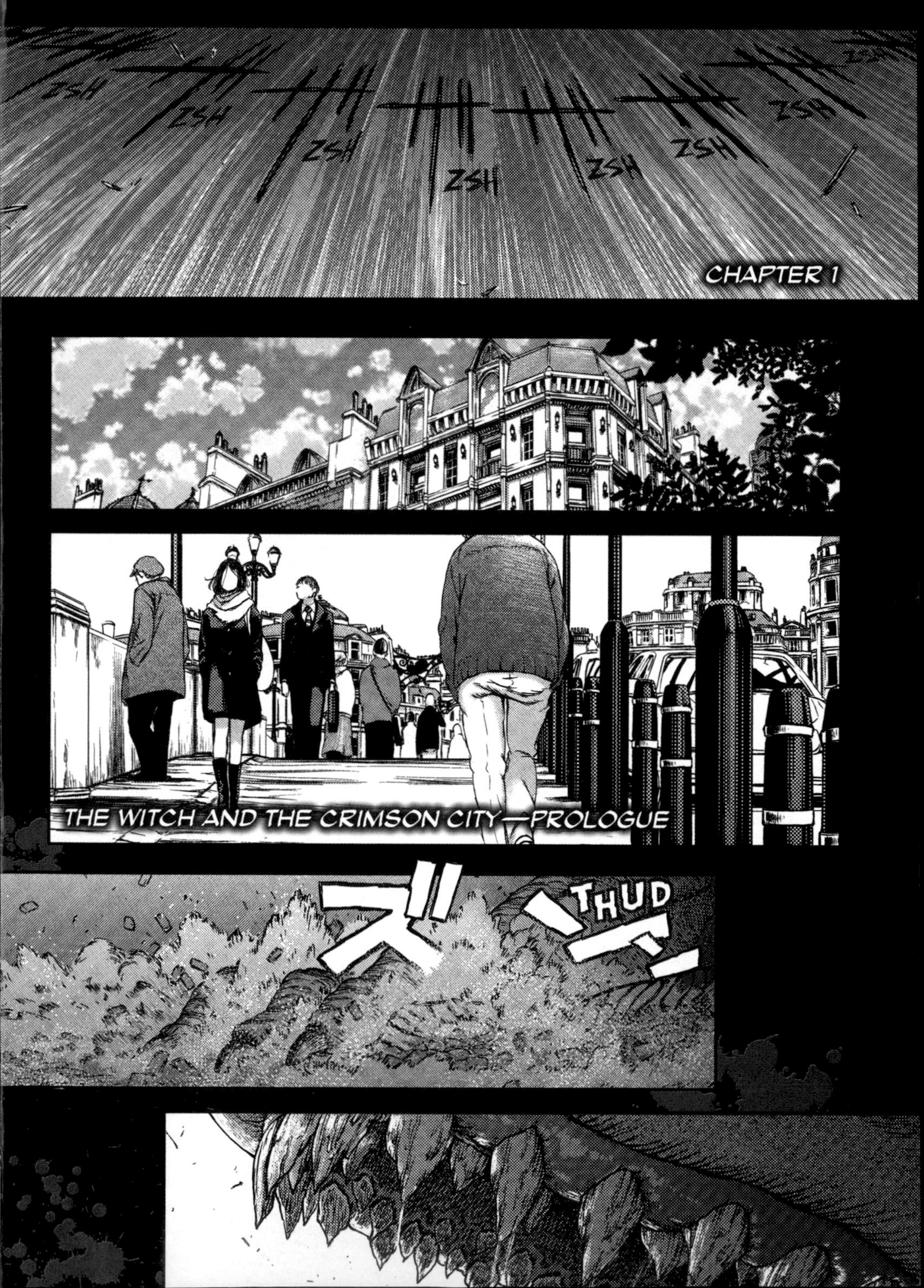
ZSH
ZSH
ZSH
ZSH
ZSH
ZSH
ZSH
ZSH
CHAPTER 1
THE WITCH AND THE CRIMSON CITY—PROLOGUE
THUD

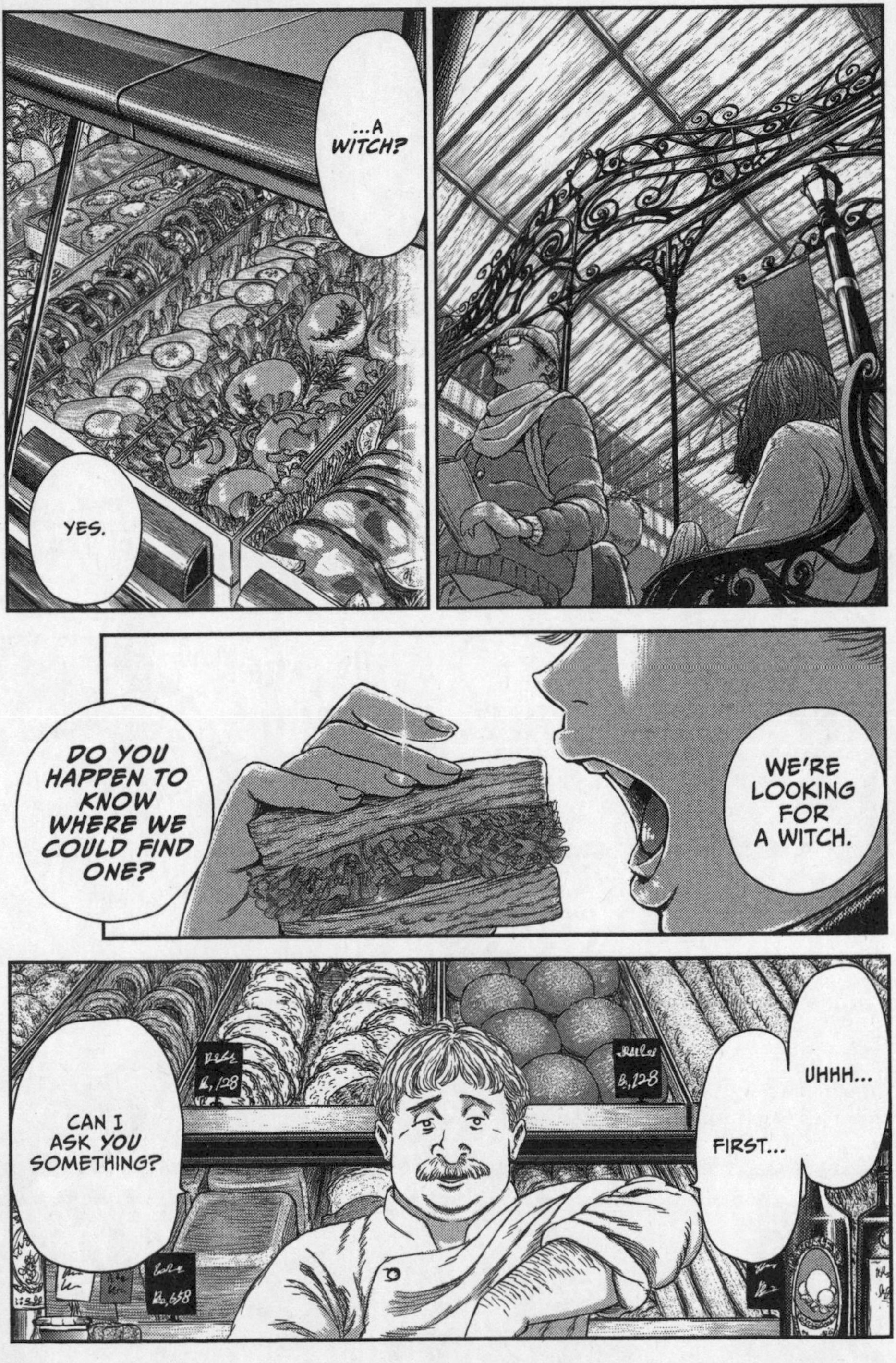
...A WITCH?
YES.
WE'RE LOOKING FOR A WITCH.
DO YOU HAPPEN TO KNOW WHERE WE COULD FIND ONE?
UHHH...
FIRST...
CAN I ASK YOU SOMETHING?

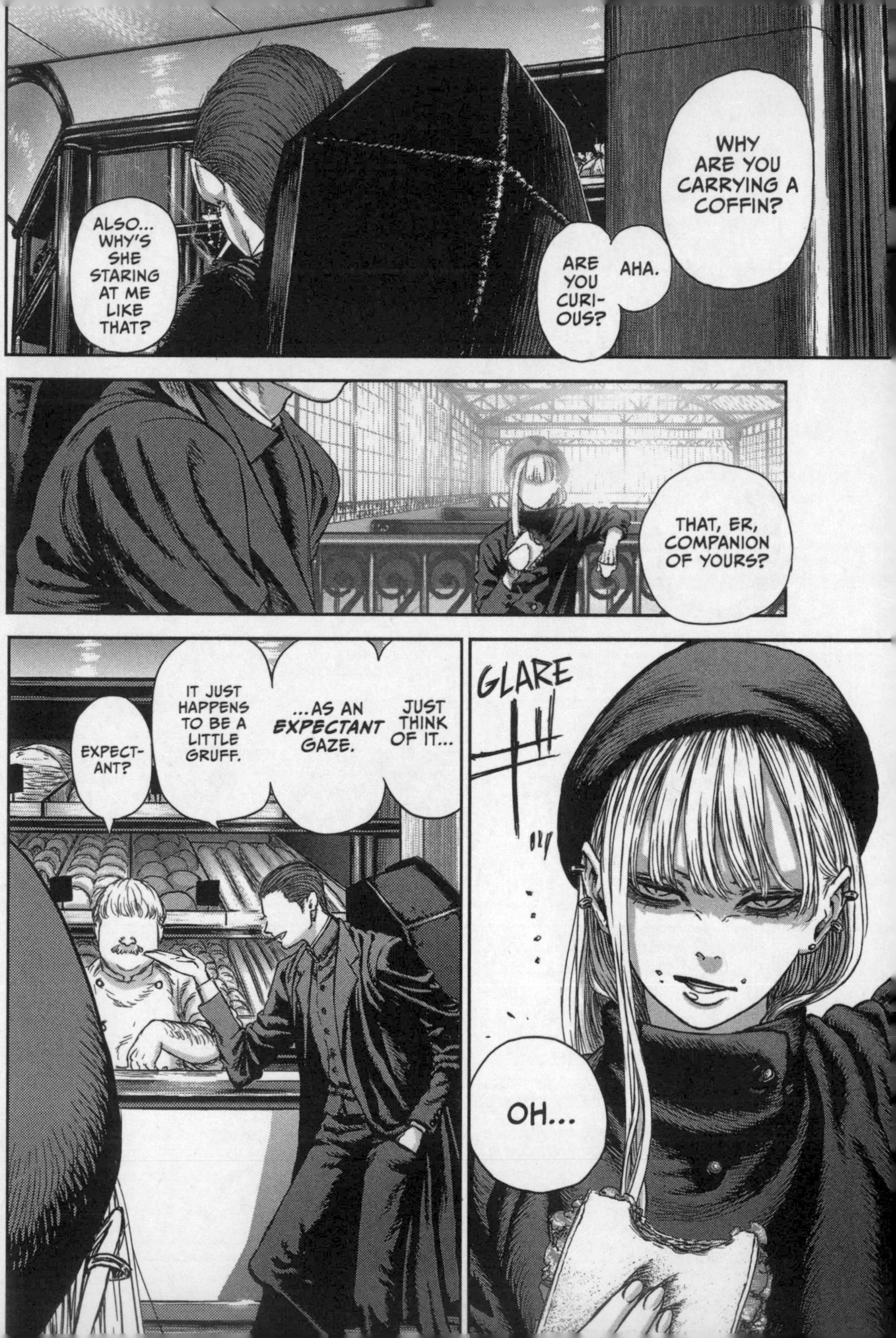
WHY ARE YOU CARRYING A COFFIN?
AHA.
ARE YOU CURI-OUS?
ALSO... WHY'S SHE STARING AT ME LIKE THAT?
THAT, ER, COMPANION OF YOURS?
GLARE
OH...
JUST THINK OF IT...
...AS AN *EXPECTANT* GAZE.
IT JUST HAPPENS TO BE A LITTLE GRUFF.
EXPECT-ANT?

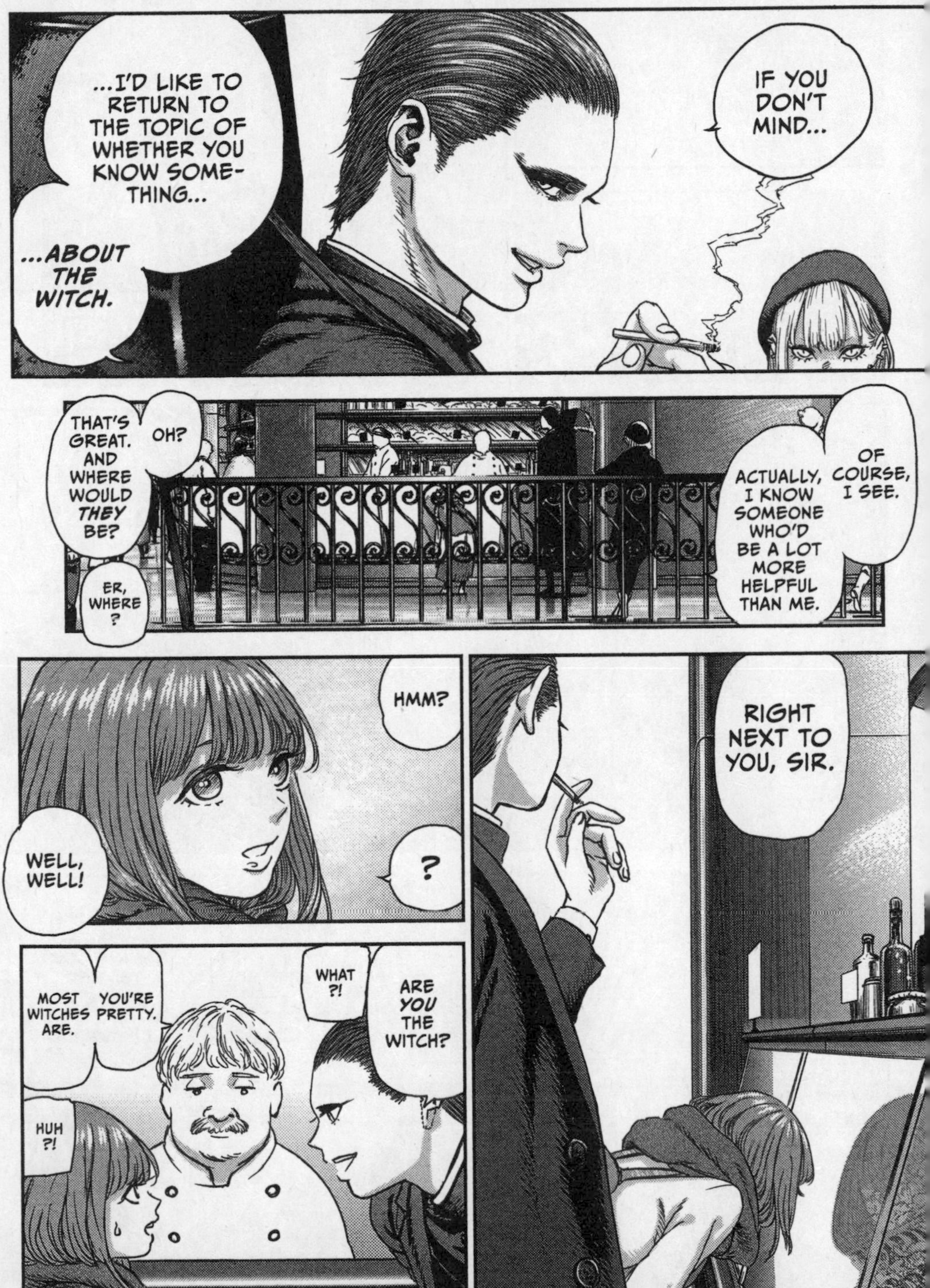
IF YOU DON'T MIND...
...I'D LIKE TO RETURN TO THE TOPIC OF WHETHER YOU KNOW SOME-THING...
...*ABOUT THE WITCH.*
OF COURSE, I SEE.
ACTUALLY, I KNOW SOMEONE WHO'D BE A LOT MORE HELPFUL THAN ME.
OH?
THAT'S GREAT. AND WHERE WOULD *THEY* BE?
ER, WHERE?
RIGHT NEXT TO YOU, SIR.
HMM?
?
WELL, WELL!
ARE *YOU* THE WITCH?
WHAT?!
YOU'RE PRETTY.
MOST WITCHES ARE.
HUH?!

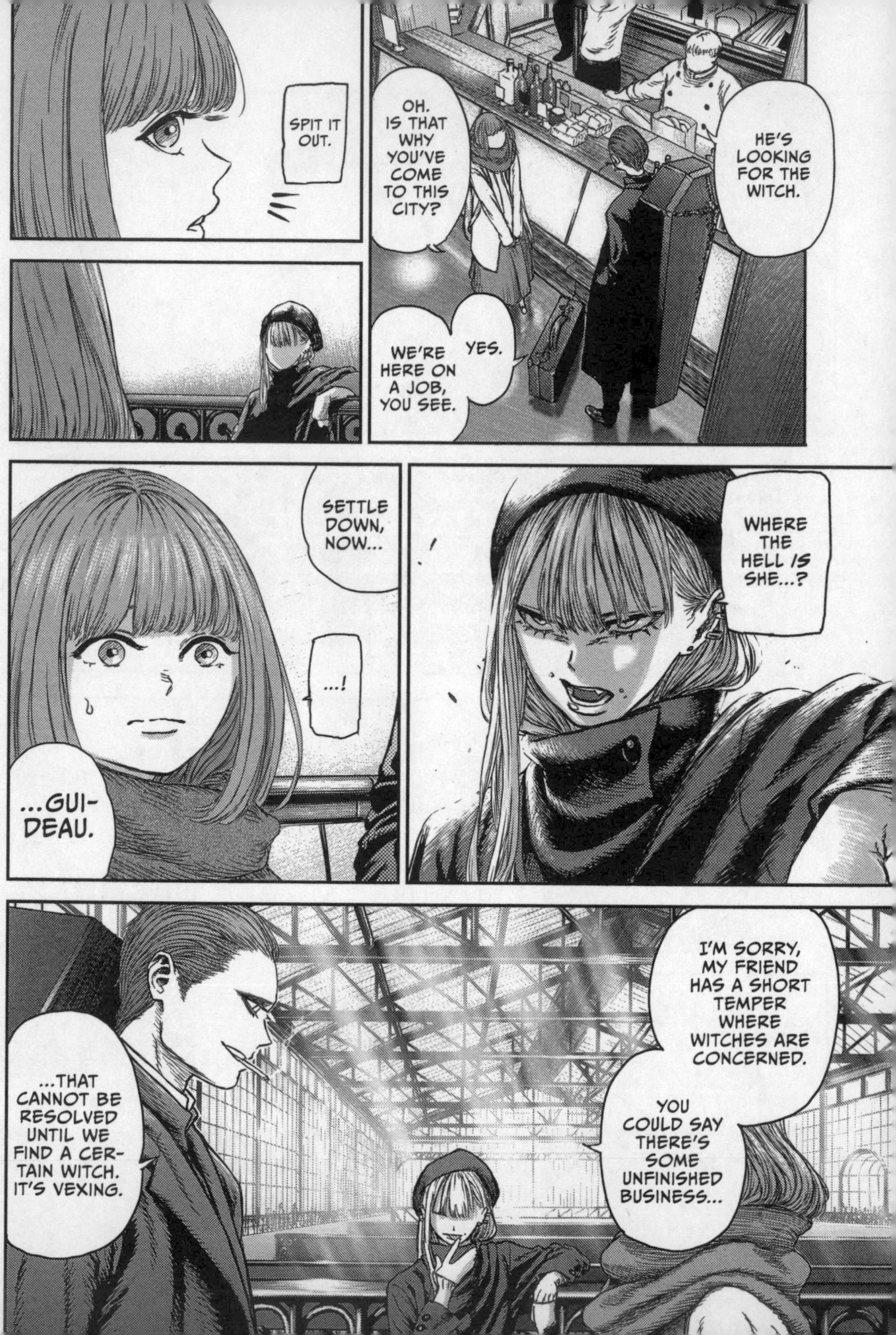
HE'S LOOKING FOR THE WITCH.
OH. IS THAT WHY YOU'VE COME TO THIS CITY?
YES.
WE'RE HERE ON A JOB, YOU SEE.
SPIT IT OUT.
WHERE THE HELL *IS* SHE...?
SETTLE DOWN, NOW...
...!
...GUI-DEAU.
I'M SORRY, MY FRIEND HAS A SHORT TEMPER WHERE WITCHES ARE CONCERNED.
YOU COULD SAY THERE'S SOME UNFINISHED BUSINESS...
...THAT CANNOT BE RESOLVED UNTIL WE FIND A CER-TAIN WITCH. IT'S VEXING.

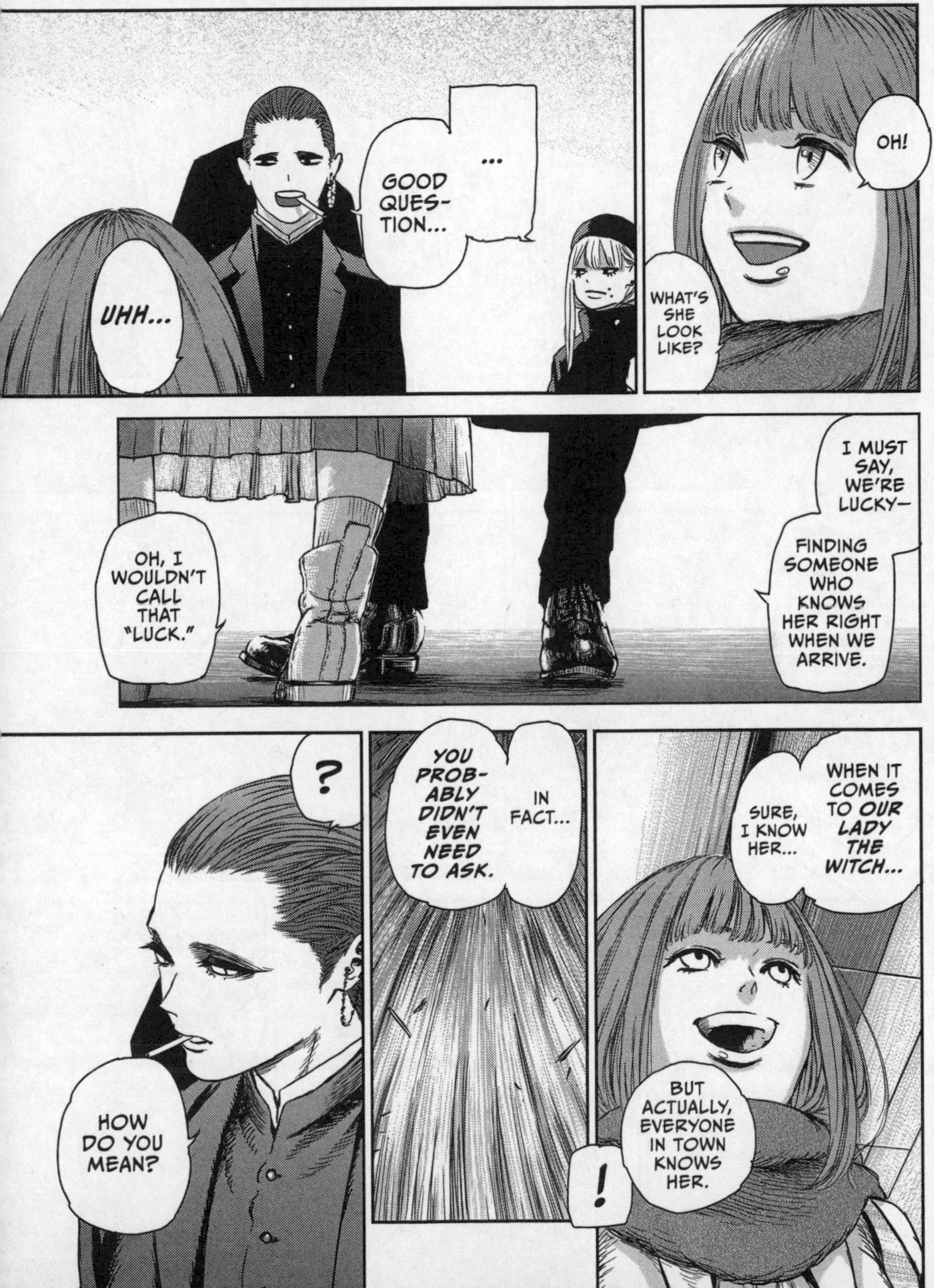
OH!
WHAT'S SHE LOOK LIKE?
... GOOD QUESTION...
UHH...
I MUST SAY, WE'RE LUCKY—
FINDING SOMEONE WHO KNOWS HER RIGHT WHEN WE ARRIVE.
OH, I WOULDN'T CALL THAT "LUCK."
WHEN IT COMES TO OUR LADY THE WITCH...
SURE, I KNOW HER...
BUT ACTUALLY, EVERYONE IN TOWN KNOWS HER.
!
IN FACT...
YOU PROBABLY DIDN'T EVEN NEED TO ASK.
?
HOW DO YOU MEAN?

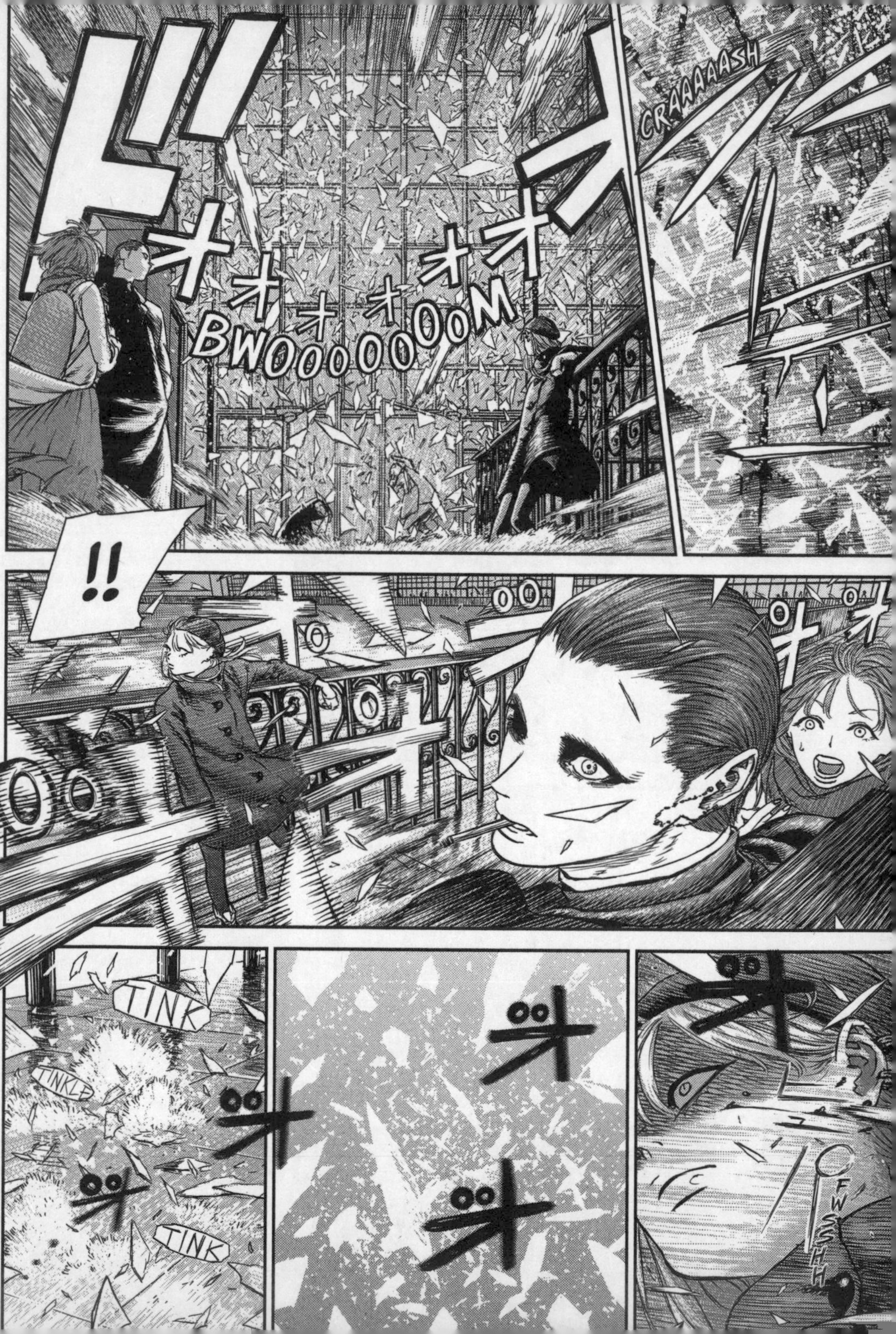
CRAAAAASH
BWOOOOOOOOM
!!
FWSSHH
TINK
TINKLE
TINK

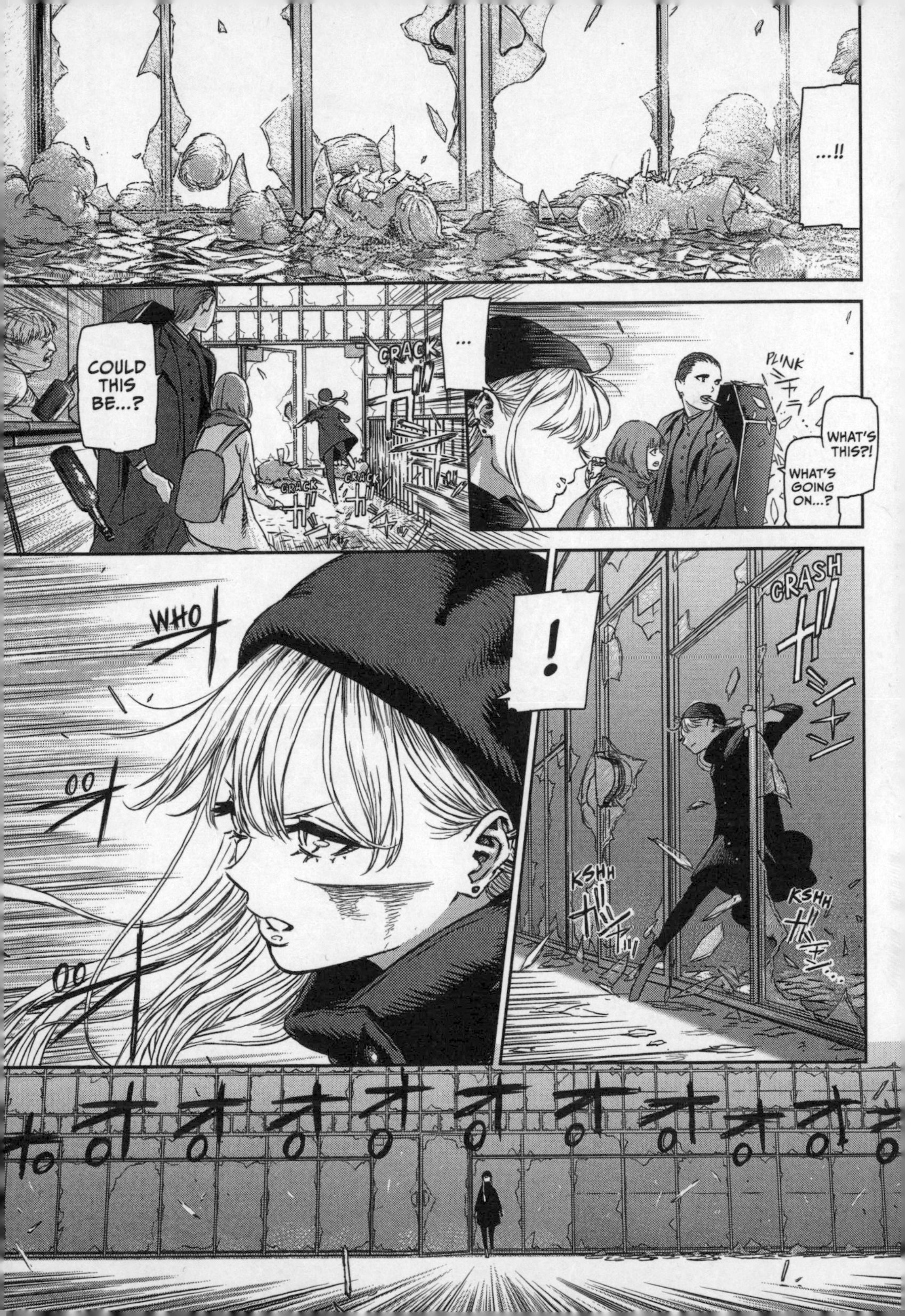
...!!
...
PLINK
WHAT'S THIS?!
WHAT'S GOING ON...?
CRACK
CRACK
CRACK
COULD THIS BE...?
CRASH
KSHH
KSHH
!
WHO
OO
OO

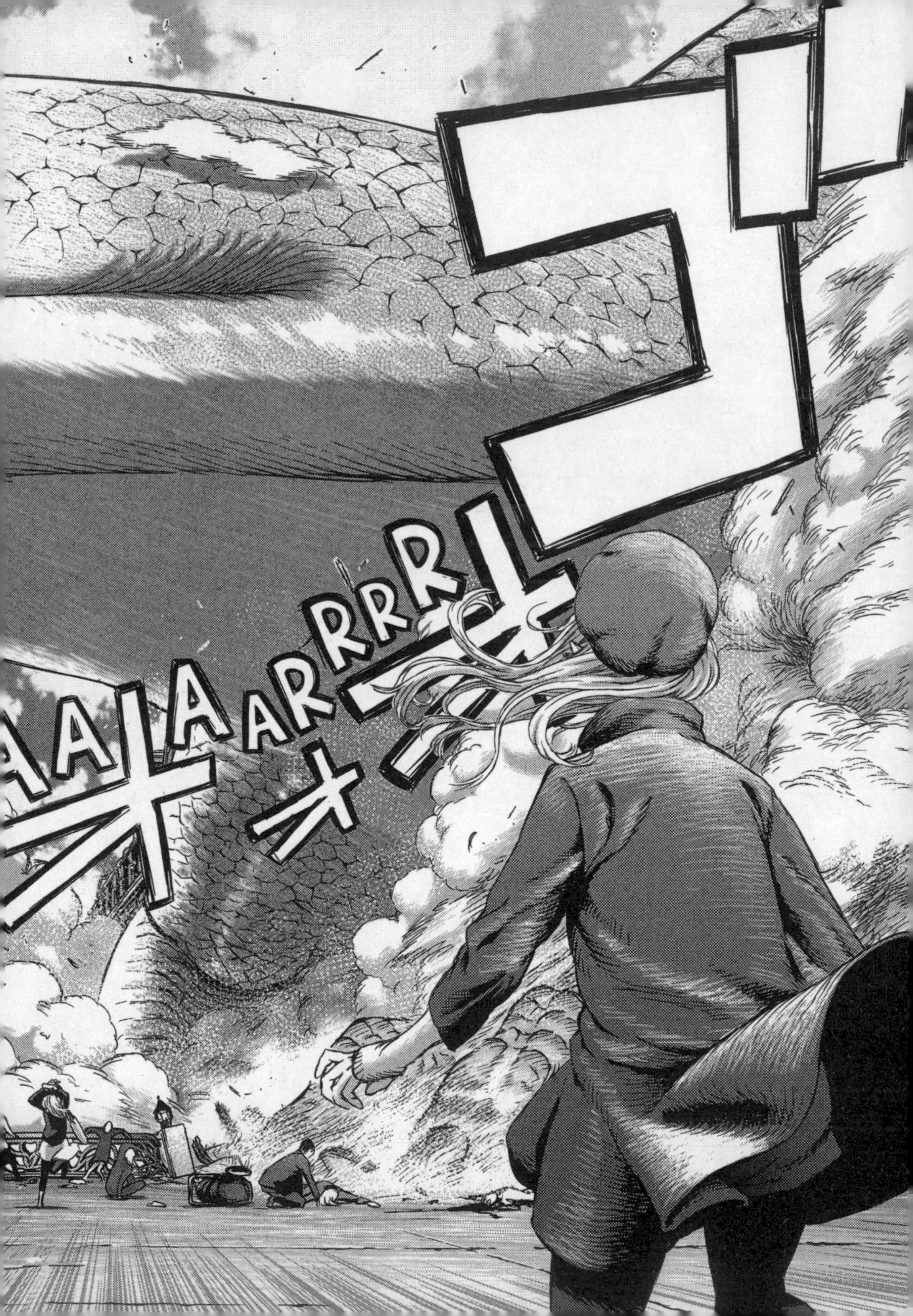
AAAARRRR

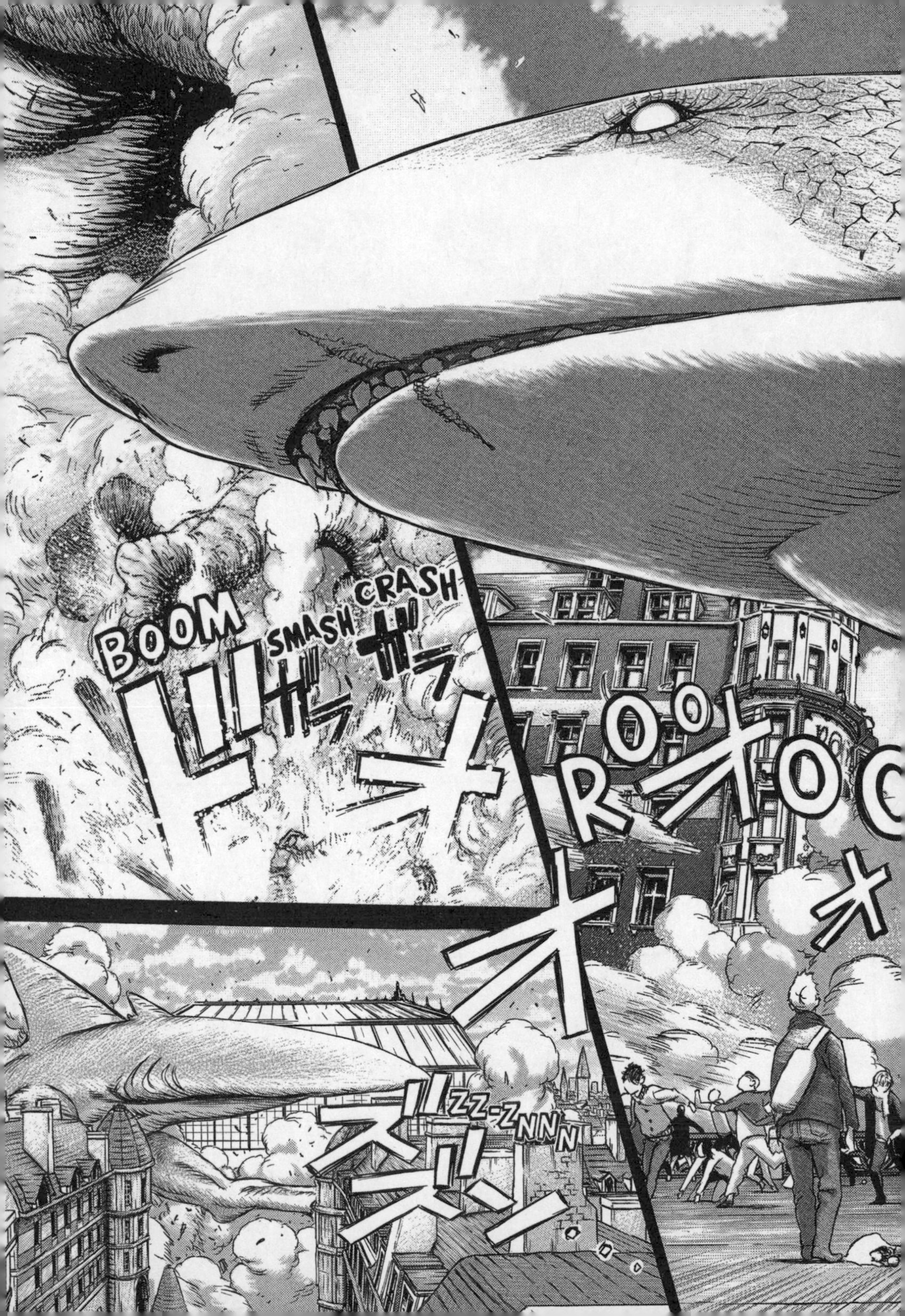
ROOOO
BOOM
SMASH
CRASH
ZZZ-ZNNNN

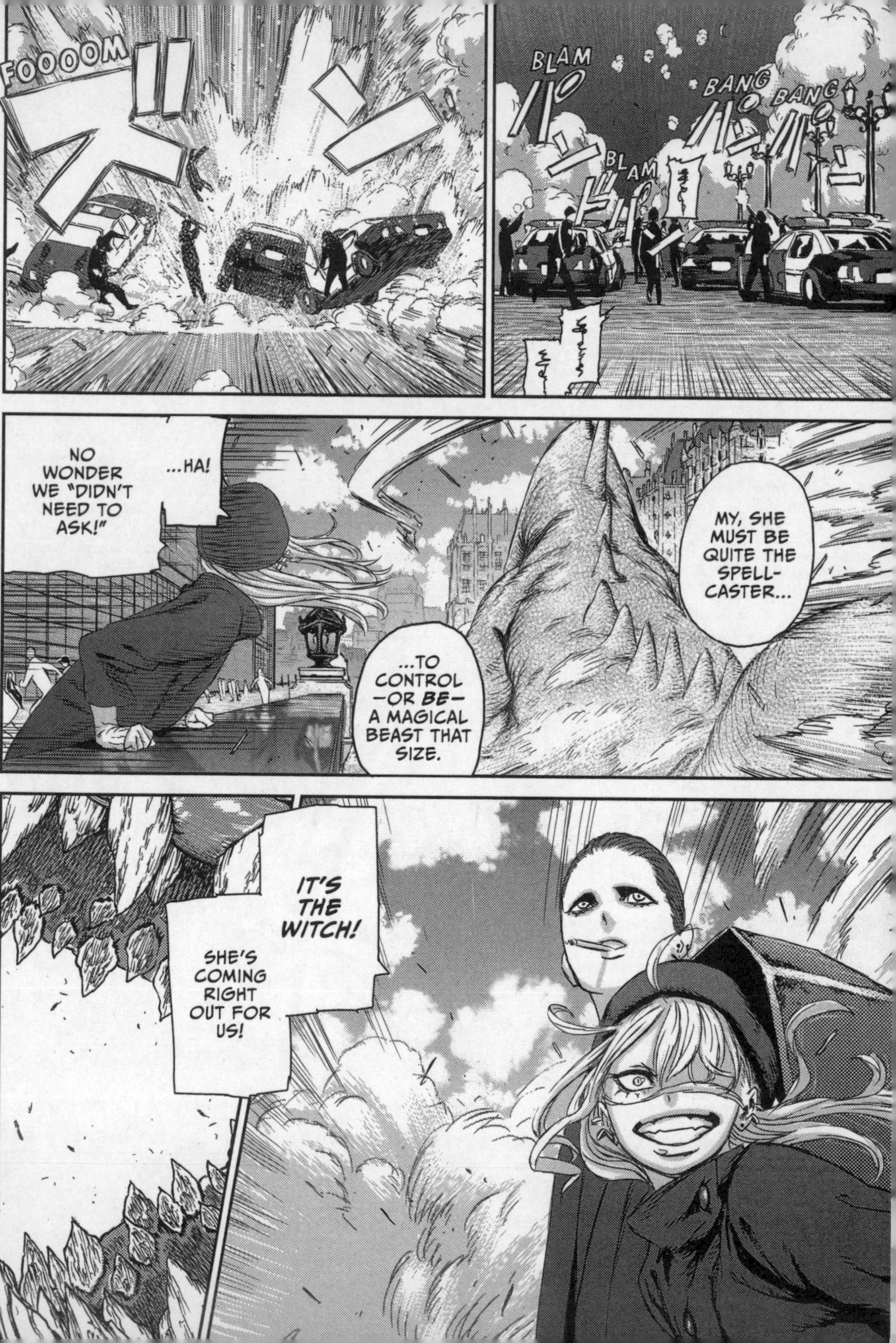
BANG
BANG
BLAM
BLAM
FOOOOM
MY, SHE MUST BE QUITE THE SPELL-CASTER...
...TO CONTROL —OR *BE*— A MAGICAL BEAST THAT SIZE.
...HA!
NO WONDER WE "DIDN'T NEED TO ASK!"
IT'S THE WITCH!
SHE'S COMING RIGHT OUT FOR US!

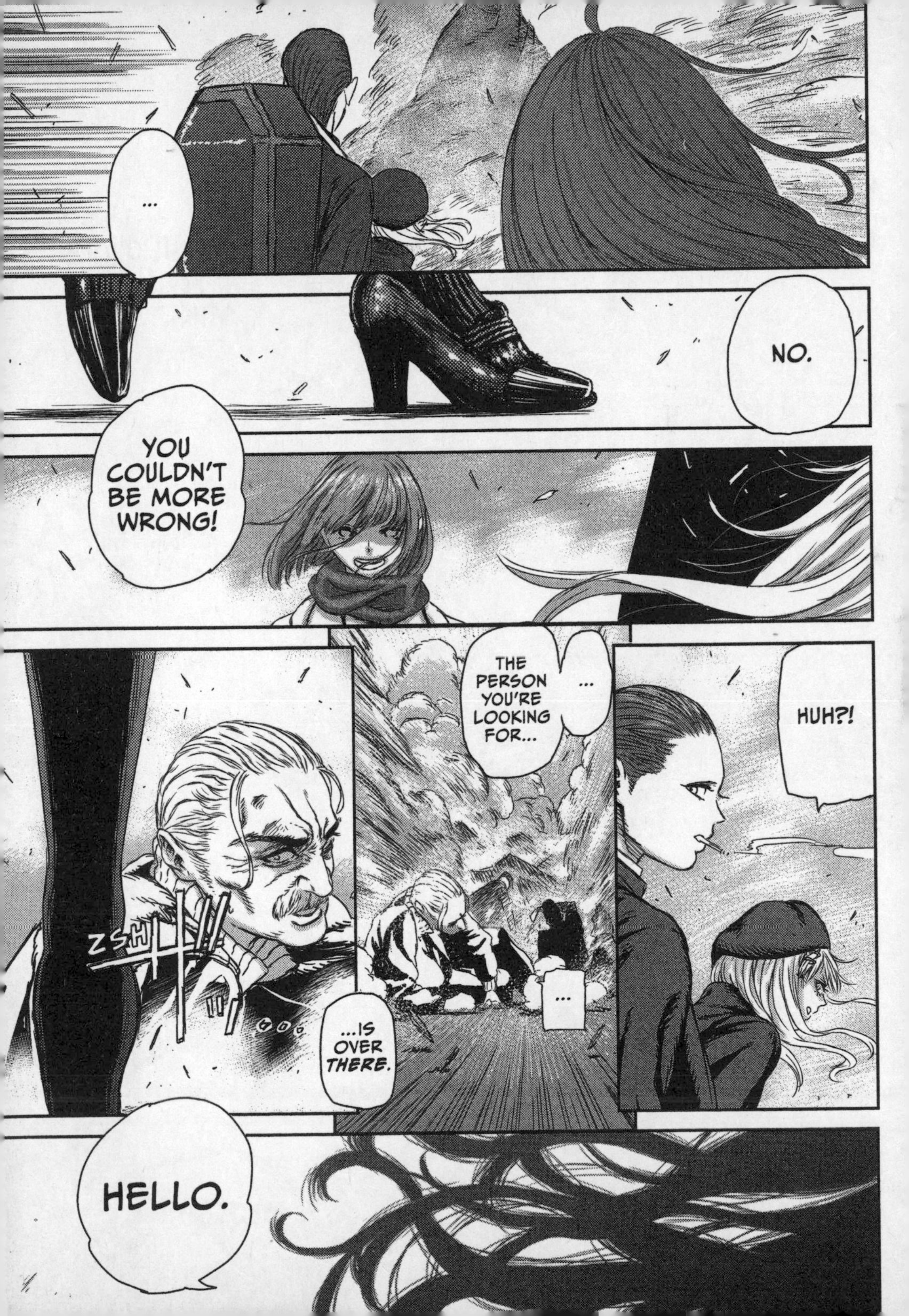
...
NO.
YOU COULDN'T BE MORE WRONG!
HUH?!
...
THE PERSON YOU'RE LOOKING FOR...
...
...IS OVER THERE.
ZSH
HELLO.

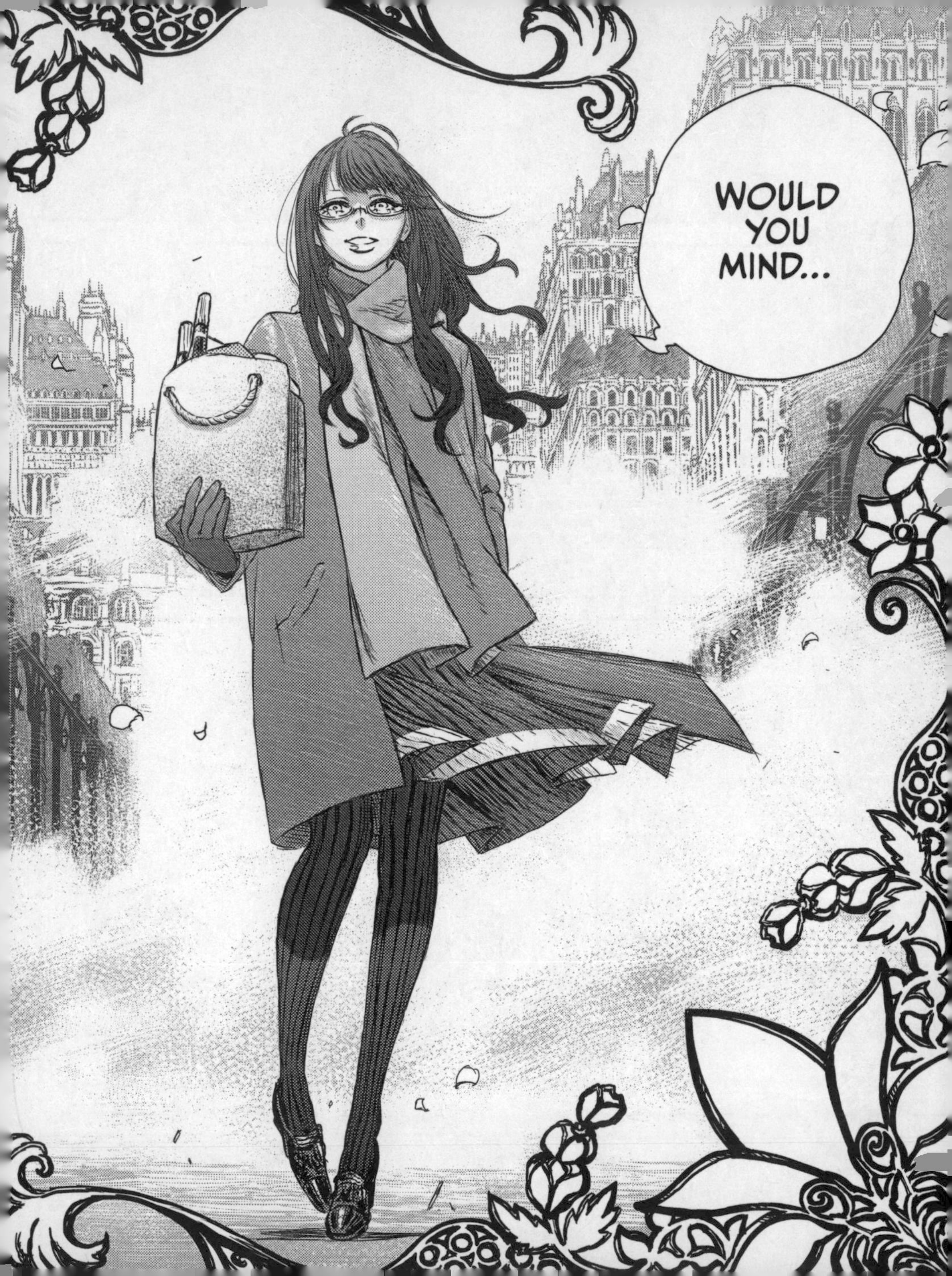
WOULD YOU MIND...

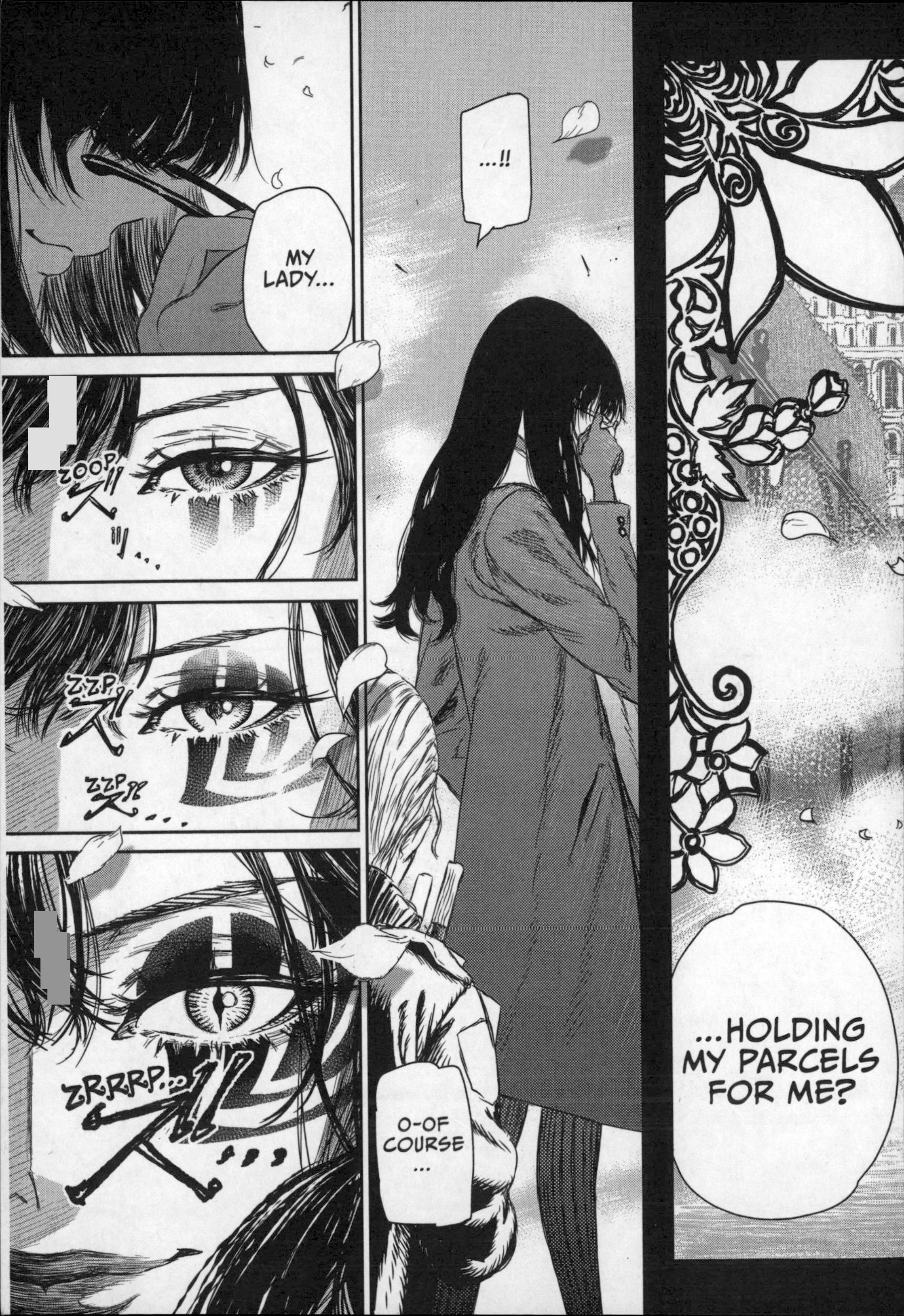
...HOLDING MY PARCELS FOR ME?
...!!
O-OF COURSE ...
MY LADY...
ZOOP
Z.Z.P.
Z.Z.P.
Z.R.R.R.P...

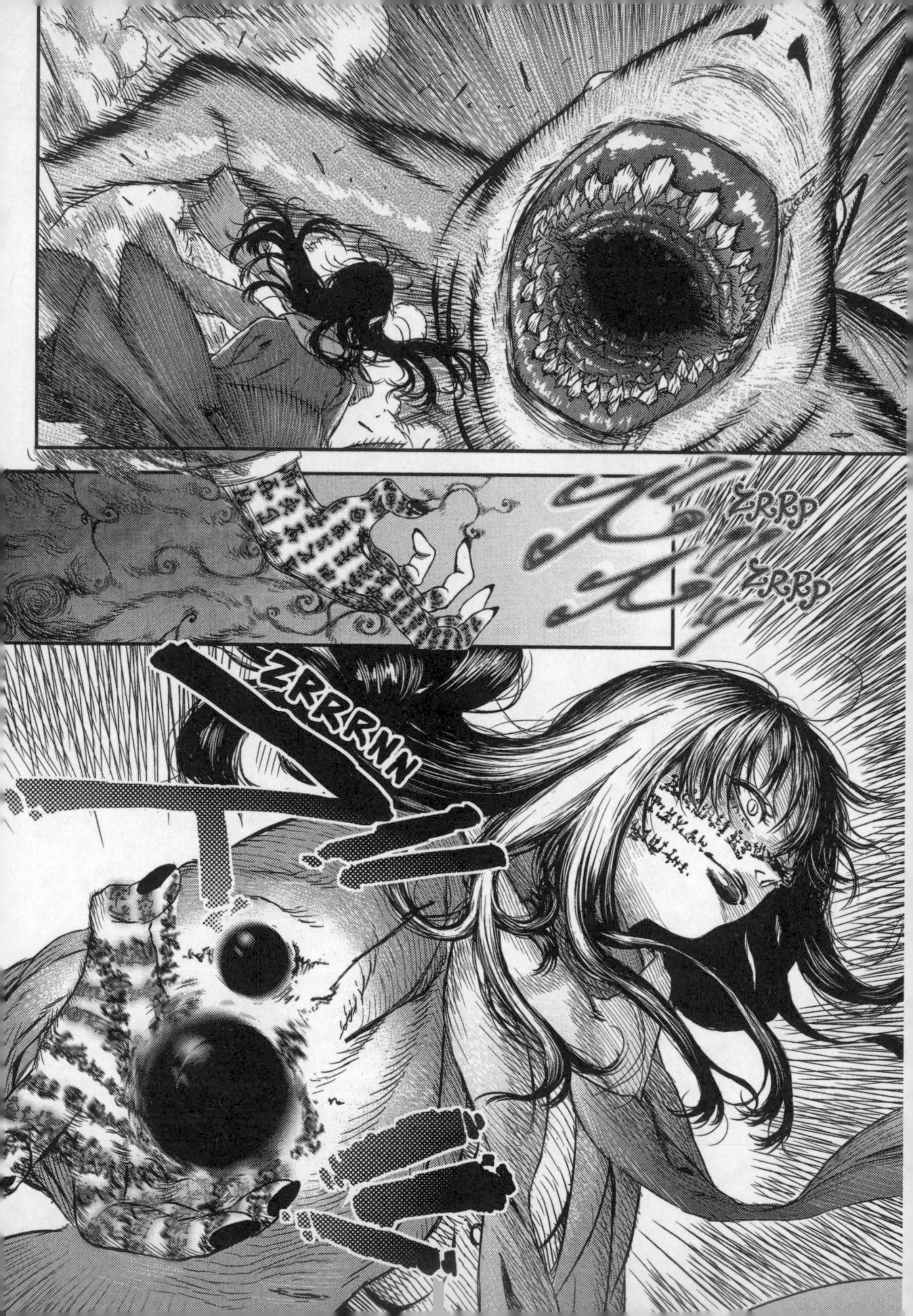
ZRRP
ZRRP
ZRRRNN

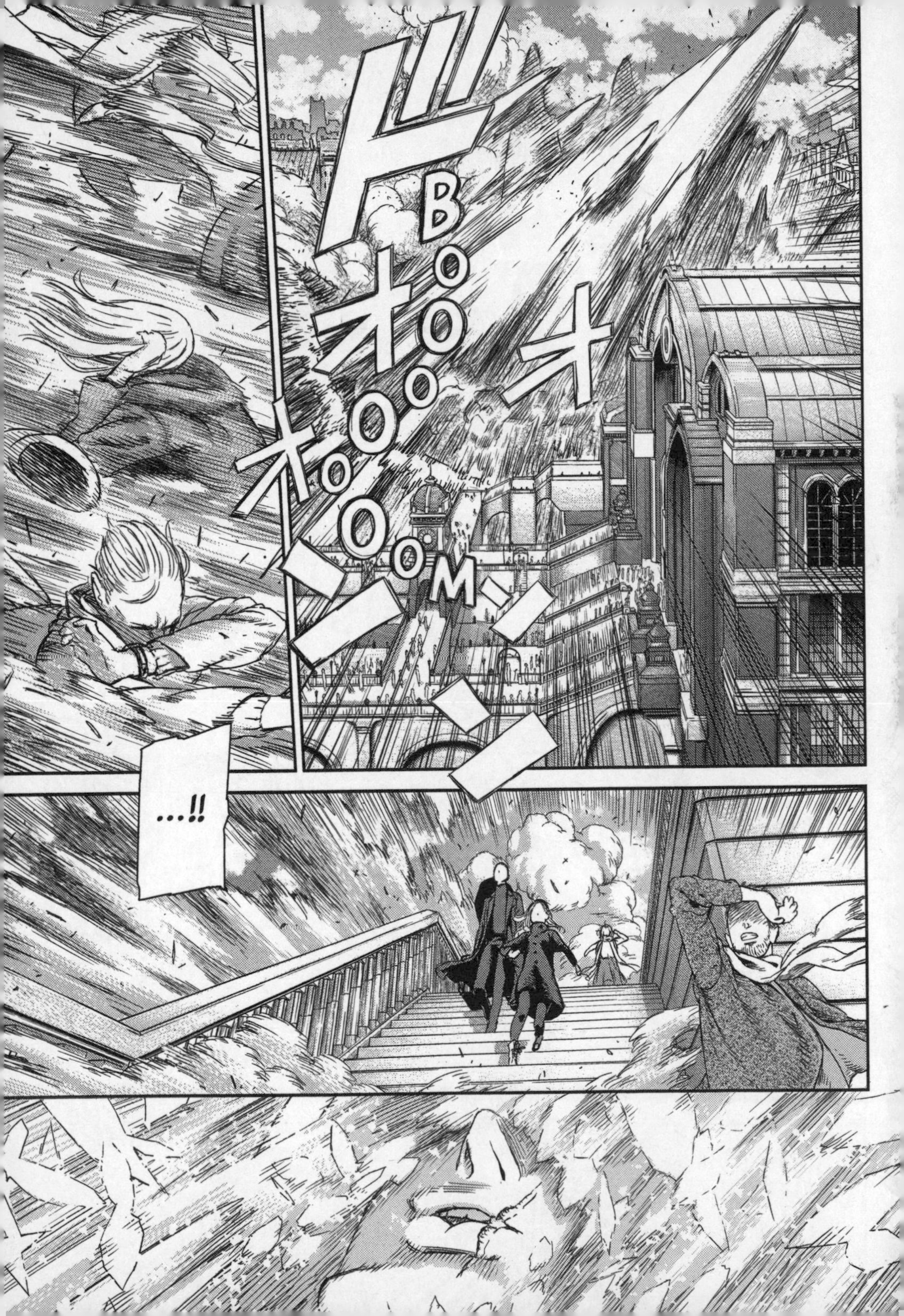
ドォオオ
BOOOOOOOM
オーーン
...!!

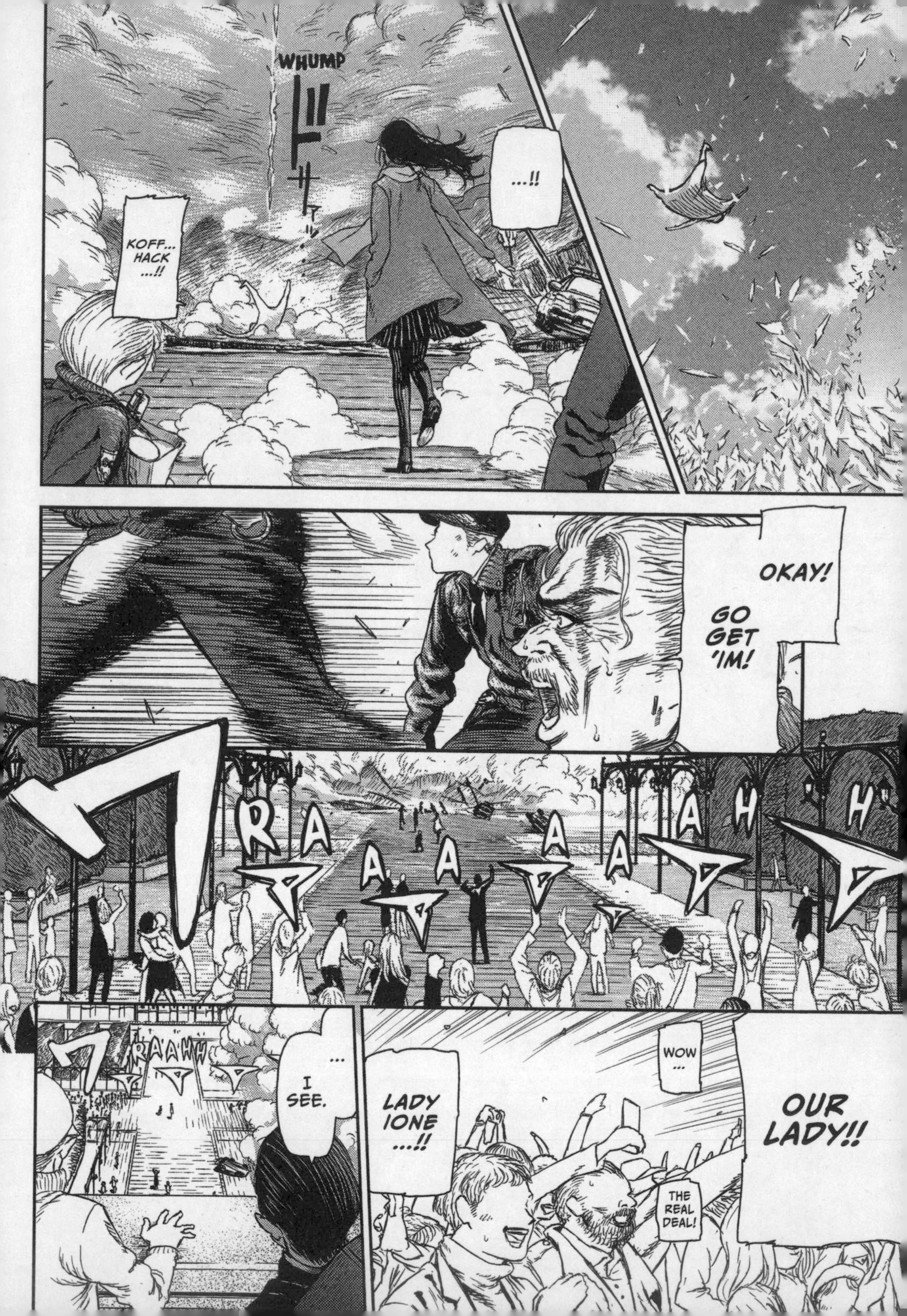

WHUMP
...!!
KOFF... HACK ...!!
OKAY!
GO GET 'IM!
RAAAAAAHH
WOW ...
OUR LADY!!
THE REAL DEAL!
LADY IONE ...!!
RAAHH
... I SEE.

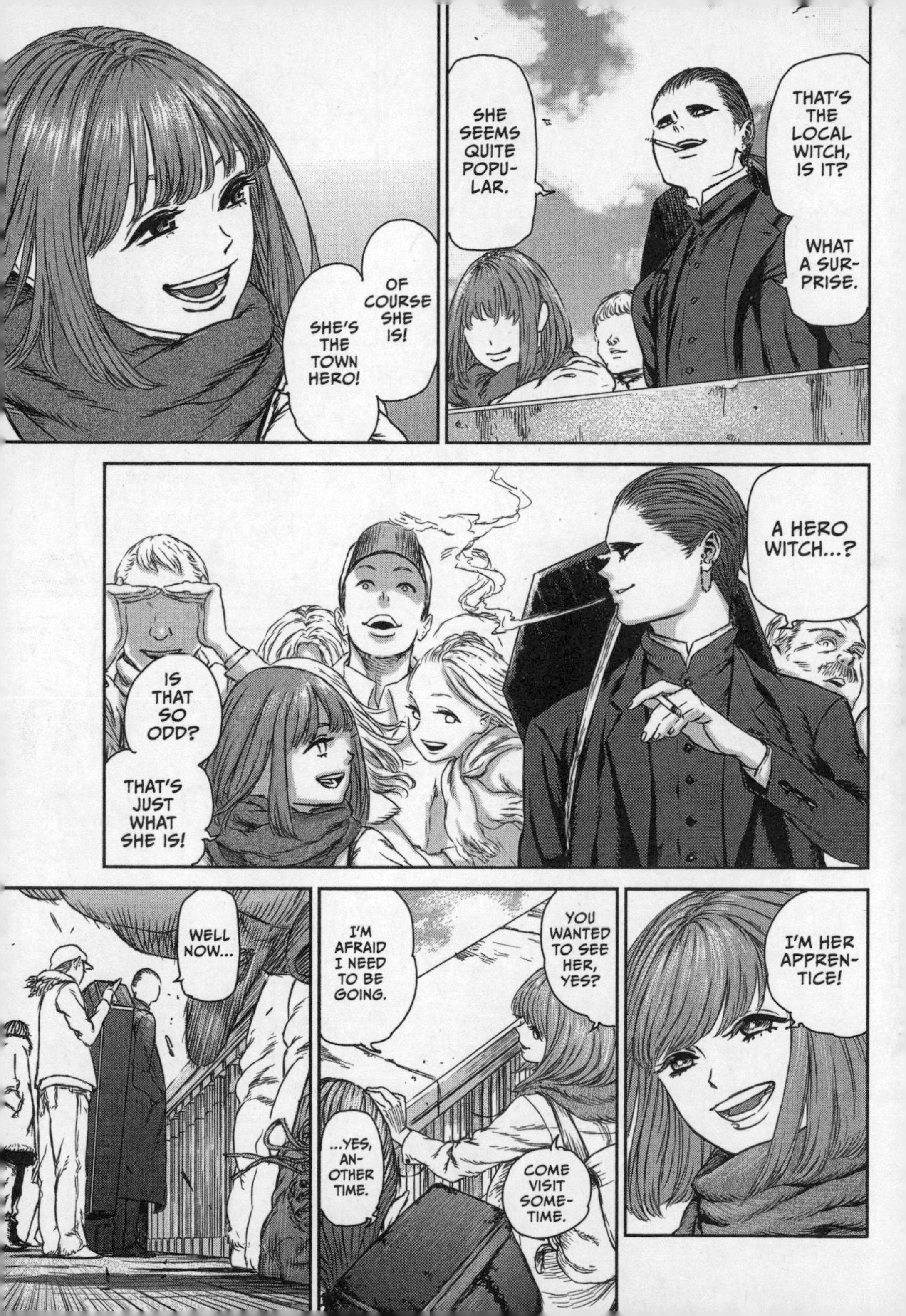
THAT'S THE LOCAL WITCH, IS IT?
WHAT A SURPRISE.
SHE SEEMS QUITE POPULAR.
OF COURSE SHE IS!
SHE'S THE TOWN HERO!
A HERO WITCH...?
IS THAT SO ODD?
THAT'S JUST WHAT SHE IS!
I'M HER APPRENTICE!
YOU WANTED TO SEE HER, YES?
I'M AFRAID I NEED TO BE GOING.
COME VISIT SOMETIME.
...YES, ANOTHER TIME.
WELL NOW...

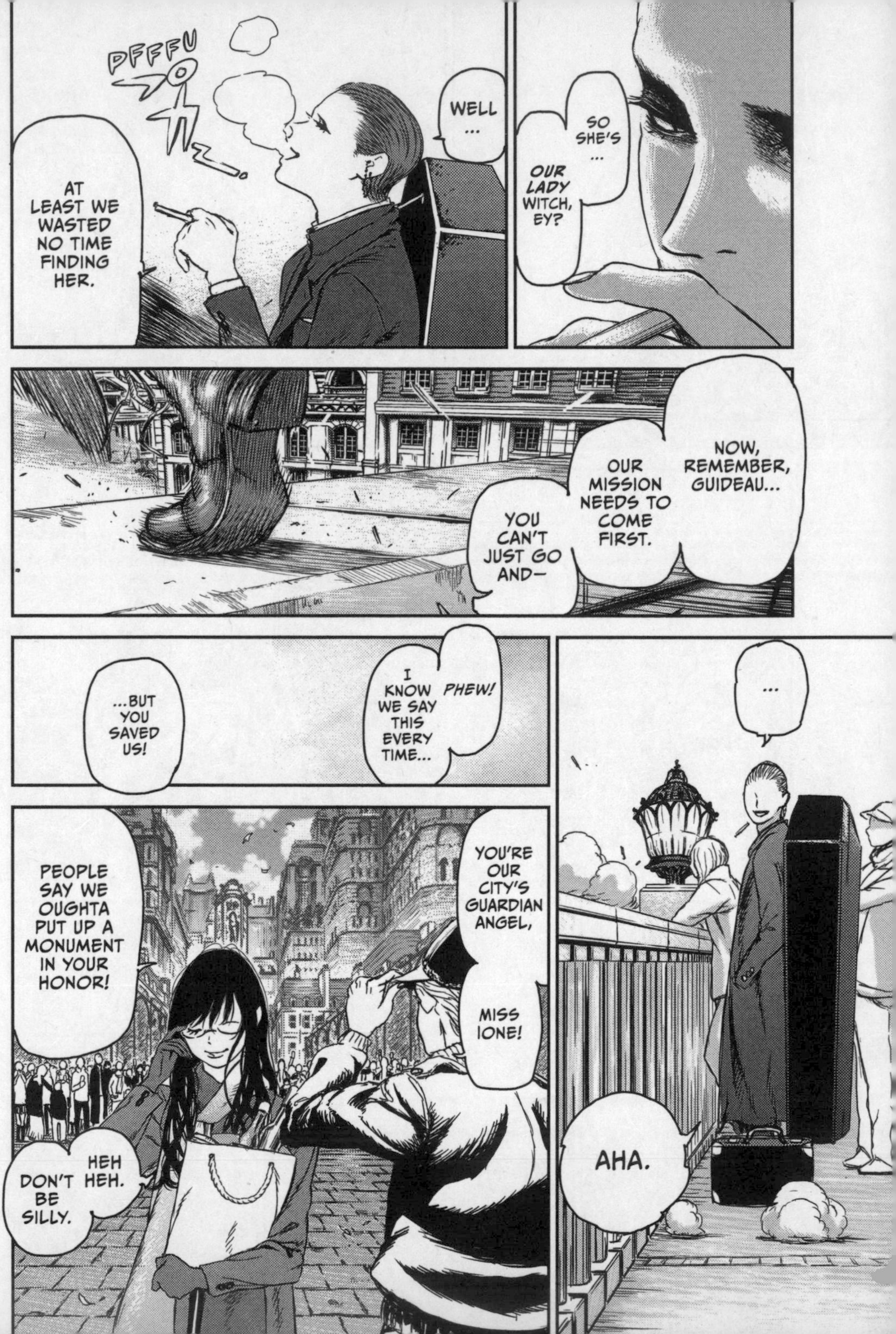
SO SHE'S... OUR LADY WITCH, EY?
WELL...
PFFFU
AT LEAST WE WASTED NO TIME FINDING HER.
NOW, REMEMBER, GUIDEAU...
OUR MISSION NEEDS TO COME FIRST.
YOU CAN'T JUST GO AND—
...
AHA.
PHEW! I KNOW WE SAY THIS EVERY TIME...
...BUT YOU SAVED US!
YOU'RE OUR CITY'S GUARDIAN ANGEL,
MISS IONE!
PEOPLE SAY WE OUGHTA PUT UP A MONUMENT IN YOUR HONOR!
HEH HEH. DON'T BE SILLY.

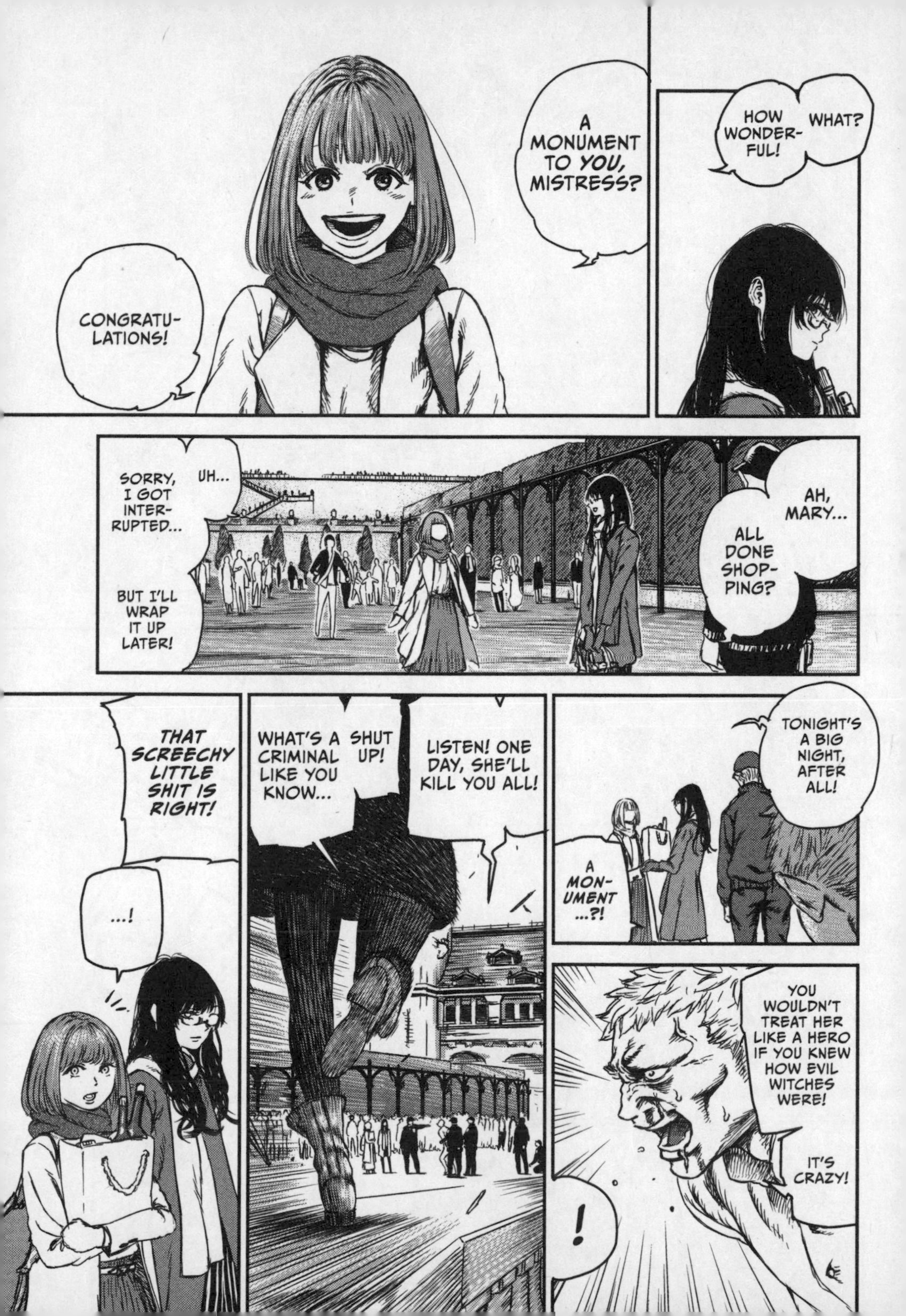
WHAT?
HOW WONDERFUL!
A MONUMENT TO *YOU*, MISTRESS?
CONGRATULATIONS!
AH, MARY...
ALL DONE SHOPPING?
UH...
SORRY, I GOT INTERRUPTED...
BUT I'LL WRAP IT UP LATER!
TONIGHT'S A BIG NIGHT, AFTER ALL!
A MONUMENT ...?!
YOU WOULDN'T TREAT HER LIKE A HERO IF YOU KNEW HOW EVIL WITCHES WERE!
IT'S CRAZY!
!
LISTEN! ONE DAY, SHE'LL KILL YOU ALL!
SHUT UP!
WHAT'S A CRIMINAL LIKE YOU KNOW...
THAT SCREECHY LITTLE SHIT IS RIGHT!
...!

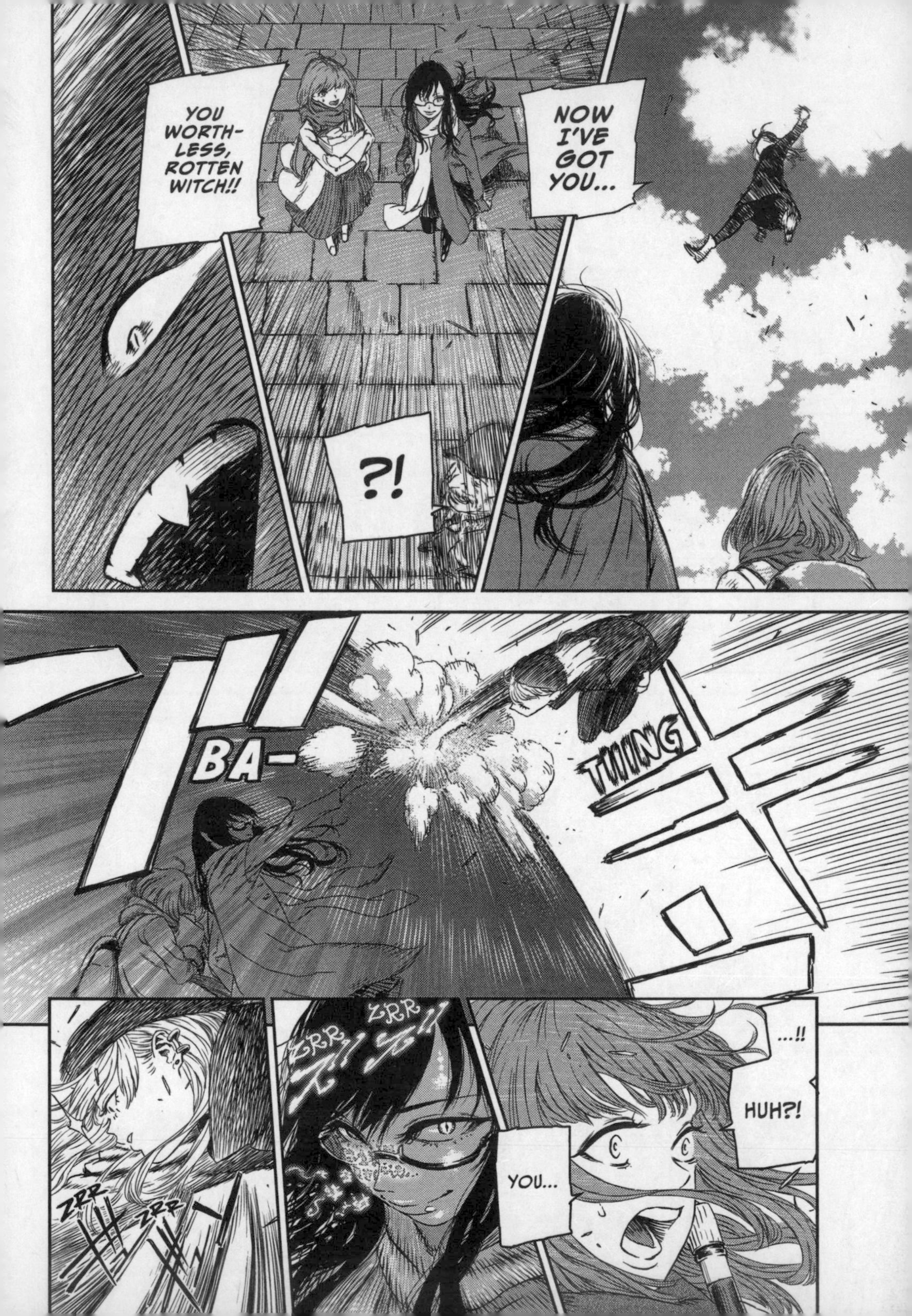

NOW I'VE GOT YOU...
YOU WORTHLESS, ROTTEN WITCH!!
?!
THING
BA-
...!!
HUH?!
YOU...
ZRR
ZRR
ZRR
ZRR

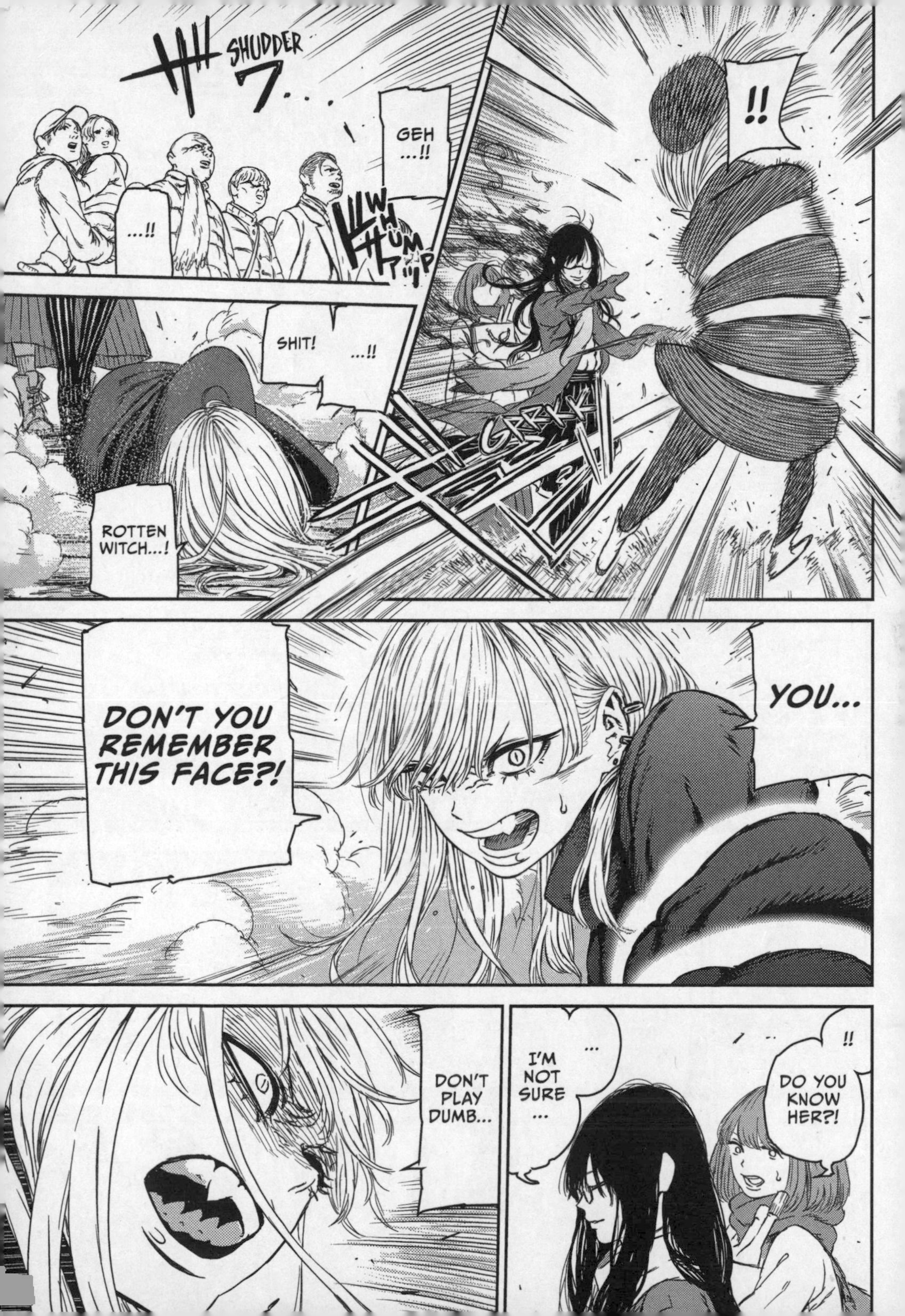
!!
GRKK
GEH ...!!
WHUMP
SHUDDER
...!!
...!!
SHIT!
ROTTEN WITCH...!
YOU...
DON'T YOU REMEMBER THIS FACE?!
!!
DO YOU KNOW HER?!
...
I'M NOT SURE ...
DON'T PLAY DUMB...

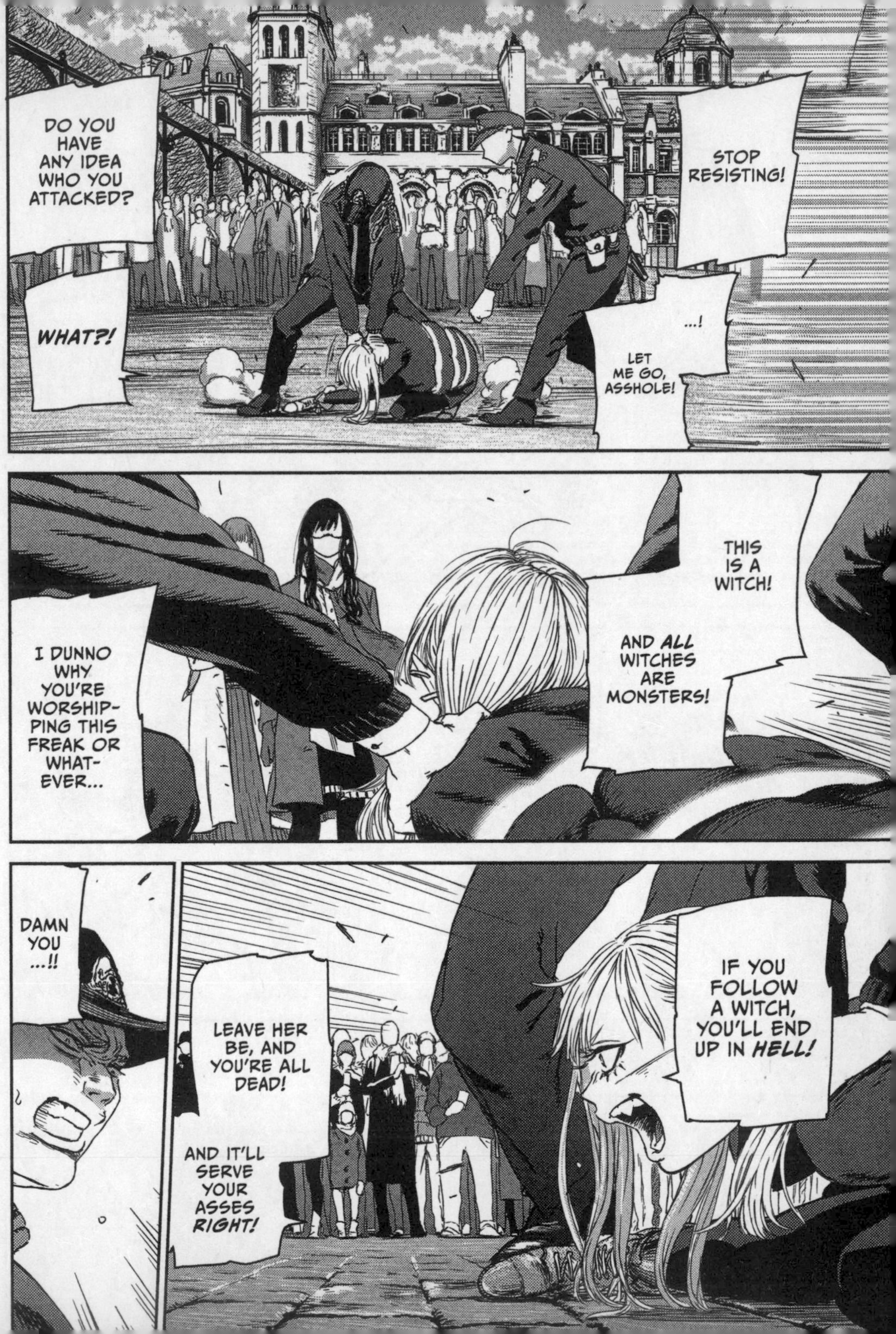
STOP RESISTING!
...!
LET ME GO, ASSHOLE!
DO YOU HAVE ANY IDEA WHO YOU ATTACKED?
WHAT?!
THIS IS A WITCH!
AND *ALL* WITCHES ARE MONSTERS!
I DUNNO WHY YOU'RE WORSHIP-PING THIS FREAK OR WHAT-EVER...
IF YOU FOLLOW A WITCH, YOU'LL END UP IN *HELL!*
LEAVE HER BE, AND YOU'RE ALL DEAD!
AND IT'LL SERVE YOUR ASSES *RIGHT!*
DAMN YOU ...!!

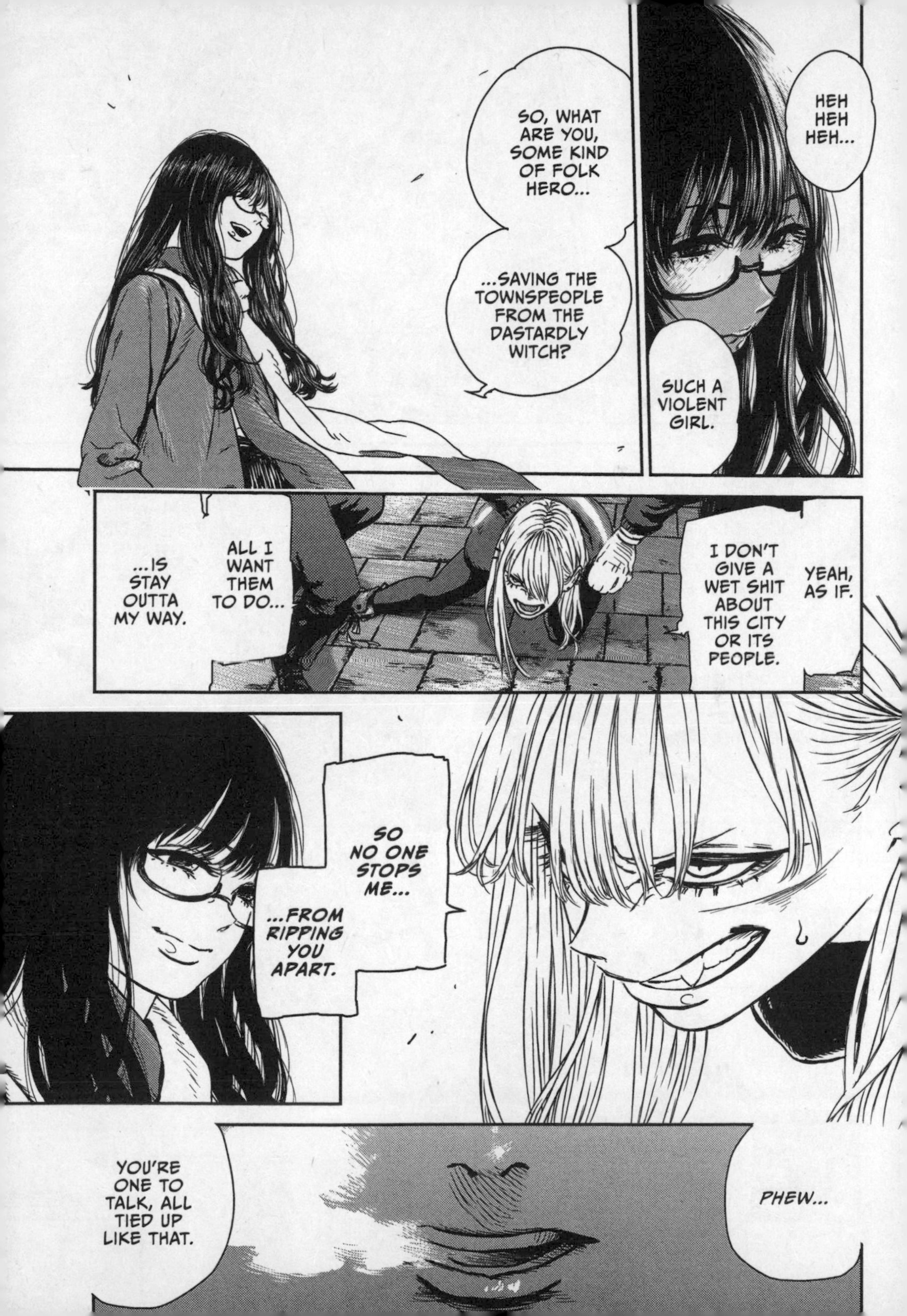
HEH HEH HEH...
SUCH A VIOLENT GIRL.
SO, WHAT ARE YOU, SOME KIND OF FOLK HERO...
...SAVING THE TOWNSPEOPLE FROM THE DASTARDLY WITCH?
YEAH, AS IF.
I DON'T GIVE A WET SHIT ABOUT THIS CITY OR ITS PEOPLE.
ALL I WANT THEM TO DO...
...IS STAY OUTTA MY WAY.
SO NO ONE STOPS ME...
...FROM RIPPING YOU APART.
PHEW...
YOU'RE ONE TO TALK, ALL TIED UP LIKE THAT.

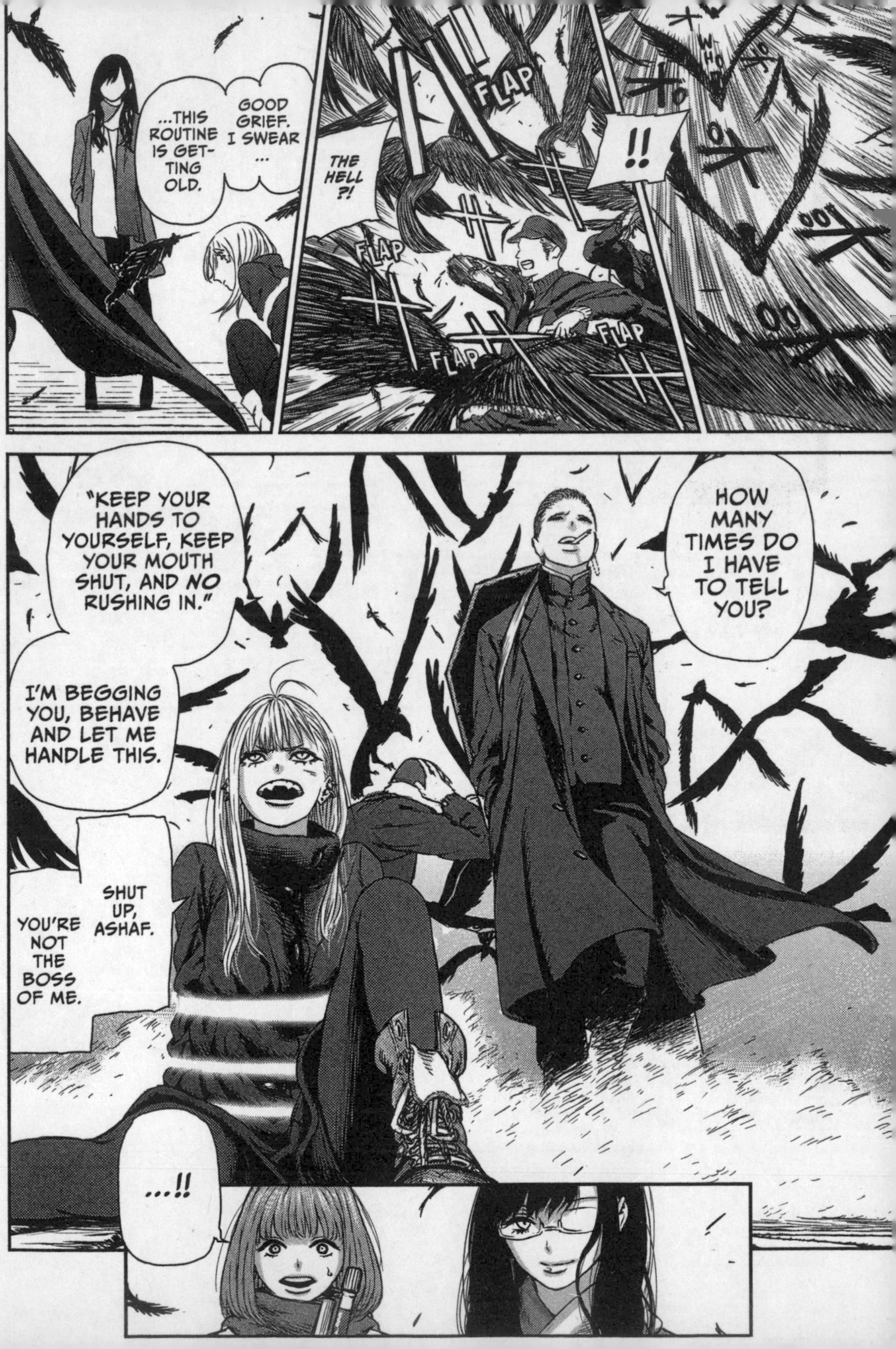
!!
FLAP
THE HELL ?!
FLAP
FLAP
FLAP
GOOD GRIEF. I SWEAR ...
...THIS ROUTINE IS GETTING OLD.
HOW MANY TIMES DO I HAVE TO TELL YOU?
"KEEP YOUR HANDS TO YOURSELF, KEEP YOUR MOUTH SHUT, AND *NO* RUSHING IN."
I'M BEGGING YOU, BEHAVE AND LET ME HANDLE THIS.
SHUT UP, ASHAF.
YOU'RE NOT THE BOSS OF ME.
...!!

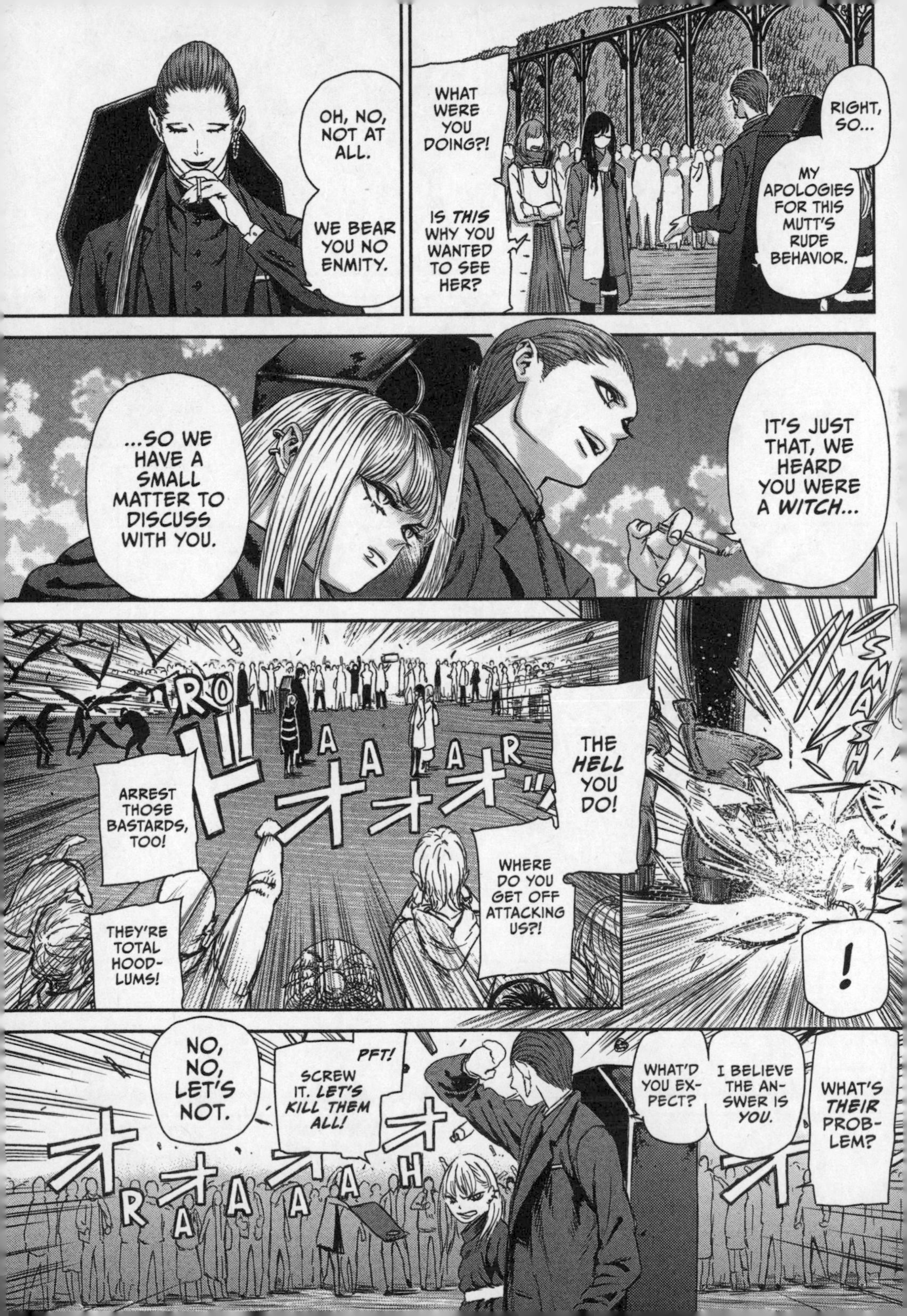
RIGHT, SO...
MY APOLOGIES FOR THIS MUTT'S RUDE BEHAVIOR.
WHAT WERE YOU DOING?!
IS *THIS* WHY YOU WANTED TO SEE HER?
OH, NO, NOT AT ALL.
WE BEAR YOU NO ENMITY.
IT'S JUST THAT, WE HEARD YOU WERE A *WITCH*...
...SO WE HAVE A SMALL MATTER TO DISCUSS WITH YOU.
SMASH
!
THE *HELL* YOU DO!
WHERE DO YOU GET OFF ATTACKING US?!
ROAAAR
ARREST THOSE BASTARDS, TOO!
THEY'RE TOTAL HOOD-LUMS!
WHAT'S *THEIR* PROB-LEM?
I BELIEVE THE AN-SWER IS *YOU*.
WHAT'D YOU EX-PECT?
PFT!
SCREW IT. *LET'S KILL THEM ALL!*
NO, NO, LET'S NOT.
RAAAAAH

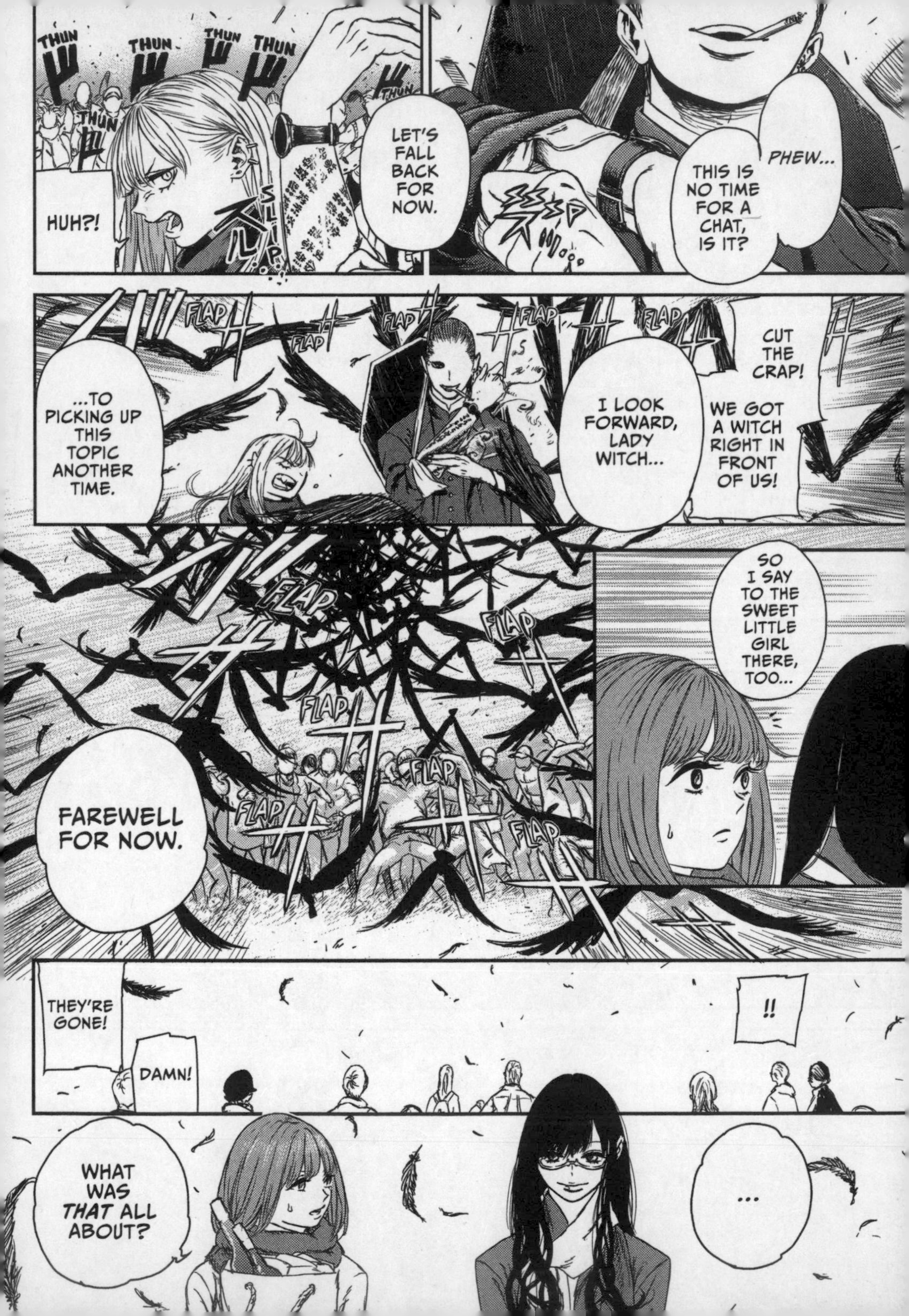
PHEW...
THIS IS NO TIME FOR A CHAT, IS IT?
THUN THUN THUN THUN THUN THUN
LET'S FALL BACK FOR NOW.
SLIP
HUH?!
FLAP
CUT THE CRAP!
WE GOT A WITCH RIGHT IN FRONT OF US!
I LOOK FORWARD, LADY WITCH...
...TO PICKING UP THIS TOPIC ANOTHER TIME.
SO I SAY TO THE SWEET LITTLE GIRL THERE, TOO...
FLAP
FAREWELL FOR NOW.
!!
THEY'RE GONE!
DAMN!
...
WHAT WAS THAT ALL ABOUT?

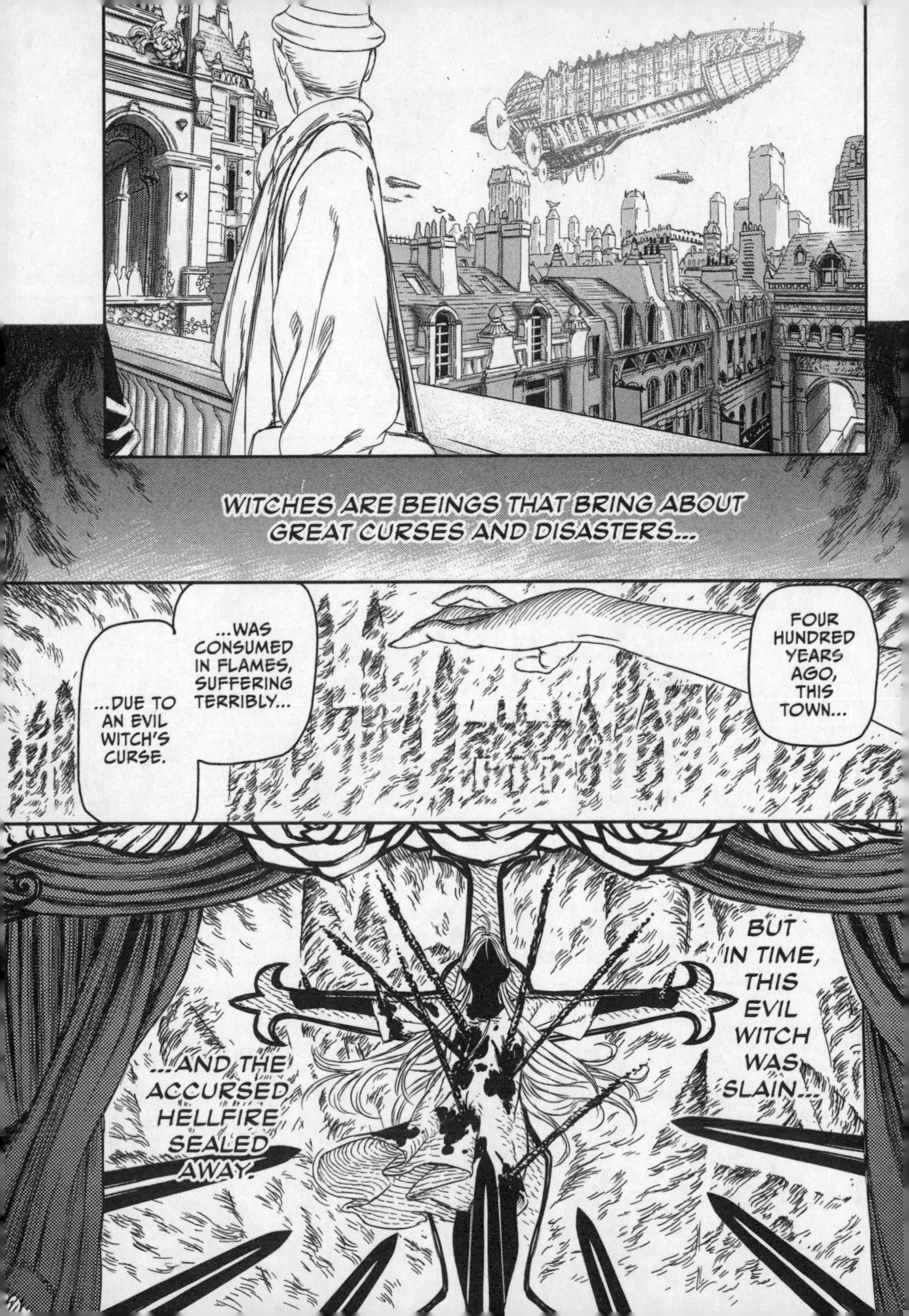
WITCHES ARE BEINGS THAT BRING ABOUT GREAT CURSES AND DISASTERS...
FOUR HUNDRED YEARS AGO, THIS TOWN...
...WAS CONSUMED IN FLAMES, SUFFERING TERRIBLY...
...DUE TO AN EVIL WITCH'S CURSE.
BUT IN TIME, THIS EVIL WITCH WAS SLAIN...
...AND THE ACCURSED HELLFIRE SEALED AWAY.

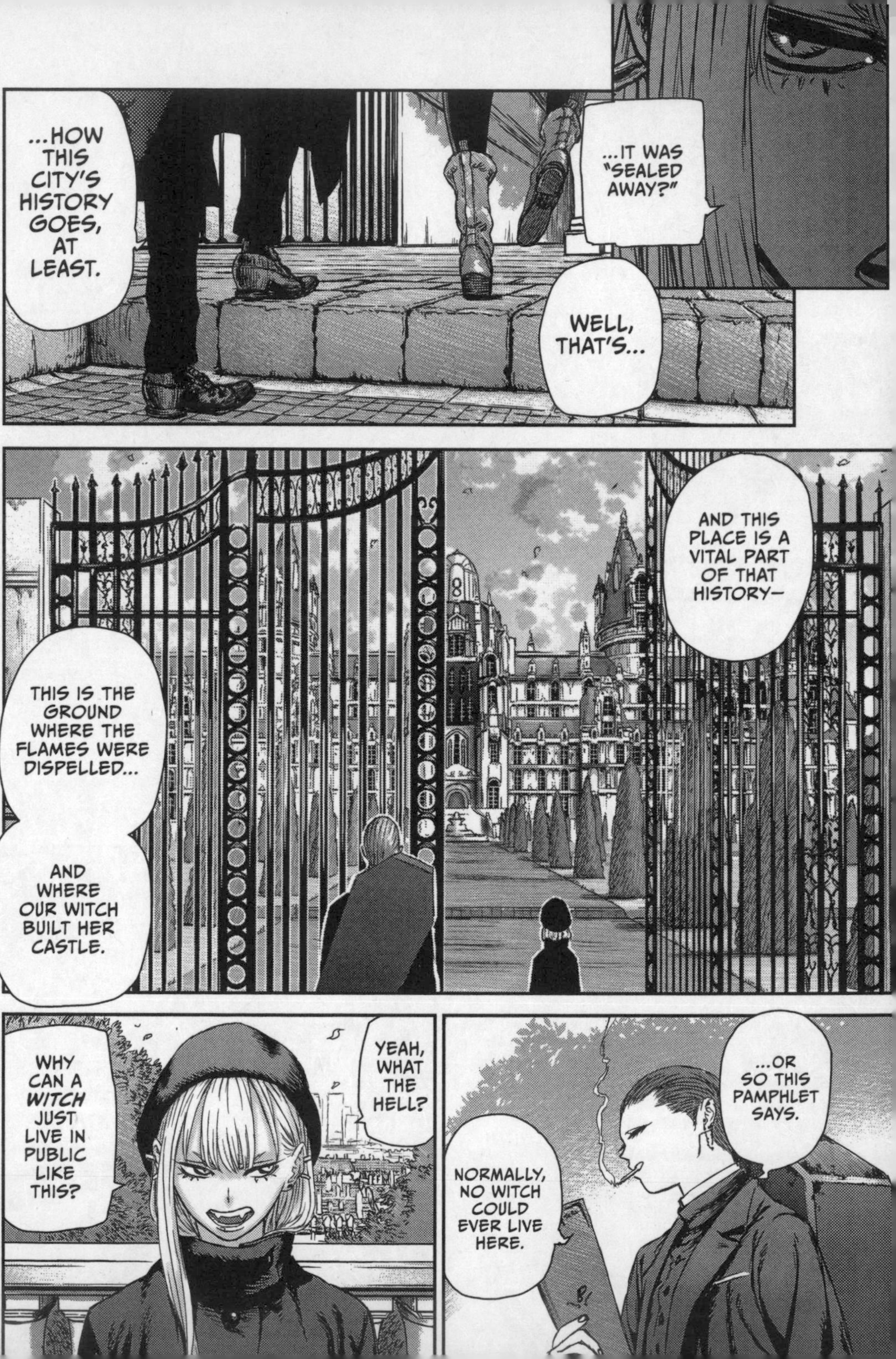
...IT WAS "SEALED AWAY?"
WELL, THAT'S...
...HOW THIS CITY'S HISTORY GOES, AT LEAST.
AND THIS PLACE IS A VITAL PART OF THAT HISTORY—
THIS IS THE GROUND WHERE THE FLAMES WERE DISPELLED...
AND WHERE OUR WITCH BUILT HER CASTLE.
...OR SO THIS PAMPHLET SAYS.
NORMALLY, NO WITCH COULD EVER LIVE HERE.
YEAH, WHAT THE HELL?
WHY CAN A *WITCH* JUST LIVE IN PUBLIC LIKE THIS?

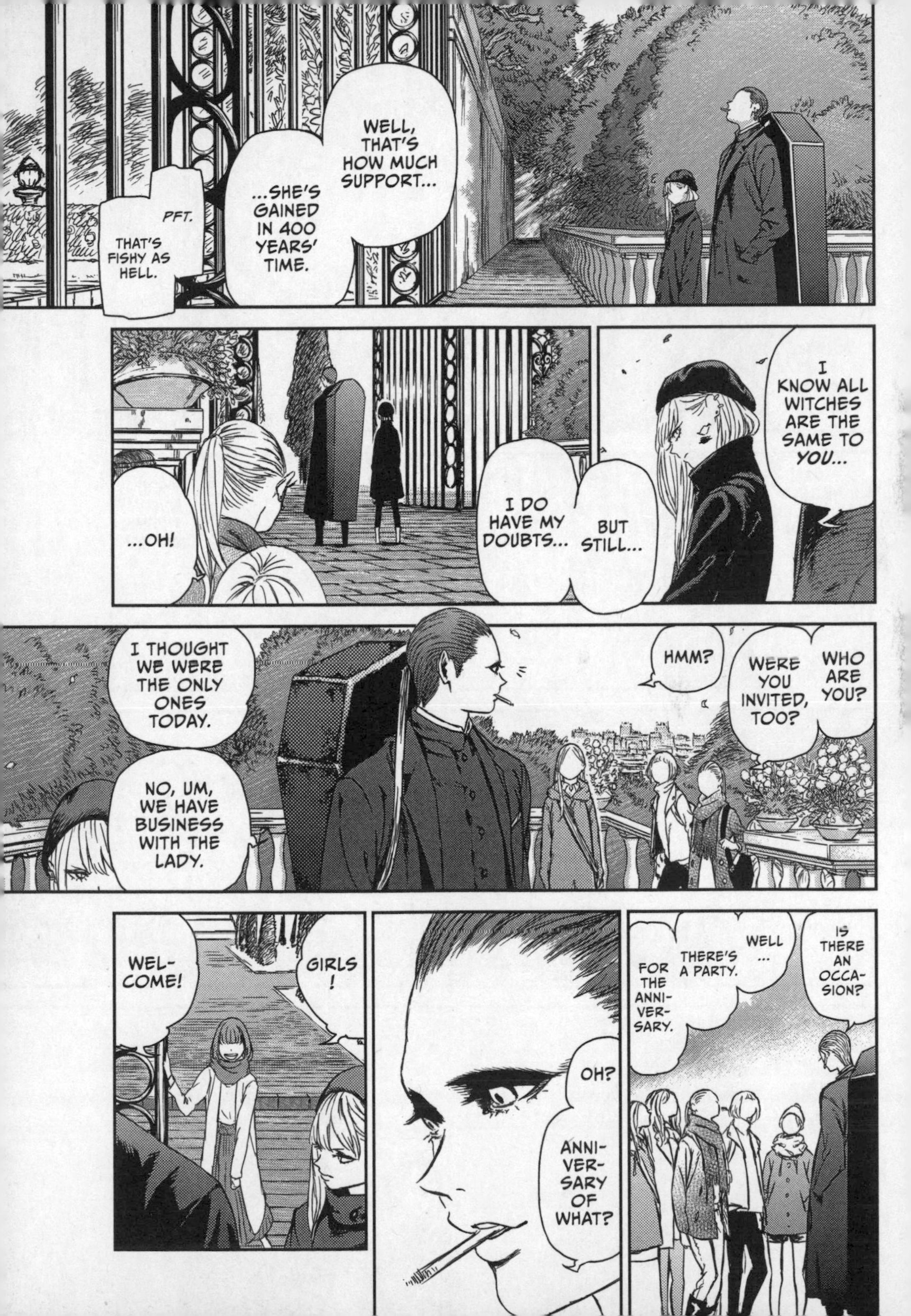
WELL, THAT'S HOW MUCH SUPPORT...
...SHE'S GAINED IN 400 YEARS' TIME.
PFT.
THAT'S FISHY AS HELL.
I KNOW ALL WITCHES ARE THE SAME TO *YOU*...
BUT STILL...
I DO HAVE MY DOUBTS...
...OH!
WHO ARE YOU?
WERE YOU INVITED, TOO?
HMM?
I THOUGHT WE WERE THE ONLY ONES TODAY.
NO, UM, WE HAVE BUSINESS WITH THE LADY.
IS THERE AN OCCASION?
WELL...
THERE'S A PARTY.
FOR THE ANNIVERSARY.
OH?
ANNIVERSARY OF WHAT?
GIRLS!
WELCOME!

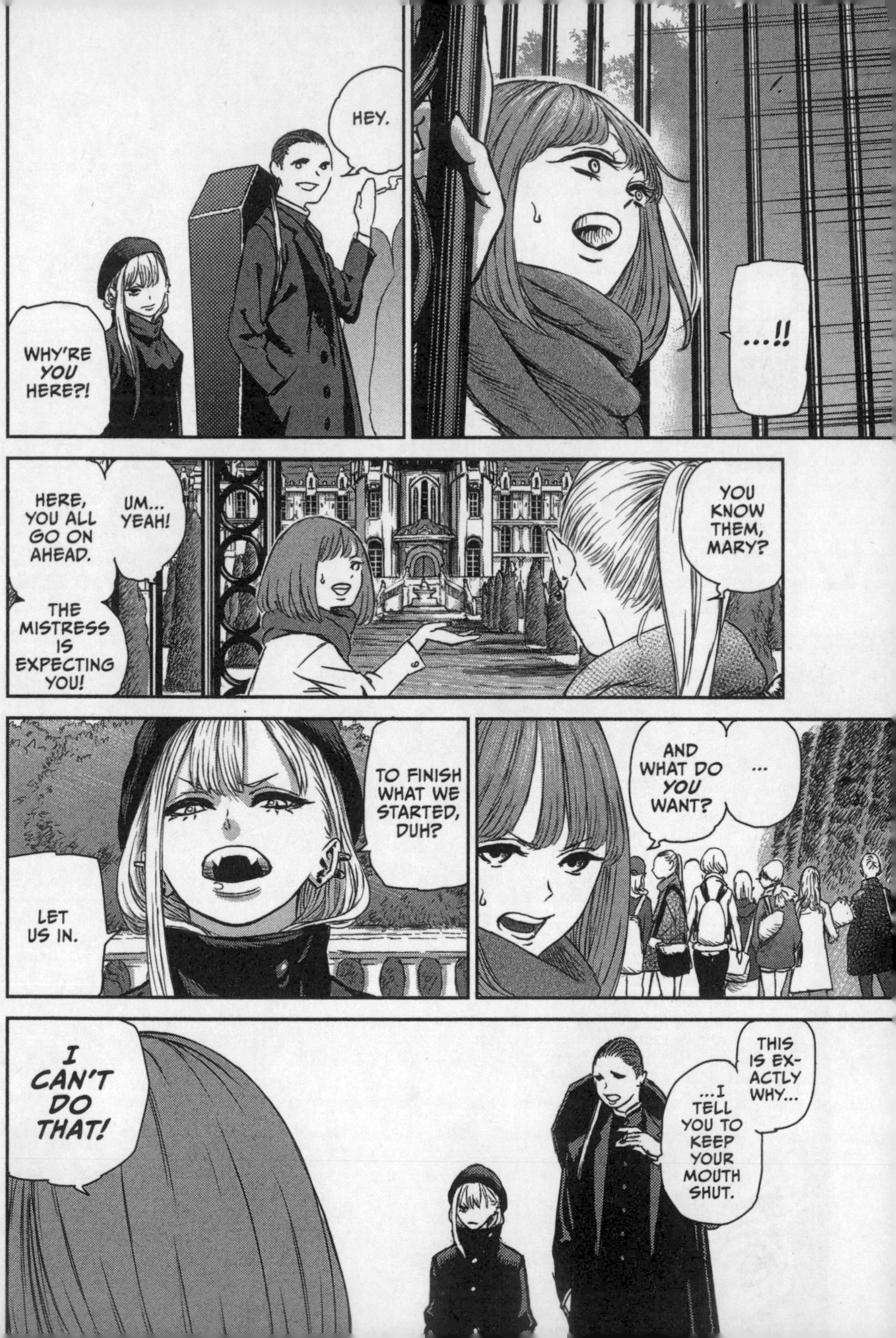
...!!
HEY.
WHY'RE YOU HERE?!
YOU KNOW THEM, MARY?
UM... YEAH!
HERE, YOU ALL GO ON AHEAD.
THE MISTRESS IS EXPECTING YOU!
...
AND WHAT DO YOU WANT?
TO FINISH WHAT WE STARTED, DUH?
LET US IN.
THIS IS EX-ACTLY WHY...
...I TELL YOU TO KEEP YOUR MOUTH SHUT.
I CAN'T DO THAT!

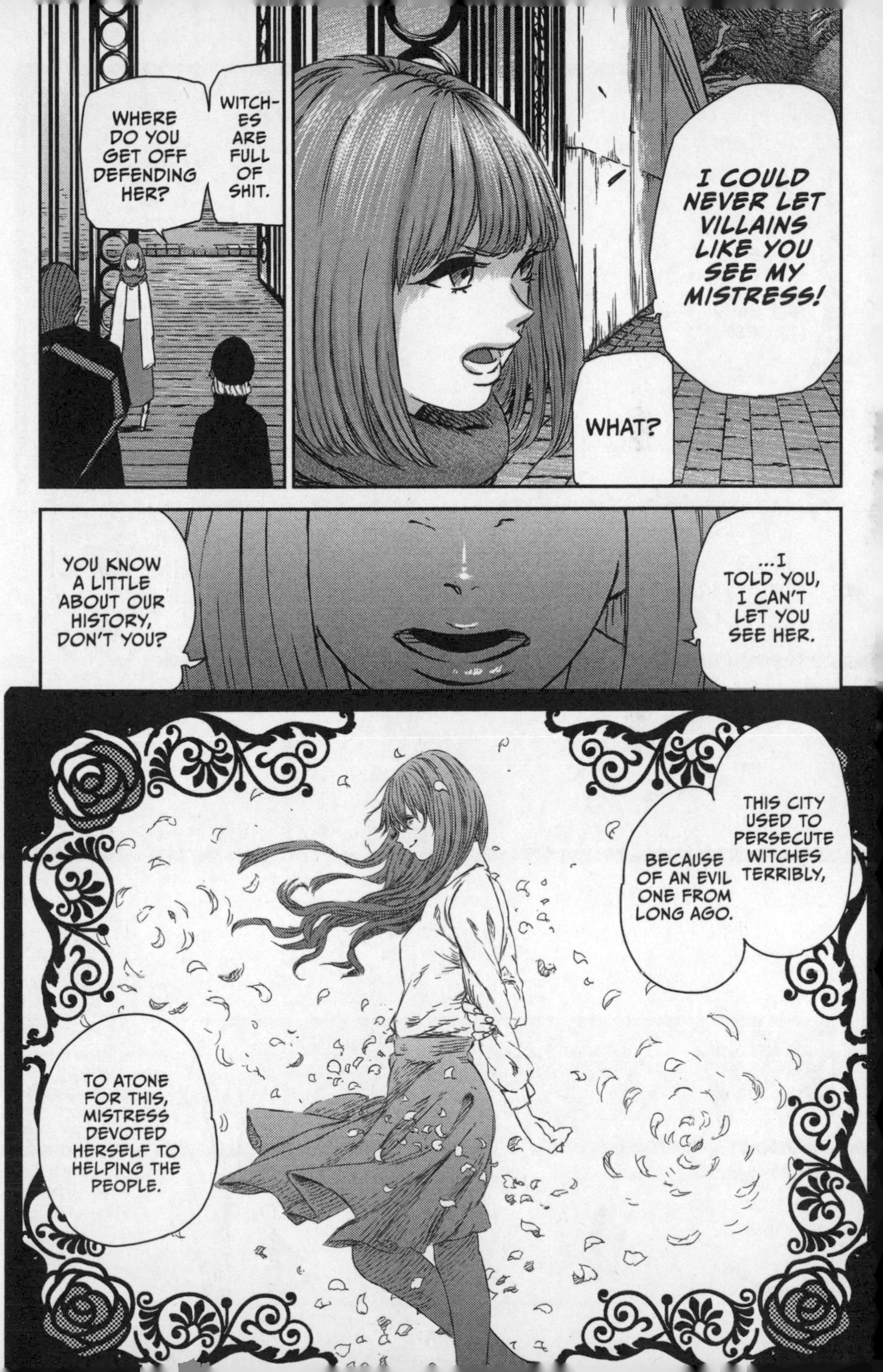
I COULD NEVER LET VILLAINS LIKE YOU SEE MY MISTRESS!
WHAT?
WITCHES ARE FULL OF SHIT.
WHERE DO YOU GET OFF DEFENDING HER?
...I TOLD YOU, I CAN'T LET YOU SEE HER.
YOU KNOW A LITTLE ABOUT OUR HISTORY, DON'T YOU?
THIS CITY USED TO PERSECUTE WITCHES TERRIBLY,
BECAUSE OF AN EVIL ONE FROM LONG AGO.
TO ATONE FOR THIS, MISTRESS DEVOTED HERSELF TO HELPING THE PEOPLE.

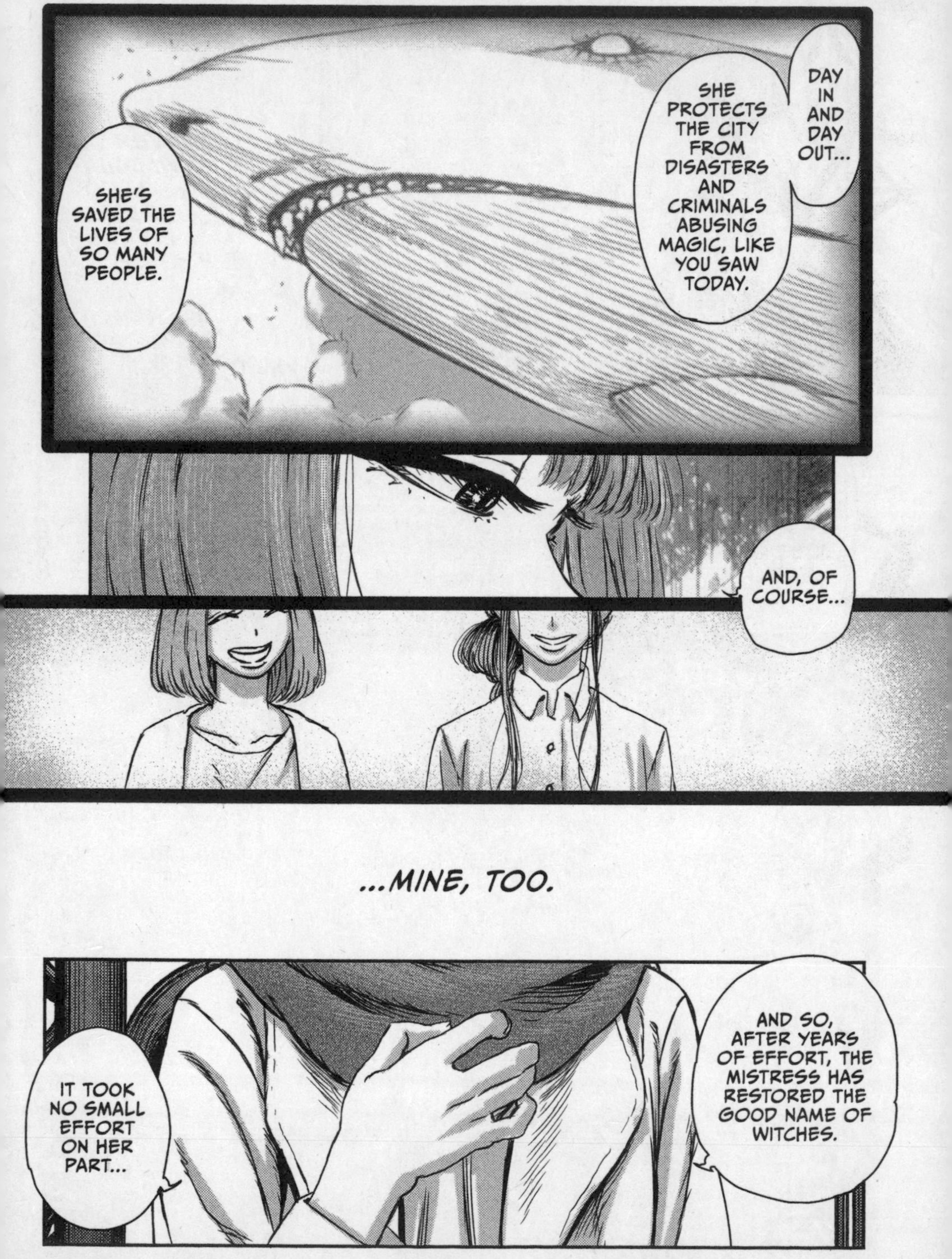
DAY IN AND DAY OUT...
SHE PROTECTS THE CITY FROM DISASTERS AND CRIMINALS ABUSING MAGIC, LIKE YOU SAW TODAY.
SHE'S SAVED THE LIVES OF SO MANY PEOPLE.
AND, OF COURSE...
...MINE, TOO.
AND SO, AFTER YEARS OF EFFORT, THE MISTRESS HAS RESTORED THE GOOD NAME OF WITCHES.
IT TOOK NO SMALL EFFORT ON HER PART...

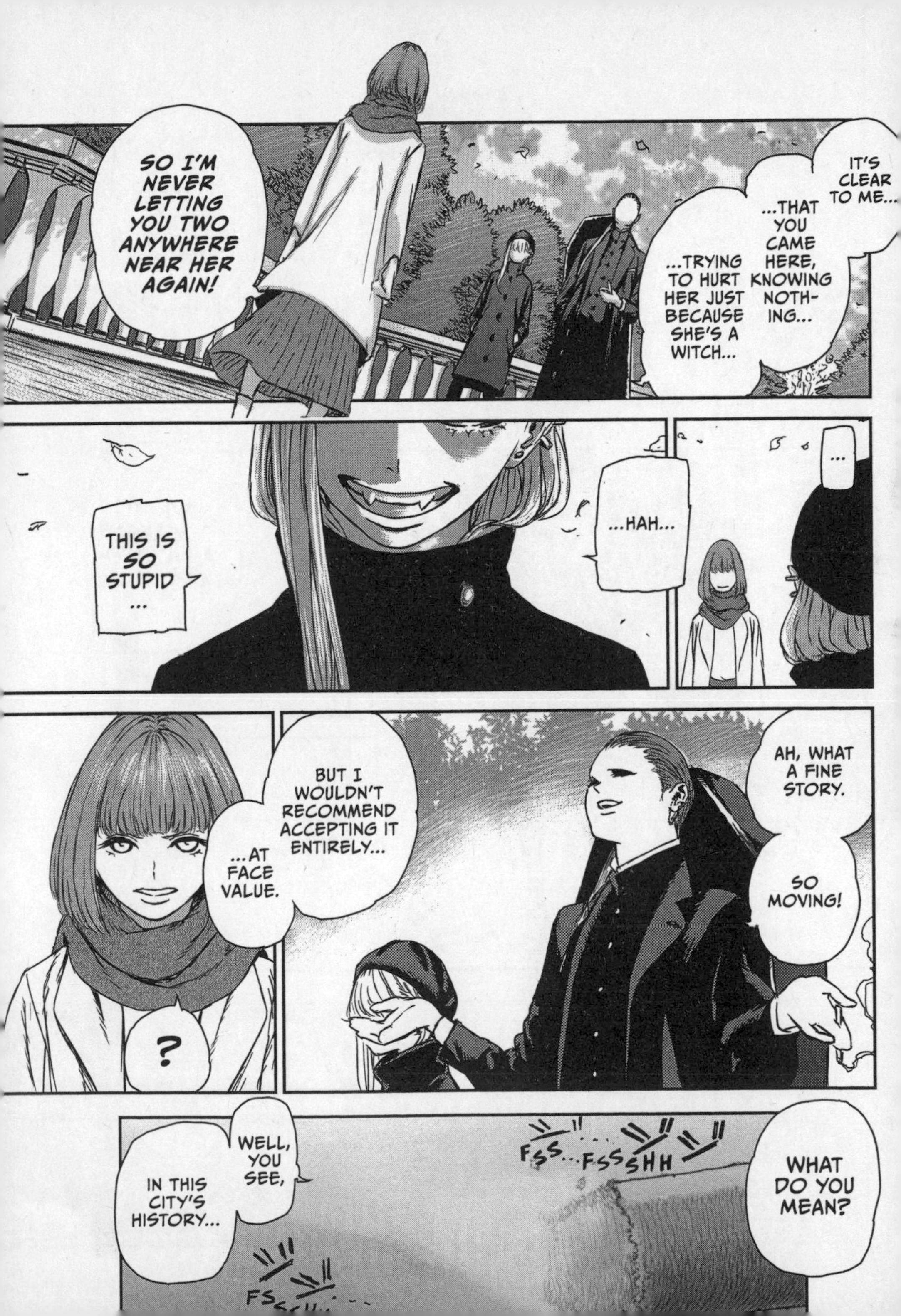
IT'S CLEAR TO ME...
...THAT YOU CAME HERE, KNOWING NOTH-ING...
...TRYING TO HURT HER JUST BECAUSE SHE'S A WITCH...
SO I'M NEVER LETTING YOU TWO ANYWHERE NEAR HER AGAIN!
...
...HAH...
THIS IS SO STUPID ...
AH, WHAT A FINE STORY.
SO MOVING!
BUT I WOULDN'T RECOMMEND ACCEPTING IT ENTIRELY...
...AT FACE VALUE.
?
WHAT DO YOU MEAN?
FSS...FSSSHH
WELL, YOU SEE,
IN THIS CITY'S HISTORY...
FS

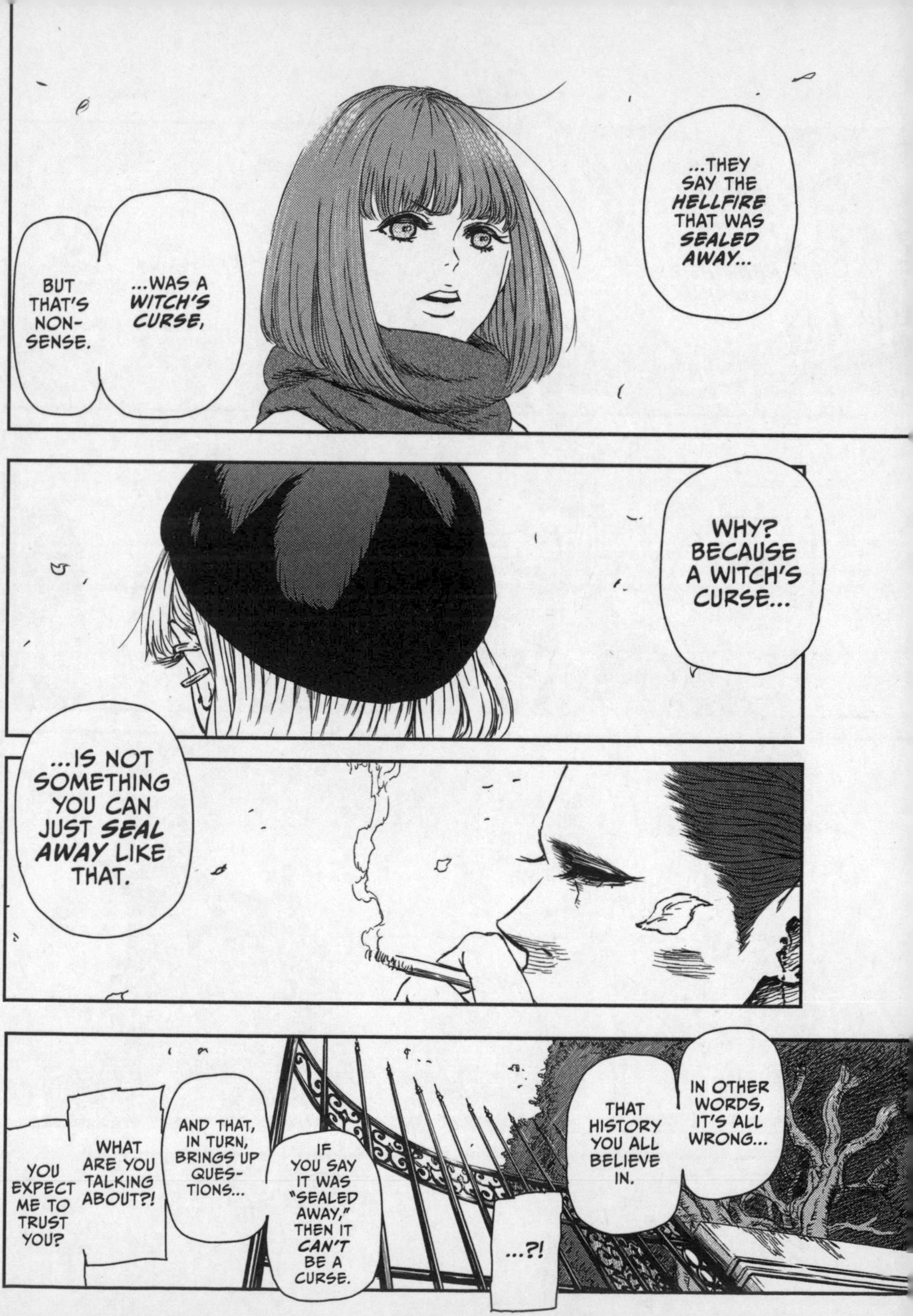
...THEY SAY THE HELLFIRE THAT WAS SEALED AWAY...
...WAS A WITCH'S CURSE,
BUT THAT'S NON-SENSE.
WHY? BECAUSE A WITCH'S CURSE...
...IS NOT SOMETHING YOU CAN JUST SEAL AWAY LIKE THAT.
IN OTHER WORDS, IT'S ALL WRONG...
THAT HISTORY YOU ALL BELIEVE IN.
...?!
IF YOU SAY IT WAS "SEALED AWAY," THEN IT CAN'T BE A CURSE.
AND THAT, IN TURN, BRINGS UP QUES-TIONS...
WHAT ARE YOU TALKING ABOUT?!
YOU EXPECT ME TO TRUST YOU?

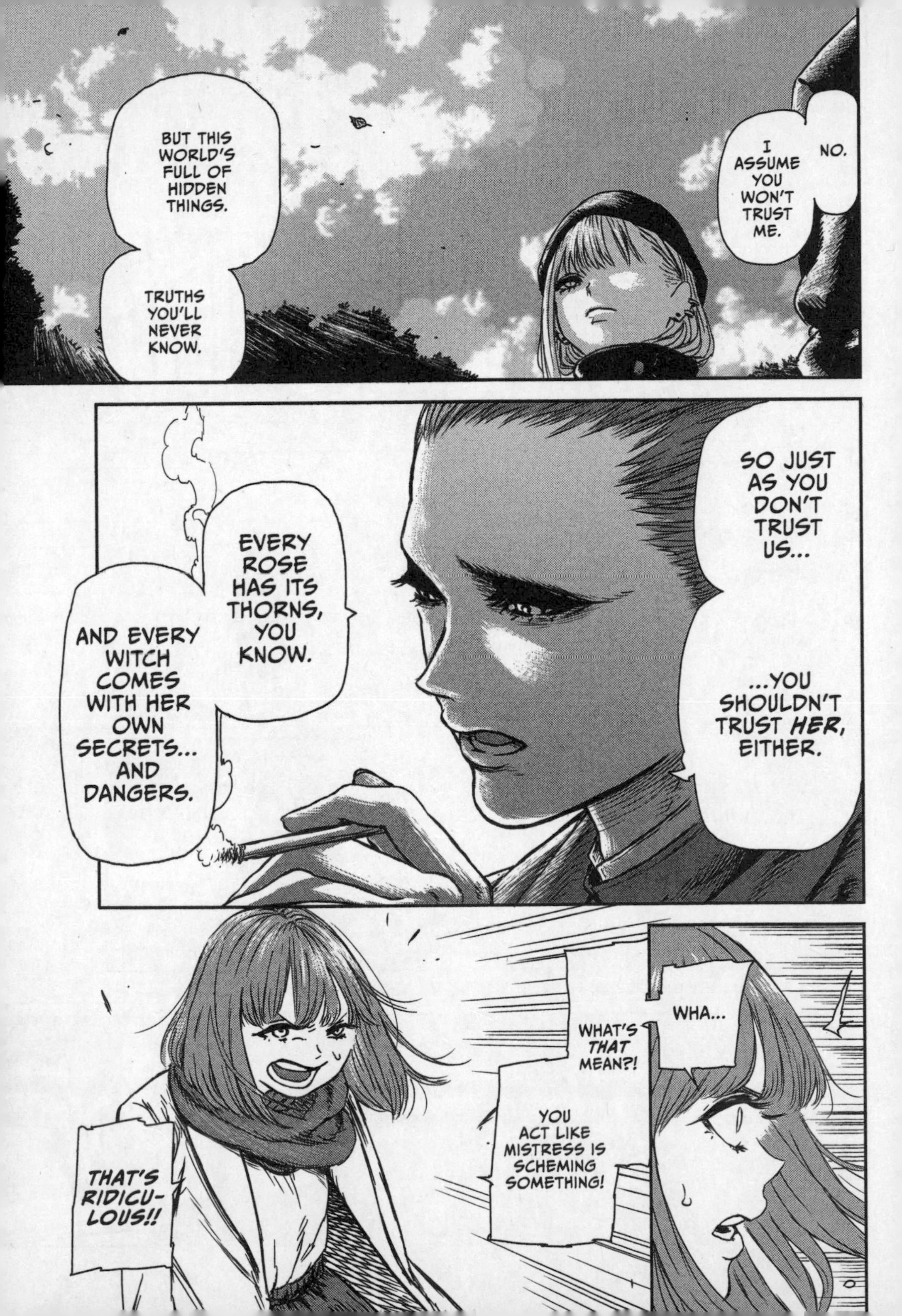
NO.
I ASSUME YOU WON'T TRUST ME.
BUT THIS WORLD'S FULL OF HIDDEN THINGS.
TRUTHS YOU'LL NEVER KNOW.
SO JUST AS YOU DON'T TRUST US...
...YOU SHOULDN'T TRUST *HER*, EITHER.
EVERY ROSE HAS ITS THORNS, YOU KNOW.
AND EVERY WITCH COMES WITH HER OWN SECRETS... AND DANGERS.
WHA...
WHAT'S *THAT* MEAN?!
YOU ACT LIKE MISTRESS IS SCHEMING SOMETHING!
THAT'S RIDICULOUS!!

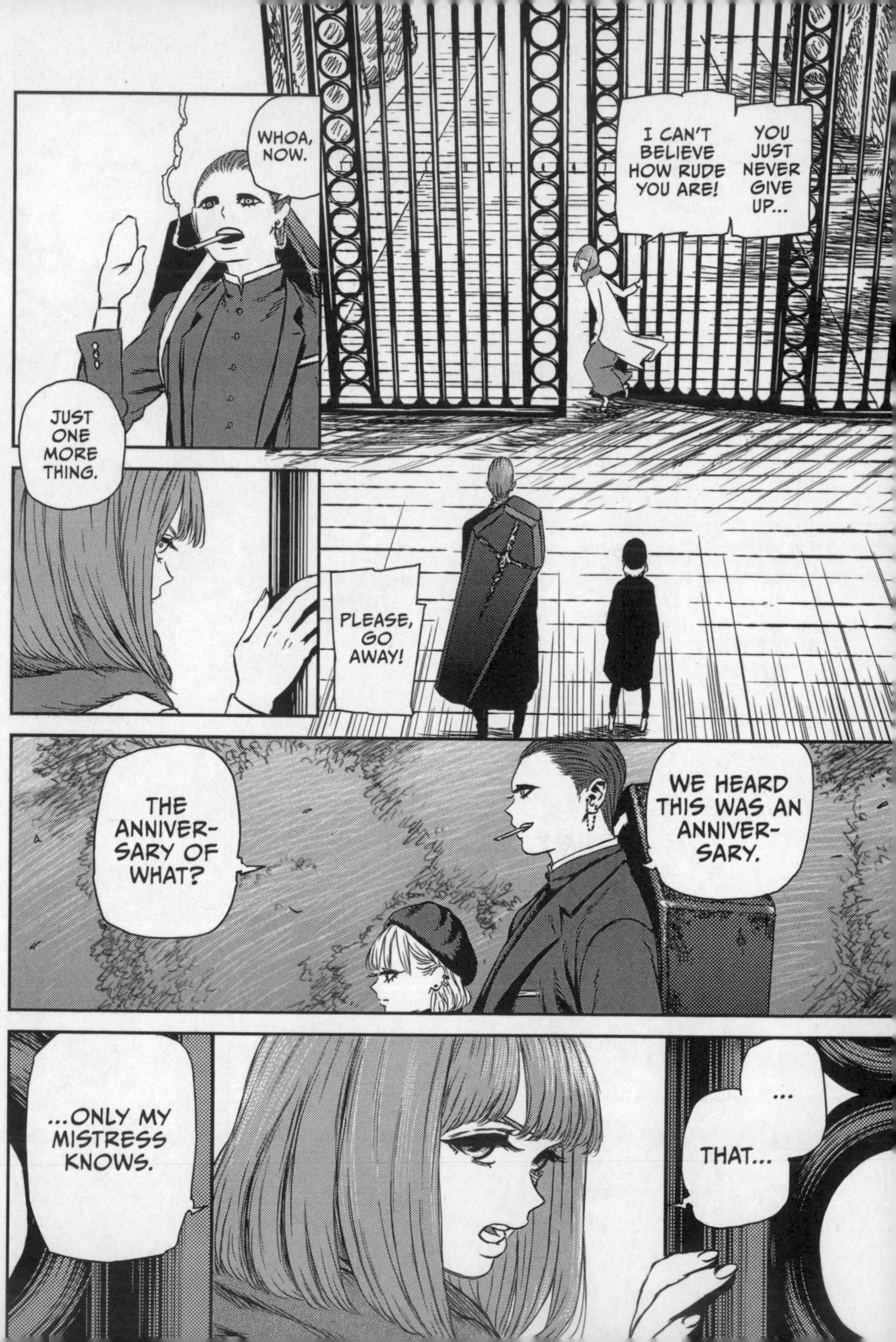
YOU JUST NEVER GIVE UP...
I CAN'T BELIEVE HOW RUDE YOU ARE!
WHOA, NOW.
JUST ONE MORE THING.
PLEASE, GO AWAY!
WE HEARD THIS WAS AN ANNIVER-SARY.
THE ANNIVER-SARY OF WHAT?
... THAT...
...ONLY MY MISTRESS KNOWS.

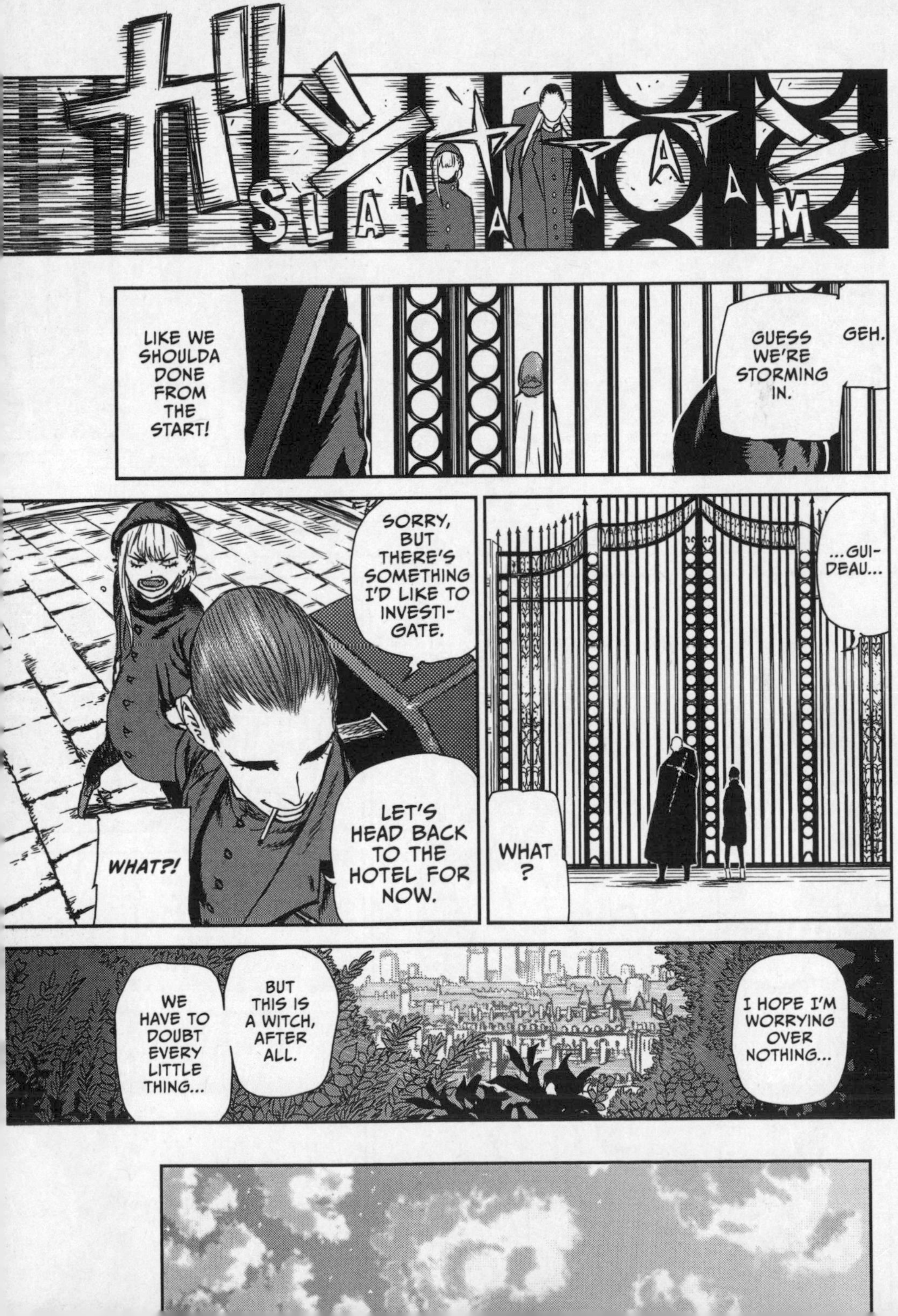
SLAAAAAAM
GEH.
GUESS WE'RE STORMING IN.
LIKE WE SHOULDA DONE FROM THE START!
...GUI-DEAU...
WHAT?
SORRY, BUT THERE'S SOMETHING I'D LIKE TO INVESTI-GATE.
LET'S HEAD BACK TO THE HOTEL FOR NOW.
WHAT?!
I HOPE I'M WORRYING OVER NOTHING...
BUT THIS IS A WITCH, AFTER ALL.
WE HAVE TO DOUBT EVERY LITTLE THING...

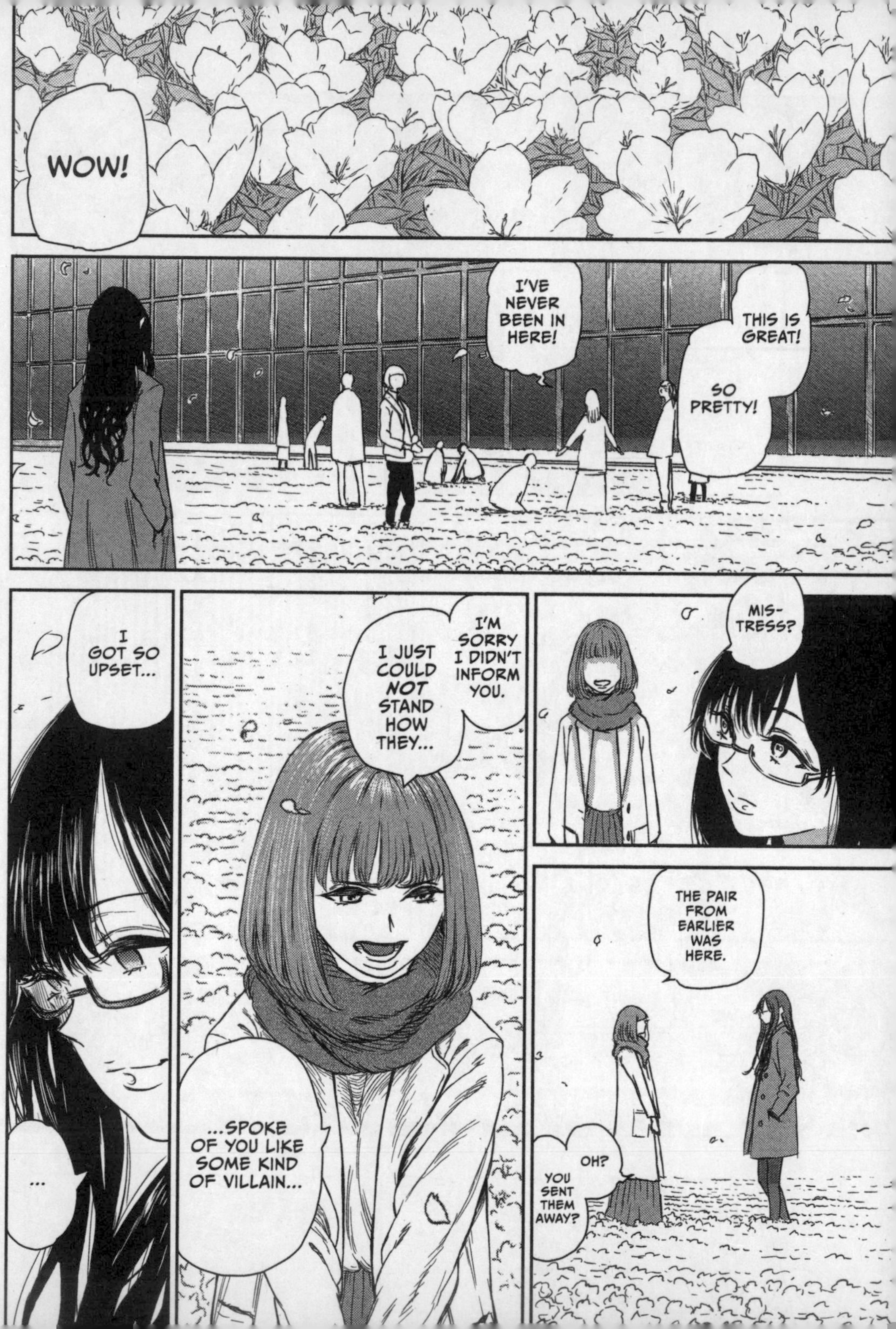
WOW!
THIS IS GREAT!
SO PRETTY!
I'VE NEVER BEEN IN HERE!
MIS-TRESS?
THE PAIR FROM EARLIER WAS HERE.
OH?
YOU SENT THEM AWAY?
I'M SORRY I DIDN'T INFORM YOU.
I JUST COULD NOT STAND HOW THEY...
...SPOKE OF YOU LIKE SOME KIND OF VILLAIN...
I GOT SO UPSET...
...

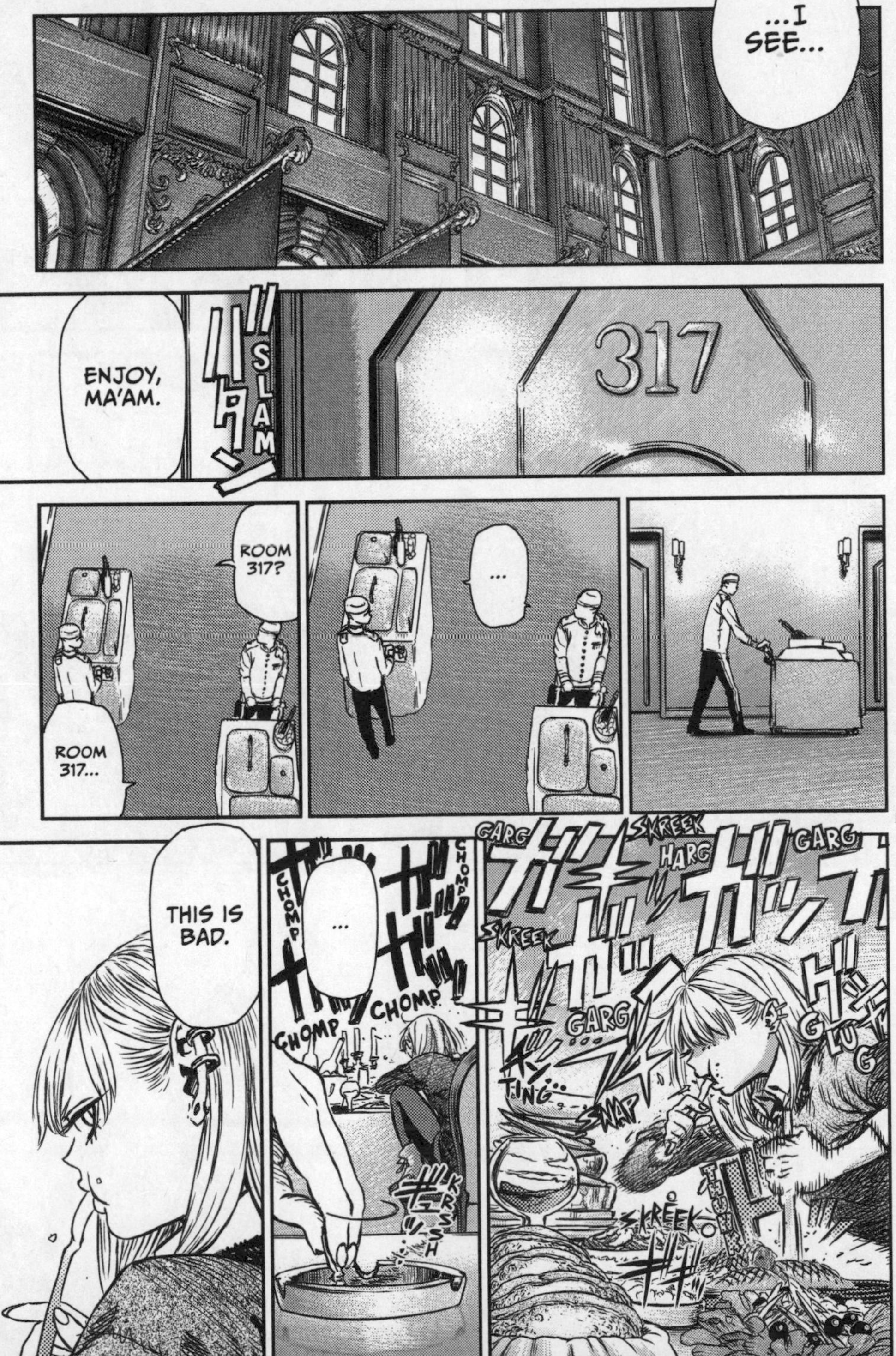

...I SEE...
SLAM
ENJOY, MA'AM.
...
ROOM 317?
ROOM 317...
GARG
SKREEK
HARG
GARG
SKREEK
GARG
GLUG
TING...
SNAP
SKREEK
CHOMP
CHOMP
...
CHOMP
CHOMP
KRSSH
THIS IS BAD.

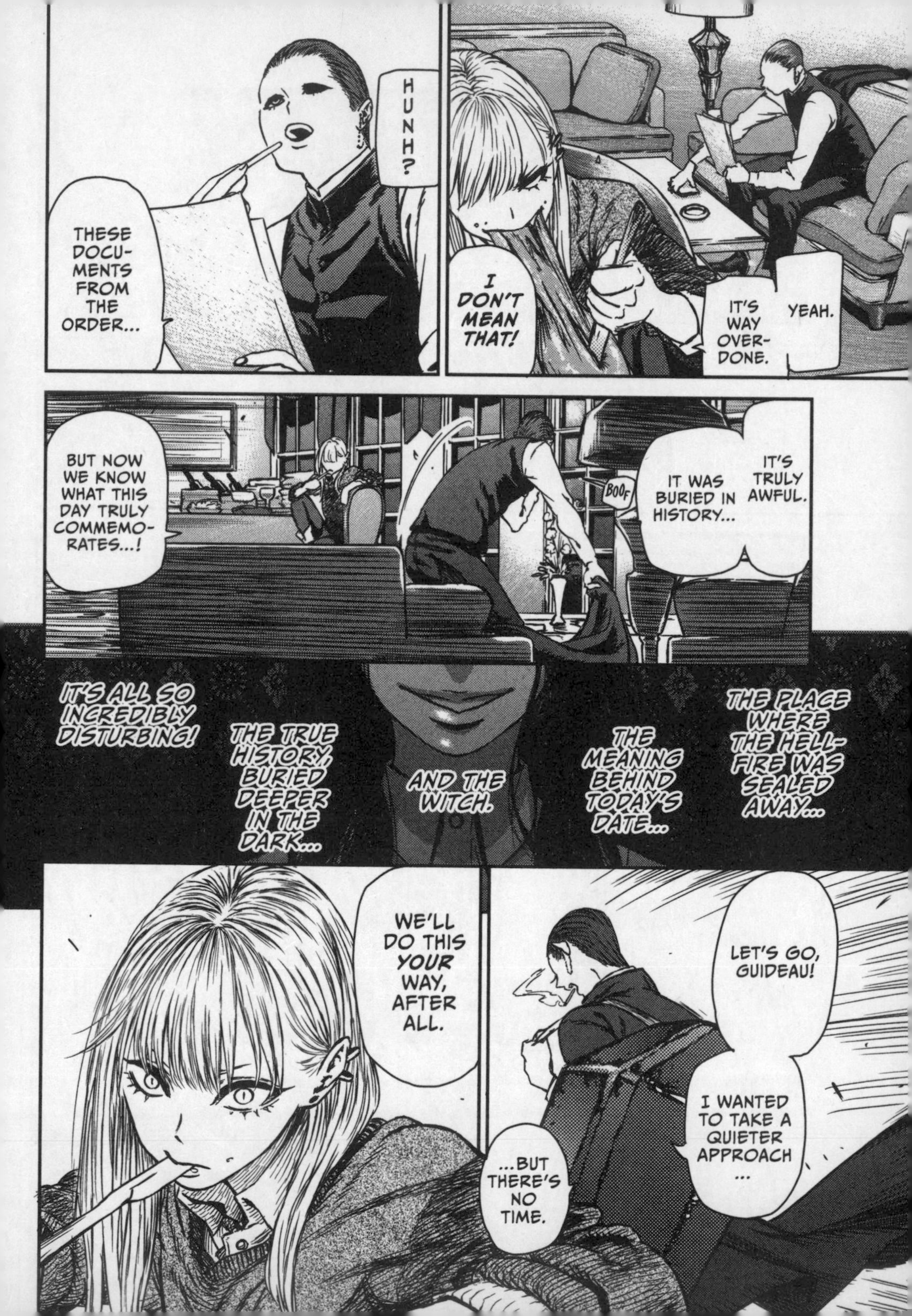
YEAH.
IT'S WAY OVER-DONE.
I DON'T MEAN THAT!
HUNH?
THESE DOCU-MENTS FROM THE ORDER...
IT'S TRULY AWFUL.
IT WAS BURIED IN HISTORY...
BOOF
BUT NOW WE KNOW WHAT THIS DAY TRULY COMMEMO-RATES...!
THE PLACE WHERE THE HELL-FIRE WAS SEALED AWAY...
THE MEANING BEHIND TODAY'S DATE...
AND THE WITCH.
THE TRUE HISTORY, BURIED DEEPER IN THE DARK...
IT'S ALL SO INCREDIBLY DISTURBING!
LET'S GO, GUIDEAU!
I WANTED TO TAKE A QUIETER APPROACH...
...BUT THERE'S NO TIME.
WE'LL DO THIS YOUR WAY, AFTER ALL.

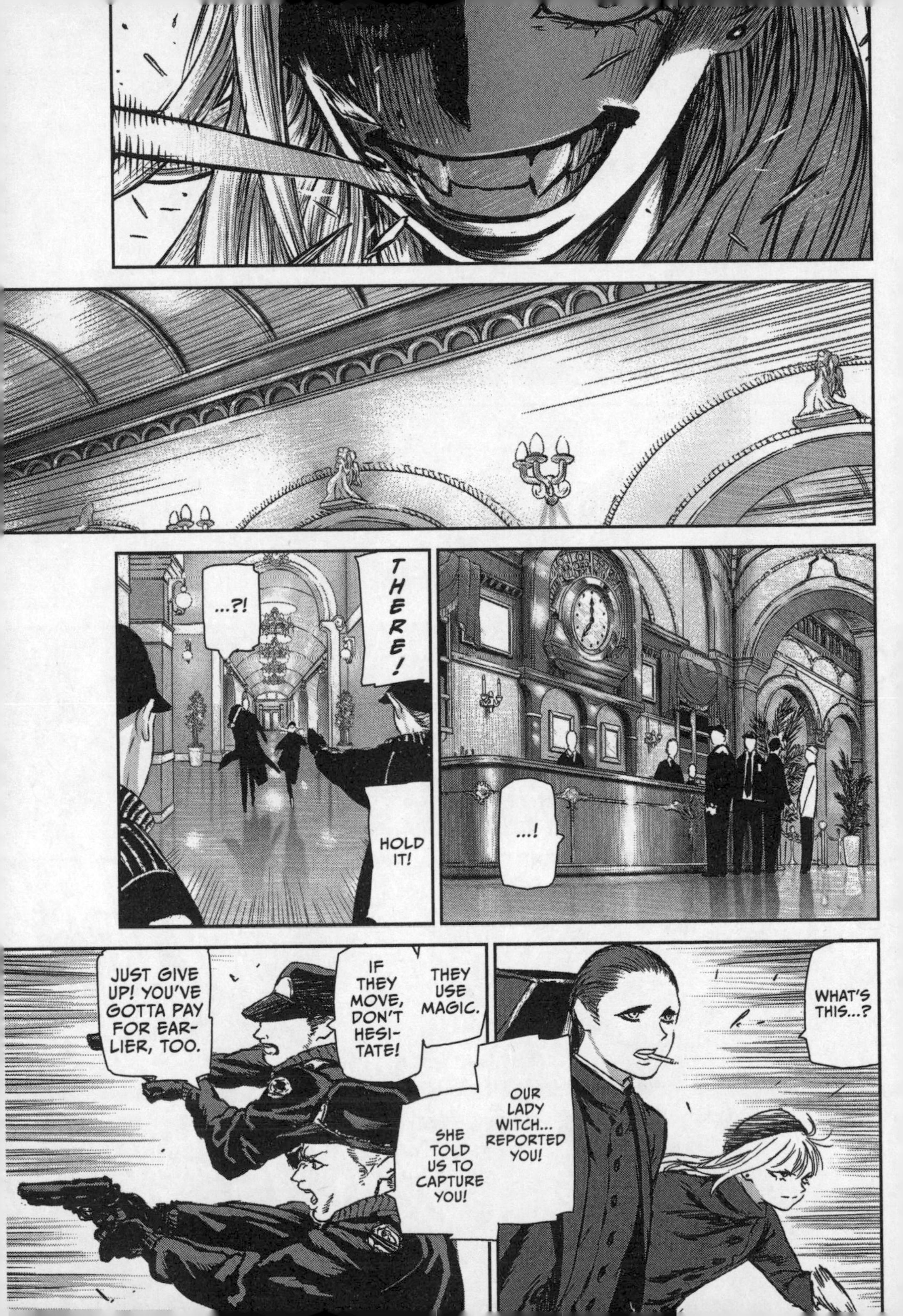
...!
THERE!
...?!
HOLD IT!
WHAT'S THIS...?
OUR LADY WITCH... REPORTED YOU!
SHE TOLD US TO CAPTURE YOU!
THEY USE MAGIC.
IF THEY MOVE, DON'T HESITATE!
JUST GIVE UP! YOU'VE GOTTA PAY FOR EARLIER, TOO.

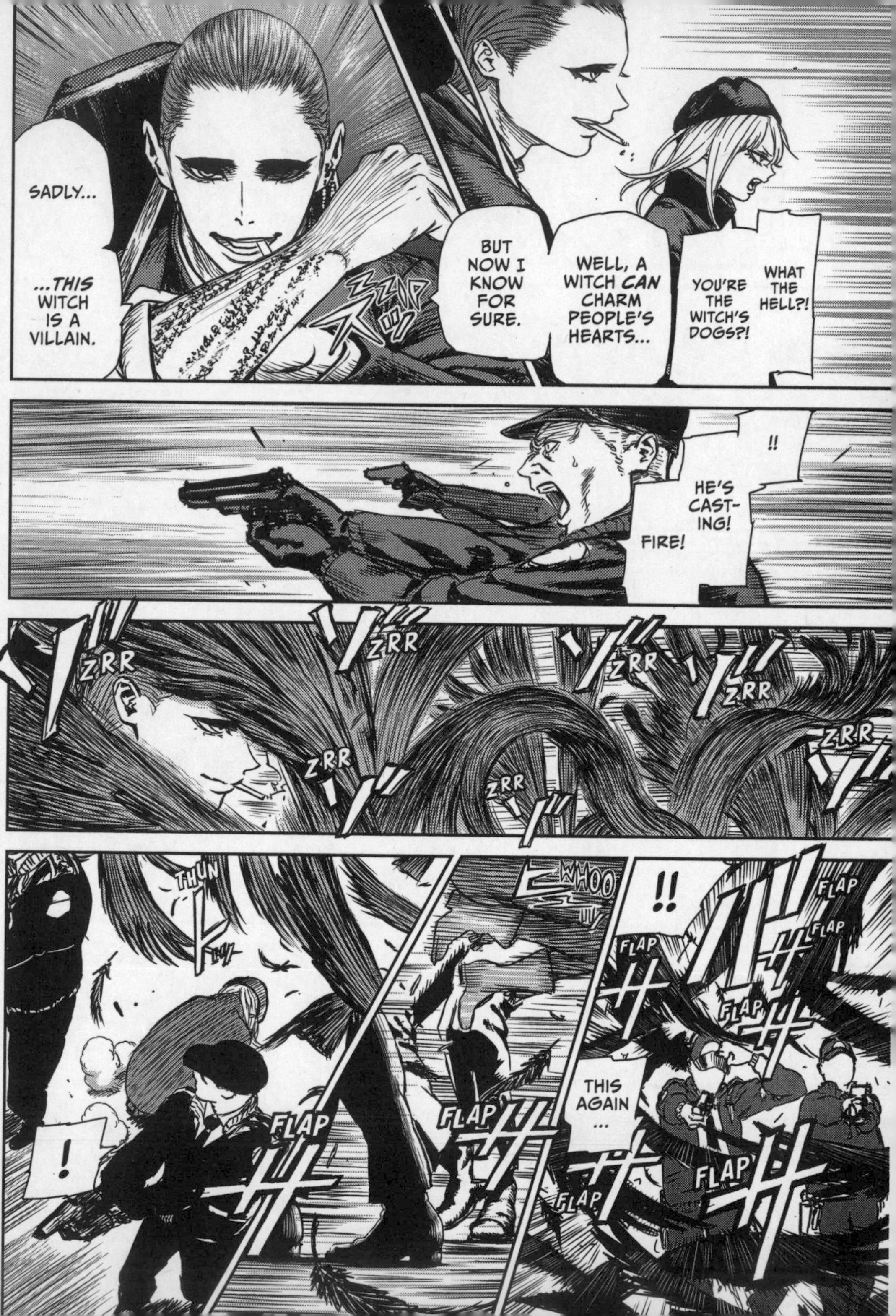
WHAT THE HELL?!
YOU'RE THE WITCH'S DOGS?!
WELL, A WITCH *CAN* CHARM PEOPLE'S HEARTS...
BUT NOW I KNOW FOR SURE.
ZZZIP
SADLY...
...*THIS* WITCH IS A VILLAIN.
!!
HE'S CASTING!
FIRE!
ZRR
ZRR
ZRR
ZRR
ZRR
ZRR
ZRR
FLAP
FLAP
FLAP
!!
FLAP
THIS AGAIN ...
FLAP
FLAP
WHOO
FLAP
THUN
!
FLAP

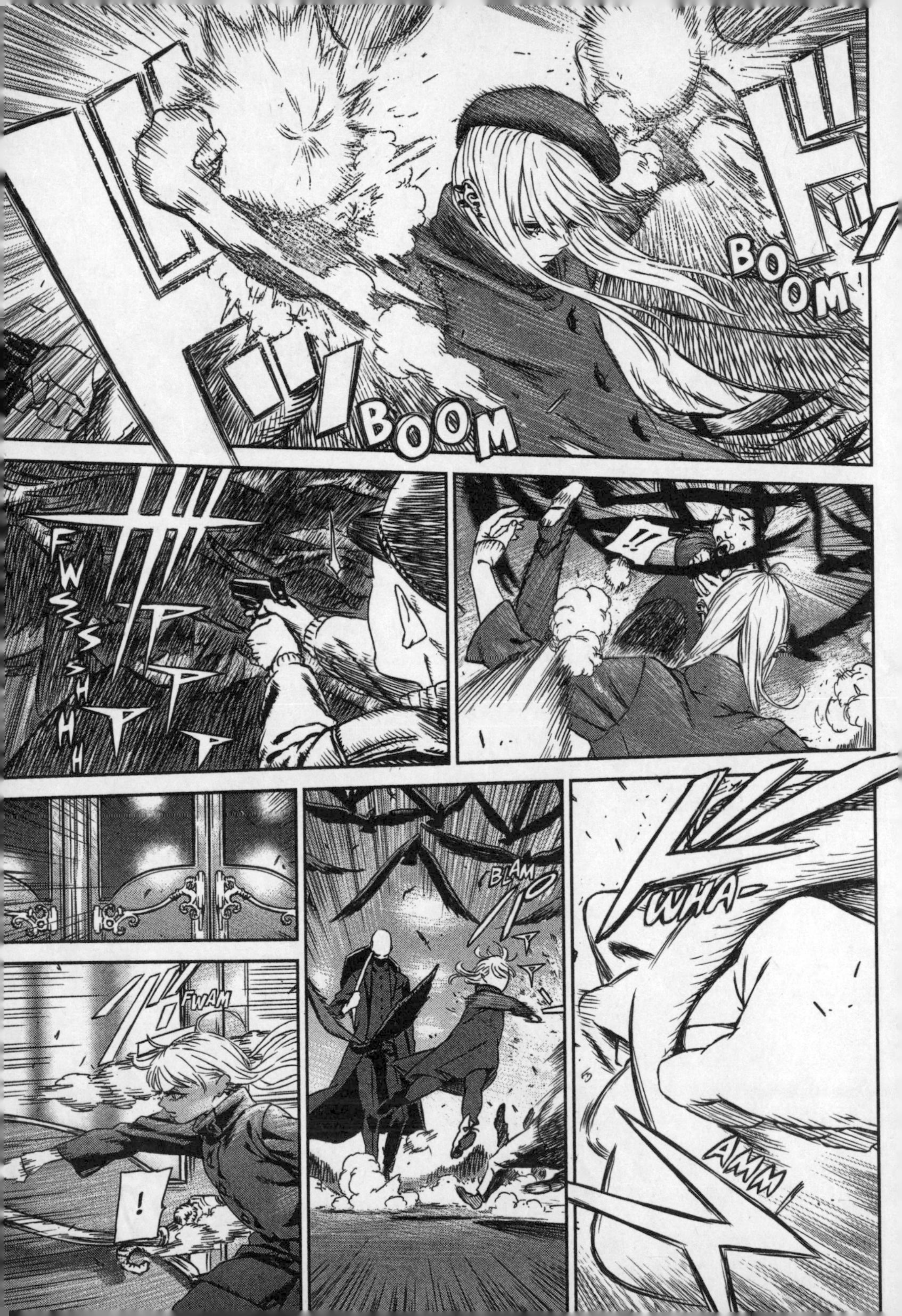
BOOM
BOOM
!!
FWSSSHHH
WHA-
AMM
BLAM
FWAM
!

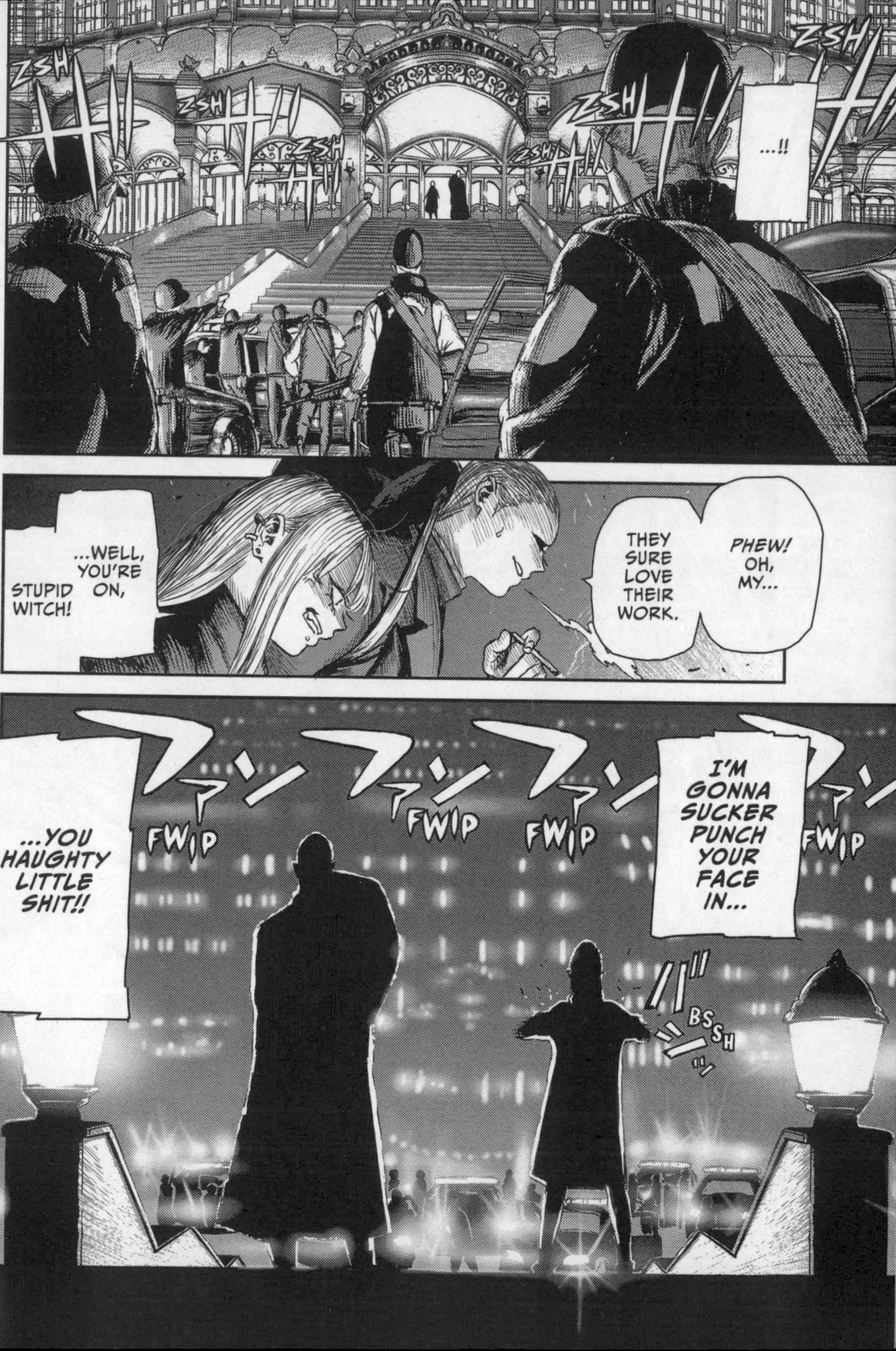
ZSH
ZSH
ZSH
ZSH
ZSH
ZSH
...!!
PHEW! OH, MY...
THEY SURE LOVE THEIR WORK.
...WELL, YOU'RE ON, STUPID WITCH!
FWIP
FWIP
FWIP
FWIP
I'M GONNA SUCKER PUNCH YOUR FACE IN...
...YOU HAUGHTY LITTLE SHIT!!
BSSH

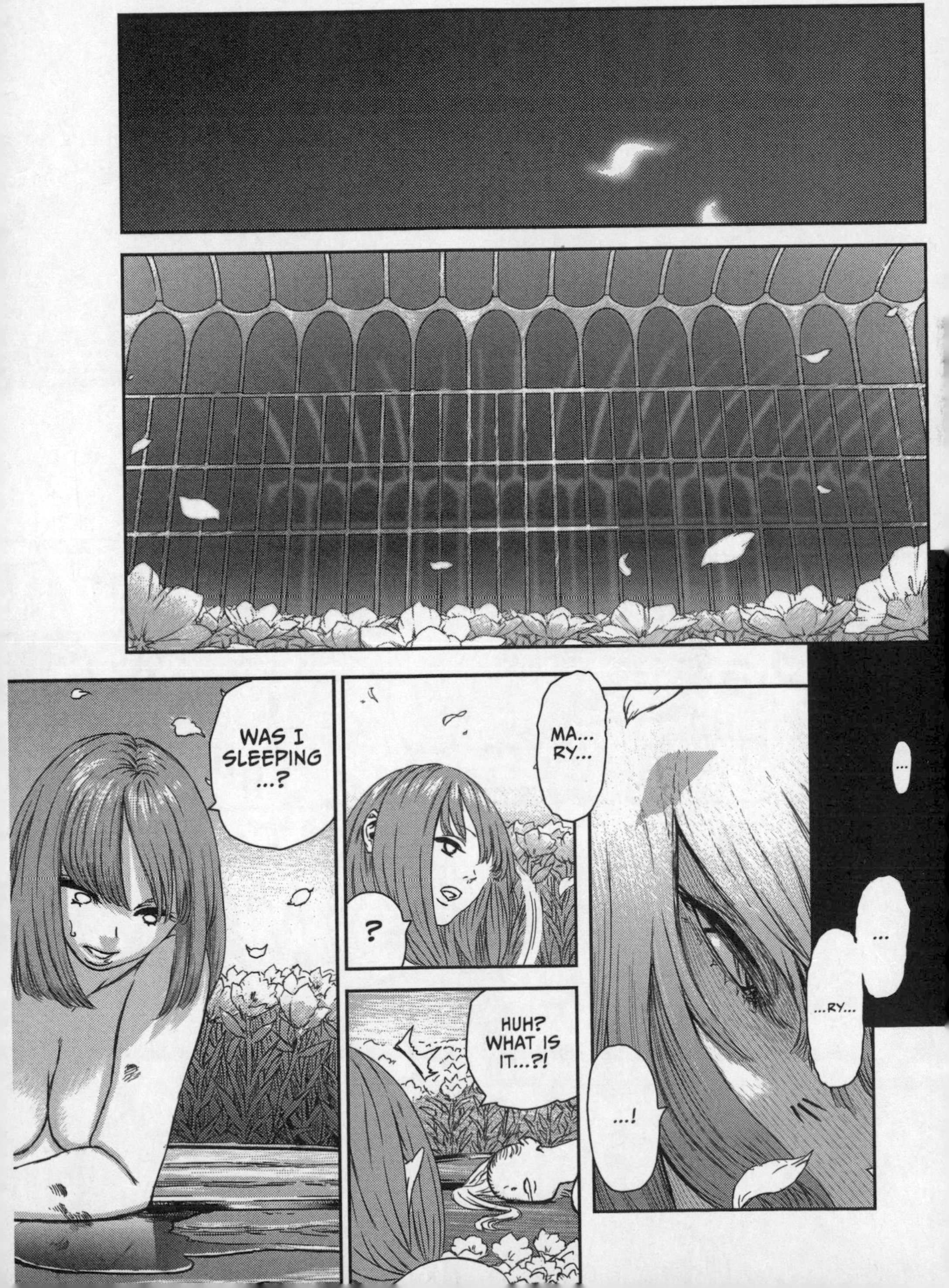
...
...
...RY...
...!
MA... RY...
?
HUH? WHAT IS IT...?!
WAS I SLEEPING ...?

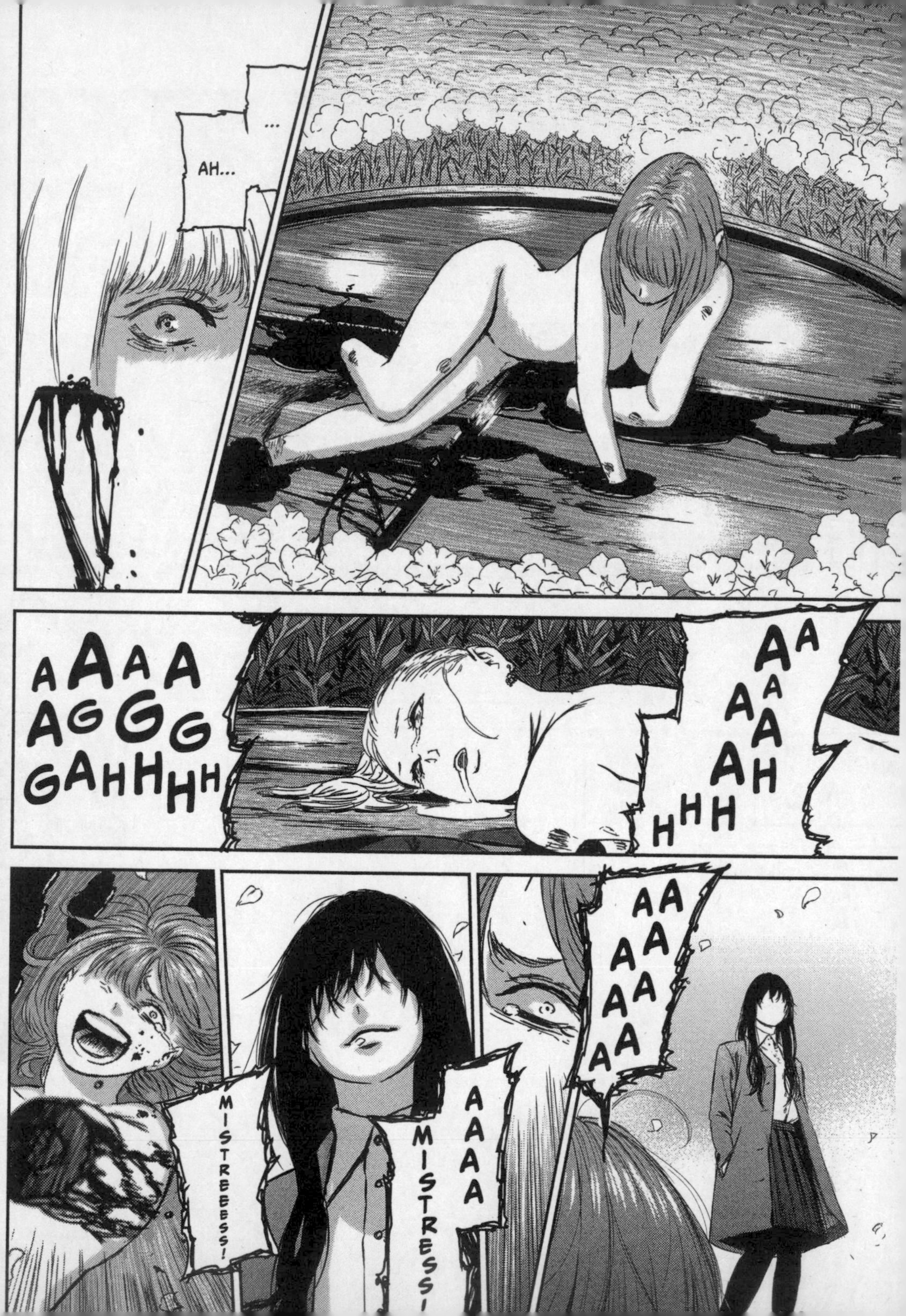
...
AH...
AAAAAAAHHHH
AAAAAGGGGGAHHHHH
AAAAAAAAAA
AAAA
MISTRESS!
MISTREEESS!

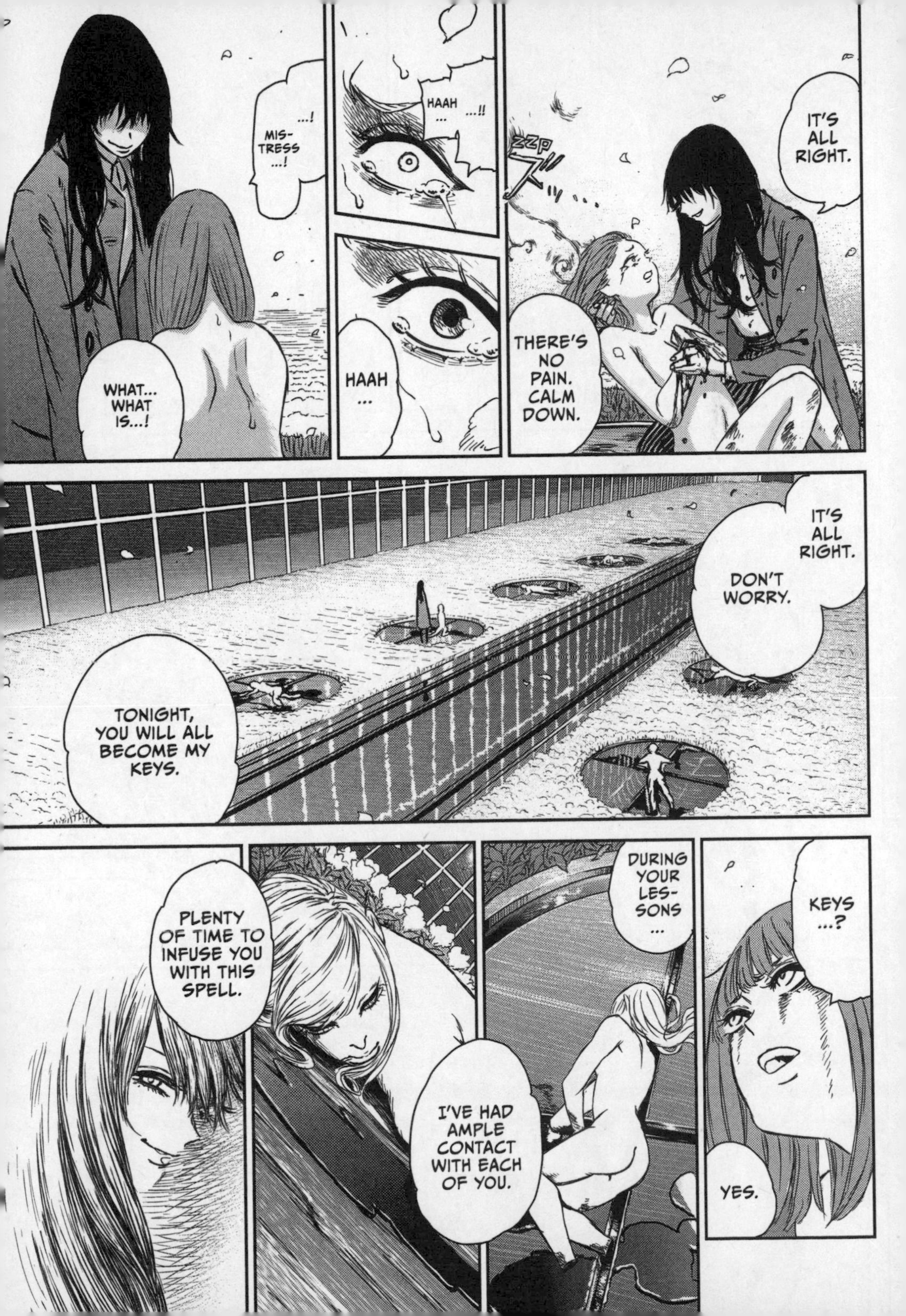
IT'S ALL RIGHT.
ZZP
THERE'S NO PAIN. CALM DOWN.
HAAH ... ...!!
HAAH ...
...! MISTRESS ...!
WHAT... WHAT IS...!
IT'S ALL RIGHT.
DON'T WORRY.
TONIGHT, YOU WILL ALL BECOME MY KEYS.
KEYS ...?
YES.
DURING YOUR LESSONS ...
I'VE HAD AMPLE CONTACT WITH EACH OF YOU.
PLENTY OF TIME TO INFUSE YOU WITH THIS SPELL.

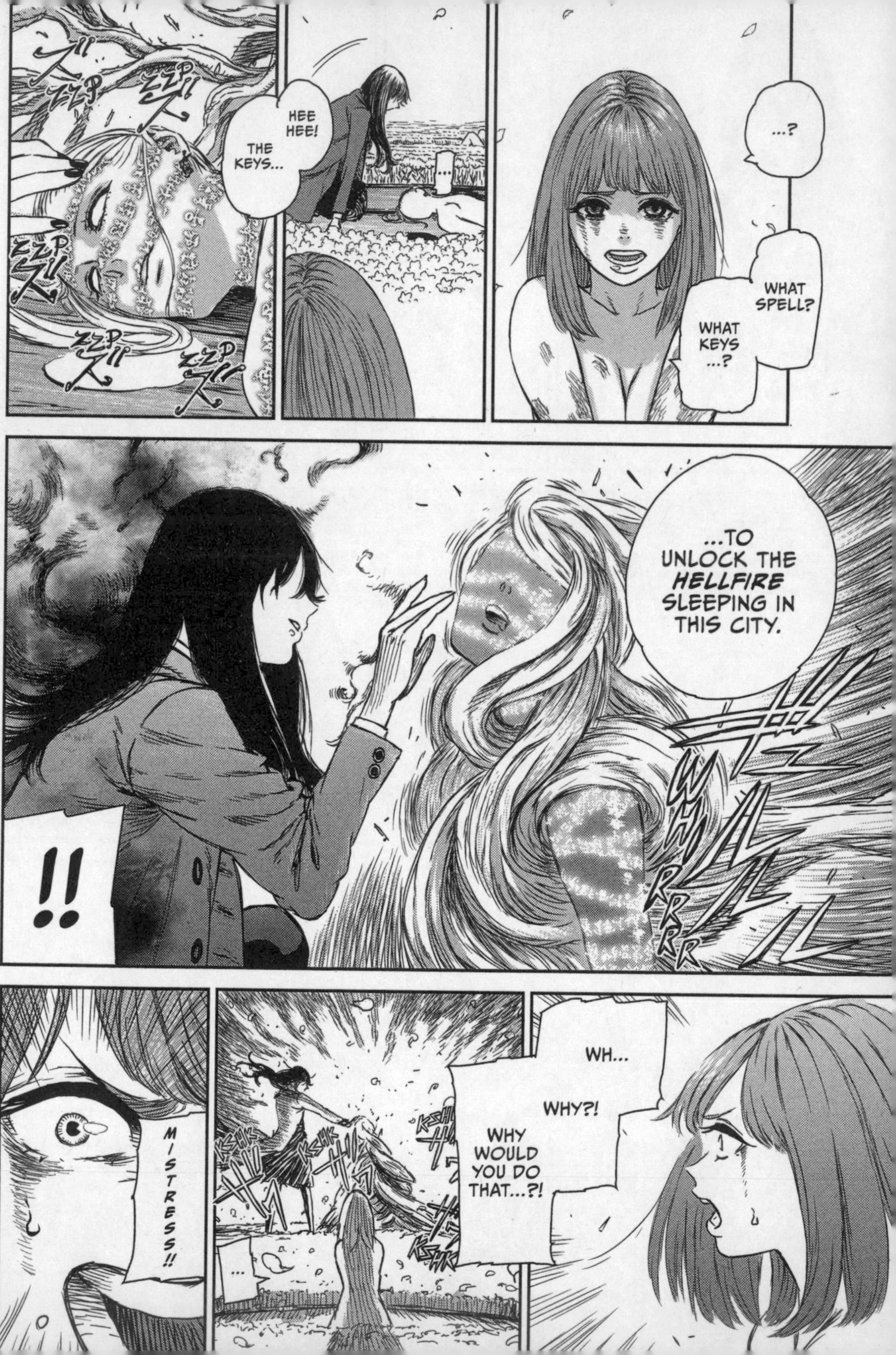
...?
WHAT SPELL? WHAT KEYS ...?
...
HEE HEE! THE KEYS...
ZZZP!!
ZZZP!!
ZZZP!!
ZZZP!!
ZZZP!!
...TO UNLOCK THE HELLFIRE SLEEPING IN THIS CITY.
WHHIRRRR
!!
WH...
WHY?!
WHY WOULD YOU DO THAT...?!
KSHK
KSHK
...
MISTRESS!!

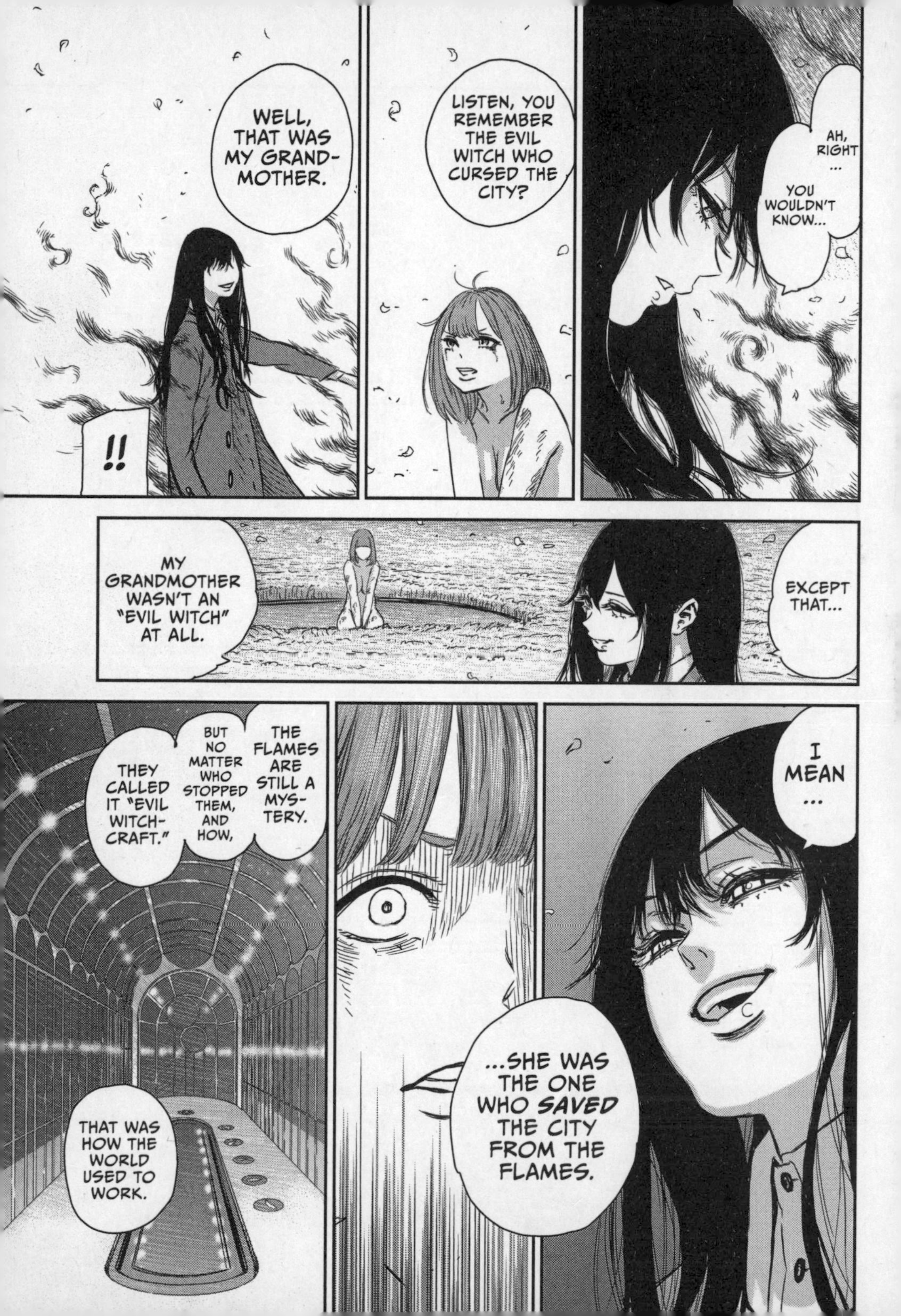
AH, RIGHT ... YOU WOULDN'T KNOW...
LISTEN, YOU REMEMBER THE EVIL WITCH WHO CURSED THE CITY?
WELL, THAT WAS MY GRANDMOTHER.
!!
EXCEPT THAT...
MY GRANDMOTHER WASN'T AN "EVIL WITCH" AT ALL.
I MEAN ...
...SHE WAS THE ONE WHO *SAVED* THE CITY FROM THE FLAMES.
THE FLAMES ARE STILL A MYSTERY.
BUT NO MATTER WHO STOPPED THEM, AND HOW,
THEY CALLED IT "EVIL WITCHCRAFT."
THAT WAS HOW THE WORLD USED TO WORK.

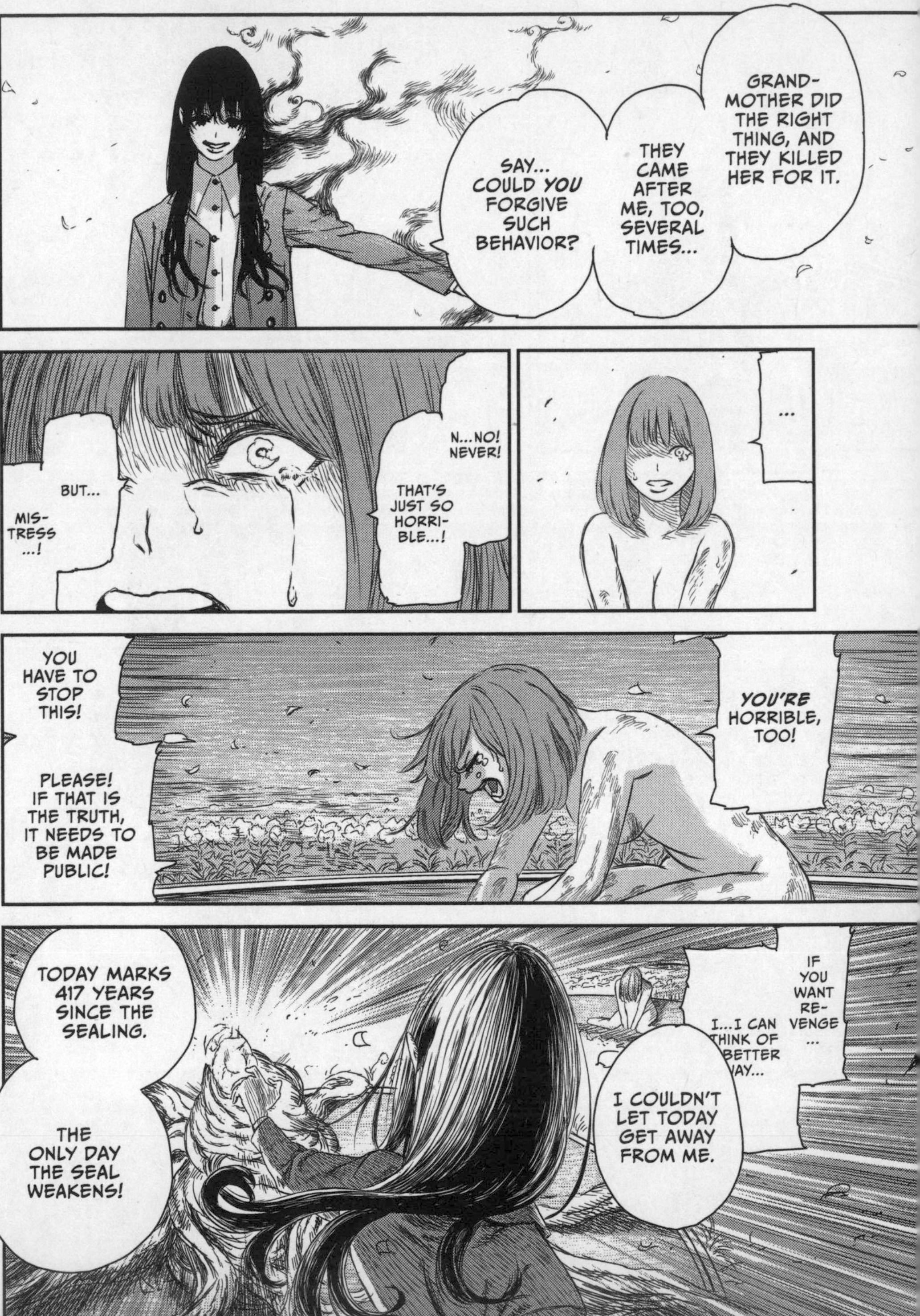
GRAND-MOTHER DID THE RIGHT THING, AND THEY KILLED HER FOR IT.
THEY CAME AFTER ME, TOO, SEVERAL TIMES...
SAY... COULD *YOU* FORGIVE SUCH BEHAVIOR?
...
N...NO! NEVER!
THAT'S JUST SO HORRI-BLE...!
BUT...
MIS-TRESS ...!
YOU'RE HORRIBLE, TOO!
YOU HAVE TO STOP THIS!
PLEASE! IF THAT IS THE TRUTH, IT NEEDS TO BE MADE PUBLIC!
IF YOU WANT RE-VENGE ...
I...I CAN THINK OF
I COULDN'T LET TODAY GET AWAY FROM ME.
TODAY MARKS 417 YEARS SINCE THE SEALING.
THE ONLY DAY THE SEAL WEAKENS!

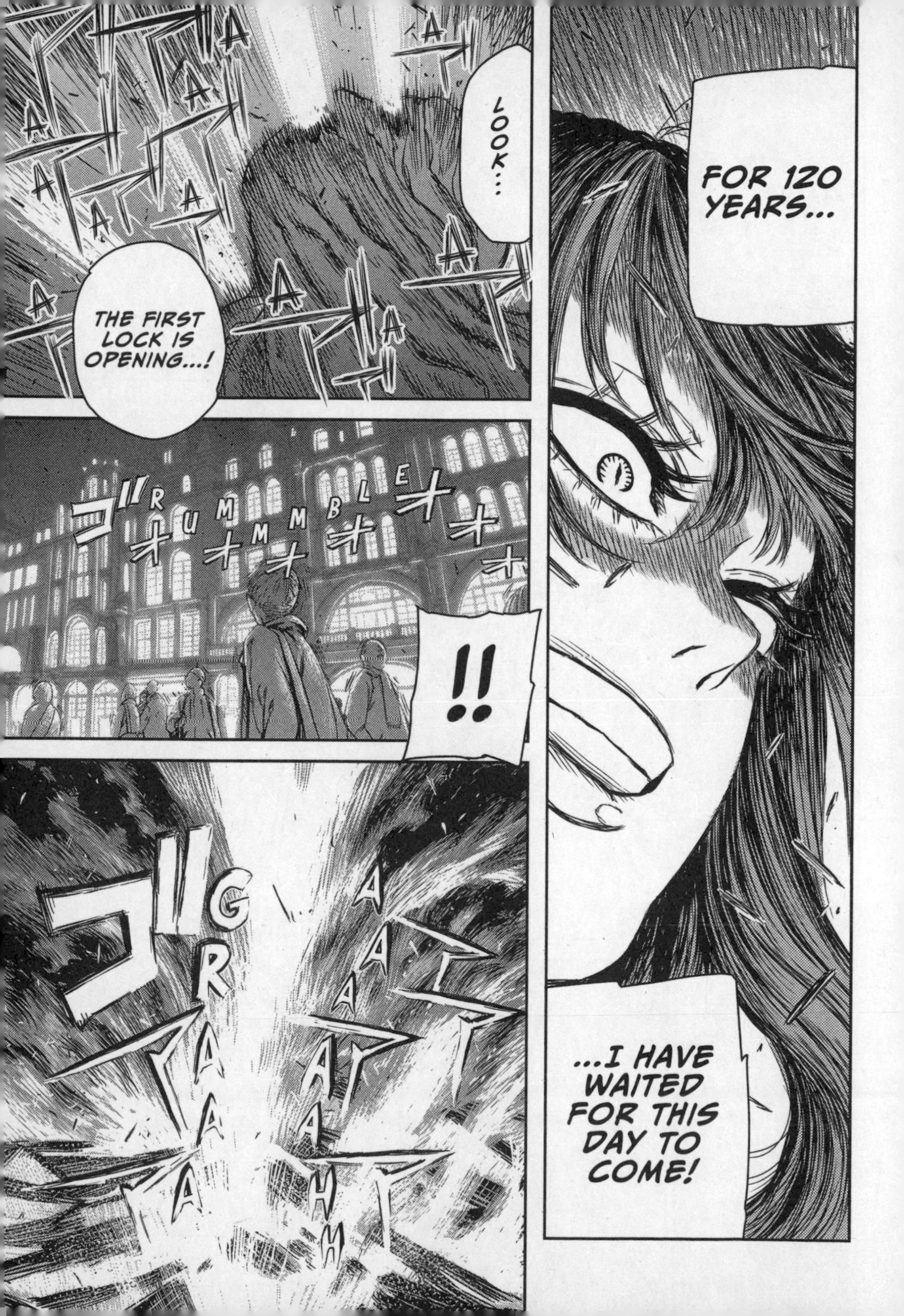
FOR 120 YEARS...
...I HAVE WAITED FOR THIS DAY TO COME!
LOOK...
THE FIRST LOCK IS OPENING...!
RUMMMMBLE
!!

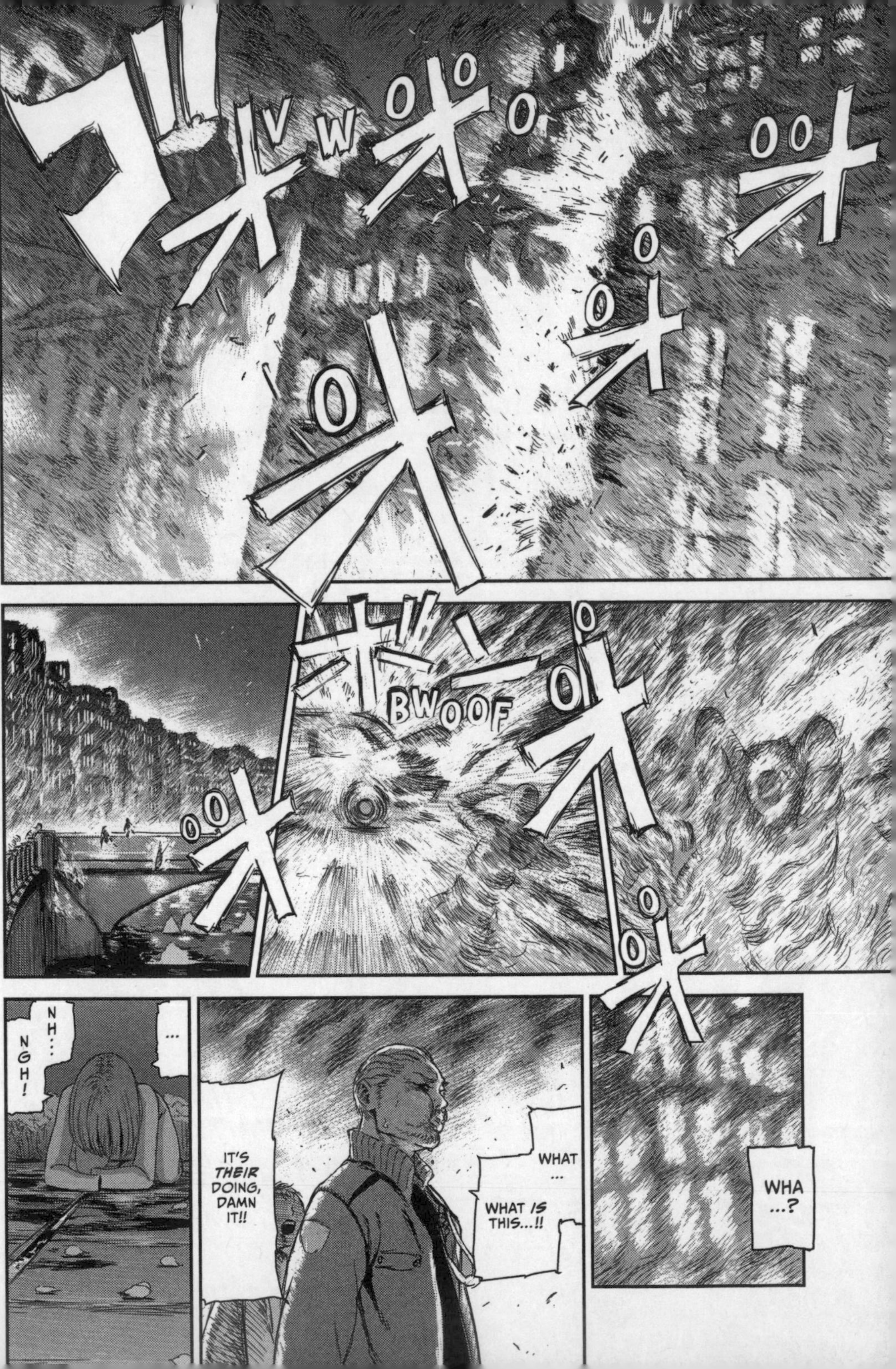
VWOOOOOOOO
BWOOF
WHA ...?
WHAT ... WHAT *IS* THIS...!!
IT'S *THEIR* DOING, DAMN IT!!
...
NH... NGH!

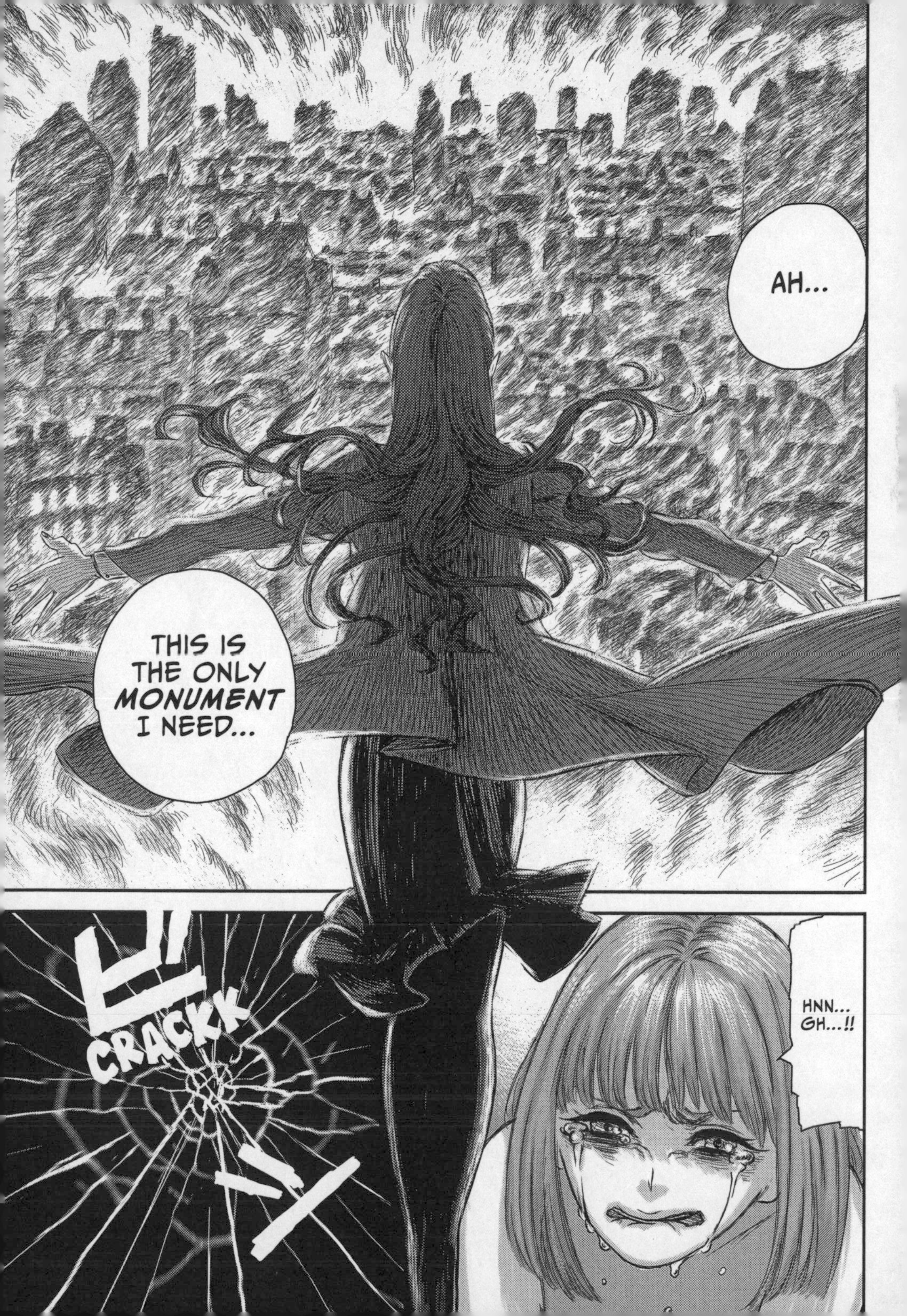
AH...
THIS IS THE ONLY *MONUMENT* I NEED...
HNN... GH...!!
CRACKK

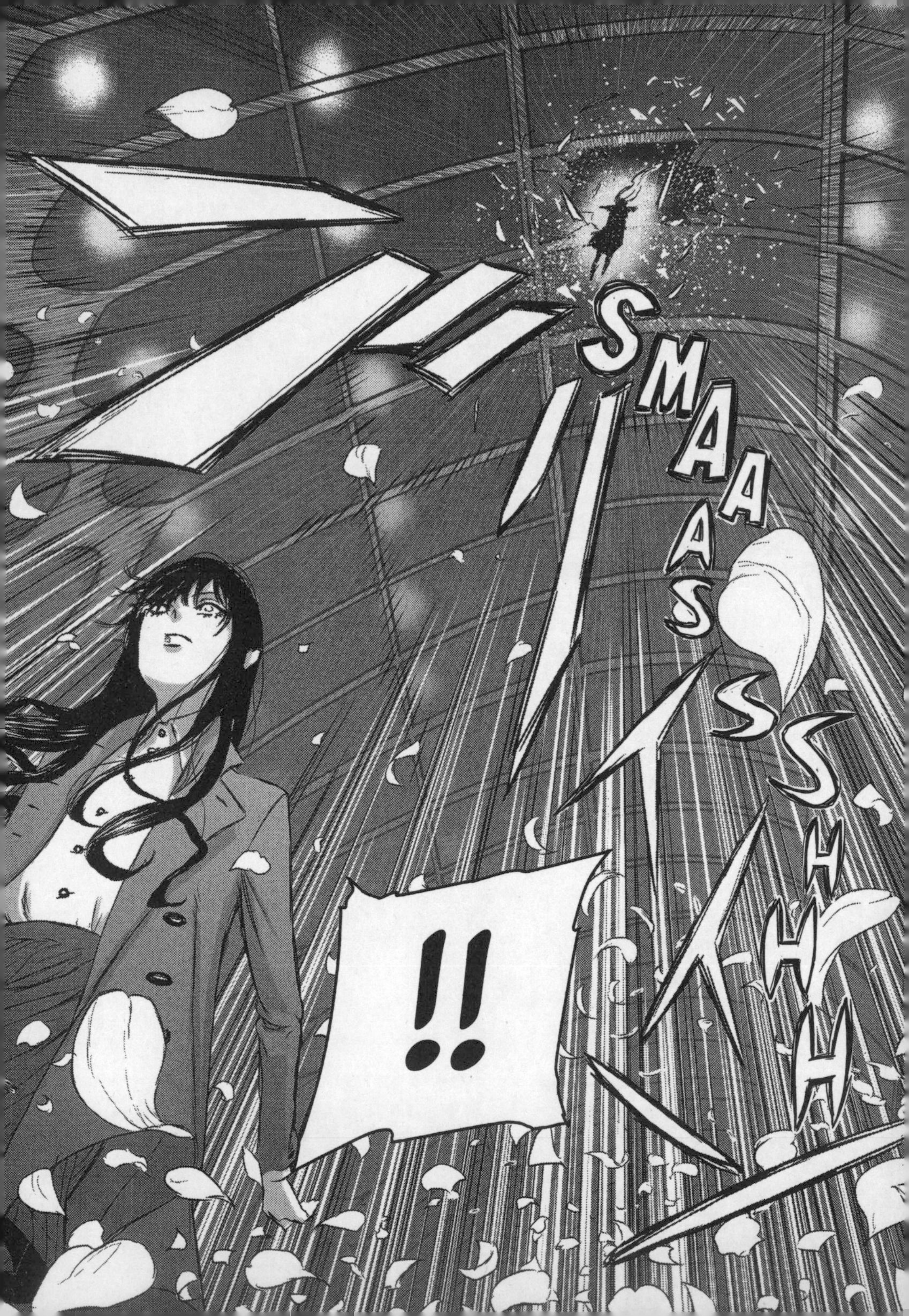
SMAAASSSHHHH
!!

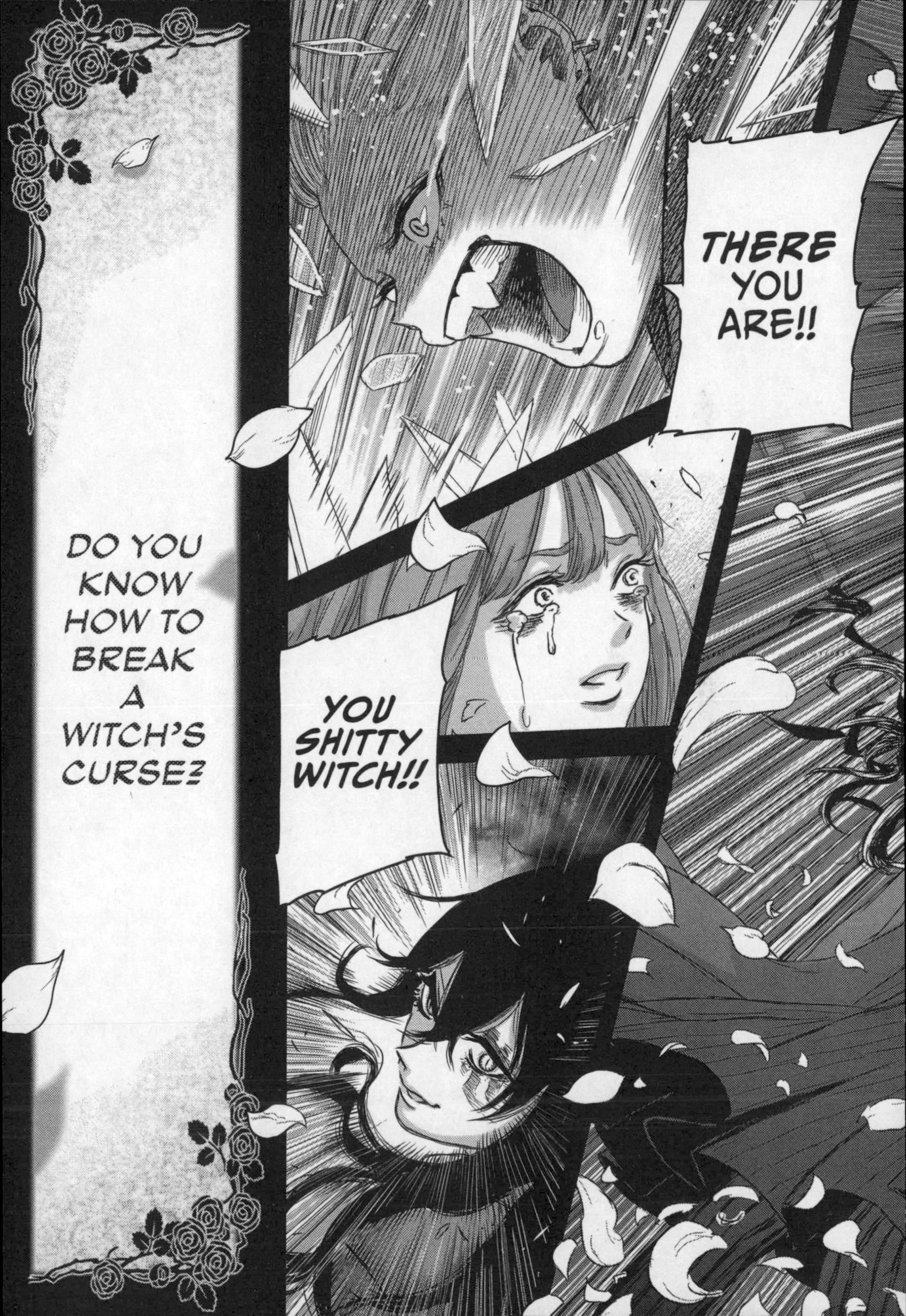
THERE YOU ARE!!
YOU SHITTY WITCH!!
DO YOU KNOW HOW TO BREAK A WITCH'S CURSE?

THE WITCH
AND THE BEAST

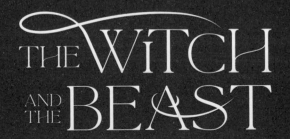

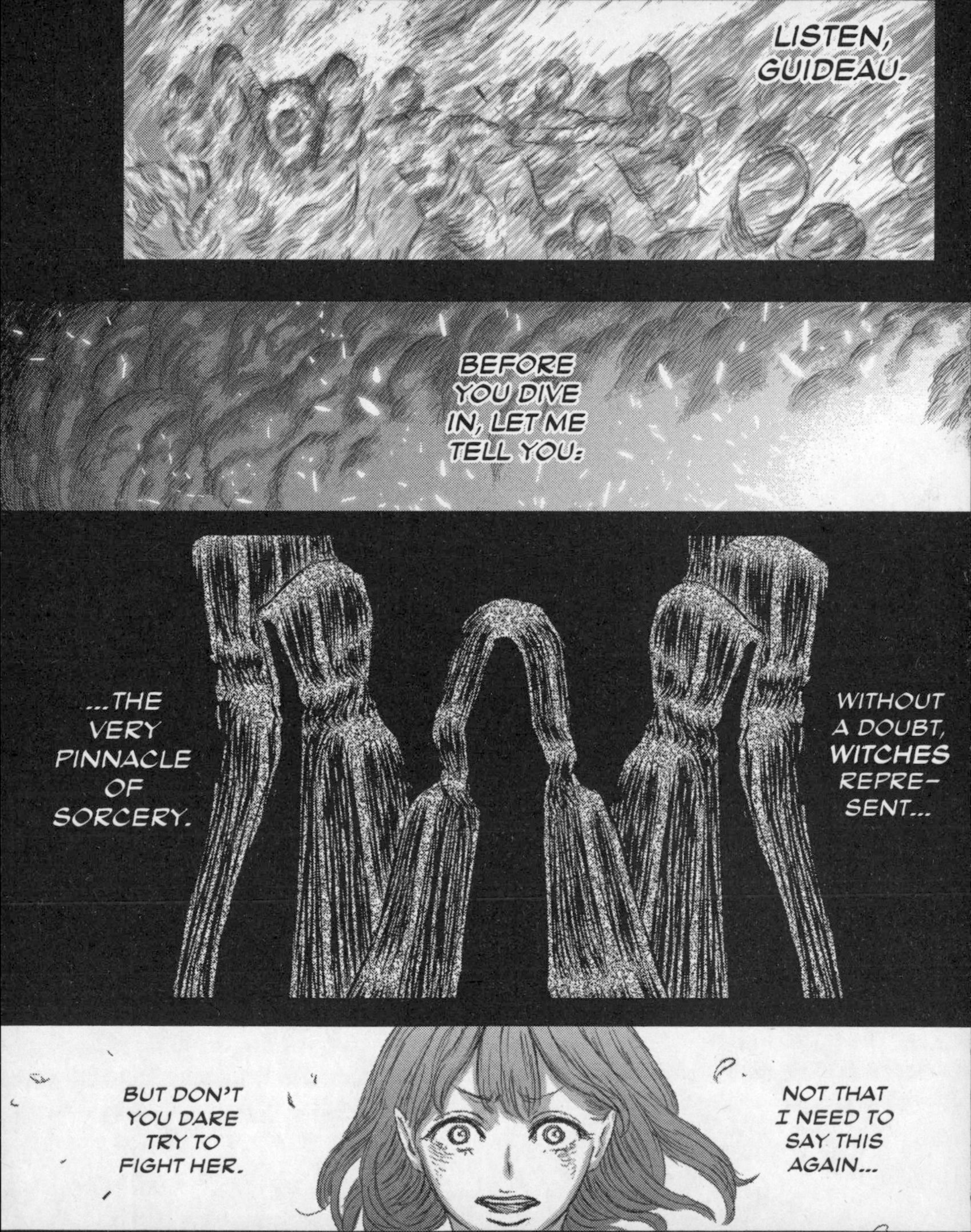
LISTEN, GUIDEAU.
BEFORE YOU DIVE IN, LET ME TELL YOU:
WITHOUT A DOUBT, WITCHES REPRESENT...
...THE VERY PINNACLE OF SORCERY.
NOT THAT I NEED TO SAY THIS AGAIN...
BUT DON'T YOU DARE TRY TO FIGHT HER.

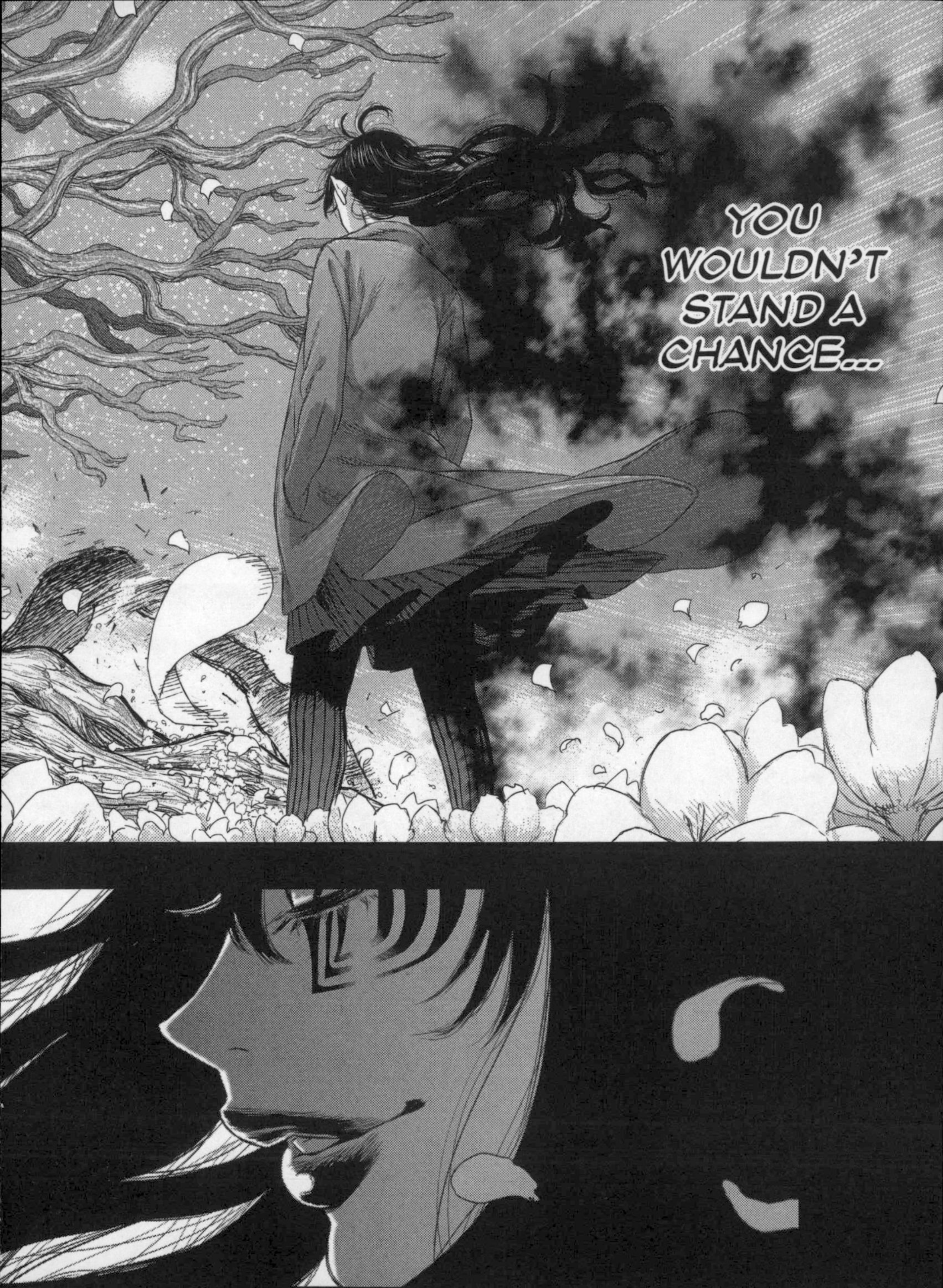
YOU WOULDN'T STAND A CHANCE...

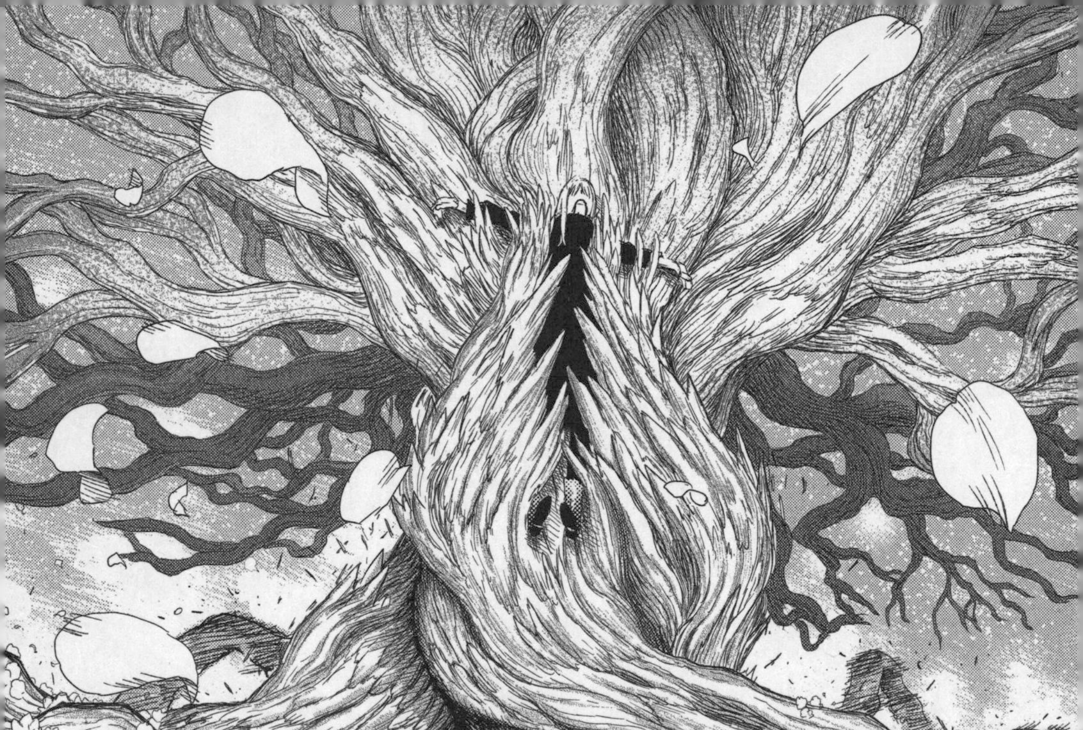

CHAPTER 2: THE WITCH AND THE CRIMSON CITY—FINAL ACT

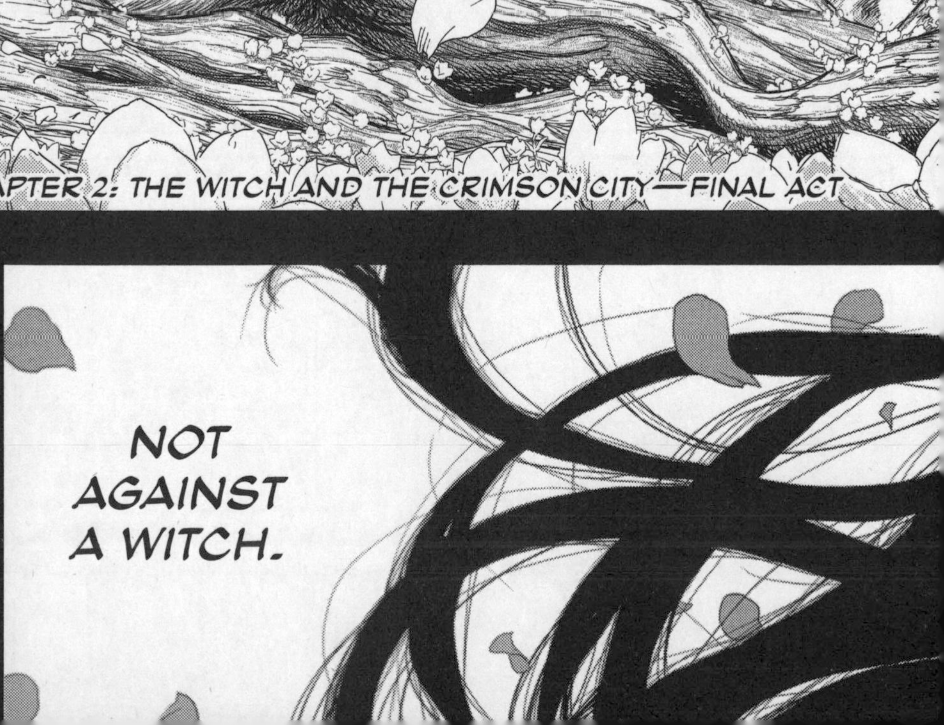
NOT AGAINST A WITCH.

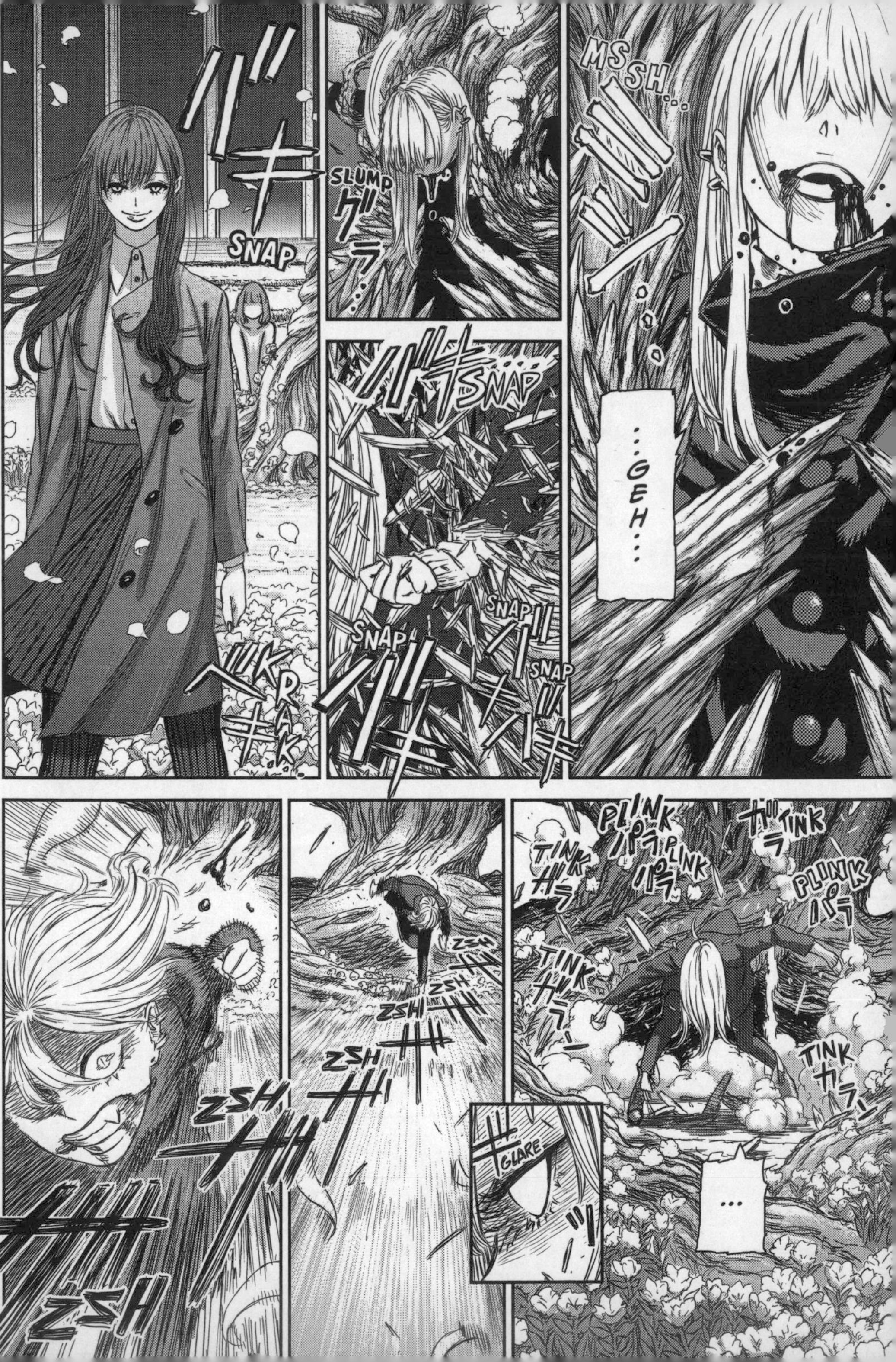
MS SH...
...GEH...
SLUMP
グラ...
SNAP
SNAP
SNAP
SNAP
SNAP
KRAK
PLINK
パラ
TINK
ガラ
PLINK
パラ
TINK
ガラ
PLINK
パラ
TINK
ガラ
TINK
カラン
...
GLARE
ZSH
ZSH
ZSH
ZSH
ZSH
ZSH

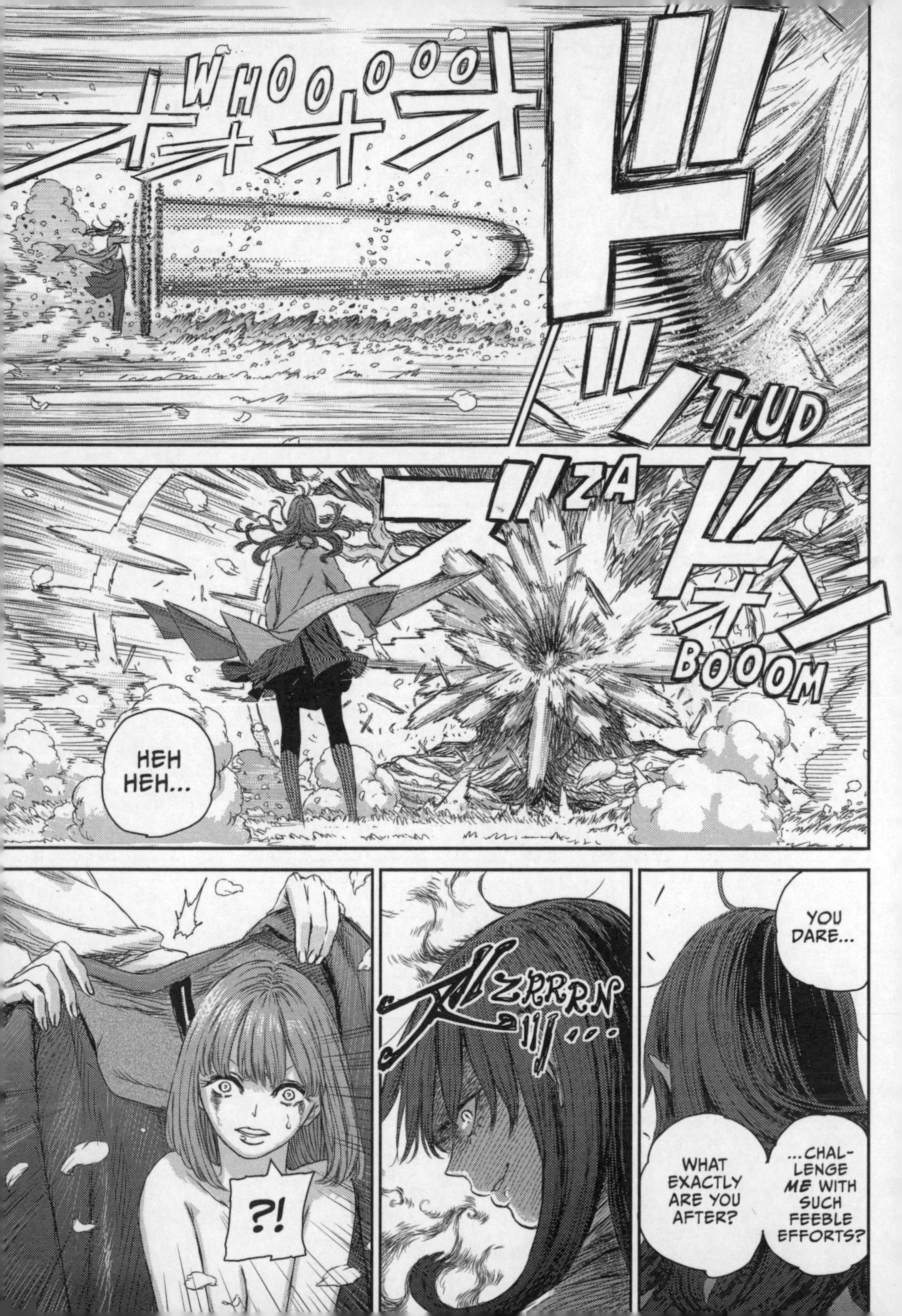
THUD
WHOOOOOO
BOOOM
ZA
HEH HEH...
YOU DARE...
...CHAL-
LENGE
ME WITH
SUCH
FEEBLE
EFFORTS?
WHAT
EXACTLY
ARE YOU
AFTER?
ZRRRN...
?!

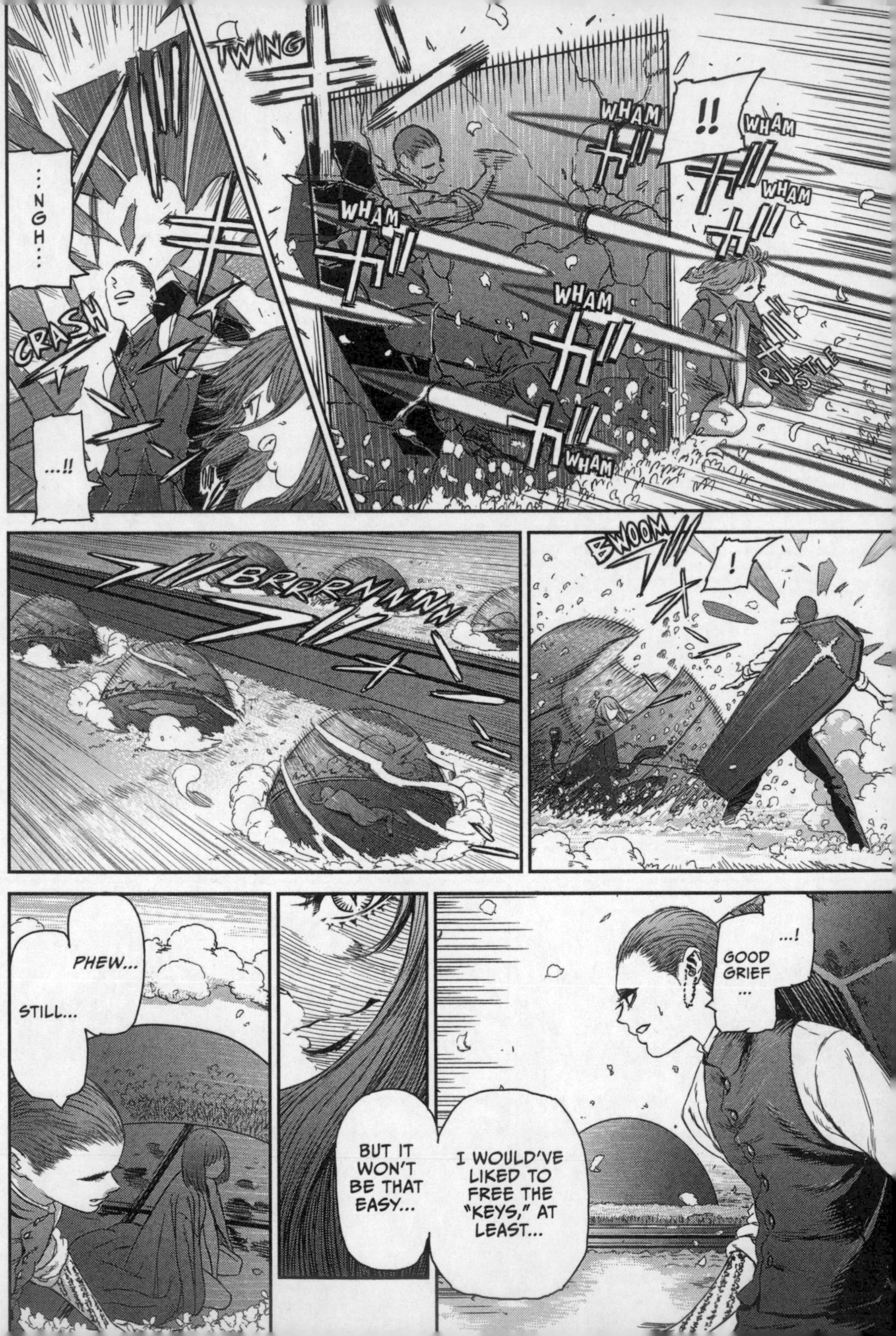
WHAM
!!
WHAM
WHAM
TWING
WHAM
...NGH...
WHAM
RUSTLE
CRASH
WHAM
...!!
BWOOM
!
BRRRRNNNNN
...!
GOOD GRIEF ...
I WOULD'VE LIKED TO FREE THE "KEYS," AT LEAST...
BUT IT WON'T BE THAT EASY...
PHEW...
STILL...

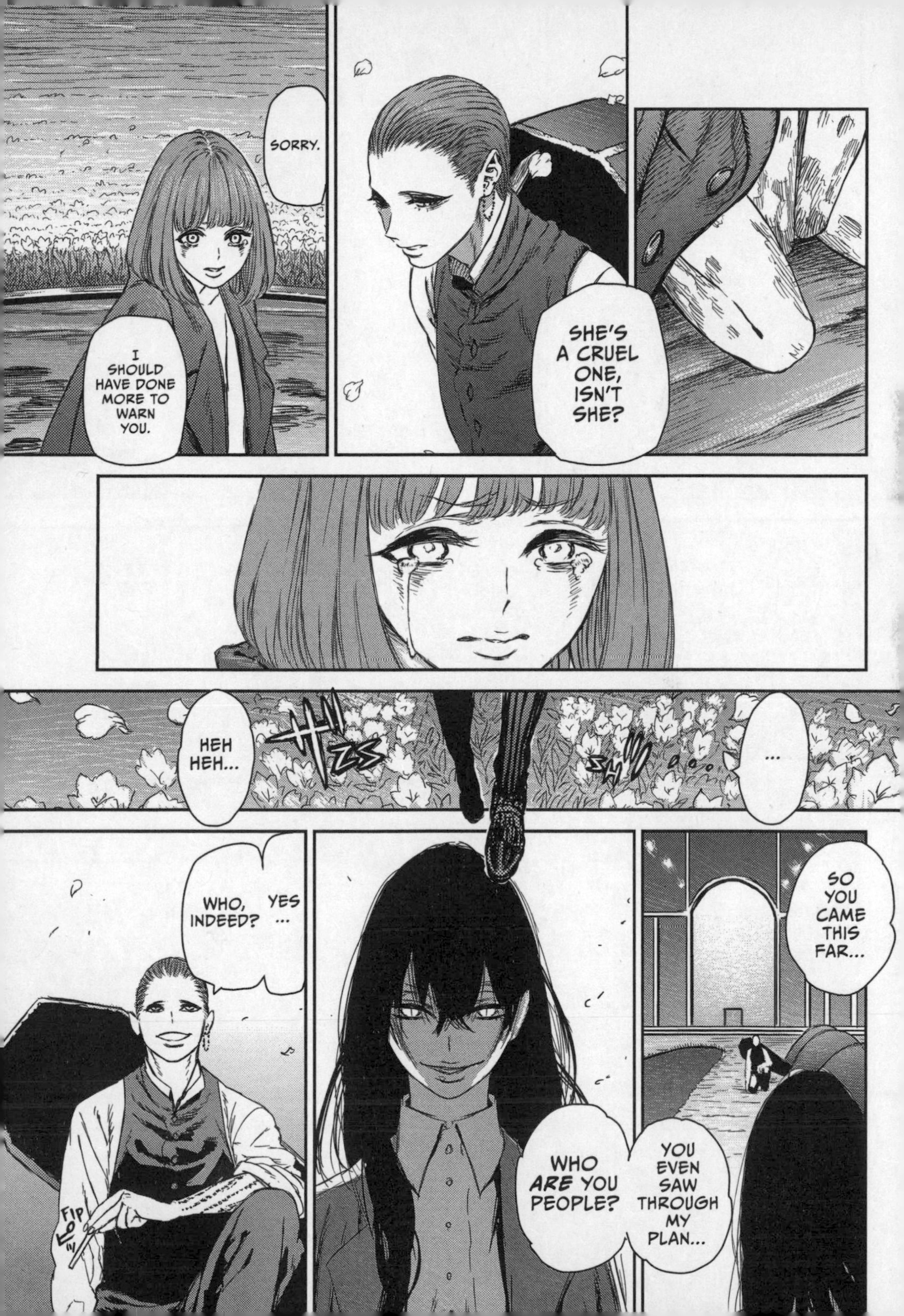
SHE'S A CRUEL ONE, ISN'T SHE?
SORRY.
I SHOULD HAVE DONE MORE TO WARN YOU.
...
HEH HEH...
SO YOU CAME THIS FAR...
YOU EVEN SAW THROUGH MY PLAN...
WHO *ARE* YOU PEOPLE?
YES... WHO, INDEED?
FLIP

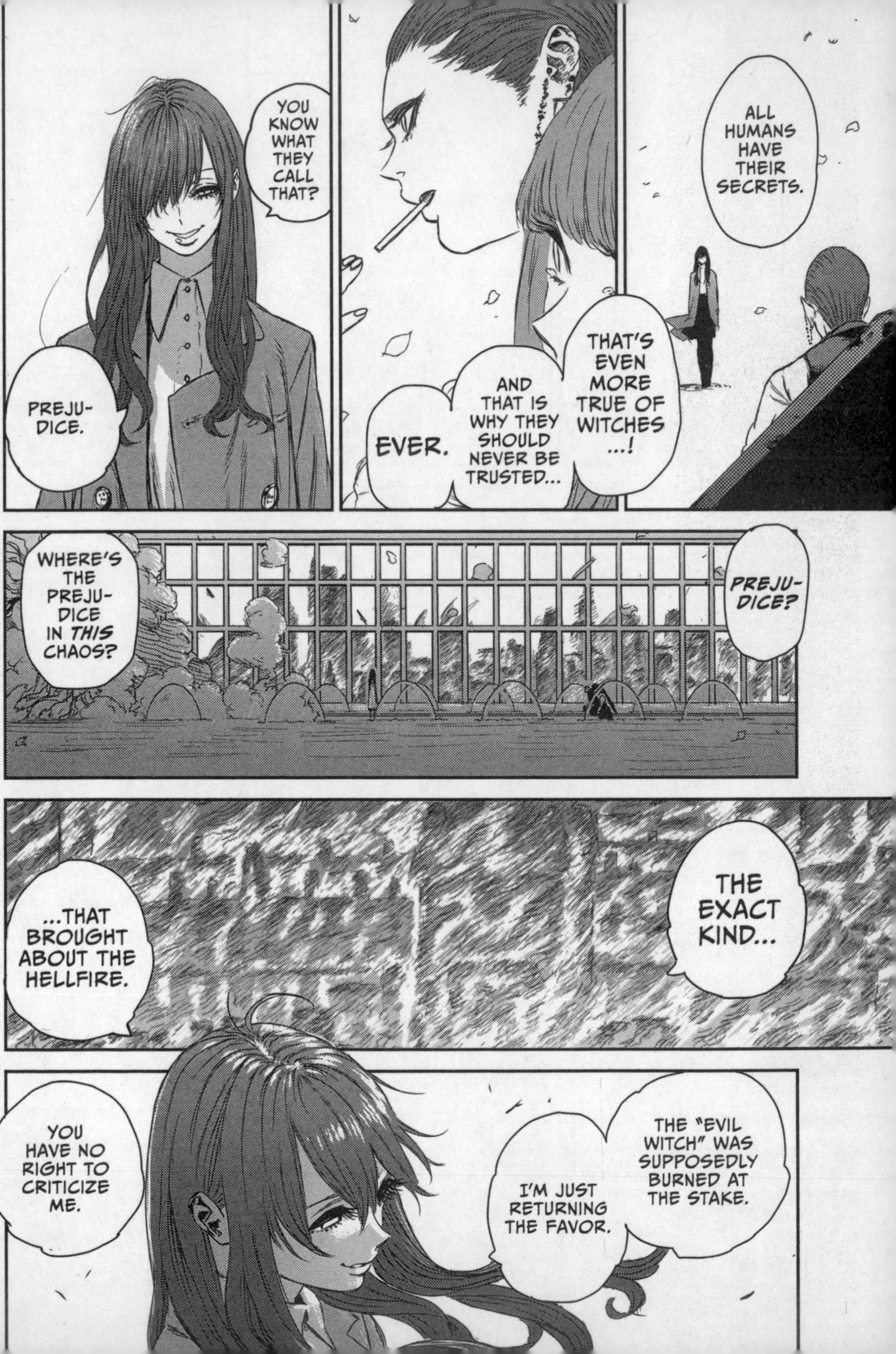
ALL HUMANS HAVE THEIR SECRETS.
THAT'S EVEN MORE TRUE OF WITCHES ...!
AND THAT IS WHY THEY SHOULD NEVER BE TRUSTED...
EVER.
YOU KNOW WHAT THEY CALL THAT?
PREJU-DICE.
PREJU-DICE?
WHERE'S THE PREJU-DICE IN THIS CHAOS?
THE EXACT KIND...
...THAT BROUGHT ABOUT THE HELLFIRE.
THE "EVIL WITCH" WAS SUPPOSEDLY BURNED AT THE STAKE.
I'M JUST RETURNING THE FAVOR.
YOU HAVE NO RIGHT TO CRITICIZE ME.

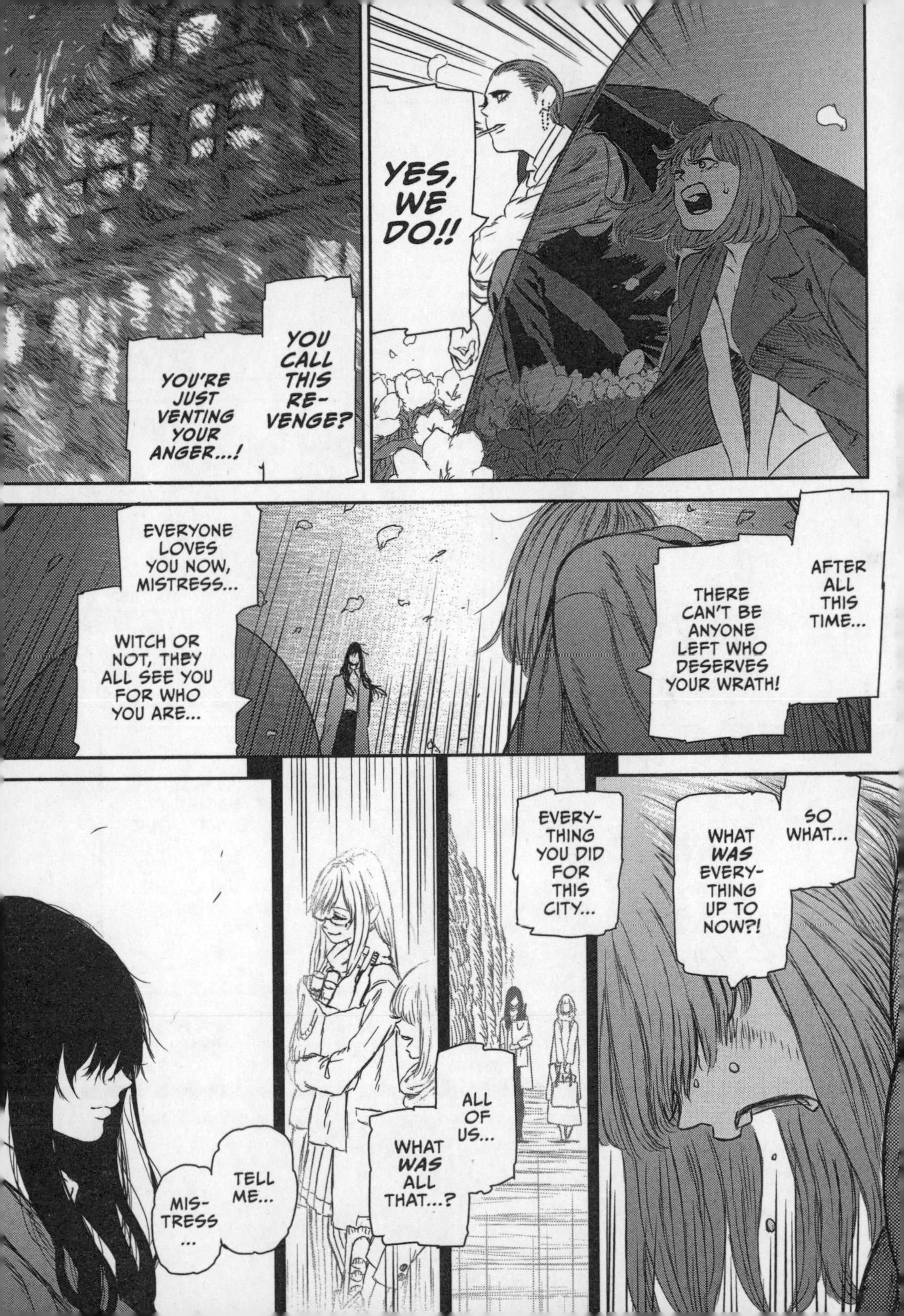
YES, WE DO!!
YOU CALL THIS RE-VENGE?
YOU'RE JUST VENTING YOUR ANGER...!
AFTER ALL THIS TIME...
THERE CAN'T BE ANYONE LEFT WHO DESERVES YOUR WRATH!
EVERYONE LOVES YOU NOW, MISTRESS...
WITCH OR NOT, THEY ALL SEE YOU FOR WHO YOU ARE...
SO WHAT...
WHAT WAS EVERY-THING UP TO NOW?!
EVERY-THING YOU DID FOR THIS CITY...
ALL OF US...
WHAT WAS ALL THAT...?
TELL ME...
MIS-TRESS...

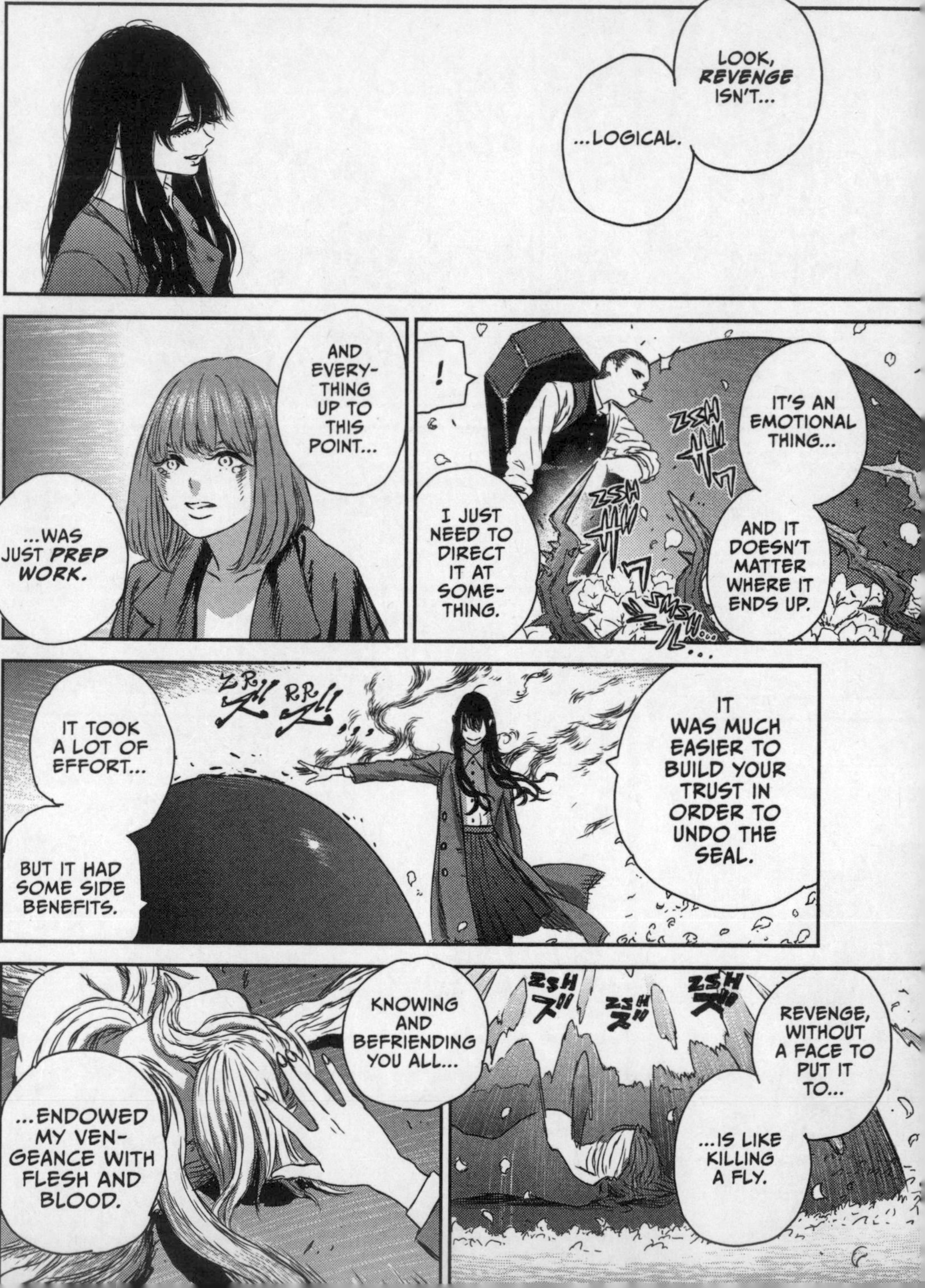
LOOK, REVENGE ISN'T...
...LOGICAL.
IT'S AN EMOTIONAL THING...
AND IT DOESN'T MATTER WHERE IT ENDS UP.
ZSH
ZSH
SMSH...
!
I JUST NEED TO DIRECT IT AT SOMETHING.
AND EVERYTHING UP TO THIS POINT...
...WAS JUST PREP WORK.
IT WAS MUCH EASIER TO BUILD YOUR TRUST IN ORDER TO UNDO THE SEAL.
RR
ZR
IT TOOK A LOT OF EFFORT...
BUT IT HAD SOME SIDE BENEFITS.
REVENGE, WITHOUT A FACE TO PUT IT TO...
...IS LIKE KILLING A FLY.
ZSH
ZSH
ZSH
KNOWING AND BEFRIENDING YOU ALL...
...ENDOWED MY VENGEANCE WITH FLESH AND BLOOD.

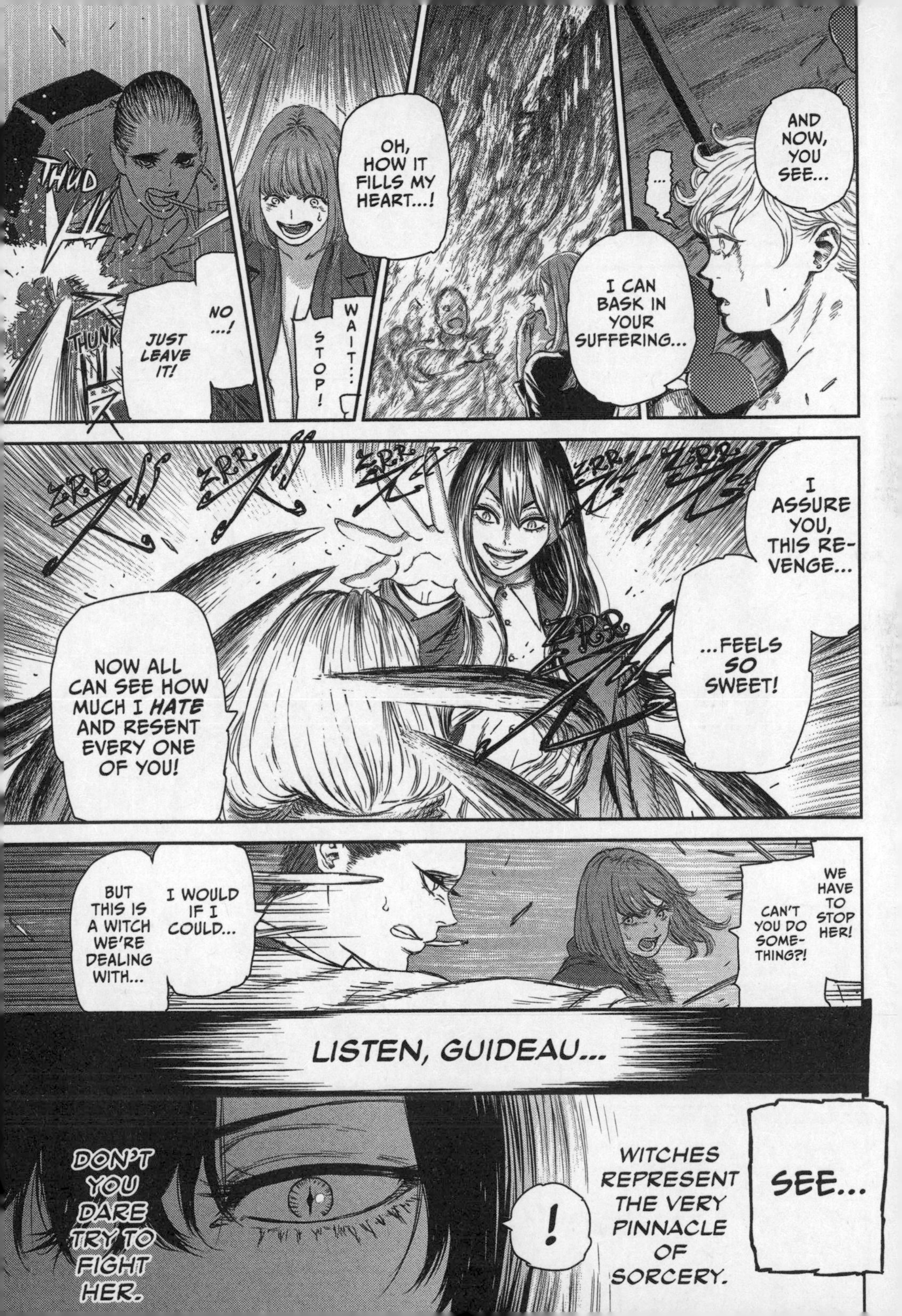
AND NOW, YOU SEE...
...
I CAN BASK IN YOUR SUFFERING...
OH, HOW IT FILLS MY HEART...!
WAIT... STOP!
NO...!
JUST LEAVE IT!
THUD
THUNK
ZRR
I ASSURE YOU, THIS RE-VENGE...
...FEELS SO SWEET!
NOW ALL CAN SEE HOW MUCH I HATE AND RESENT EVERY ONE OF YOU!
WE HAVE TO STOP HER!
CAN'T YOU DO SOME-THING?!
I WOULD IF I COULD...
BUT THIS IS A WITCH WE'RE DEALING WITH...
LISTEN, GUIDEAU...
SEE...
WITCHES REPRESENT THE VERY PINNACLE OF SORCERY.
!
DON'T YOU DARE TRY TO FIGHT HER.

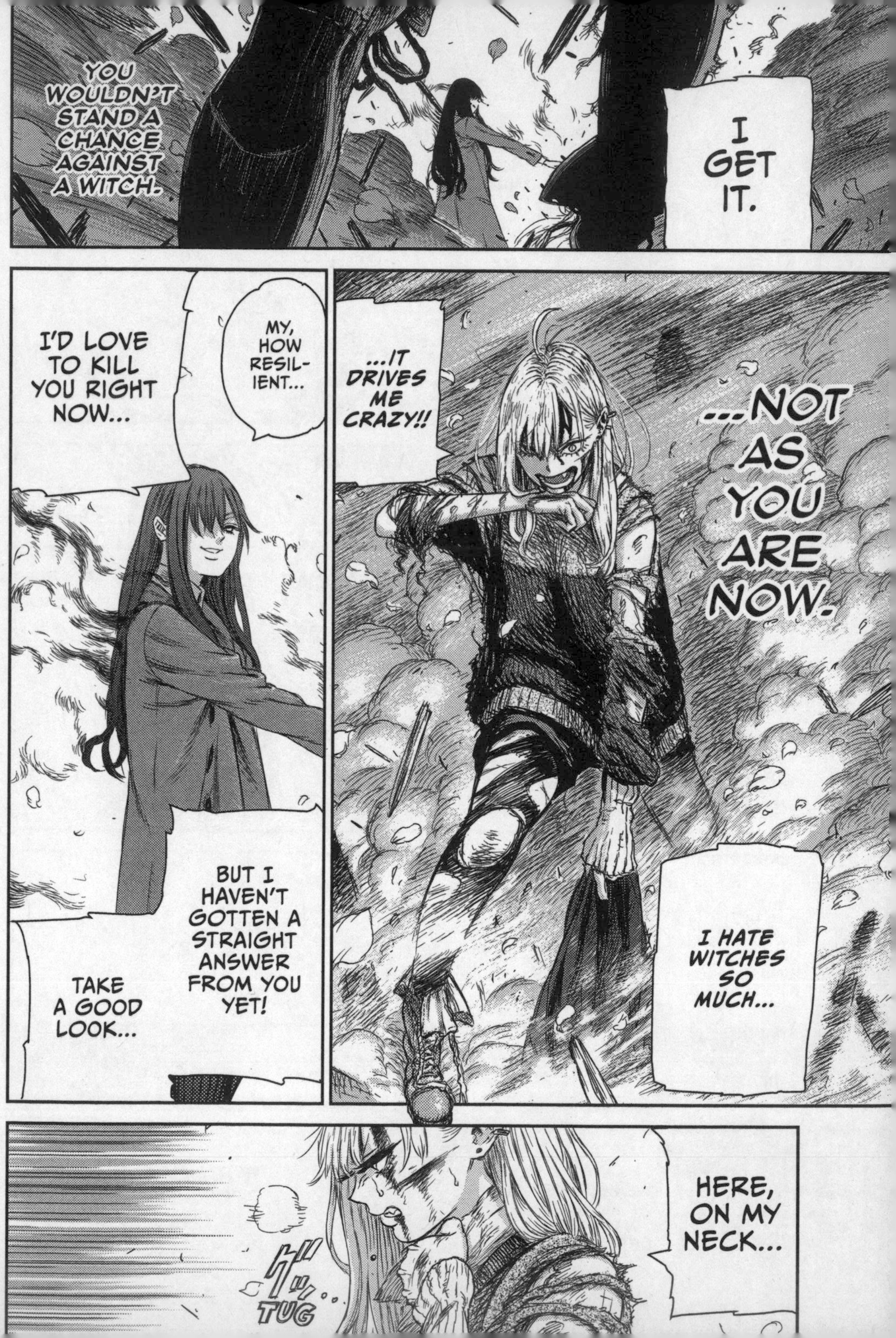
I GET IT.
YOU WOULDN'T STAND A CHANCE AGAINST A WITCH.
...NOT AS YOU ARE NOW.
...IT DRIVES ME CRAZY!!
I HATE WITCHES SO MUCH...
MY, HOW RESIL-IENT...
I'D LOVE TO KILL YOU RIGHT NOW...
BUT I HAVEN'T GOTTEN A STRAIGHT ANSWER FROM YOU YET!
TAKE A GOOD LOOK...
HERE, ON MY NECK...
グッ...
TUG

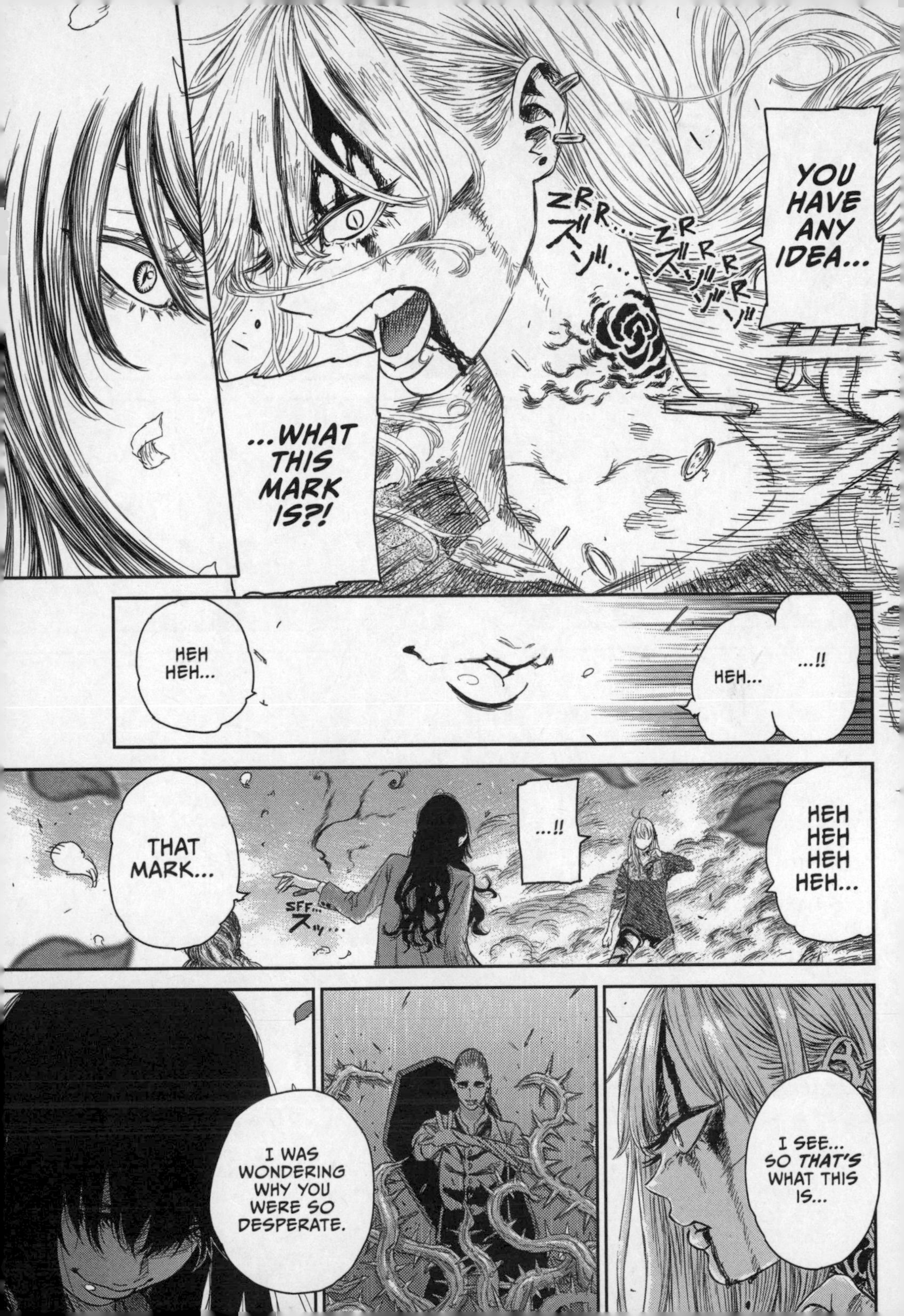
YOU HAVE ANY IDEA...
ZRR... ZRRRR
...WHAT THIS MARK IS?!
...!!
HEH...
HEH HEH...
HEH HEH HEH HEH...
...!!
SFF...
THAT MARK...
I SEE... SO THAT'S WHAT THIS IS...
I WAS WONDERING WHY YOU WERE SO DESPERATE.

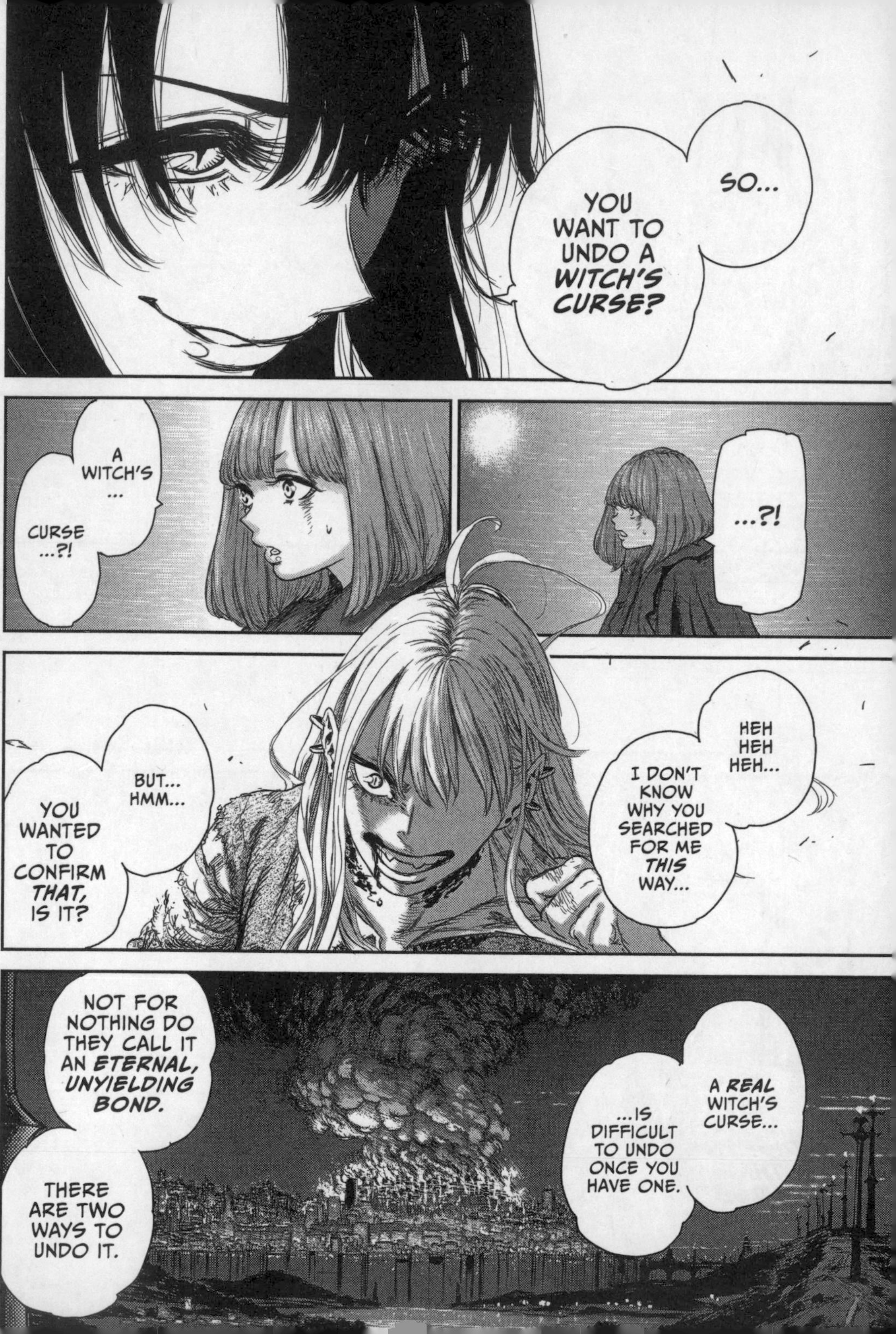
SO...
YOU WANT TO UNDO A WITCH'S CURSE?
...?!
A WITCH'S ...
CURSE ...?!
HEH HEH HEH...
I DON'T KNOW WHY YOU SEARCHED FOR ME THIS WAY...
BUT... HMM...
YOU WANTED TO CONFIRM THAT, IS IT?
A REAL WITCH'S CURSE...
...IS DIFFICULT TO UNDO ONCE YOU HAVE ONE.
NOT FOR NOTHING DO THEY CALL IT AN ETERNAL, UNYIELDING BOND.
THERE ARE TWO WAYS TO UNDO IT.

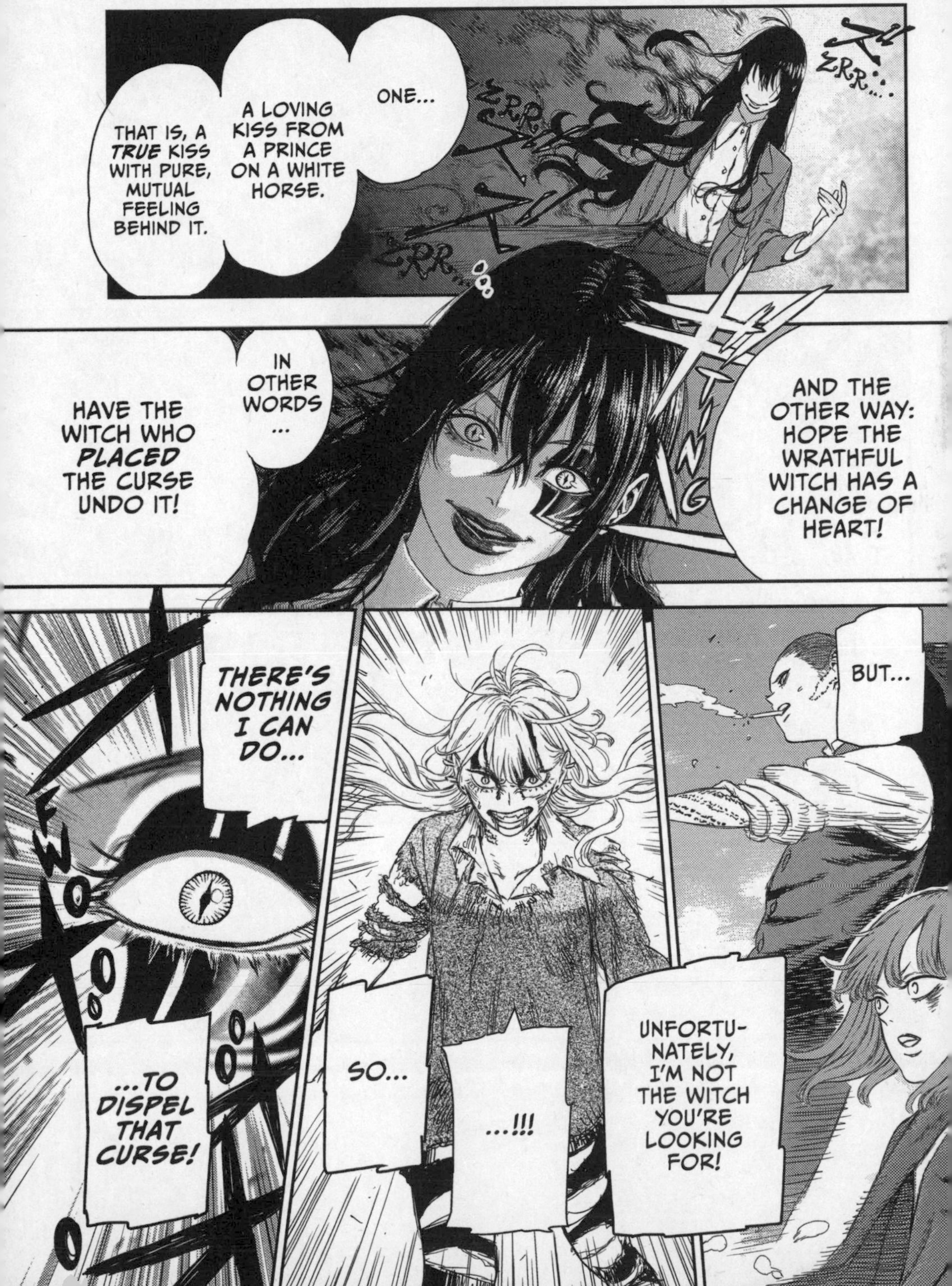
ZRR...
ONE...
A LOVING KISS FROM A PRINCE ON A WHITE HORSE.
THAT IS, A *TRUE* KISS WITH PURE, MUTUAL FEELING BEHIND IT.
ZRR...
ZRR...
TING
AND THE OTHER WAY: HOPE THE WRATHFUL WITCH HAS A CHANGE OF HEART!
IN OTHER WORDS...
HAVE THE WITCH WHO *PLACED* THE CURSE UNDO IT!
BUT...
UNFORTUNATELY, I'M NOT THE WITCH YOU'RE LOOKING FOR!
THERE'S NOTHING I CAN DO...
...!!!
SO...
...TO DISPEL THAT CURSE!
FWOOOO

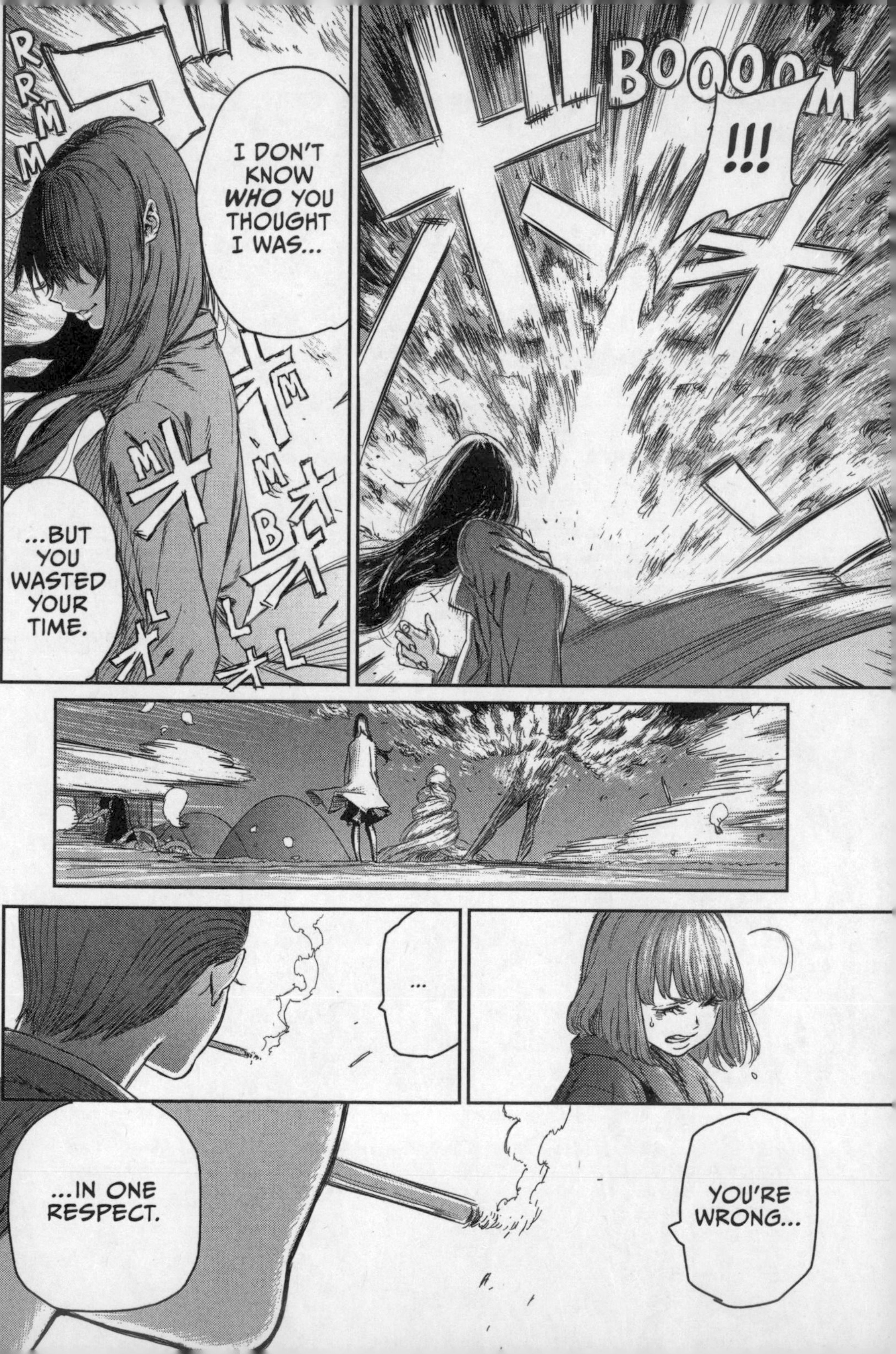
BOOOOM
!!!
RRMMM
I DON'T KNOW *WHO* YOU THOUGHT I WAS...
MMMBLLLL
...BUT YOU WASTED YOUR TIME.
...
YOU'RE WRONG...
...IN ONE RESPECT.

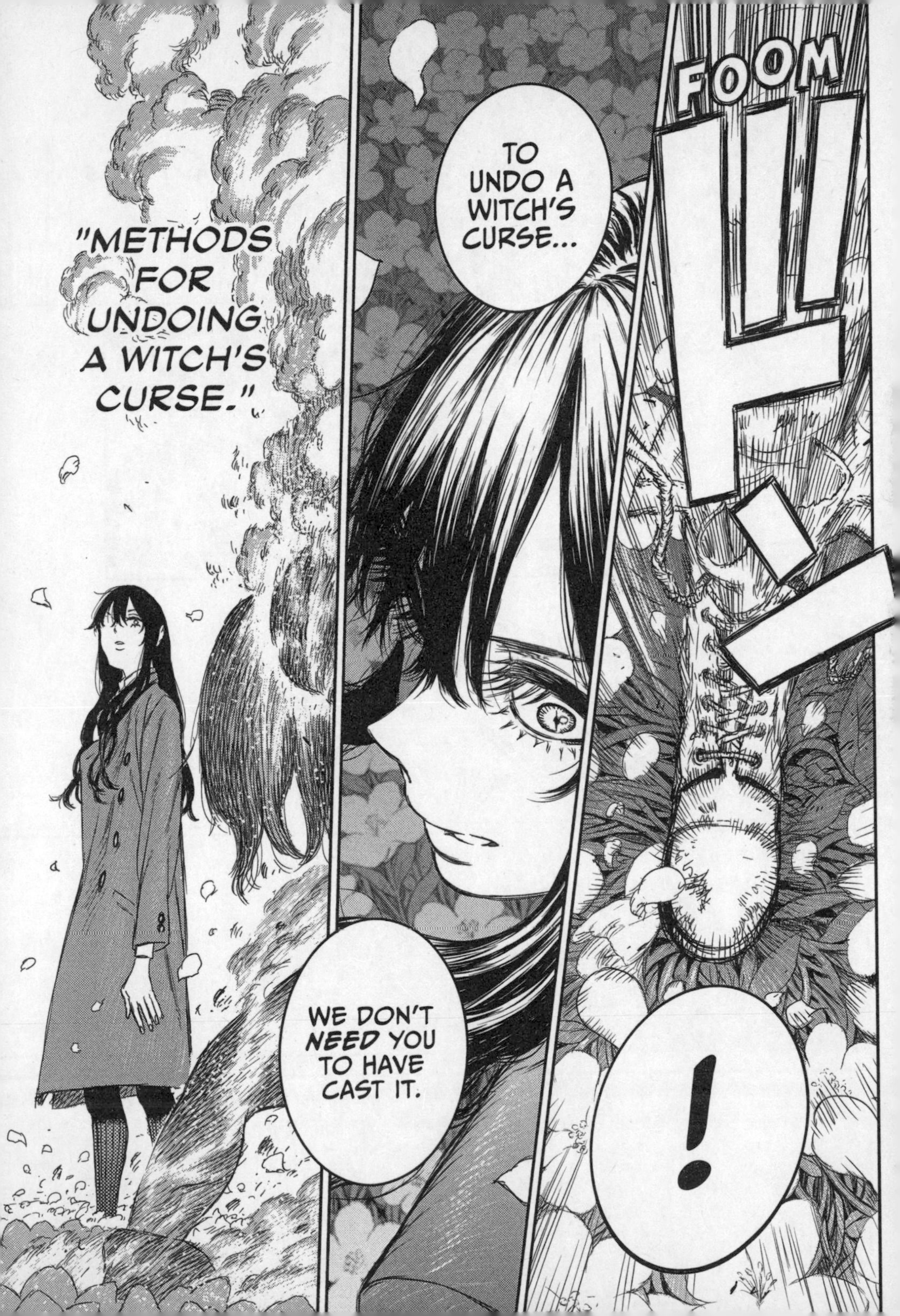
FOOM
!
TO UNDO A WITCH'S CURSE...
WE DON'T *NEED* YOU TO HAVE CAST IT.
"METHODS FOR UNDOING A WITCH'S CURSE."

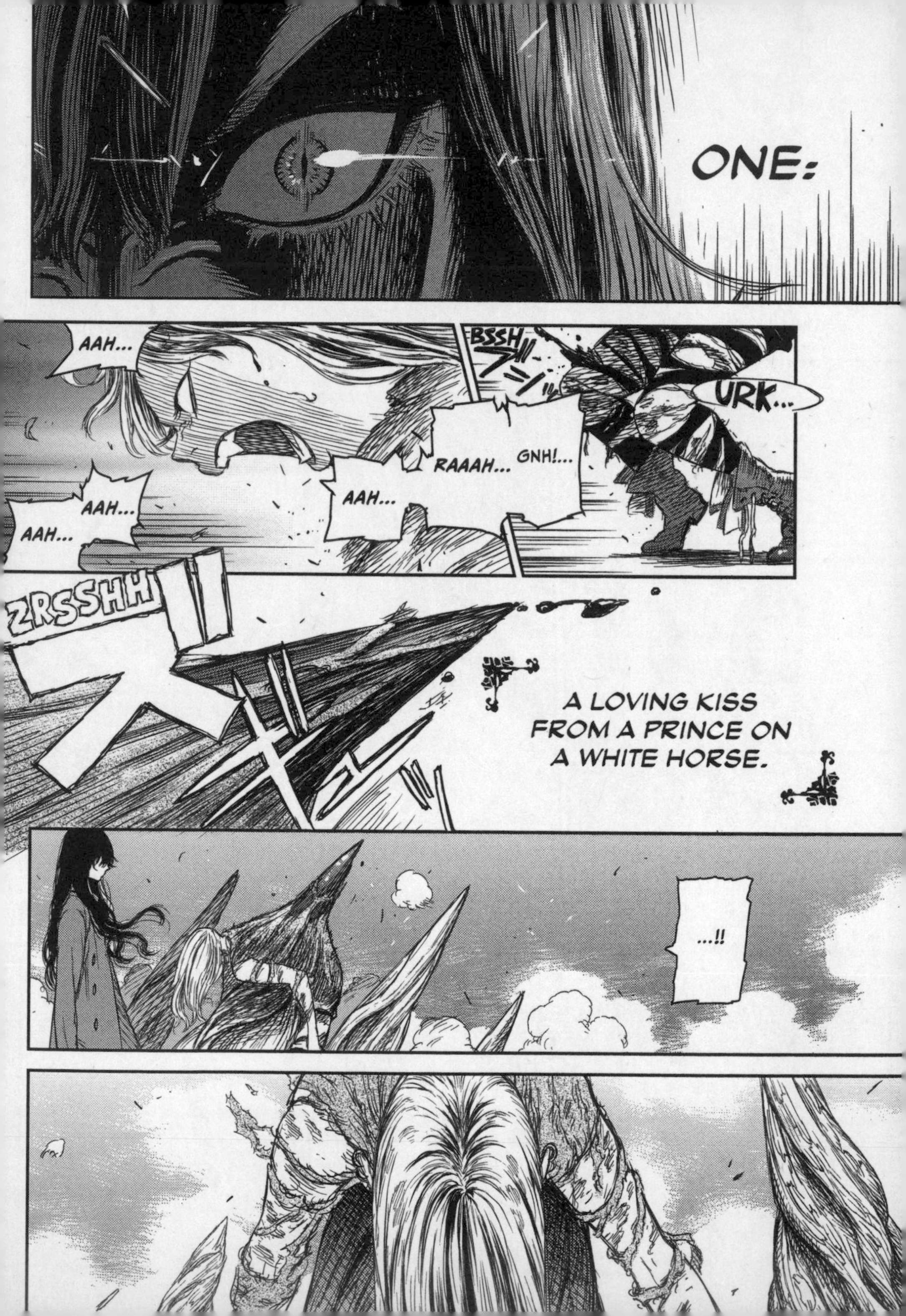
ONE:
BSSH
URK...
GNH!...
RAAAH...
AAH...
AAH...
AAH...
AAH...
A LOVING KISS FROM A PRINCE ON A WHITE HORSE.
ZRSSHH
...!!

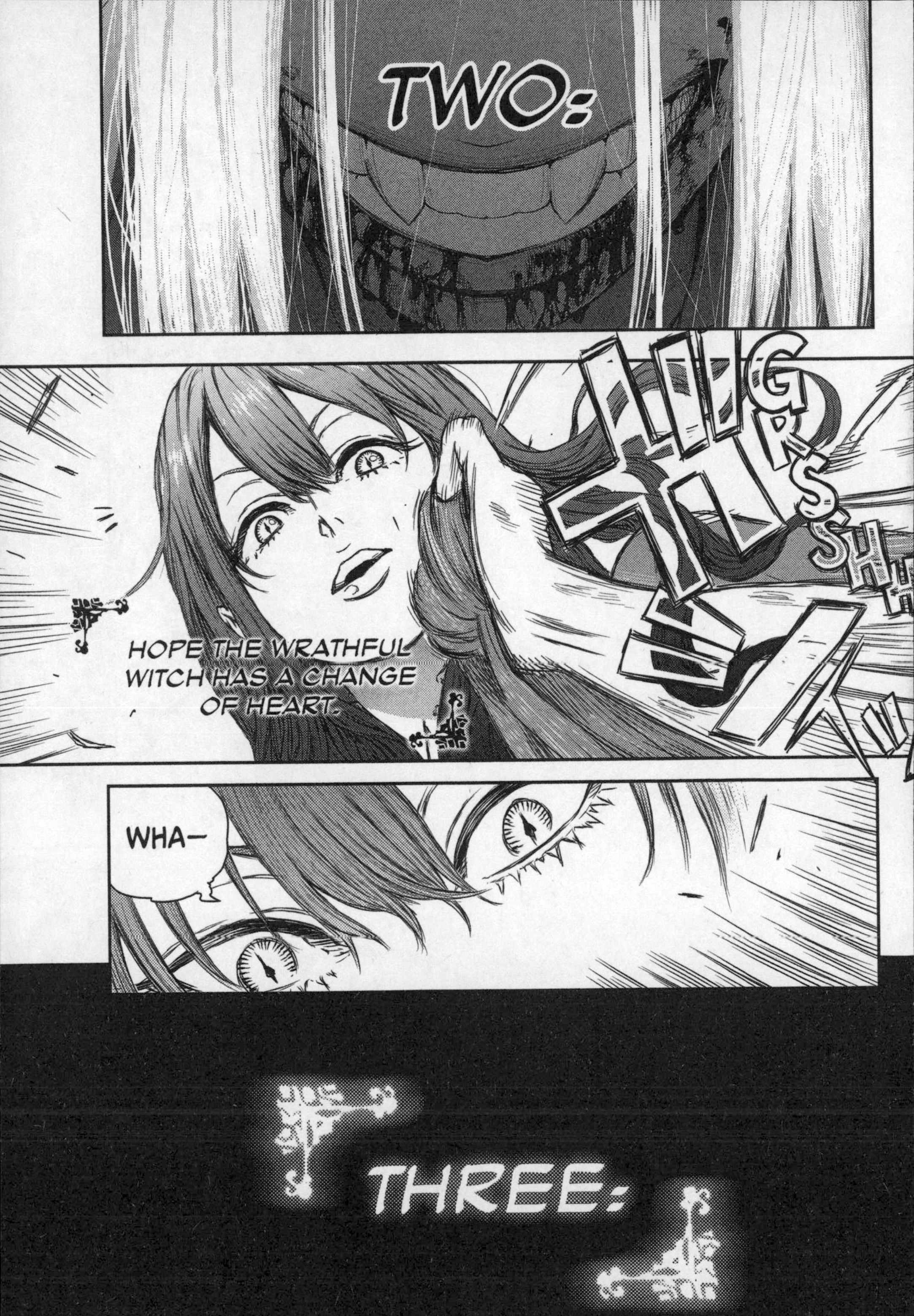
TWO:
GRSSH
HOPE THE WRATHFUL WITCH HAS A CHANGE OF HEART.
WHA–
THREE:

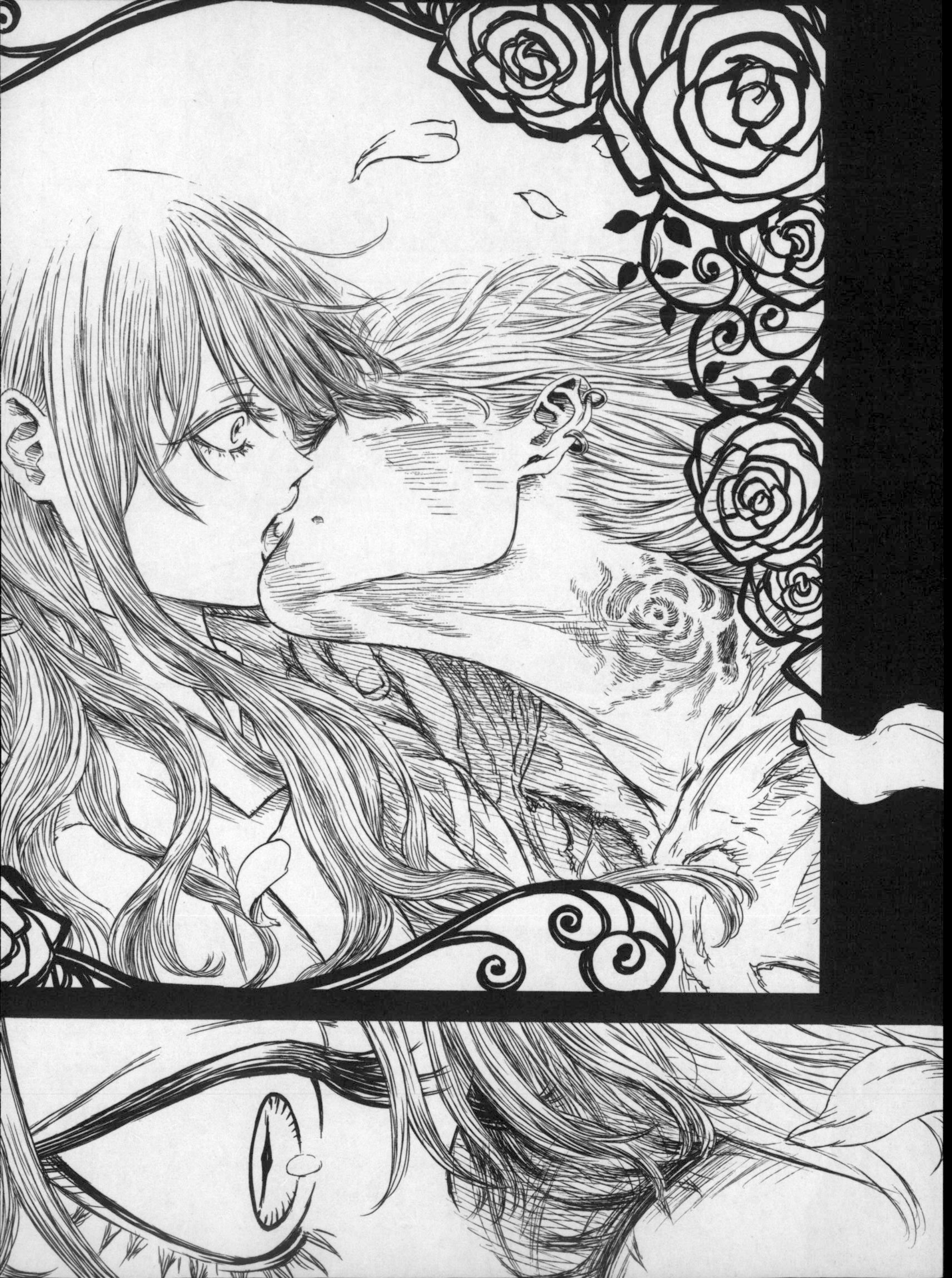

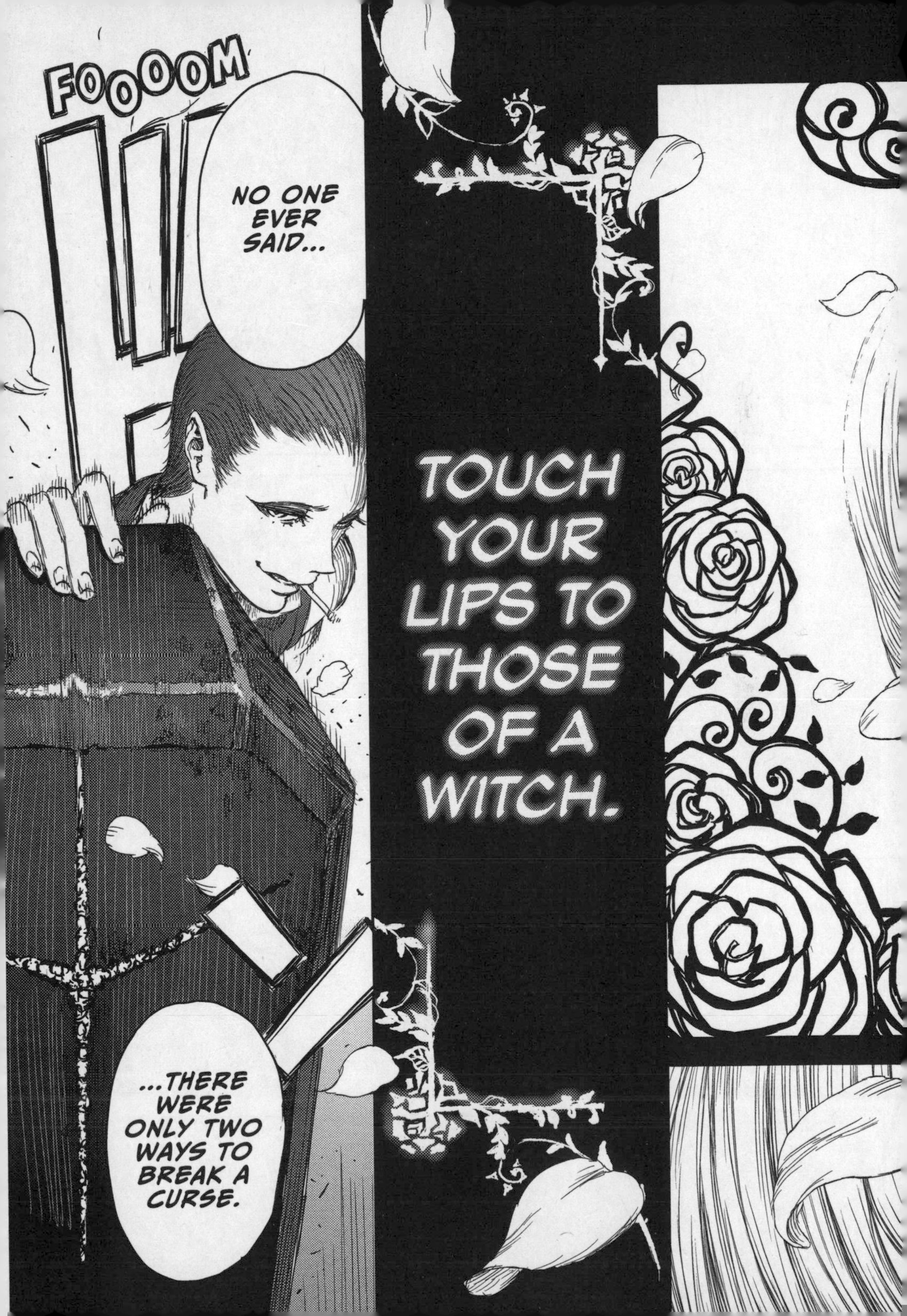
TOUCH YOUR LIPS TO THOSE OF A WITCH.
FOOOOM
NO ONE EVER SAID...
...THERE WERE ONLY TWO WAYS TO BREAK A CURSE.

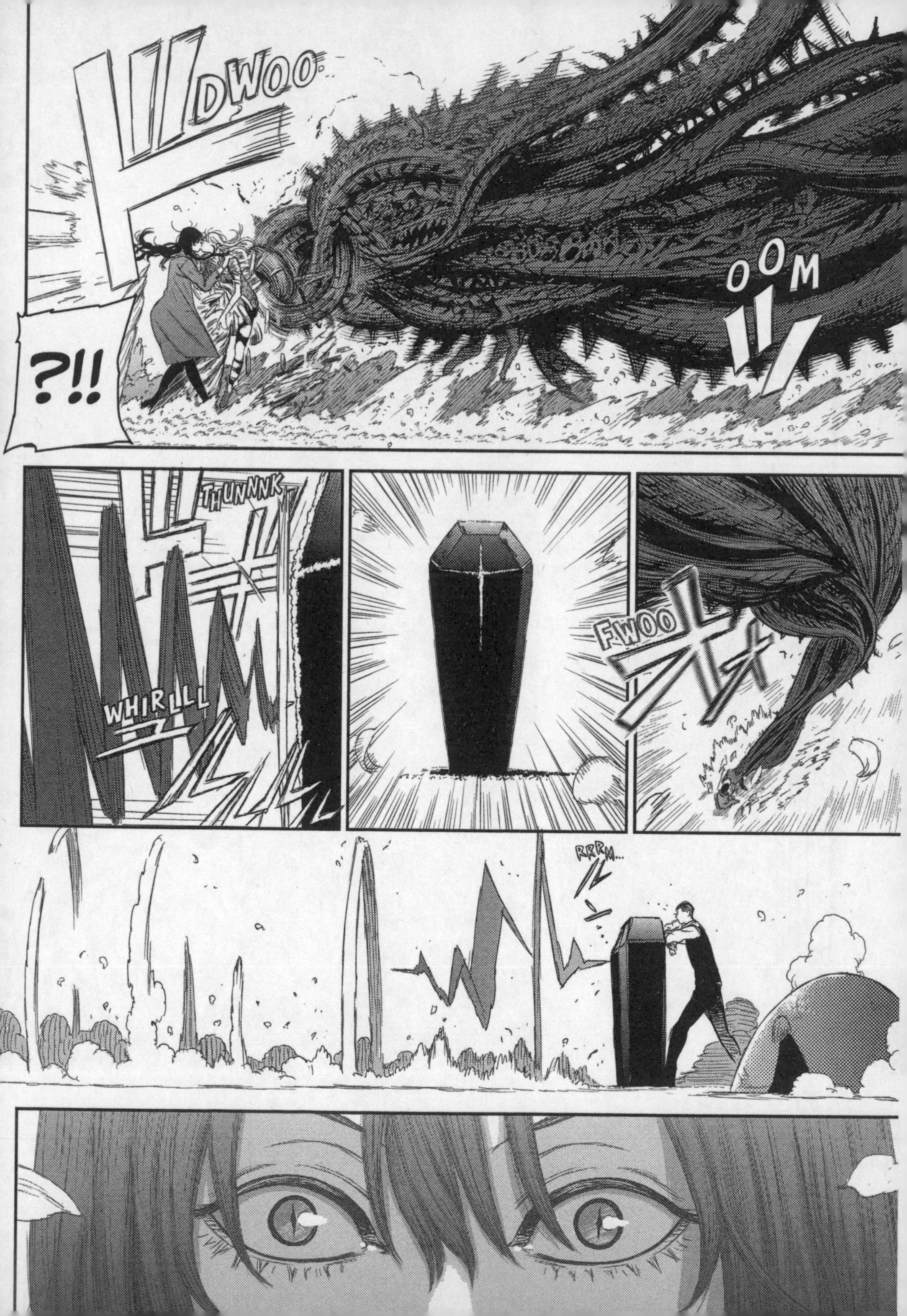
DWOO
OOM
?!!
FWOO
THUNNNK
WHIRLLL
RRRM...

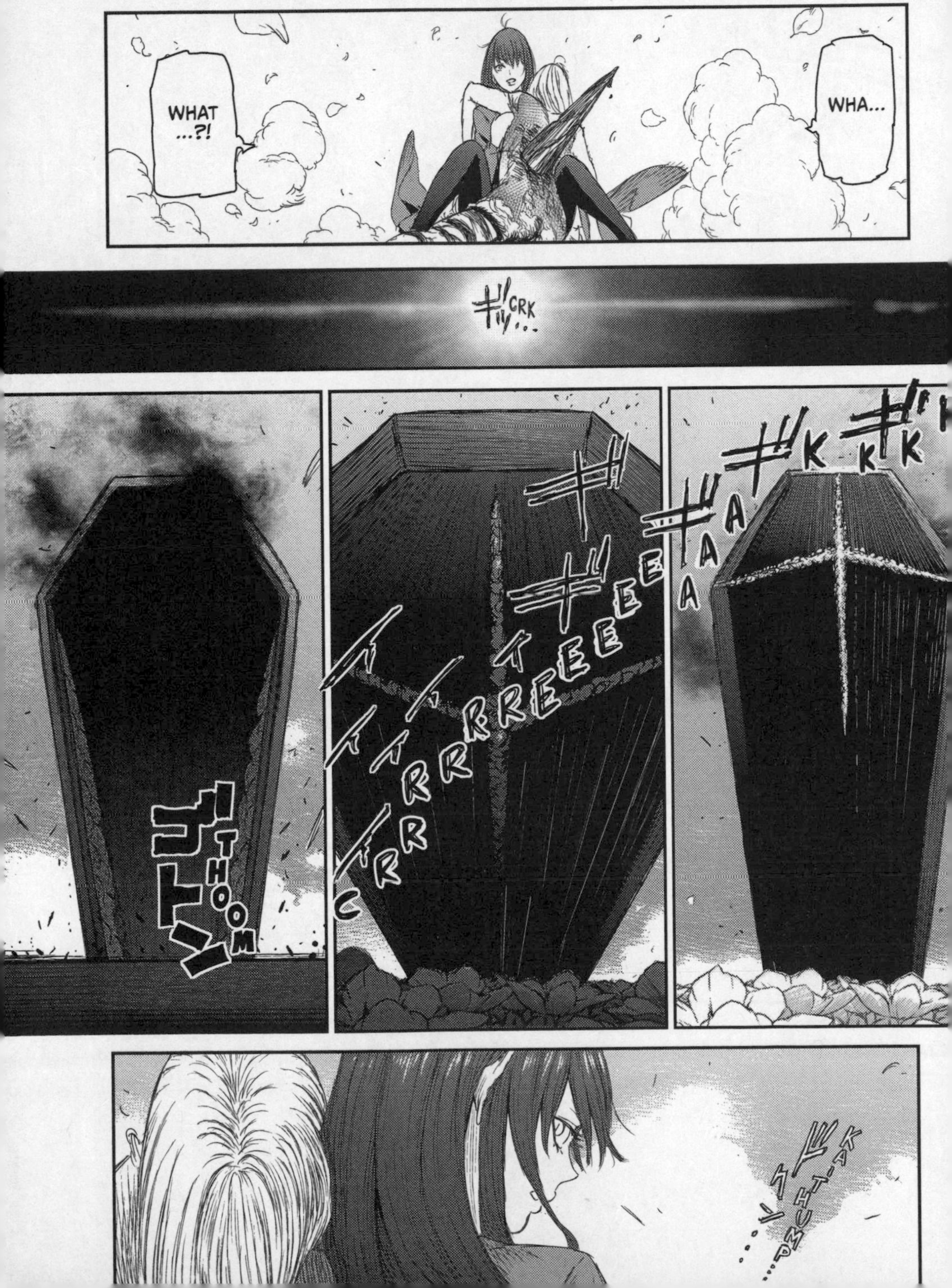
WHA...
WHAT ...?!
CRK
CRRRRRREEEEEEAAAAKKK
THOOM
KA-THUMP......

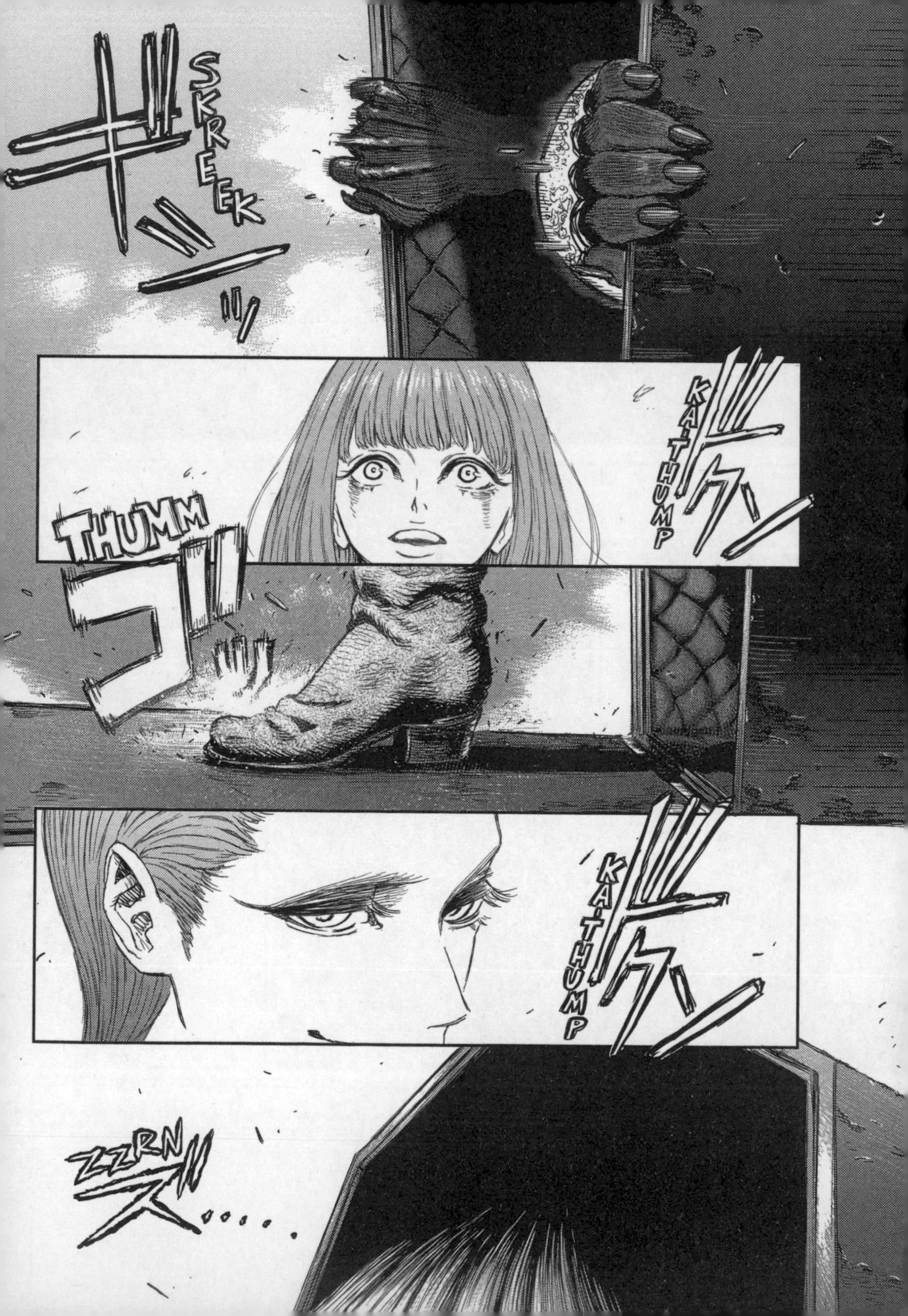

SKREEEK
KATHUMP
THUMM
KATHUMP
ZZRN

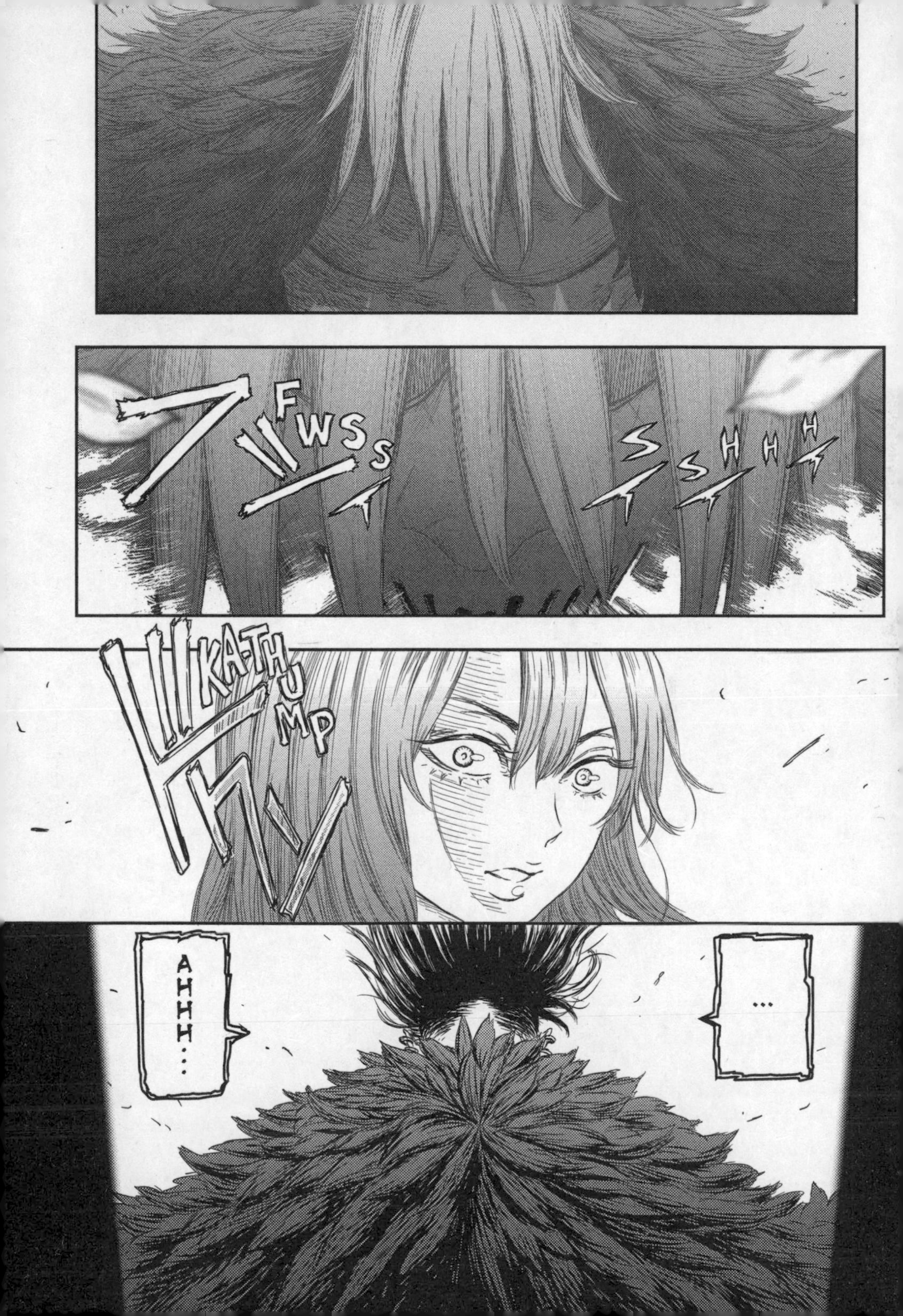
FWSSS
SSHHH
KA-THUMP
...
AHHH...

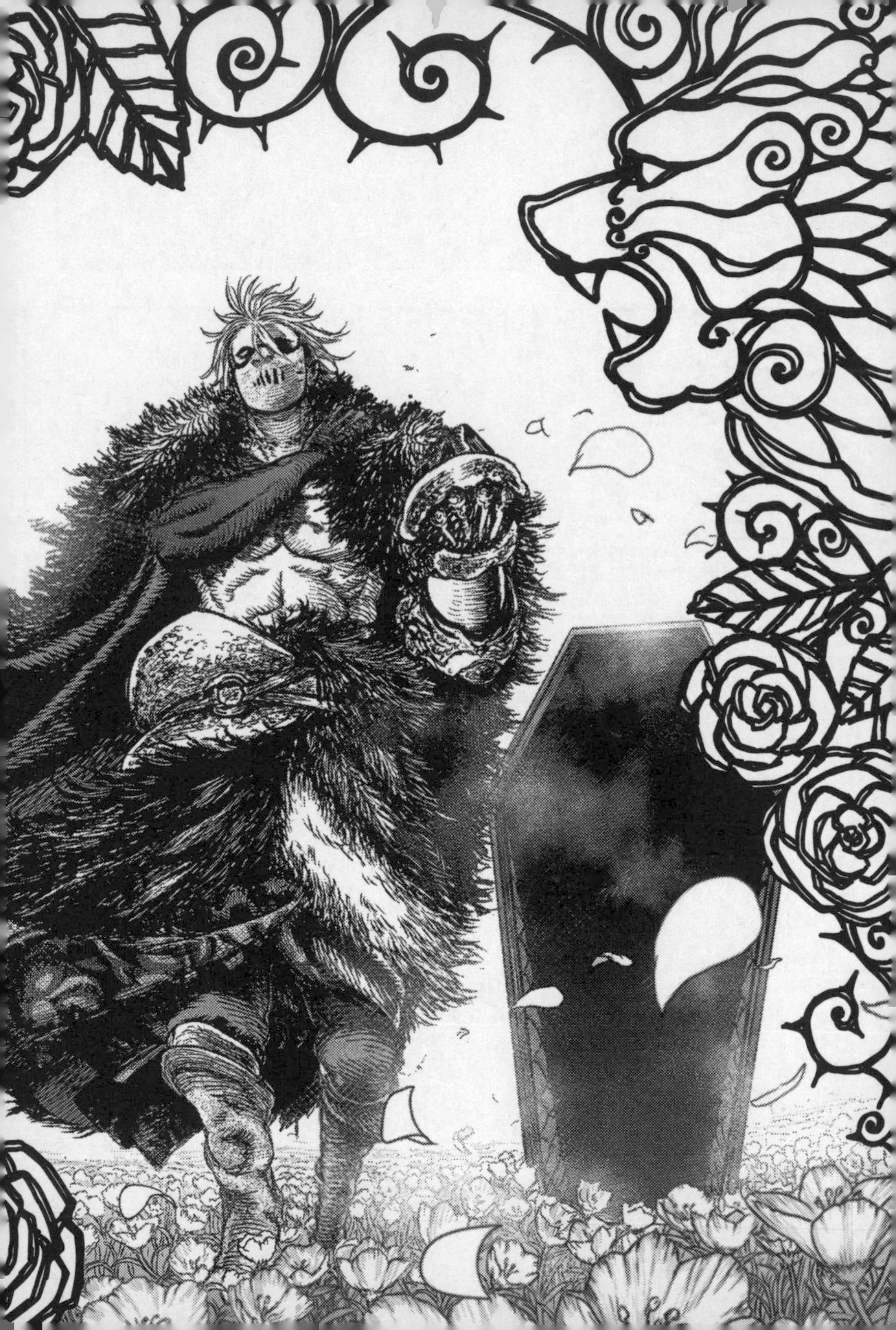

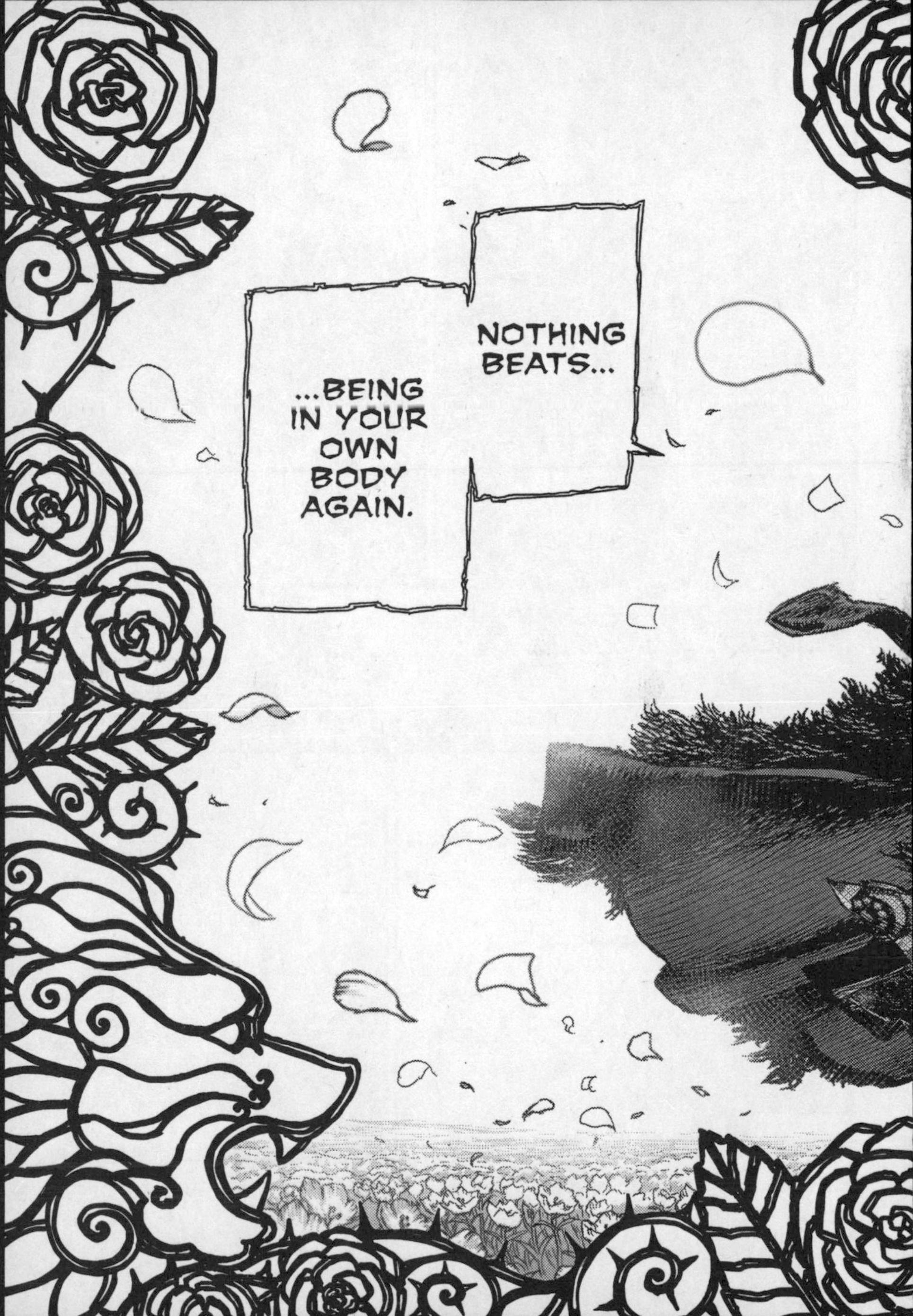
NOTHING BEATS...
...BEING IN YOUR OWN BODY AGAIN.

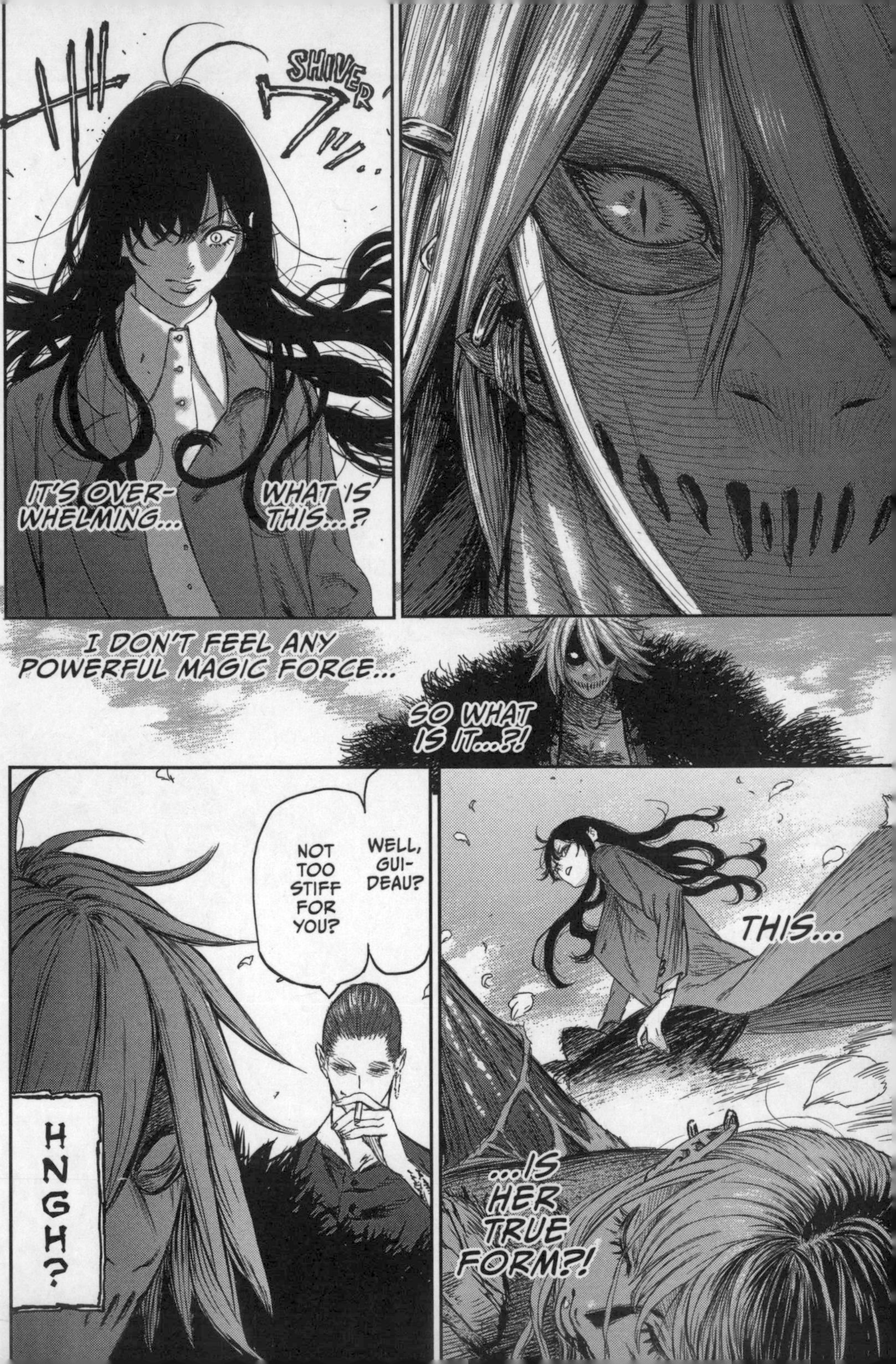
SHIVER
WHAT IS THIS...?
IT'S OVER-WHELMING...
I DON'T FEEL ANY POWERFUL MAGIC FORCE...
SO WHAT IS IT...?!
THIS...
...IS HER TRUE FORM?!
WELL, GUI-DEAU?
NOT TOO STIFF FOR YOU?
HNGH?

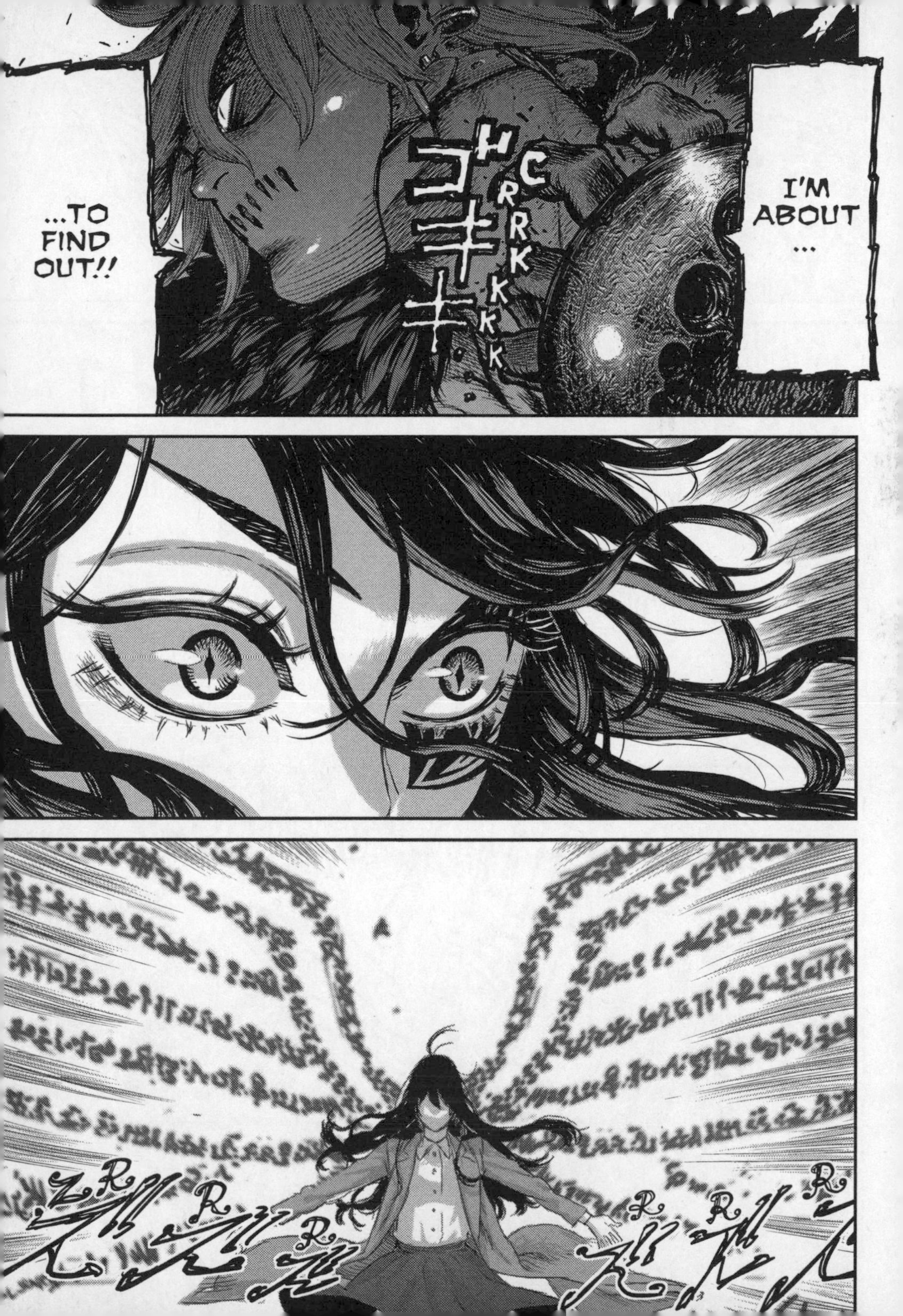
I'M ABOUT ...
CRRKKKK
...TO FIND OUT!!

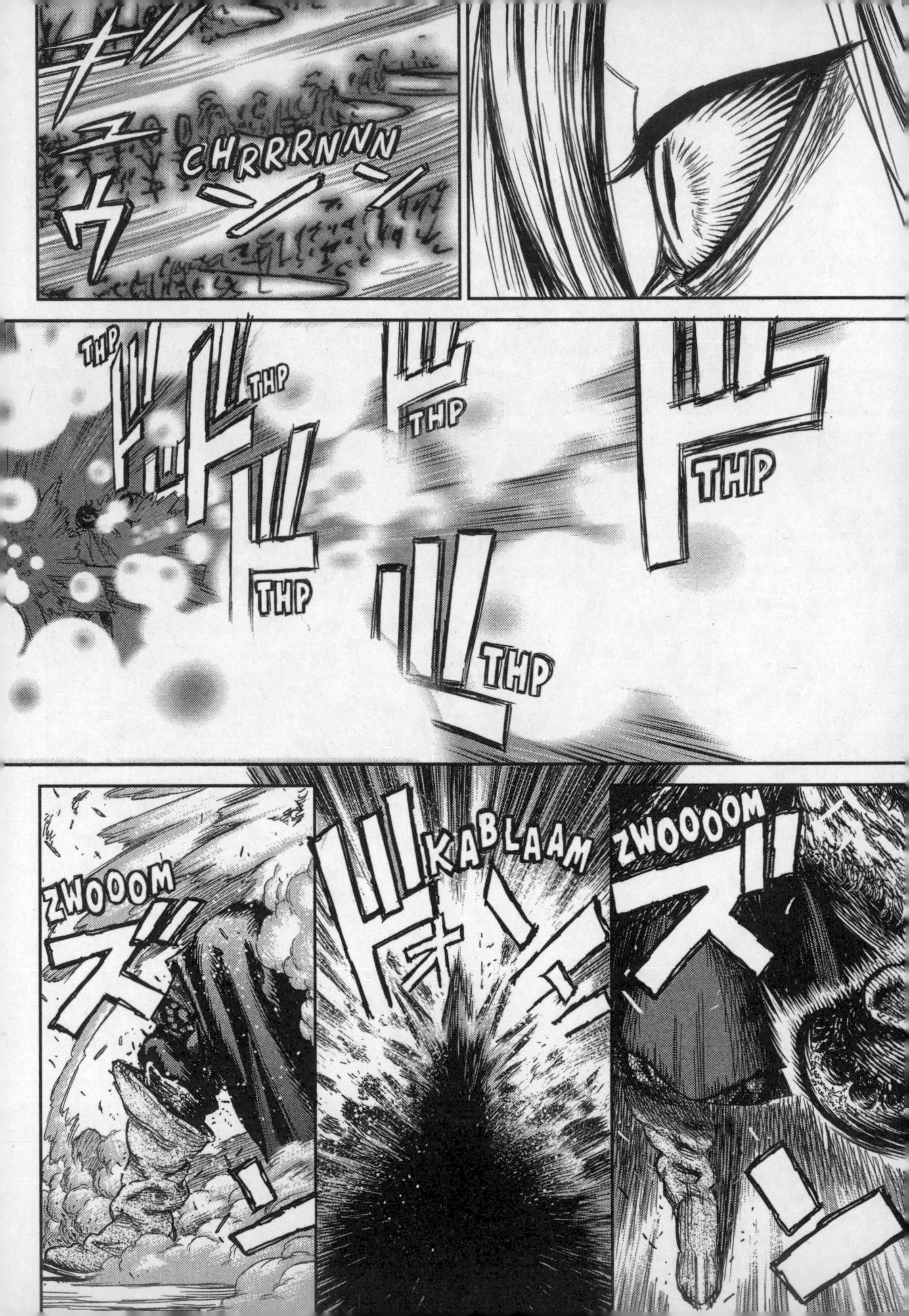
CHRRRNNN
THP
THP
THP
THP
THP
THP
ZWOOOOM
KABLAAM
ZWOOOM

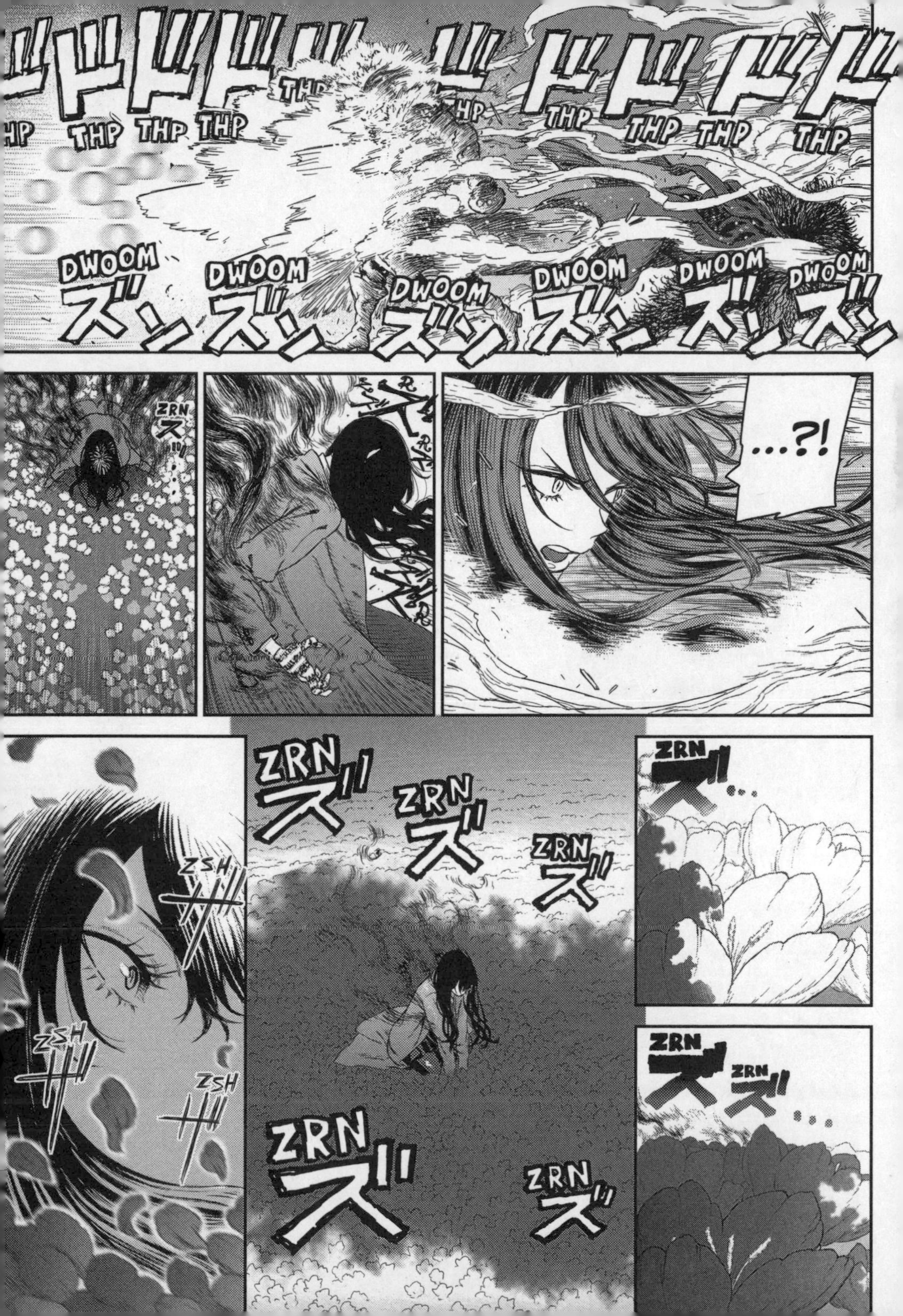
THP THP THP THP
THP THP THP THP THP
DWOOM DWOOM DWOOM DWOOM DWOOM DWOOM
...?!
ZRN
ZRN
ZRN
ZRN
ZRN
ZRN
ZRN
ZRN
ZRN
ZSH
ZSH
ZSH

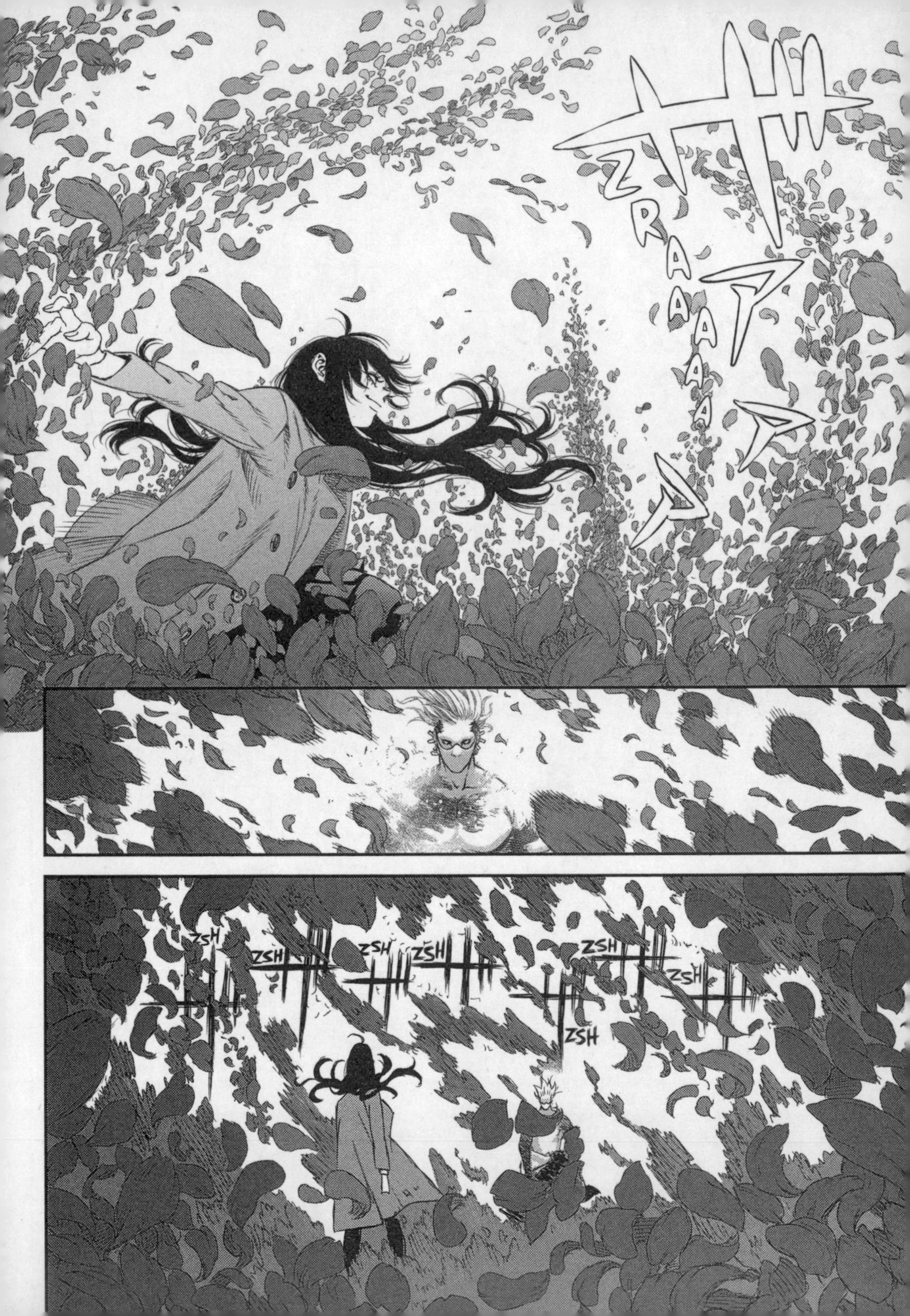

ZRAAAAAA
ZSH
ZSH
ZSH
ZSH
ZSH
ZSH
ZSH

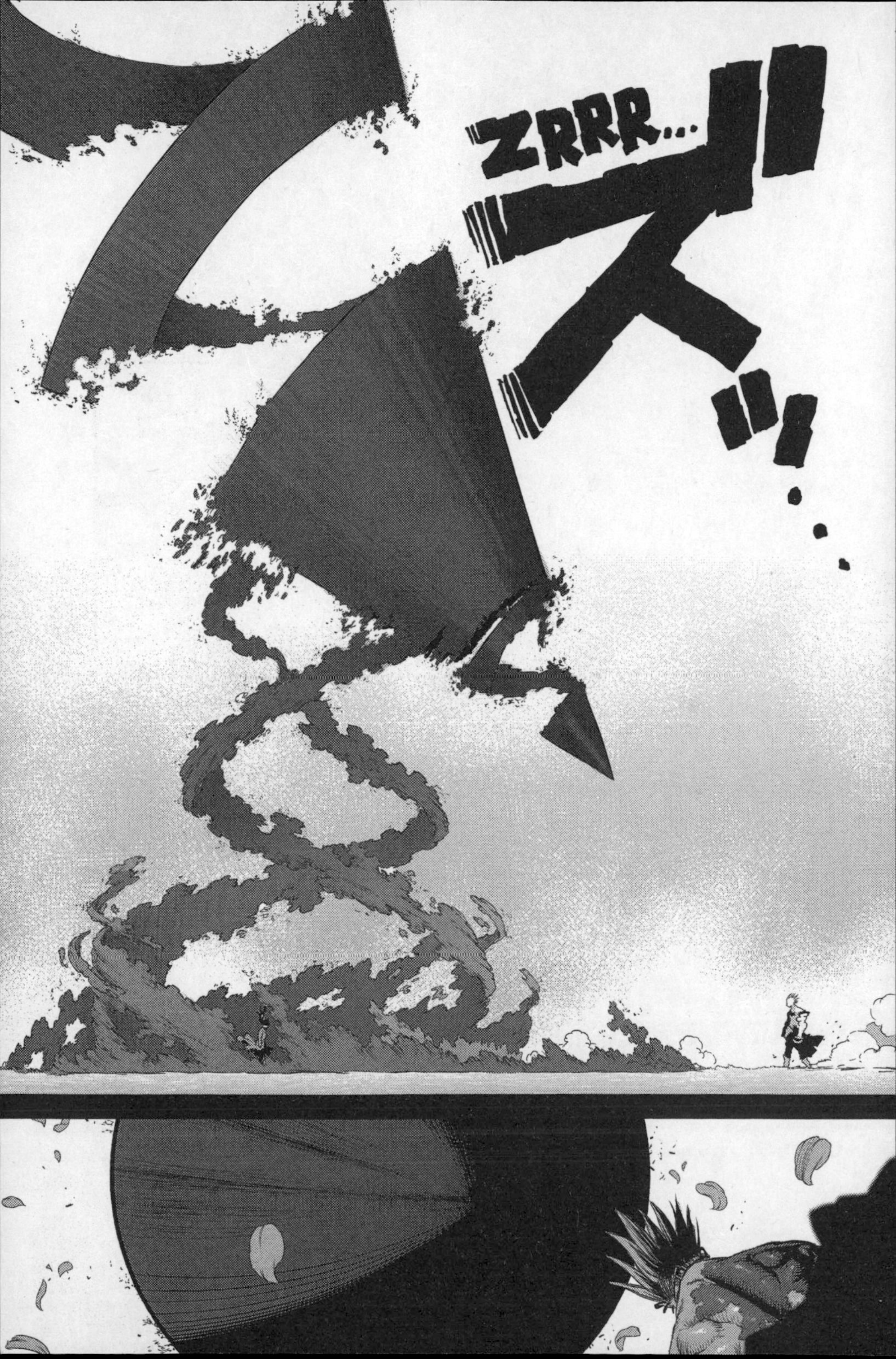
ZRRR...
ズ...

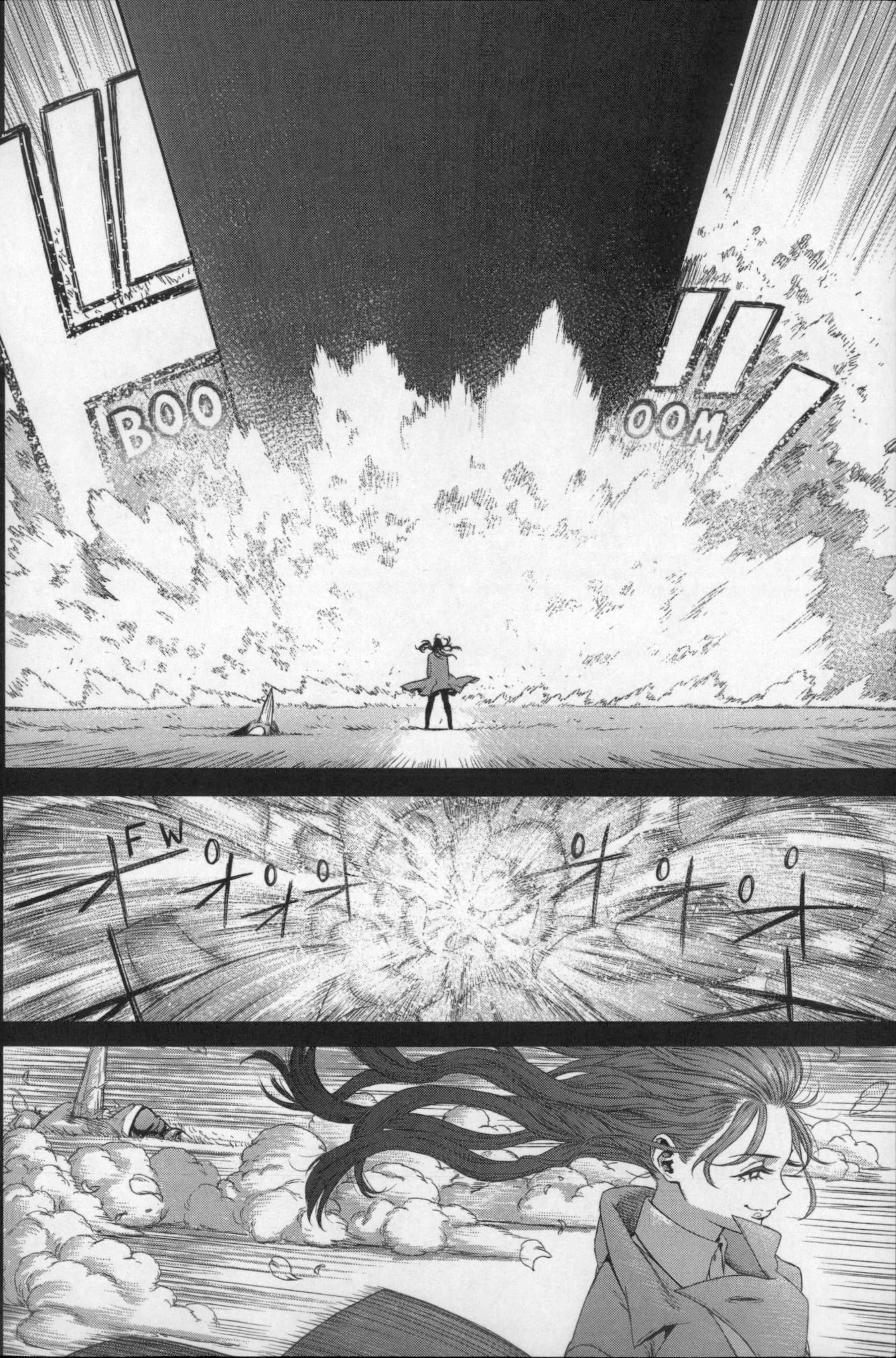
BOO
OOM
FWOOOOOOO

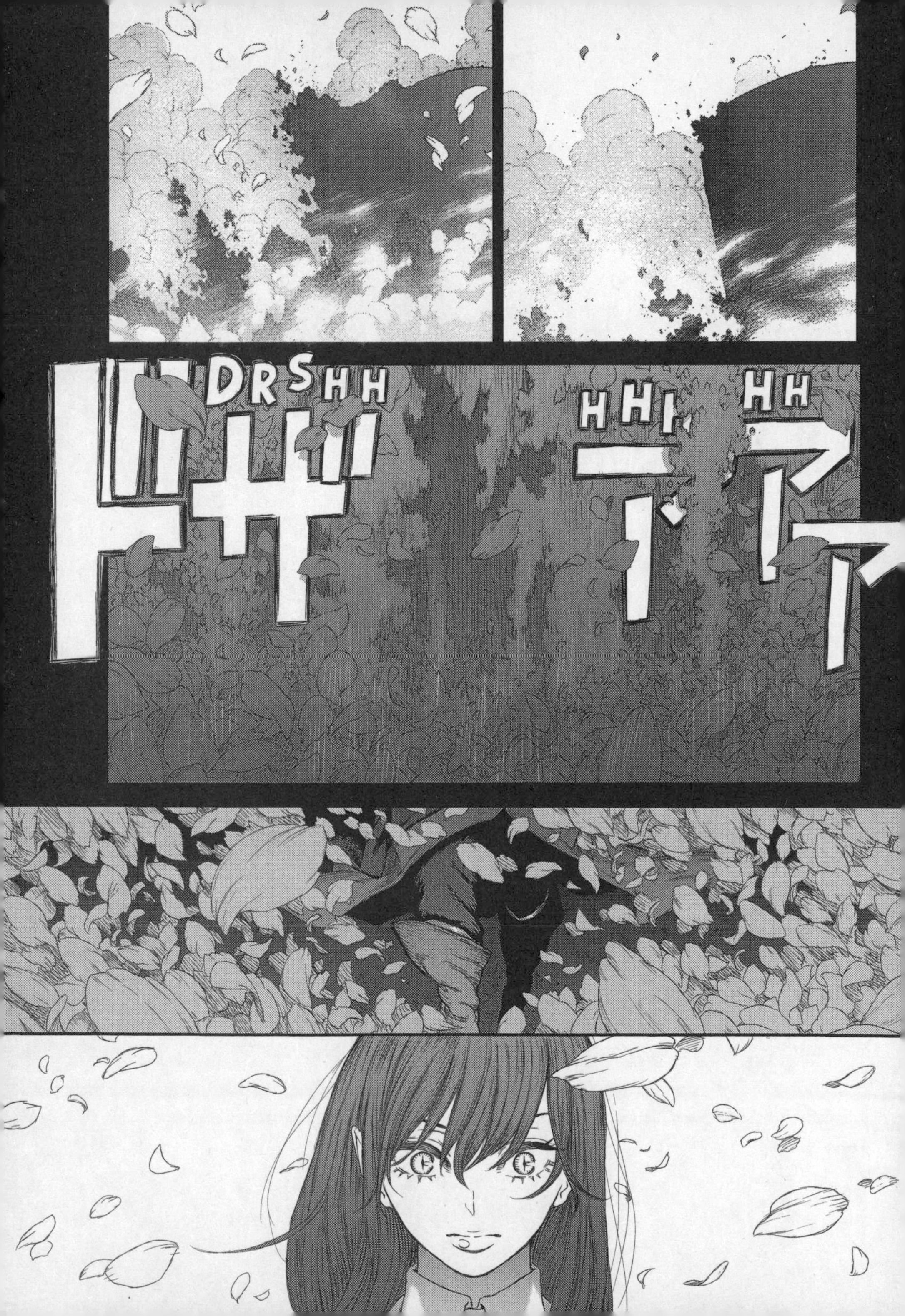
DRSHH
HHH
HH

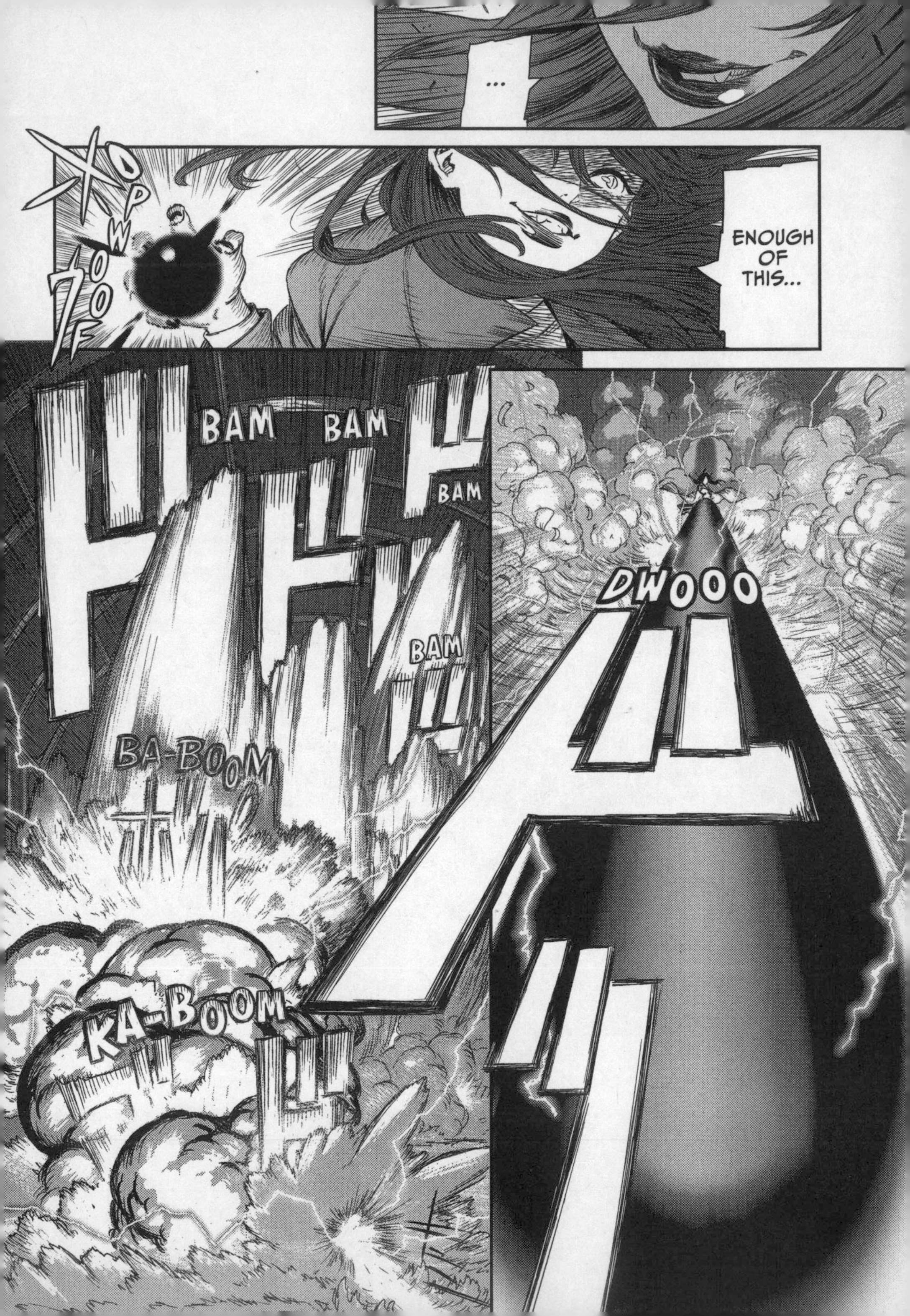
...
ENOUGH OF THIS...
DWOOO
BAM
BAM
BAM
BAM
BA-BOOM
KA-BOOM

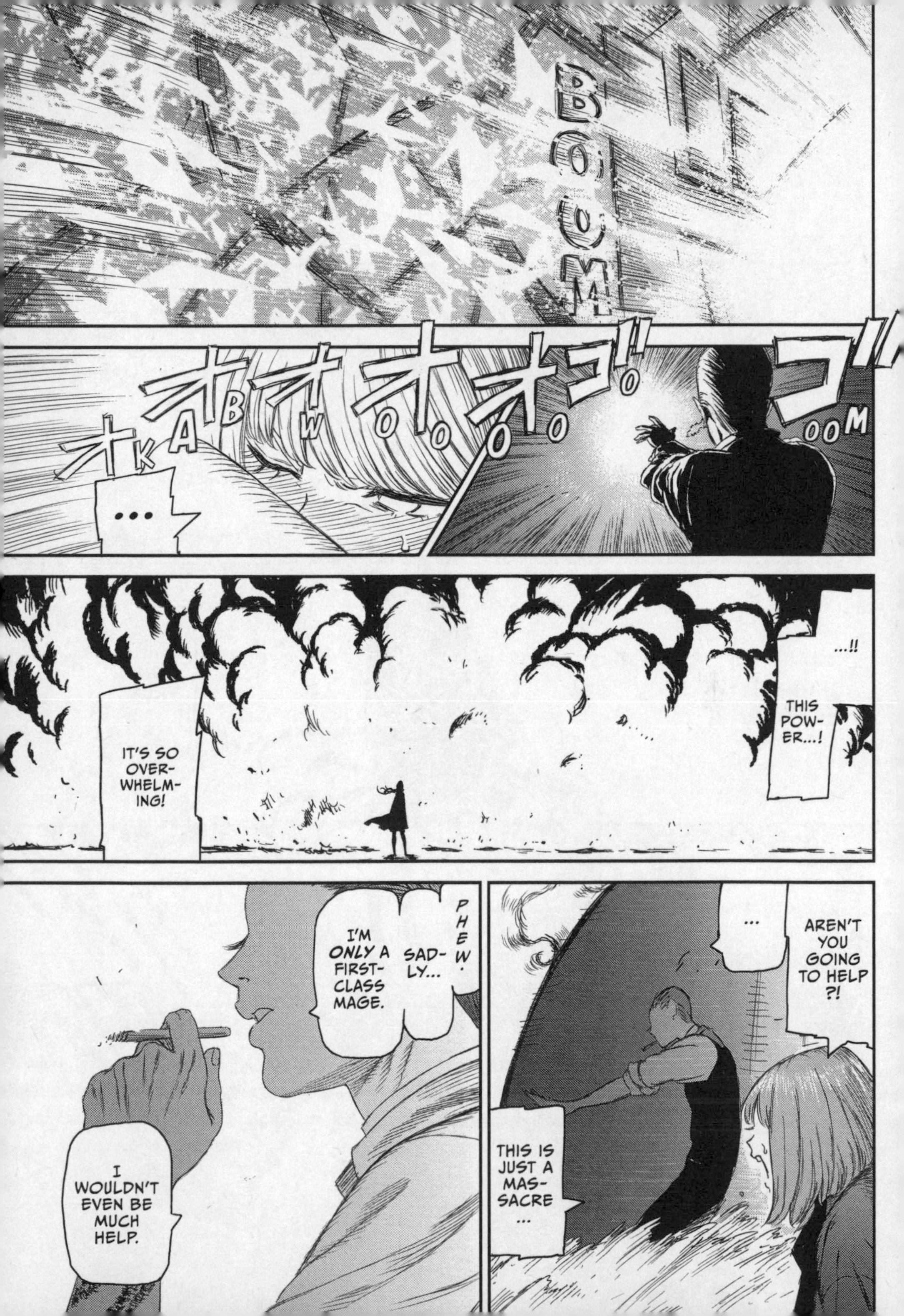
BOOM
KABWOOOOOOOM
...
...!!
THIS POW-ER...!
IT'S SO OVER-WHELM-ING!
AREN'T YOU GOING TO HELP ?!
...
THIS IS JUST A MAS-SACRE ...
PHEW.
SAD-LY...
I'M *ONLY* A FIRST-CLASS MAGE.
I WOULDN'T EVEN BE MUCH HELP.

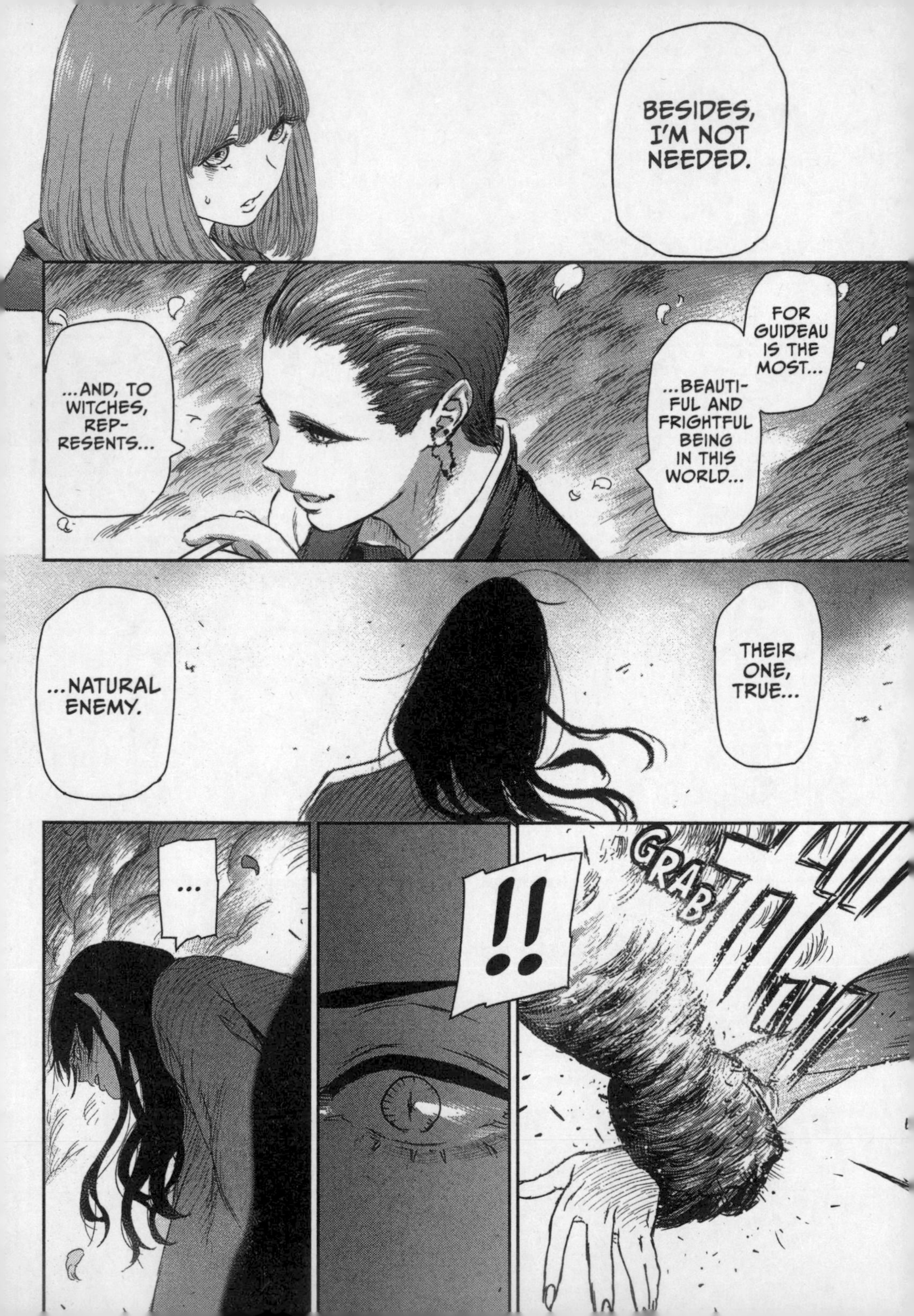
BESIDES, I'M NOT NEEDED.
FOR GUIDEAU IS THE MOST...
...BEAUTI-FUL AND FRIGHTFUL BEING IN THIS WORLD...
...AND, TO WITCHES, REP-RESENTS...
THEIR ONE, TRUE...
...NATURAL ENEMY.
GRAB
!!
...

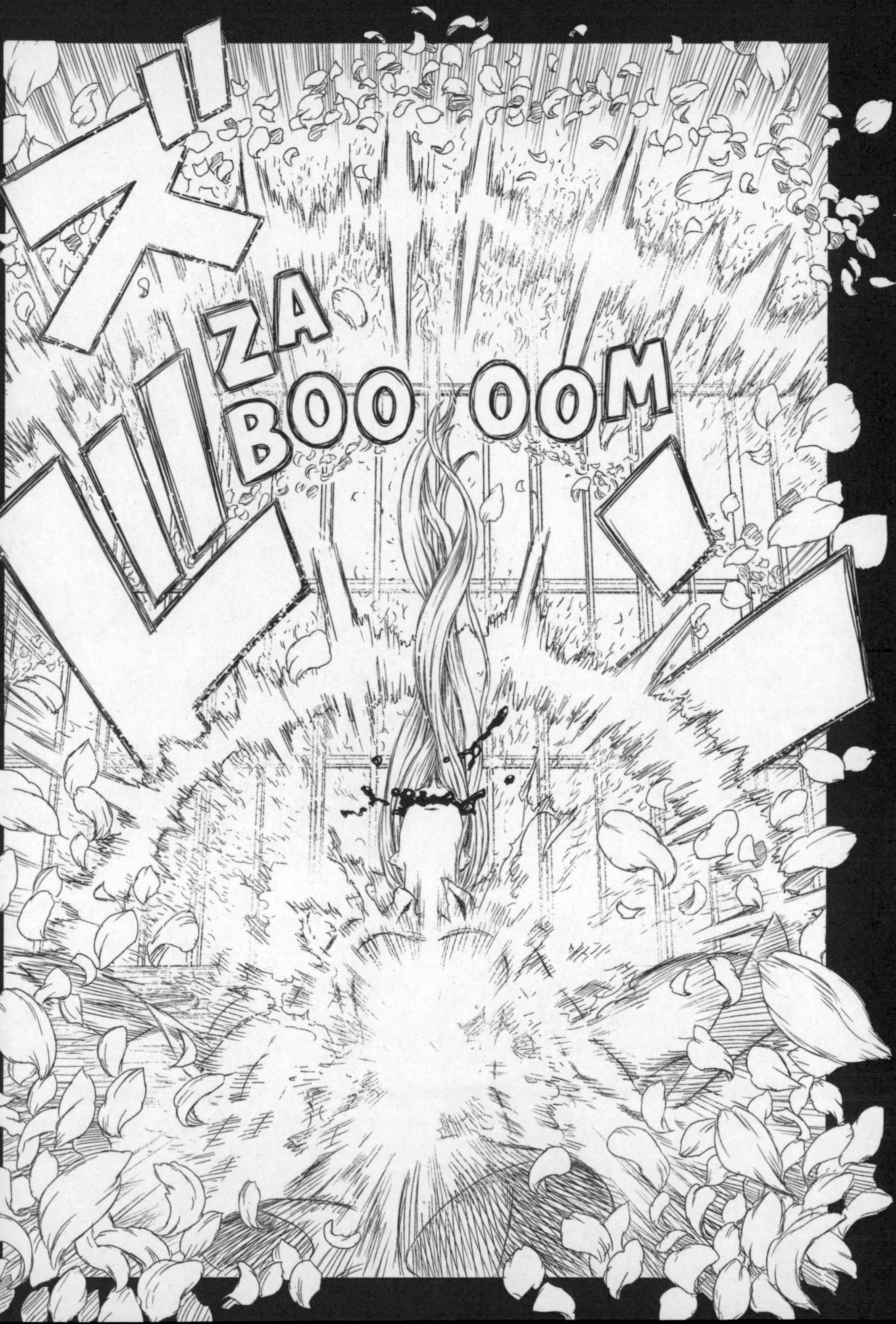
ZA
BOO OOM

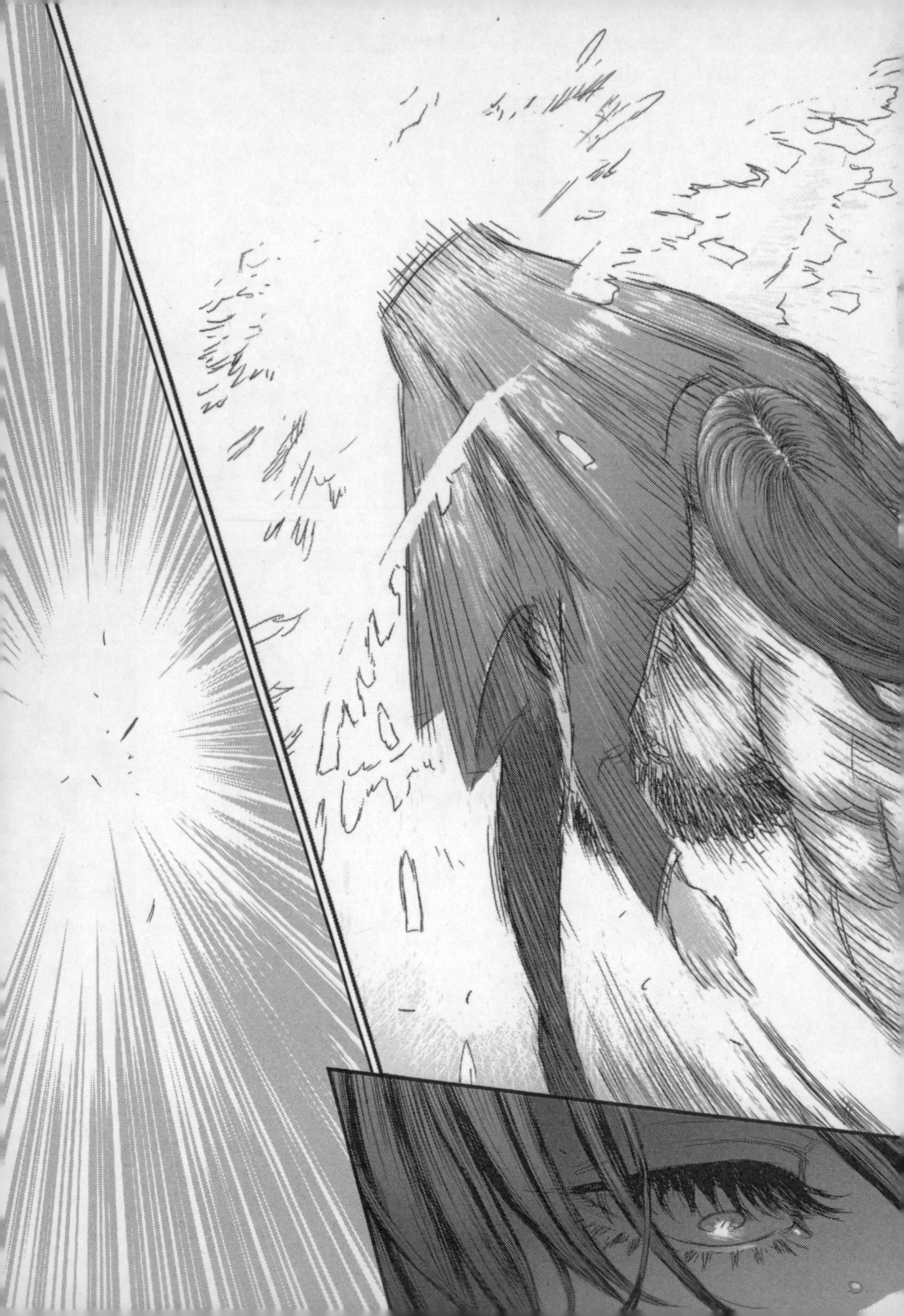

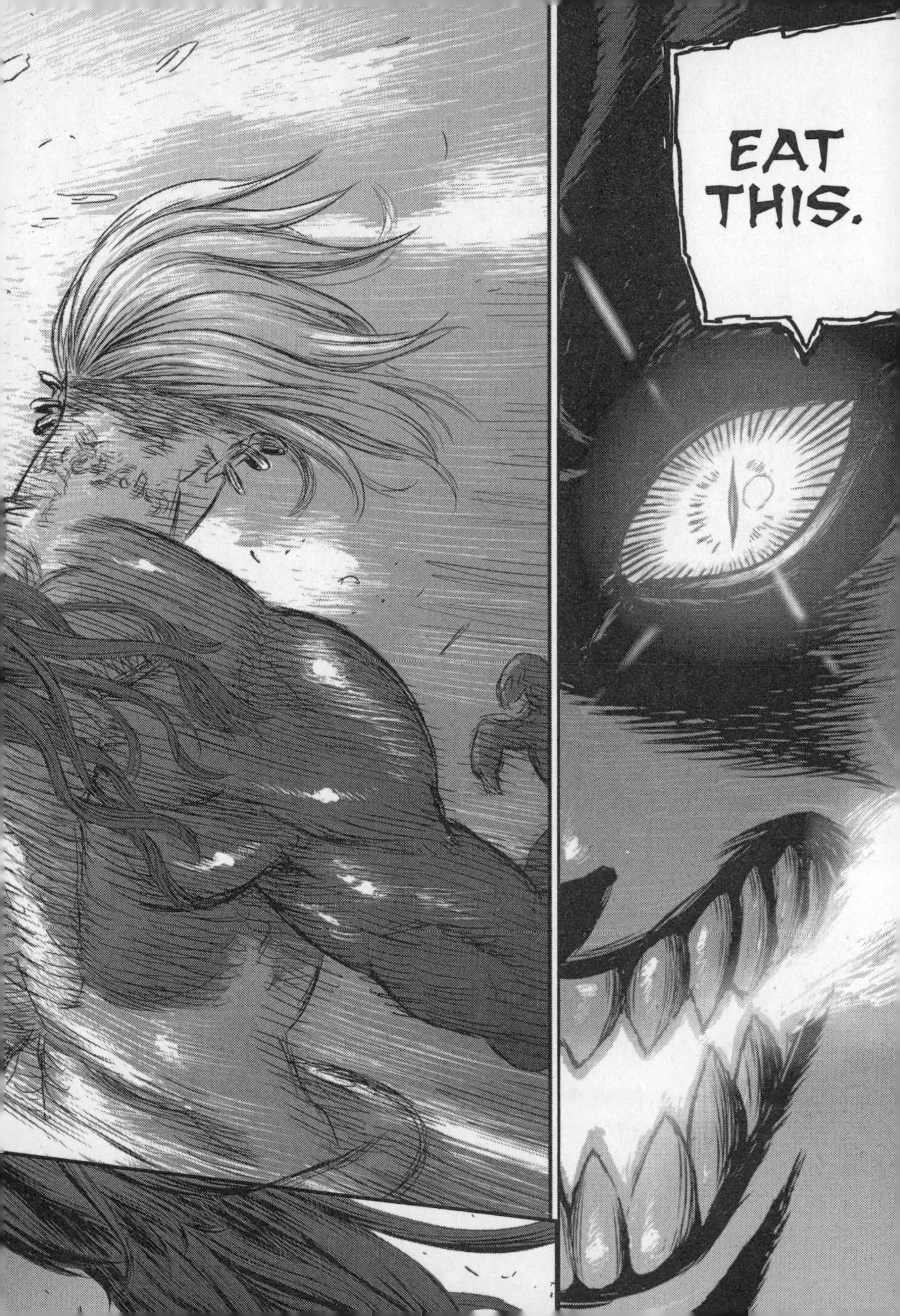
EAT THIS.

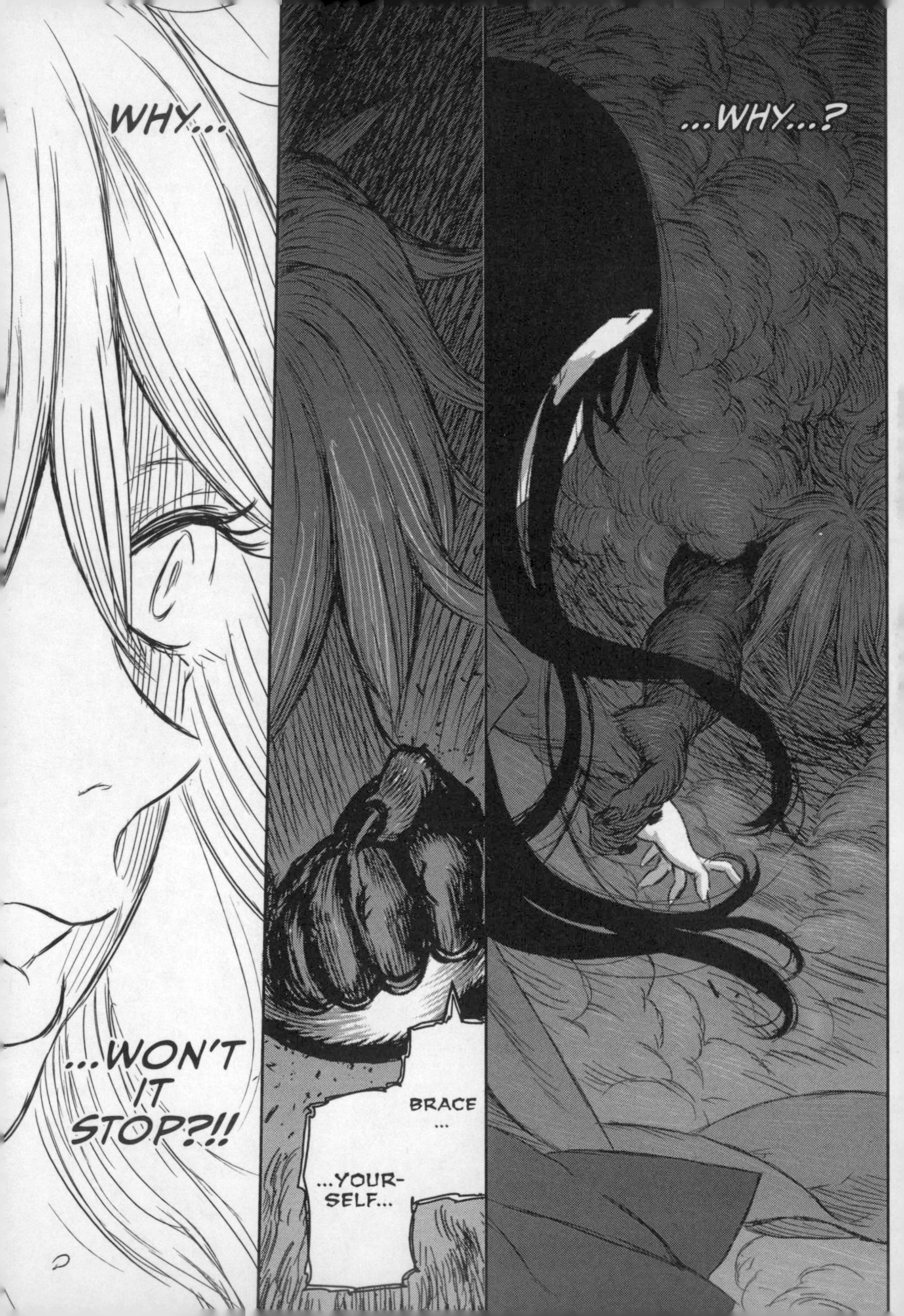
...WHY...?
BRACE ...
...YOURSELF...
WHY...
...WON'T IT STOP?!!

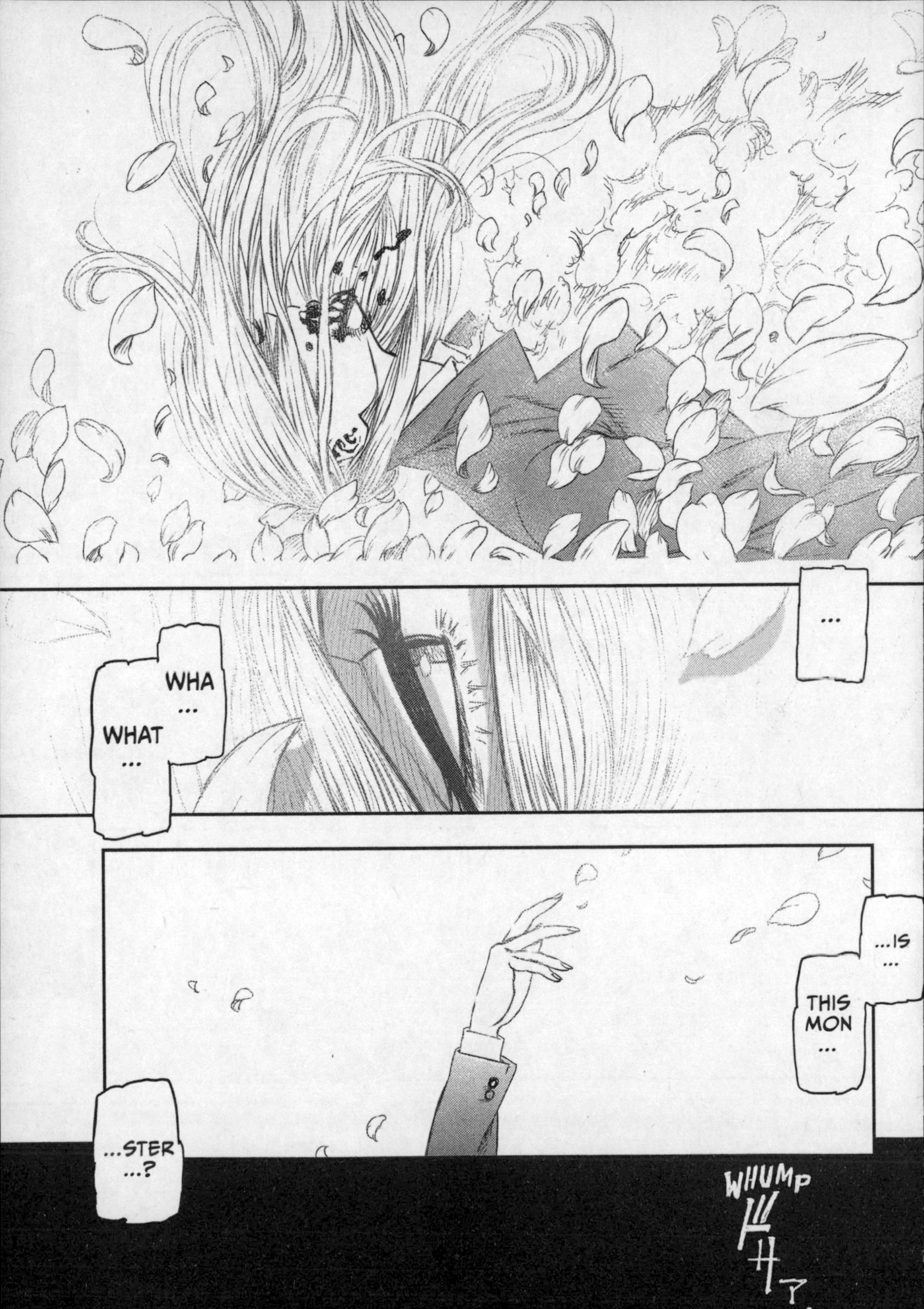
...
WHA ... WHAT ...
...IS ... THIS MON ...
...STER ...?
WHUMP
ドサァ

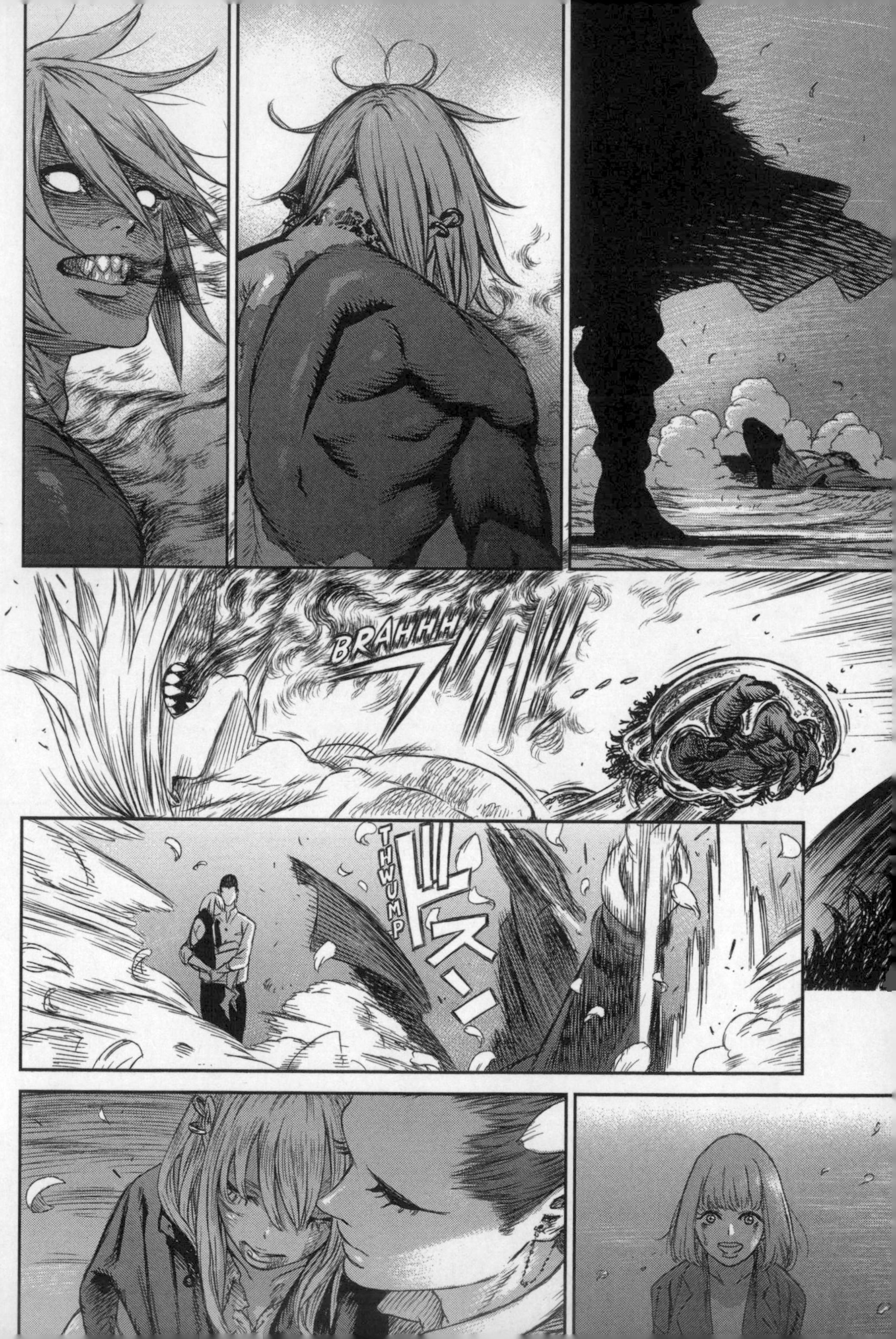
BRAHHH
THWUMP

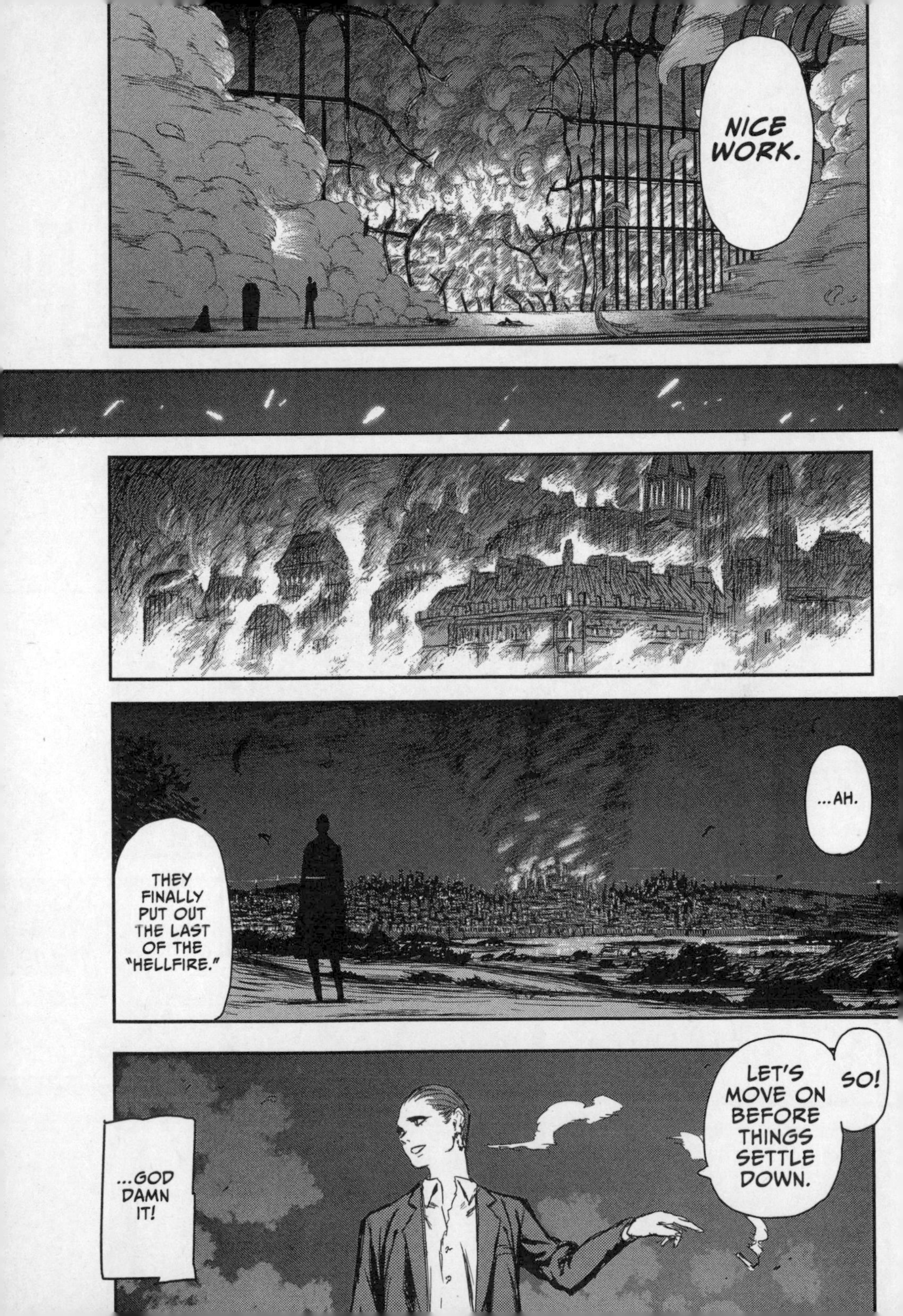
NICE WORK.
...AH.
THEY FINALLY PUT OUT THE LAST OF THE "HELLFIRE."
SO!
LET'S MOVE ON BEFORE THINGS SETTLE DOWN.
...GOD DAMN IT!

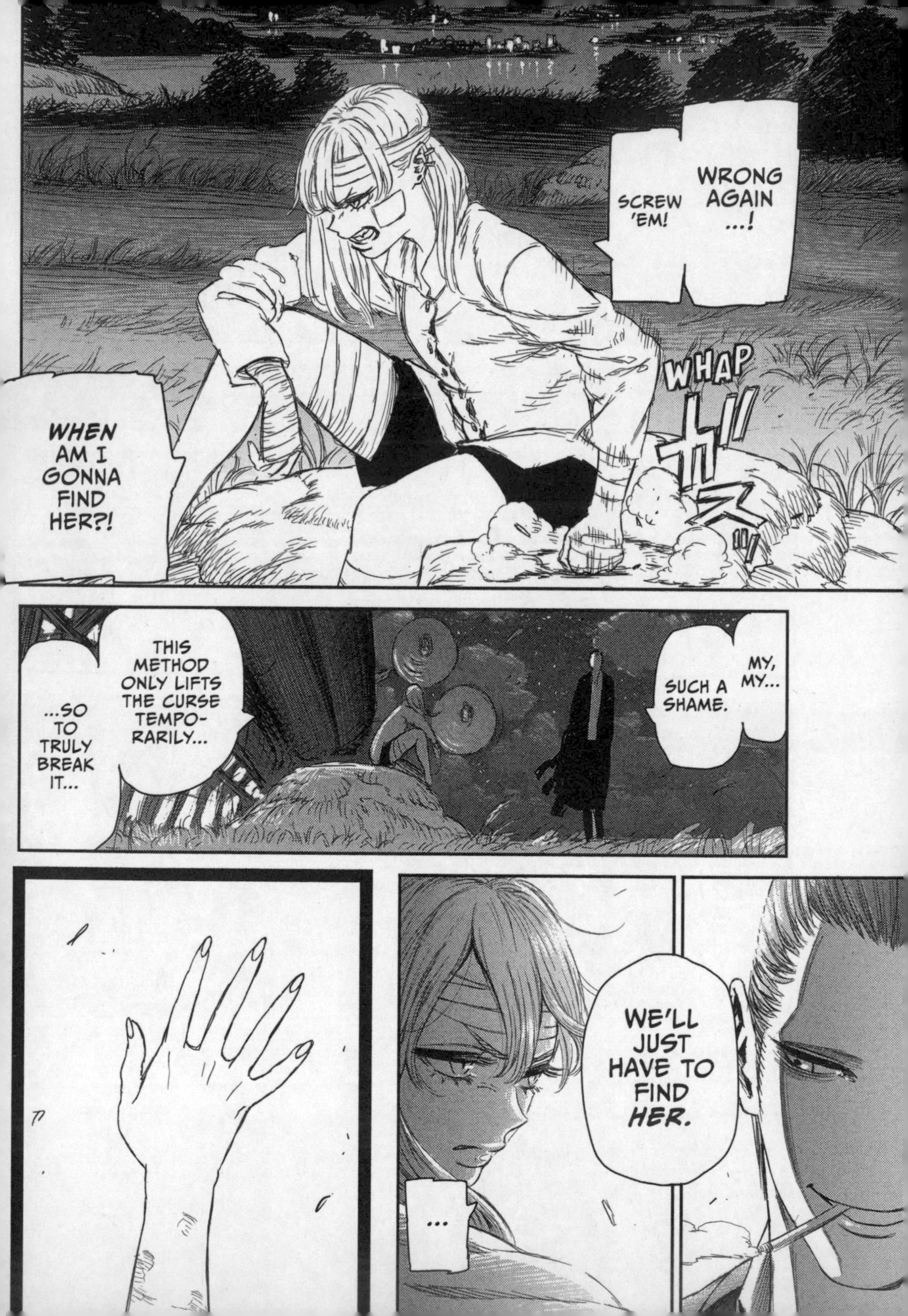
WRONG AGAIN ...!
SCREW 'EM!
WHAP
WHEN AM I GONNA FIND HER?!
MY, MY...
SUCH A SHAME.
THIS METHOD ONLY LIFTS THE CURSE TEMPO-RARILY...
...SO TO TRULY BREAK IT...
WE'LL JUST HAVE TO FIND HER.
...

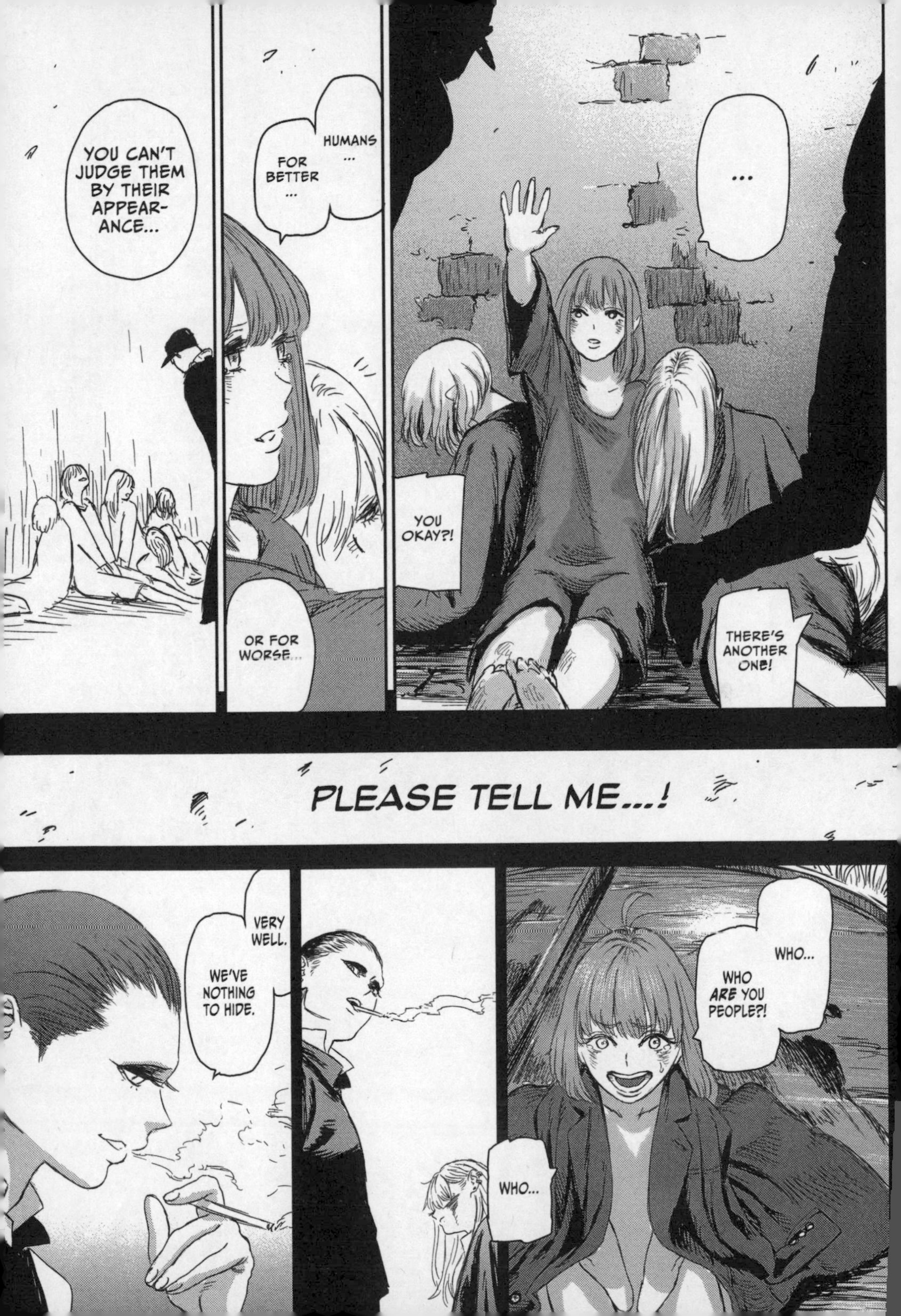
...
YOU OKAY?!
THERE'S ANOTHER ONE!
HUMANS... FOR BETTER...
OR FOR WORSE...
YOU CAN'T JUDGE THEM BY THEIR APPEARANCE...
PLEASE TELL ME...!
WHO... WHO ARE YOU PEOPLE?!
WHO...
VERY WELL. WE'VE NOTHING TO HIDE.

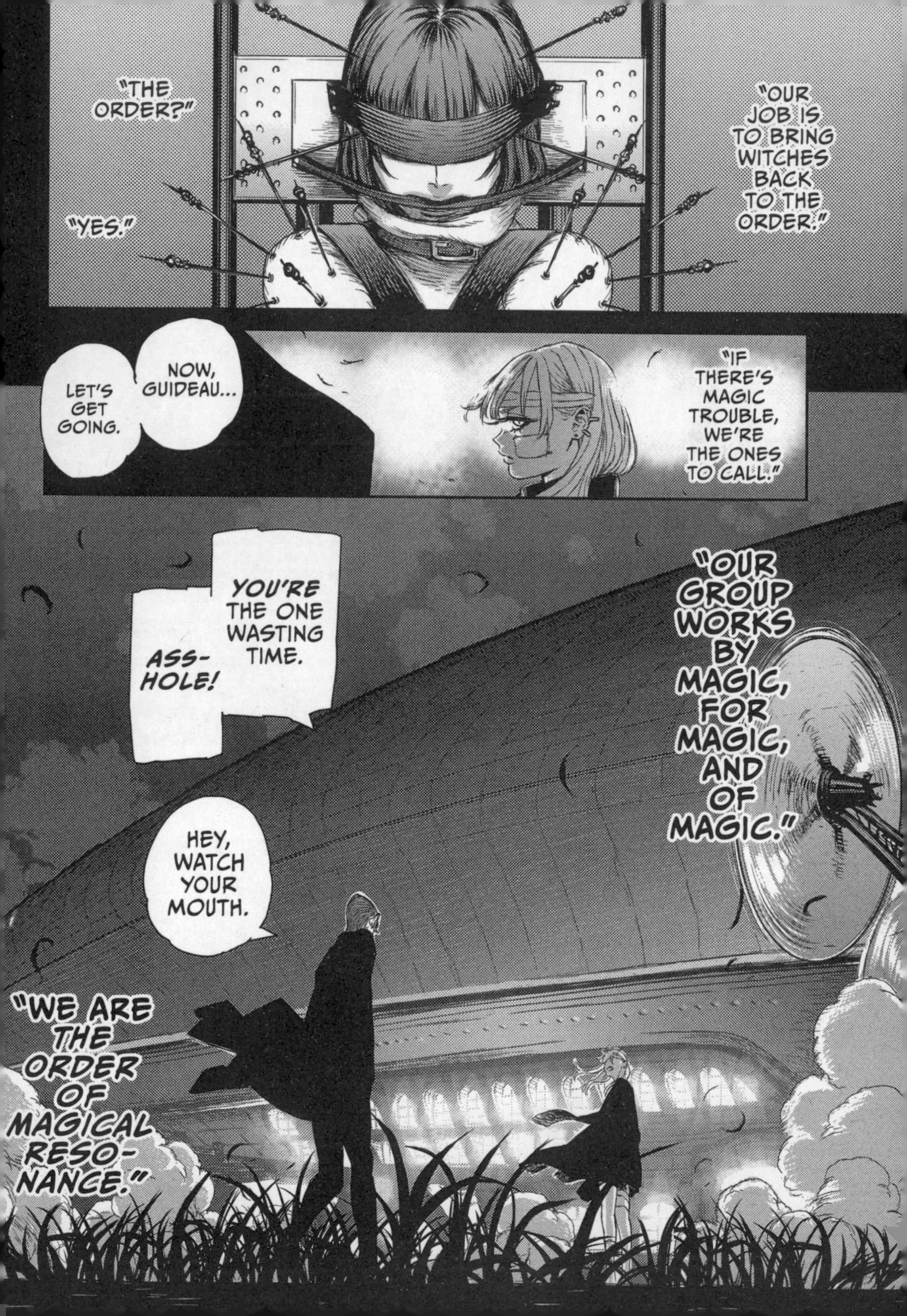
"OUR JOB IS TO BRING WITCHES BACK TO THE ORDER."
"THE ORDER?"
"YES."
"IF THERE'S MAGIC TROUBLE, WE'RE THE ONES TO CALL."
NOW, GUIDEAU...
LET'S GET GOING.
"OUR GROUP WORKS BY MAGIC, FOR MAGIC, AND OF MAGIC."
YOU'RE THE ONE WASTING TIME.
ASS-HOLE!
HEY, WATCH YOUR MOUTH.
"WE ARE THE ORDER OF MAGICAL RESO-NANCE."

THE WITCH AND THE BEAST

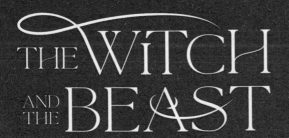

THE WITCH AND THE BEAST

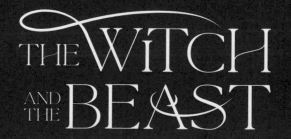

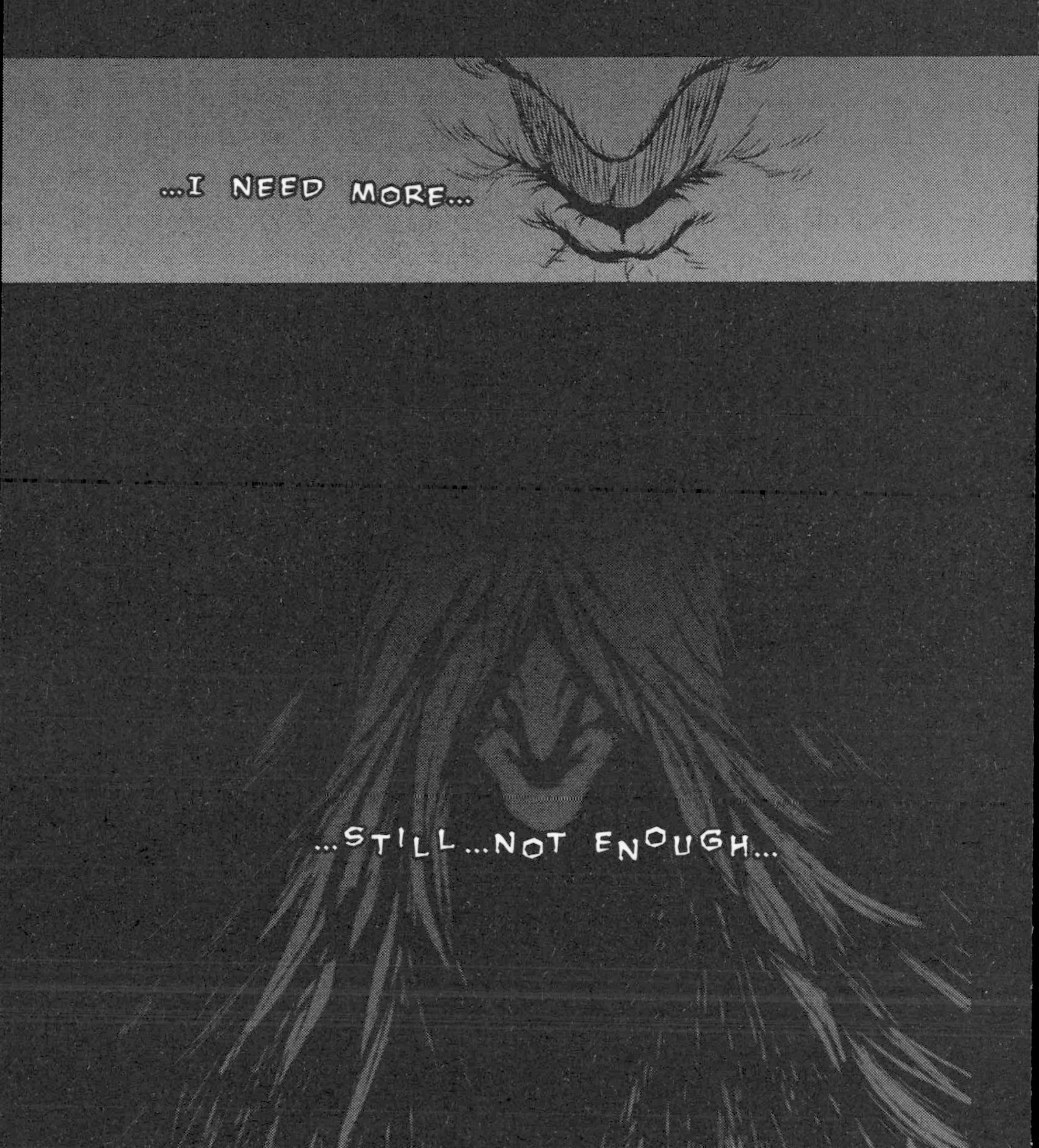
...I NEED MORE...
...STILL...NOT ENOUGH...

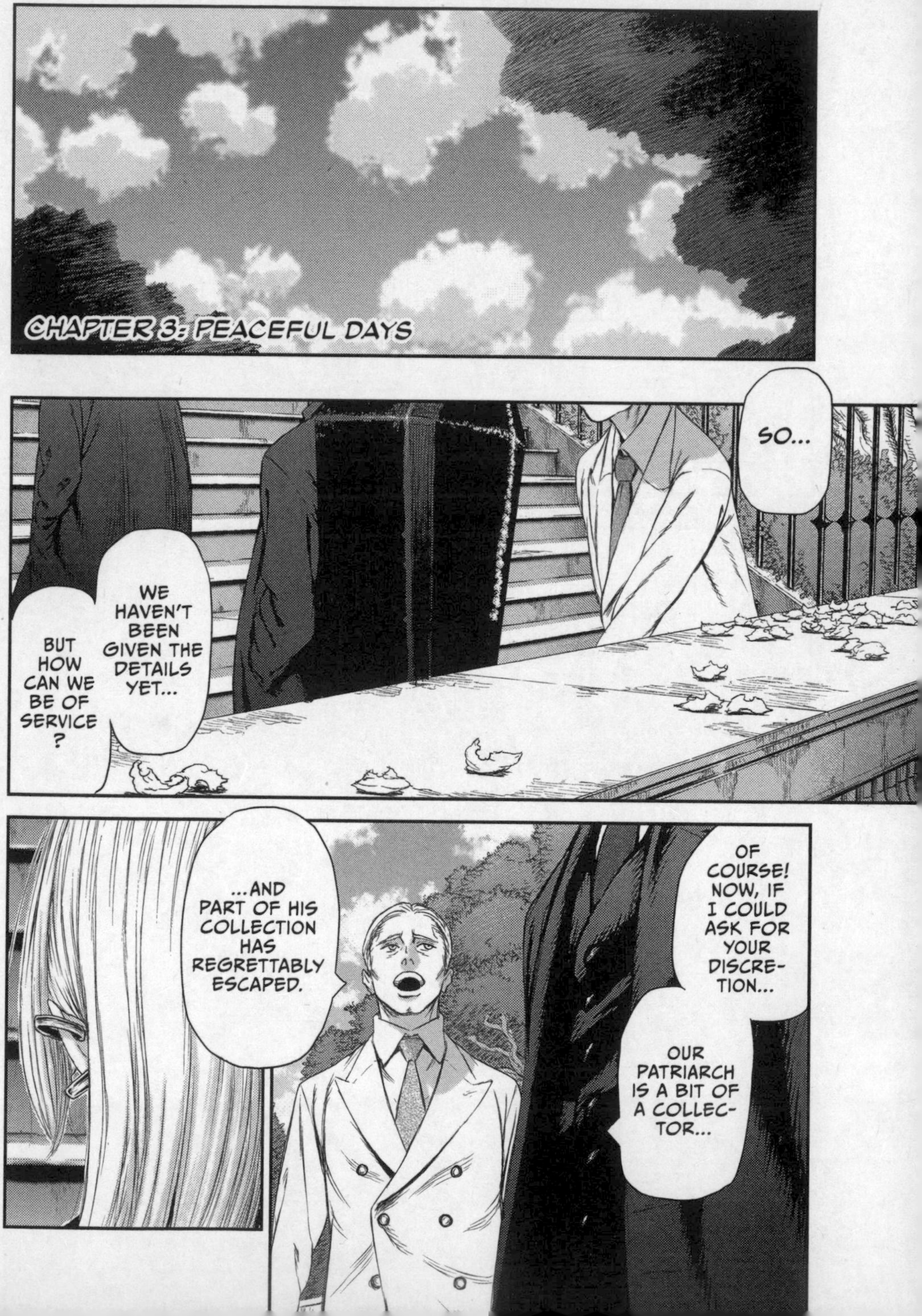
CHAPTER 3: PEACEFUL DAYS
SO...
WE HAVEN'T BEEN GIVEN THE DETAILS YET...
BUT HOW CAN WE BE OF SERVICE?
OF COURSE! NOW, IF I COULD ASK FOR YOUR DISCRETION...
OUR PATRIARCH IS A BIT OF A COLLECTOR...
...AND PART OF HIS COLLECTION HAS REGRETTABLY ESCAPED.

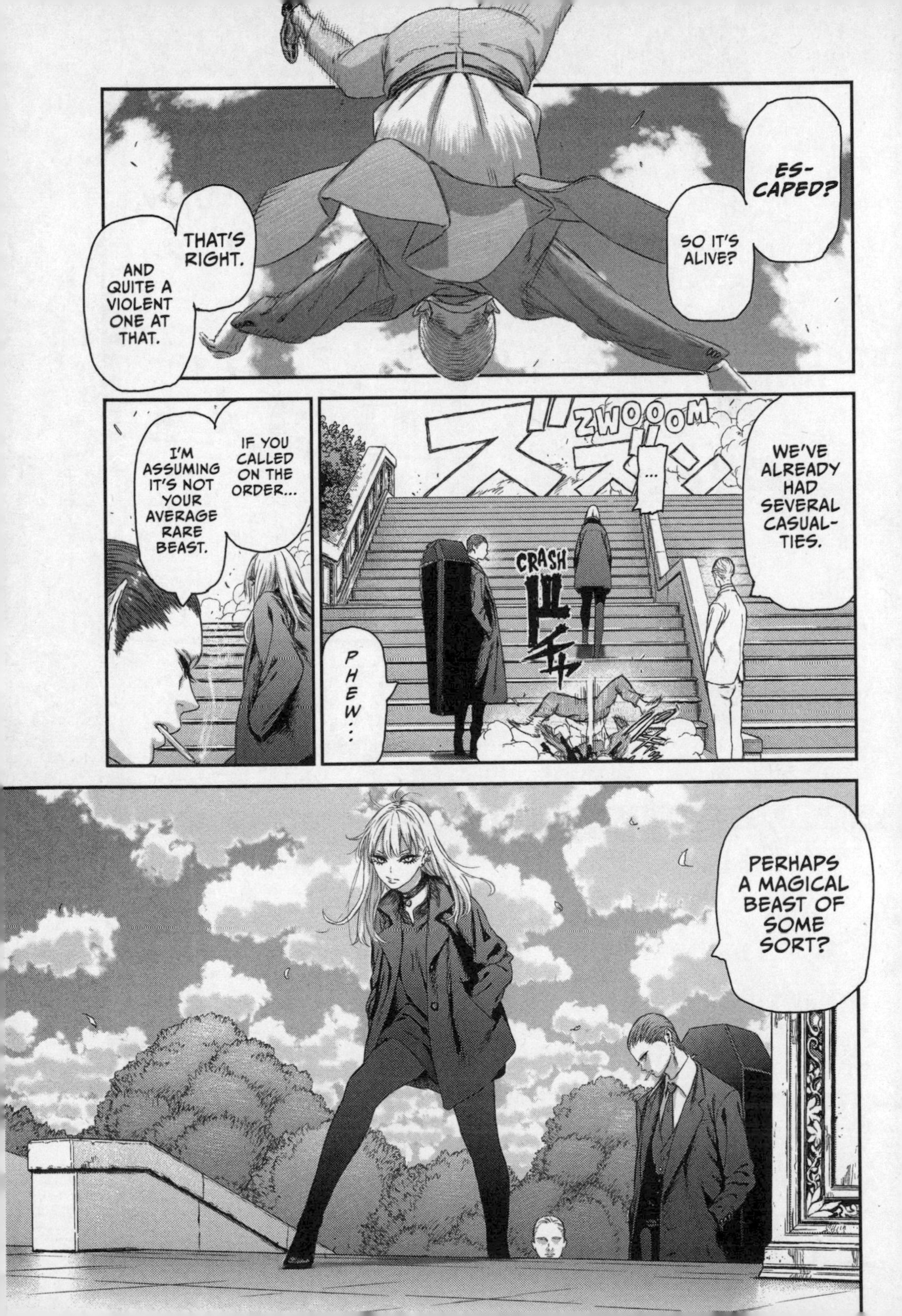
ES-CAPED?
SO IT'S ALIVE?
THAT'S RIGHT.
AND QUITE A VIOLENT ONE AT THAT.
ZWOOOM
...
WE'VE ALREADY HAD SEVERAL CASUAL-TIES.
CRASH
PHEW...
IF YOU CALLED ON THE ORDER...
I'M ASSUMING IT'S NOT YOUR AVERAGE RARE BEAST.
PERHAPS A MAGICAL BEAST OF SOME SORT?

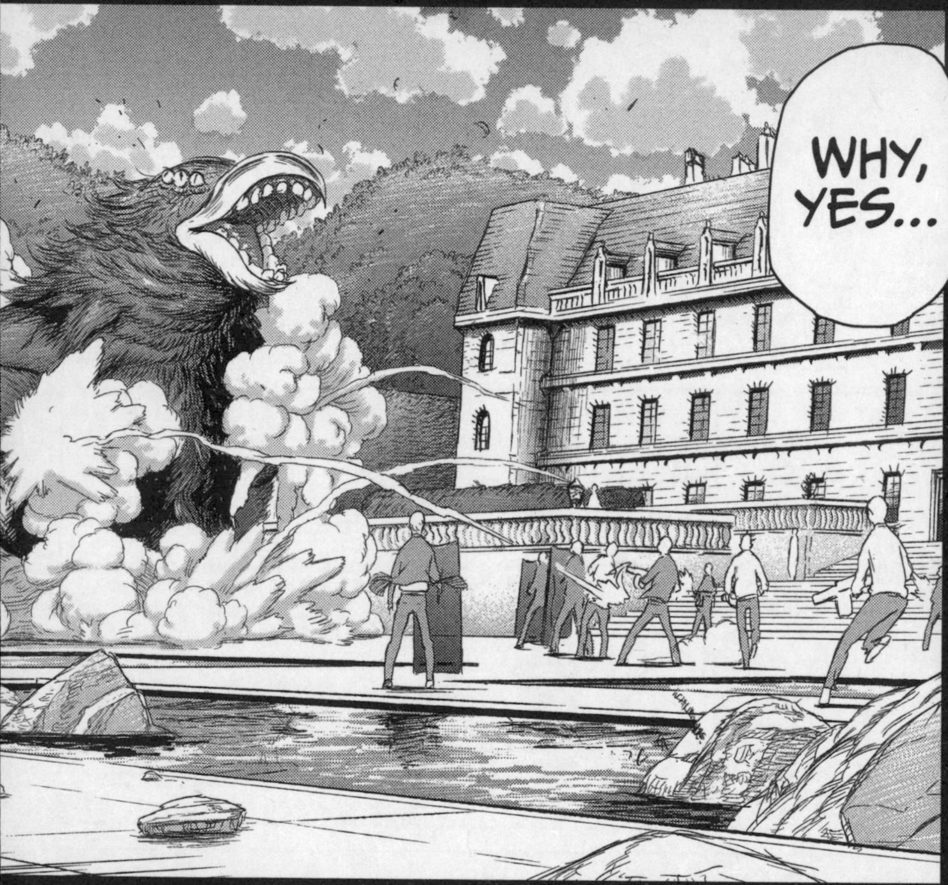
WHY, YES...
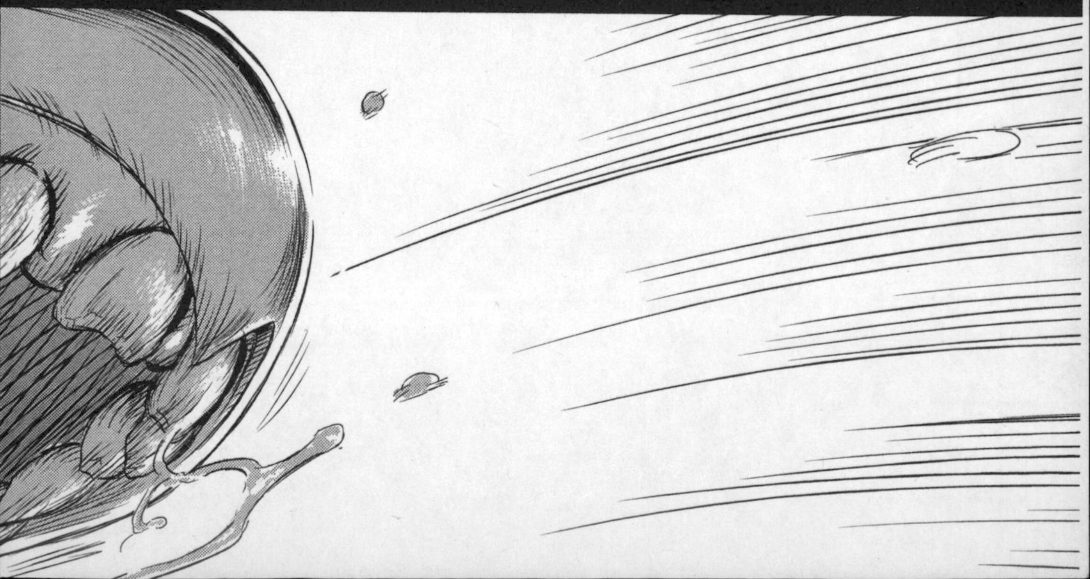

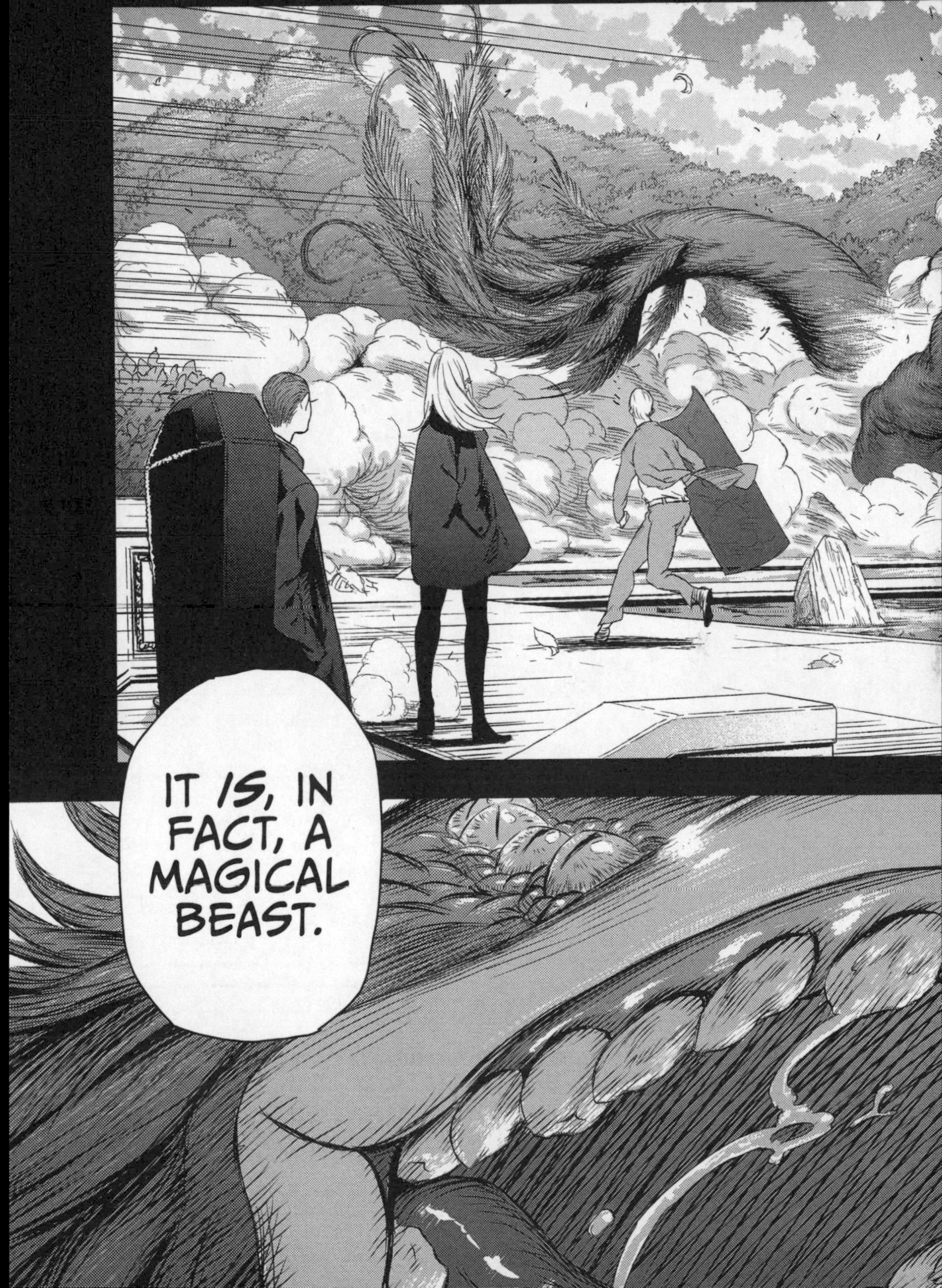
IT IS, IN FACT, A MAGICAL BEAST.

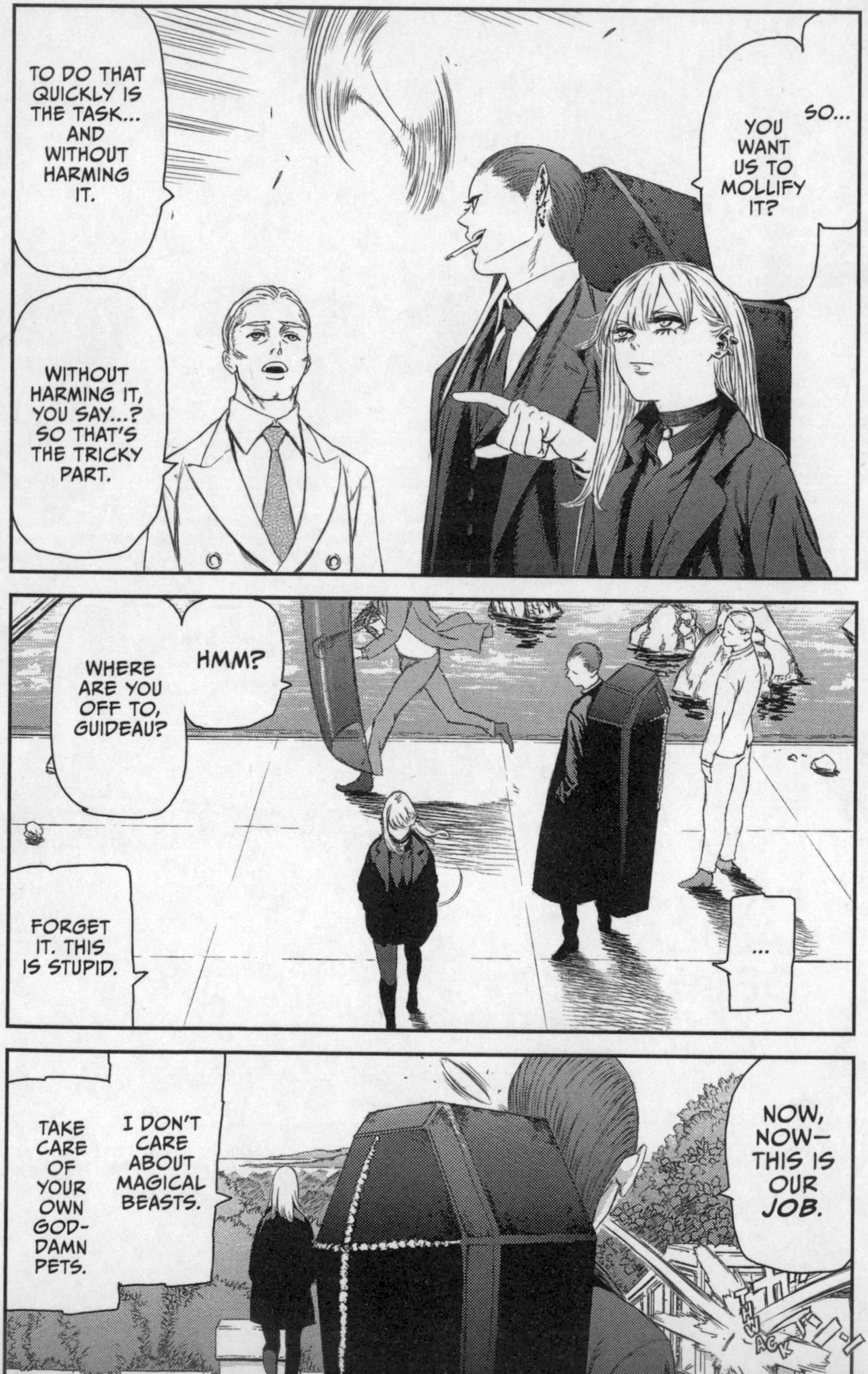
SO... YOU WANT US TO MOLLIFY IT?
TO DO THAT QUICKLY IS THE TASK... AND WITHOUT HARMING IT.
WITHOUT HARMING IT, YOU SAY...? SO THAT'S THE TRICKY PART.
HMM?
WHERE ARE YOU OFF TO, GUIDEAU?
...
FORGET IT. THIS IS STUPID.
NOW, NOW— THIS IS OUR JOB.
THWACK
I DON'T CARE ABOUT MAGICAL BEASTS.
TAKE CARE OF YOUR OWN GOD-DAMN PETS.

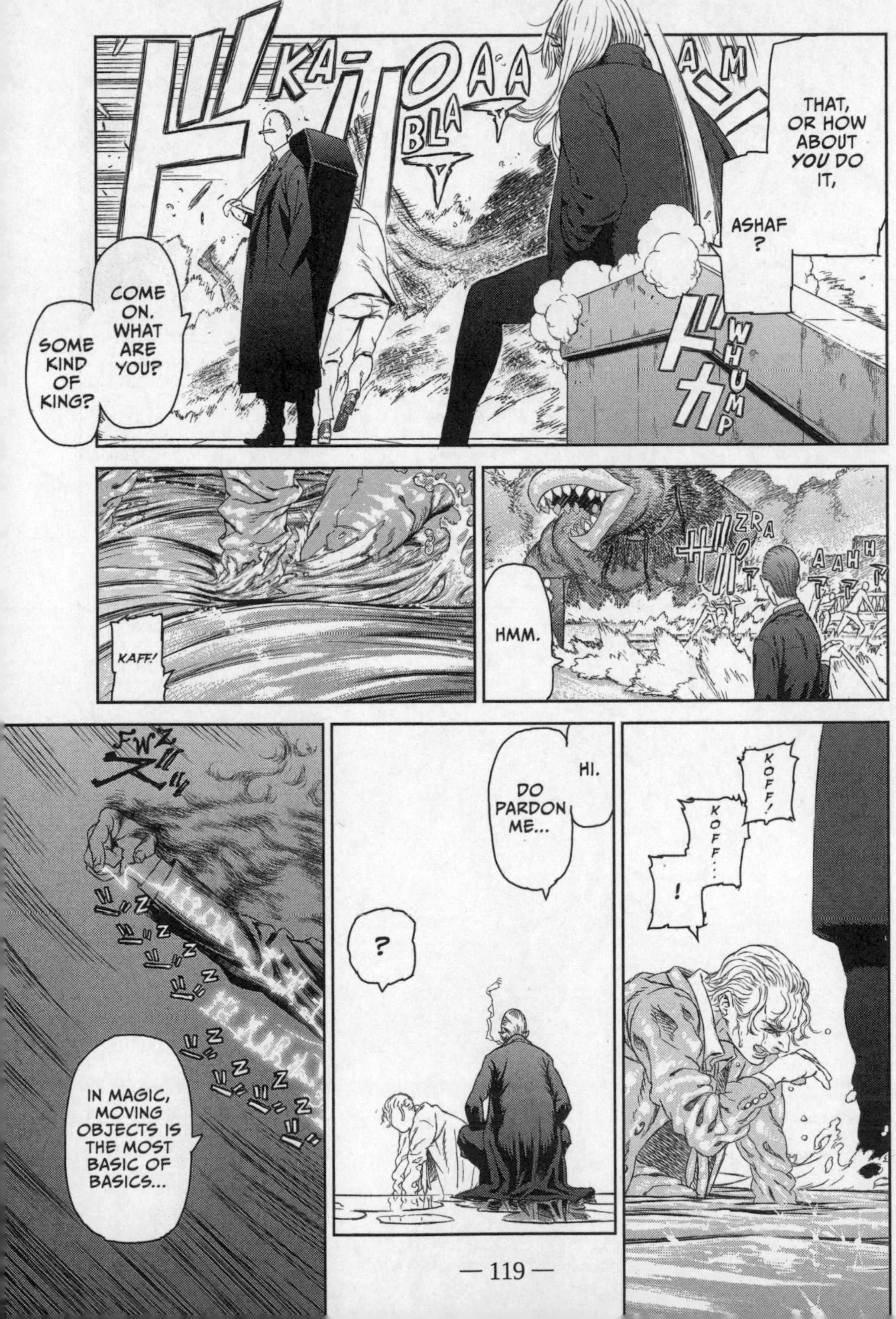
KA-BLAAAAAA-M
THAT, OR HOW ABOUT *YOU* DO IT,
ASHAF?
WHUMP
COME ON. WHAT ARE YOU?
SOME KIND OF KING?
ZRA
AAHH
HMM.
KAFF!
KOFF!
KOFF...
!
HI.
DO PARDON ME...
?
FWZZ
IN MAGIC, MOVING OBJECTS IS THE MOST BASIC OF BASICS...

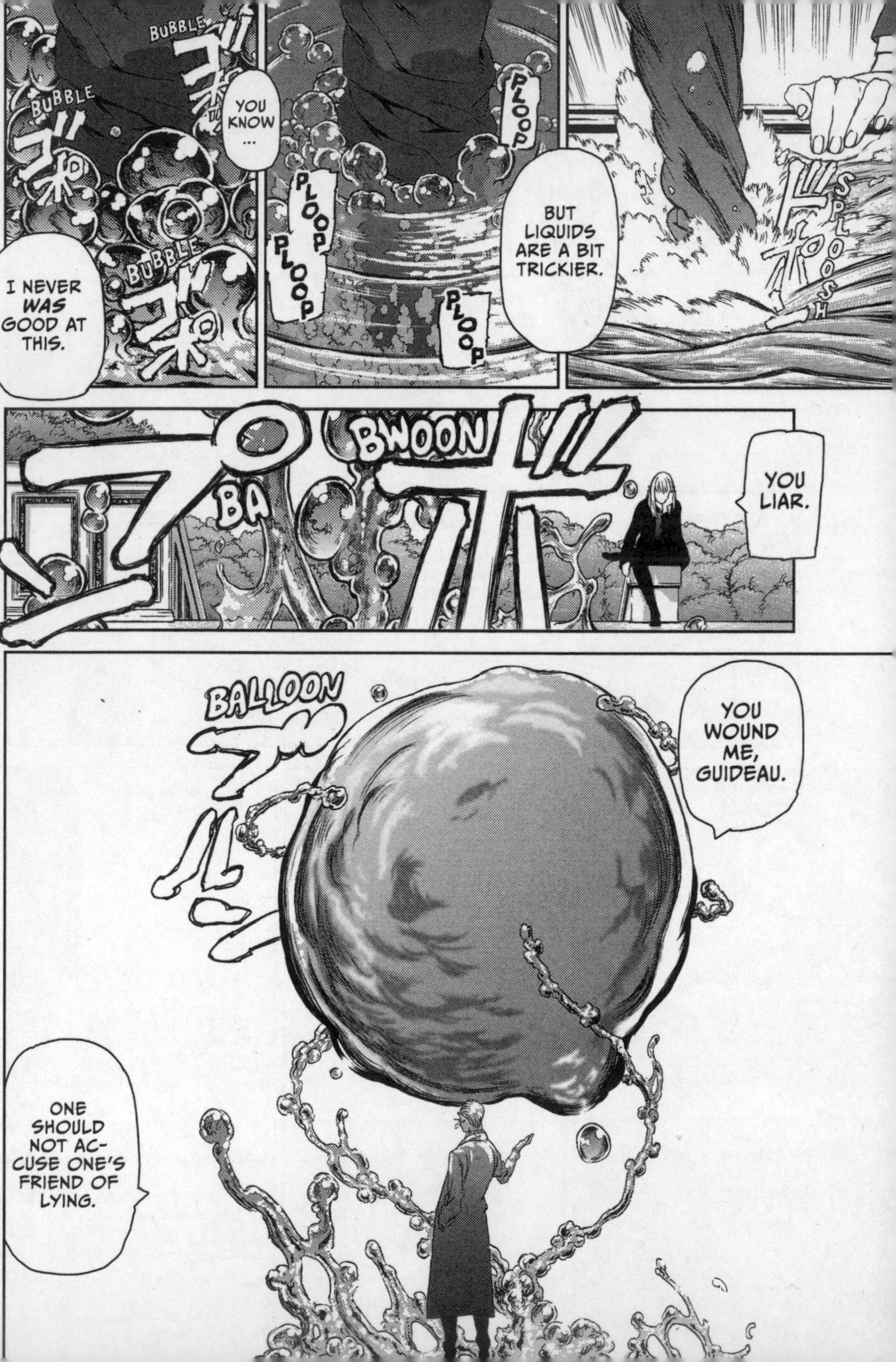

SPLOOSH
BUT LIQUIDS ARE A BIT TRICKIER.
PLOOP
PLOOP
PLOOP
PLOOP
YOU KNOW ...
BUBBLE
BUBBLE
BUBBLE
I NEVER WAS GOOD AT THIS.
YOU LIAR.
BWOON
BA
YOU WOUND ME, GUIDEAU.
BALLOON
ONE SHOULD NOT AC-CUSE ONE'S FRIEND OF LYING.

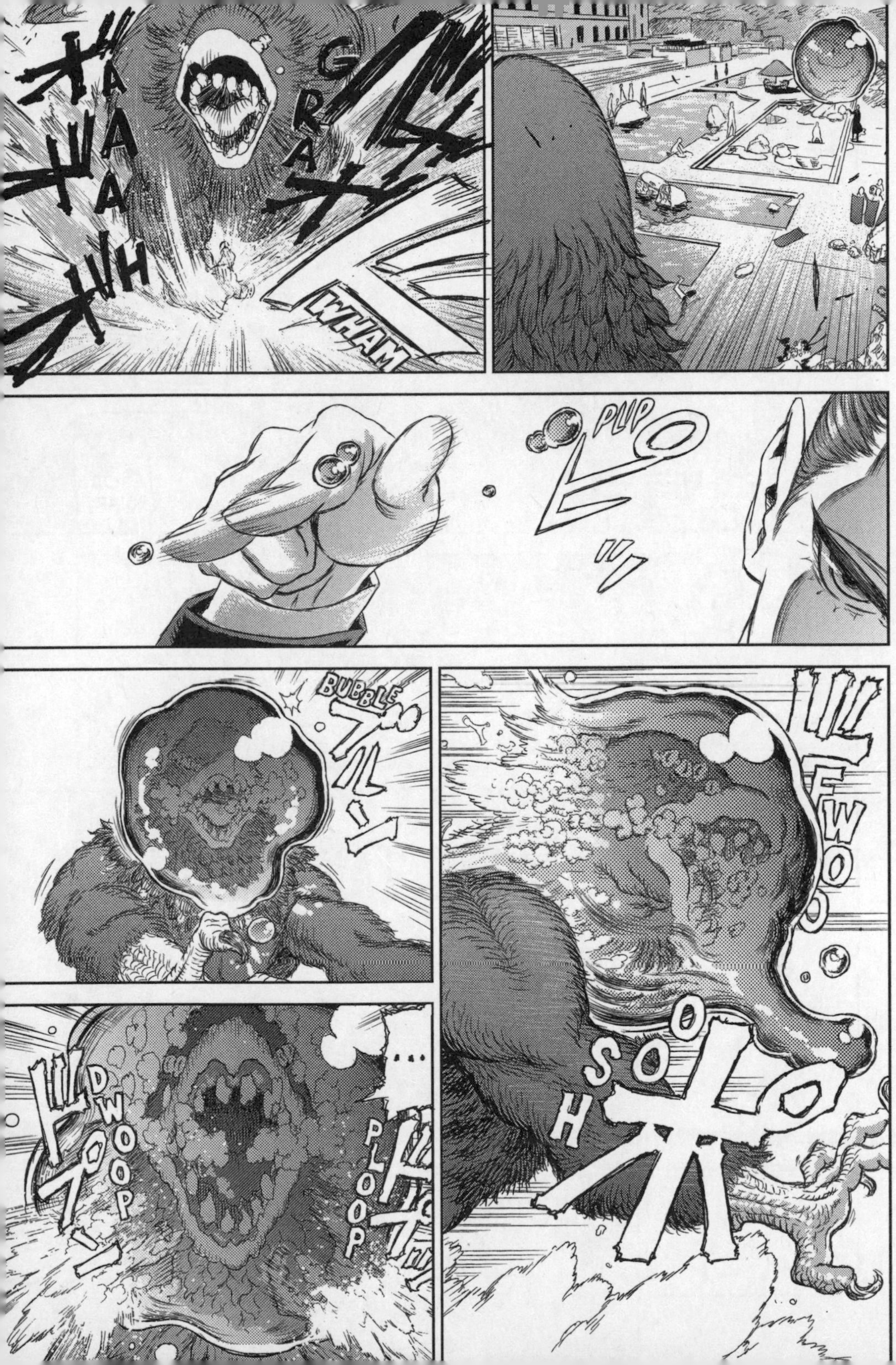
GRA
HAAAH
WHAM
PLIP
FWOOO
SOOH
BUBBLE
...
PLOOOP
DWOOOP

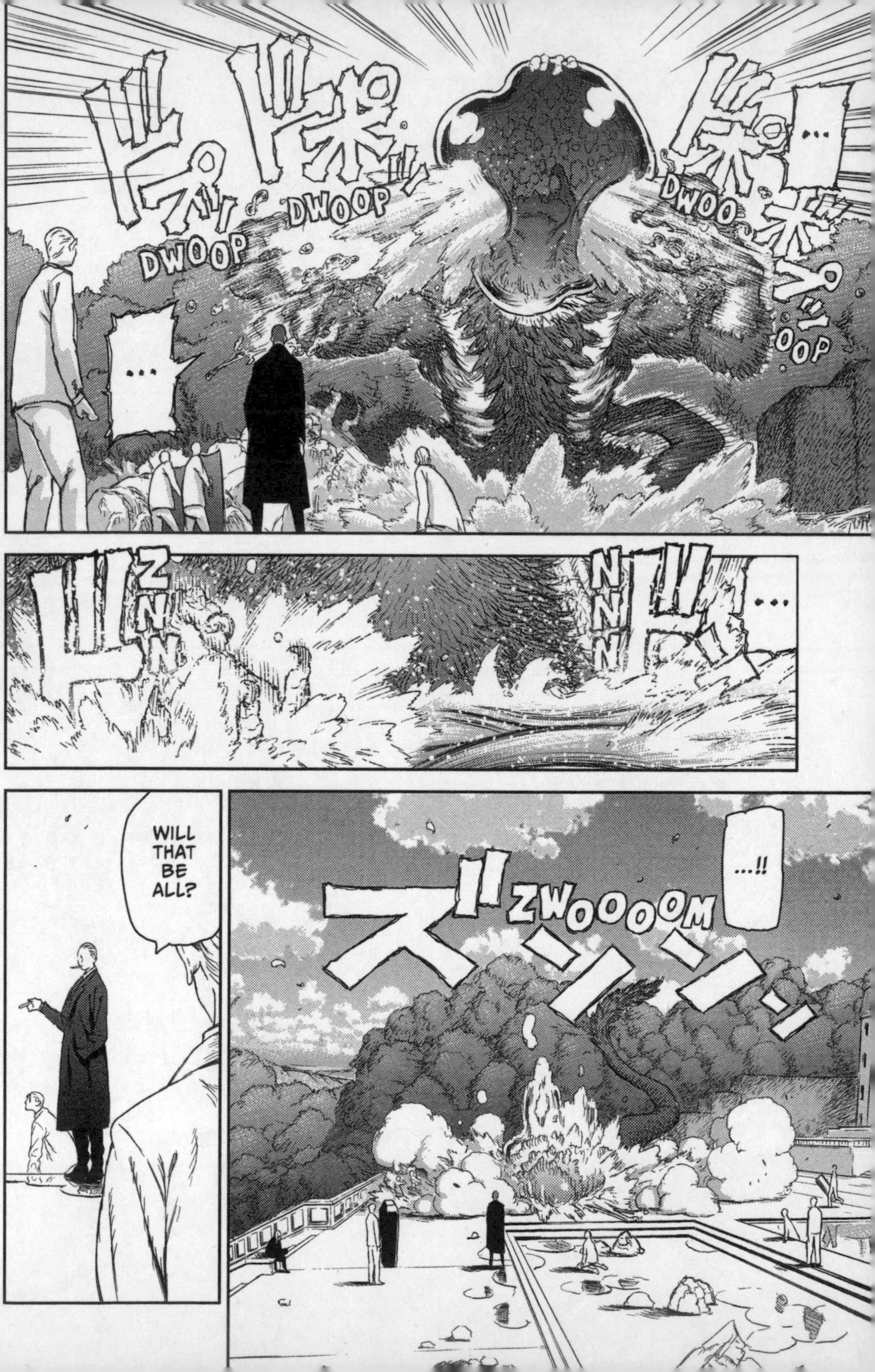
…
DWOO
OOP
DWOOP
DWOOP
…
…
NNN
ZNN
…!!
ZWOOOOM
WILL THAT BE ALL?

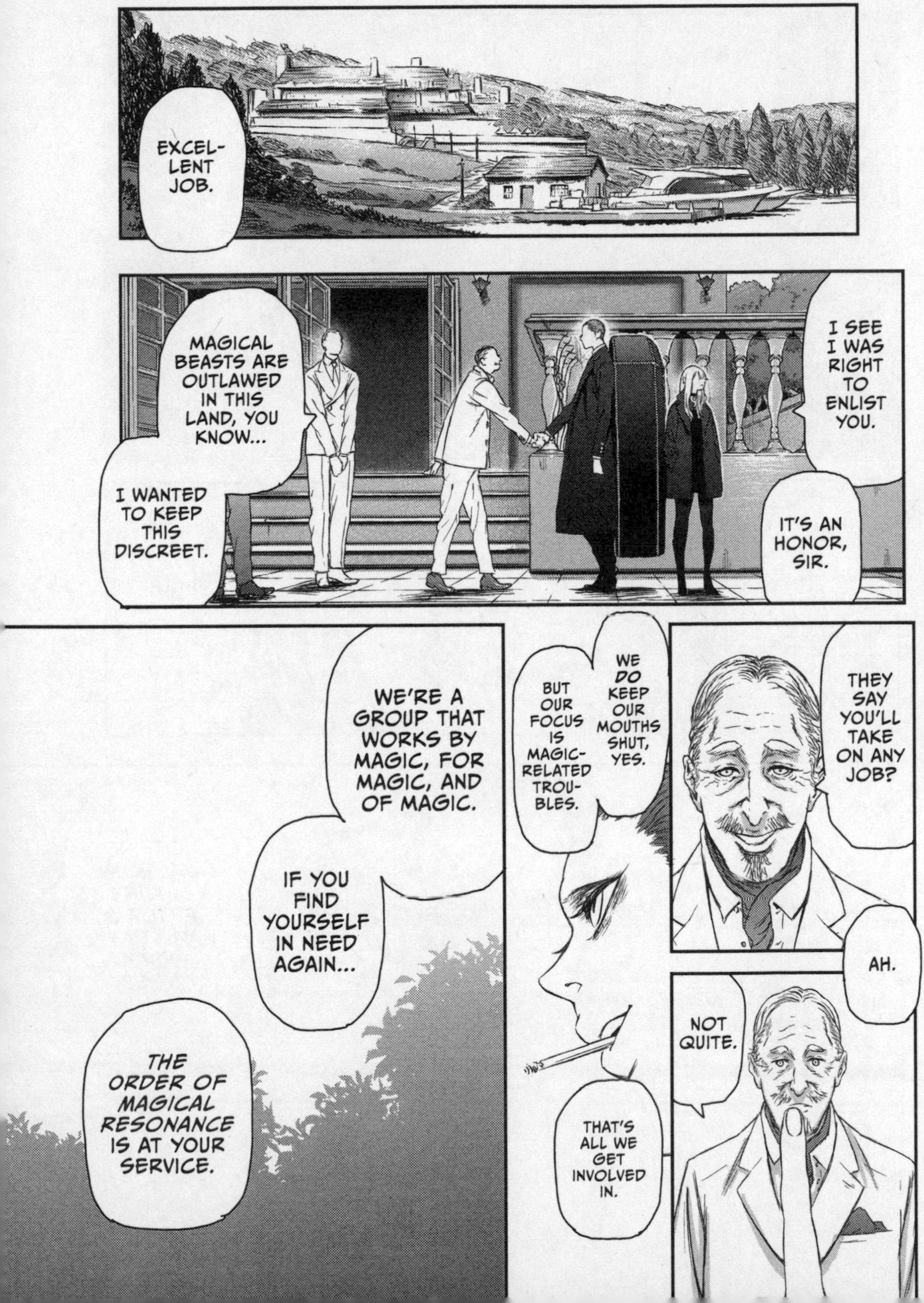
EXCEL-LENT JOB.
I SEE I WAS RIGHT TO ENLIST YOU.
IT'S AN HONOR, SIR.
MAGICAL BEASTS ARE OUTLAWED IN THIS LAND, YOU KNOW...
I WANTED TO KEEP THIS DISCREET.
THEY SAY YOU'LL TAKE ON ANY JOB?
AH.
NOT QUITE.
WE *DO* KEEP OUR MOUTHS SHUT, YES.
BUT OUR FOCUS IS MAGIC-RELATED TROU-BLES.
THAT'S ALL WE GET INVOLVED IN.
WE'RE A GROUP THAT WORKS BY MAGIC, FOR MAGIC, AND OF MAGIC.
IF YOU FIND YOURSELF IN NEED AGAIN...
THE ORDER OF MAGICAL RESONANCE IS AT YOUR SERVICE.

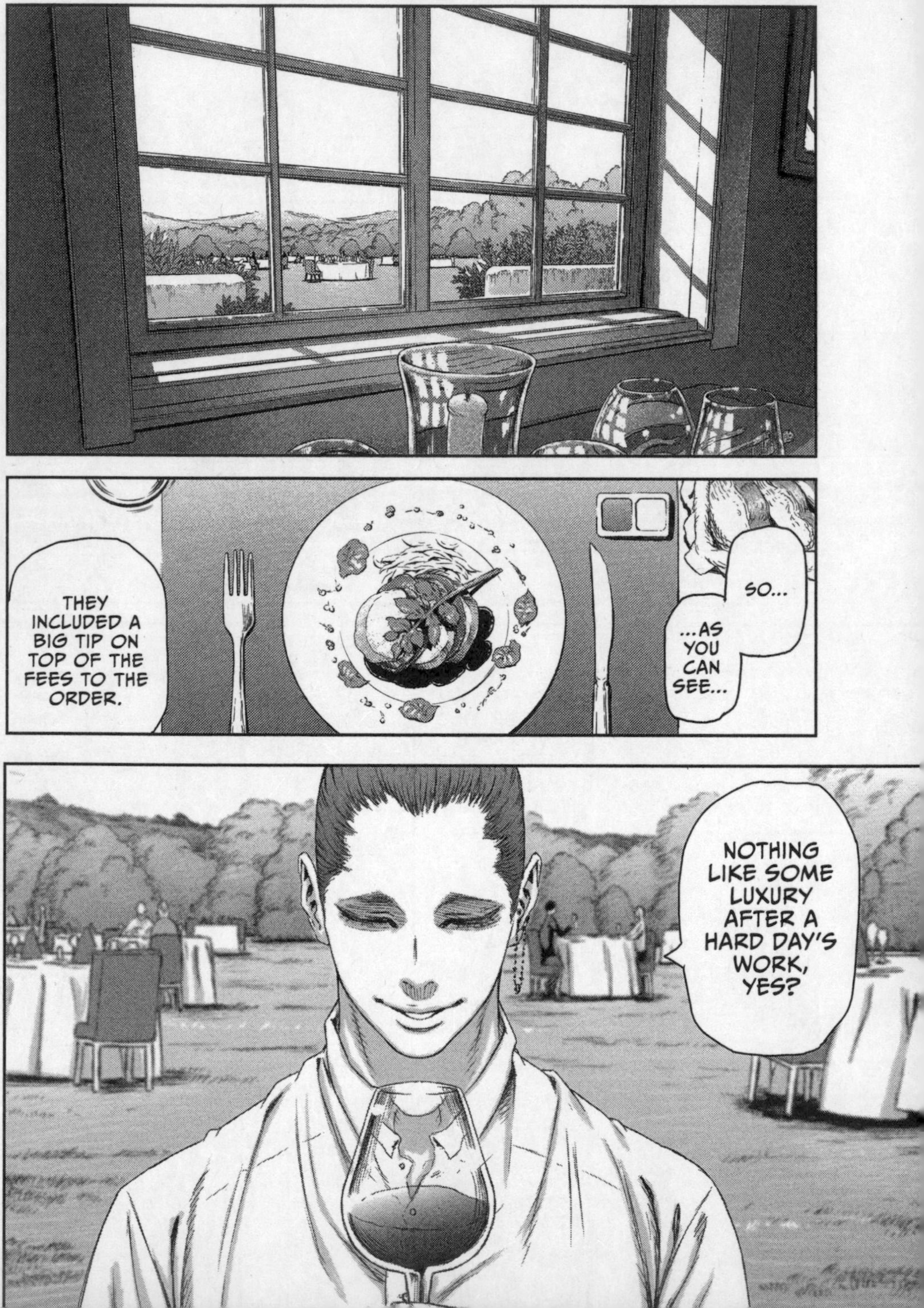
SO...
...AS YOU CAN SEE...
THEY INCLUDED A BIG TIP ON TOP OF THE FEES TO THE ORDER.
NOTHING LIKE SOME LUXURY AFTER A HARD DAY'S WORK, YES?

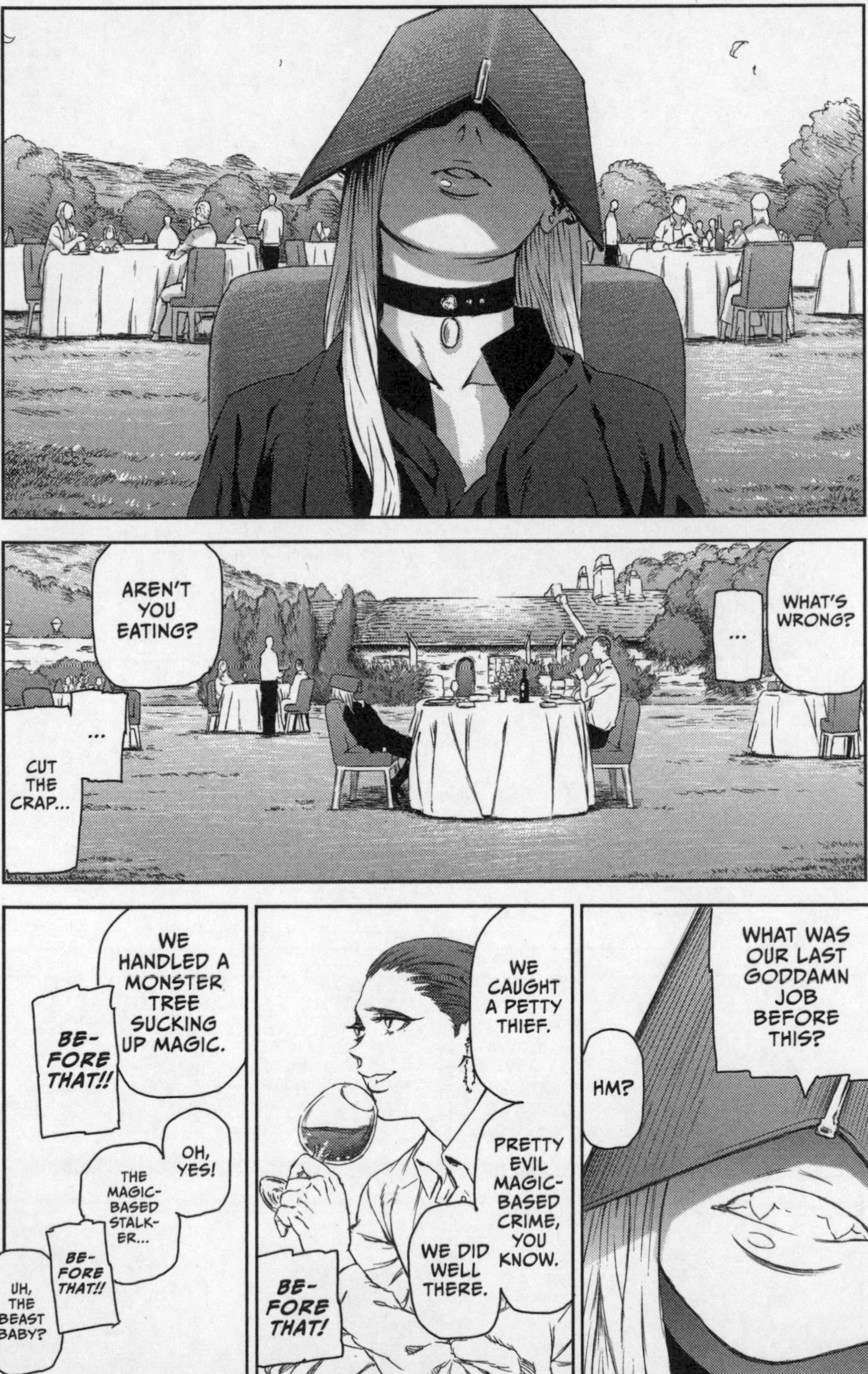
WHAT'S WRONG?
...
AREN'T YOU EATING?
...
CUT THE CRAP...
WHAT WAS OUR LAST GODDAMN JOB BEFORE THIS?
HM?
WE CAUGHT A PETTY THIEF.
PRETTY EVIL MAGIC-BASED CRIME, YOU KNOW.
WE DID WELL THERE.
BE-FORE THAT!
WE HANDLED A MONSTER TREE SUCKING UP MAGIC.
BE-FORE THAT!!
OH, YES!
THE MAGIC-BASED STALK-ER...
BE-FORE THAT!!
UH, THE BEAST BABY?

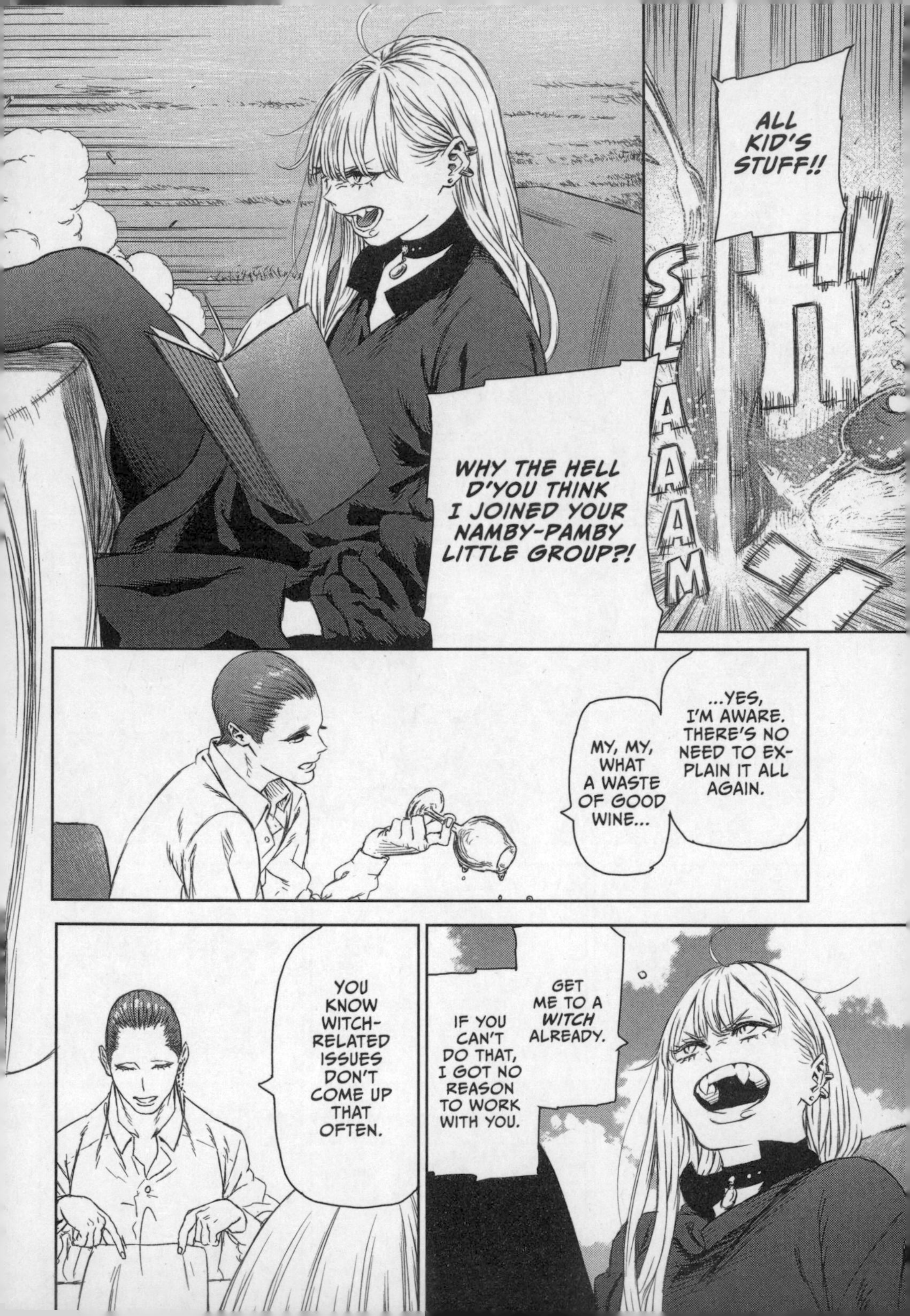
ALL KID'S STUFF!!
SLAAAAM
WHY THE HELL D'YOU THINK I JOINED YOUR NAMBY-PAMBY LITTLE GROUP?!
...YES, I'M AWARE. THERE'S NO NEED TO EX-PLAIN IT ALL AGAIN.
MY, MY, WHAT A WASTE OF GOOD WINE...
GET ME TO A *WITCH* ALREADY.
IF YOU CAN'T DO THAT, I GOT NO REASON TO WORK WITH YOU.
YOU KNOW WITCH-RELATED ISSUES DON'T COME UP THAT OFTEN.

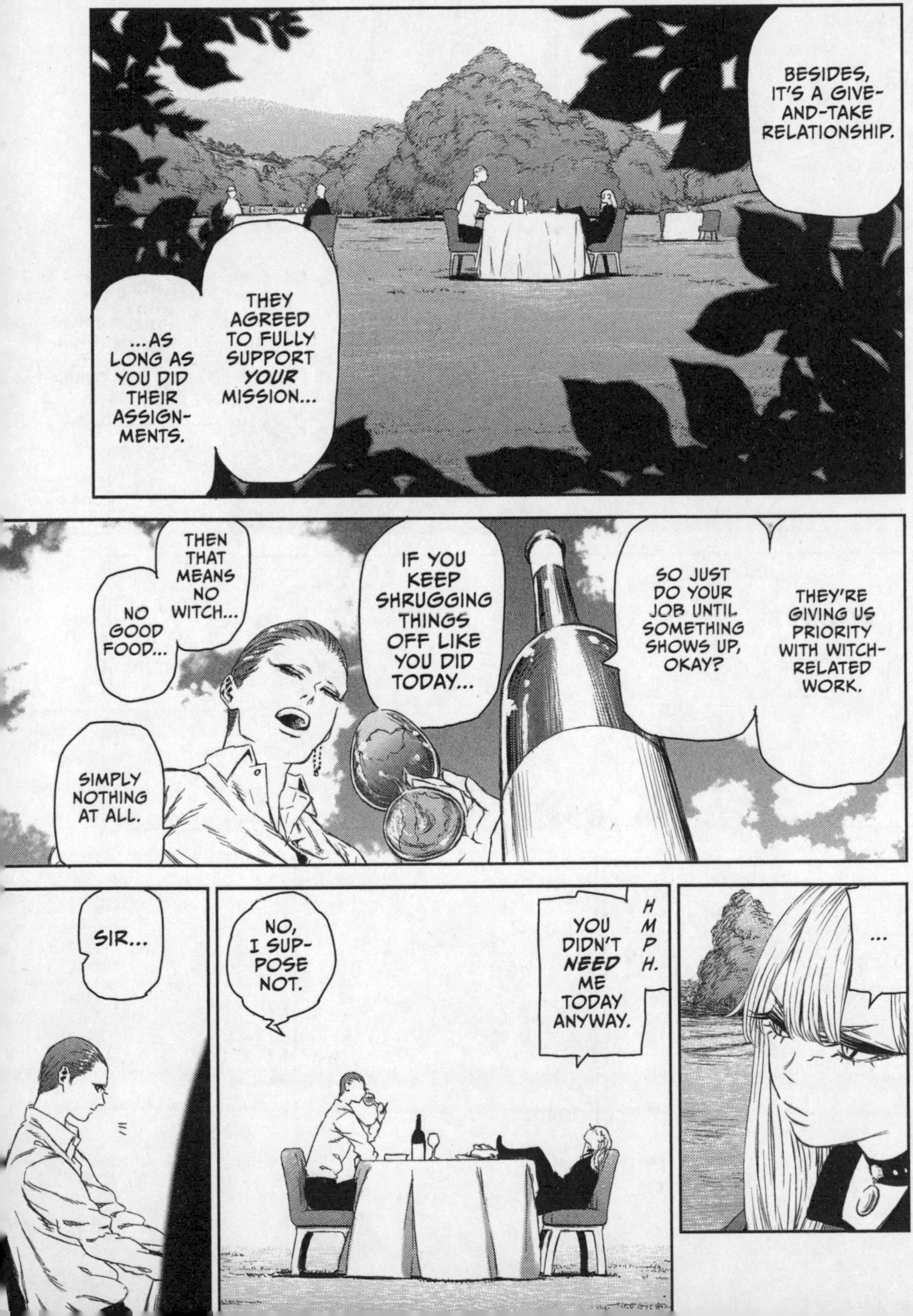
BESIDES, IT'S A GIVE-AND-TAKE RELATIONSHIP.
THEY AGREED TO FULLY SUPPORT *YOUR* MISSION...
...AS LONG AS YOU DID THEIR ASSIGNMENTS.
THEY'RE GIVING US PRIORITY WITH WITCH-RELATED WORK.
SO JUST DO YOUR JOB UNTIL SOMETHING SHOWS UP, OKAY?
IF YOU KEEP SHRUGGING THINGS OFF LIKE YOU DID TODAY...
THEN THAT MEANS NO WITCH...
NO GOOD FOOD...
SIMPLY NOTHING AT ALL.
...
HMPH.
YOU DIDN'T *NEED* ME TODAY ANYWAY.
NO, I SUPPOSE NOT.
SIR...

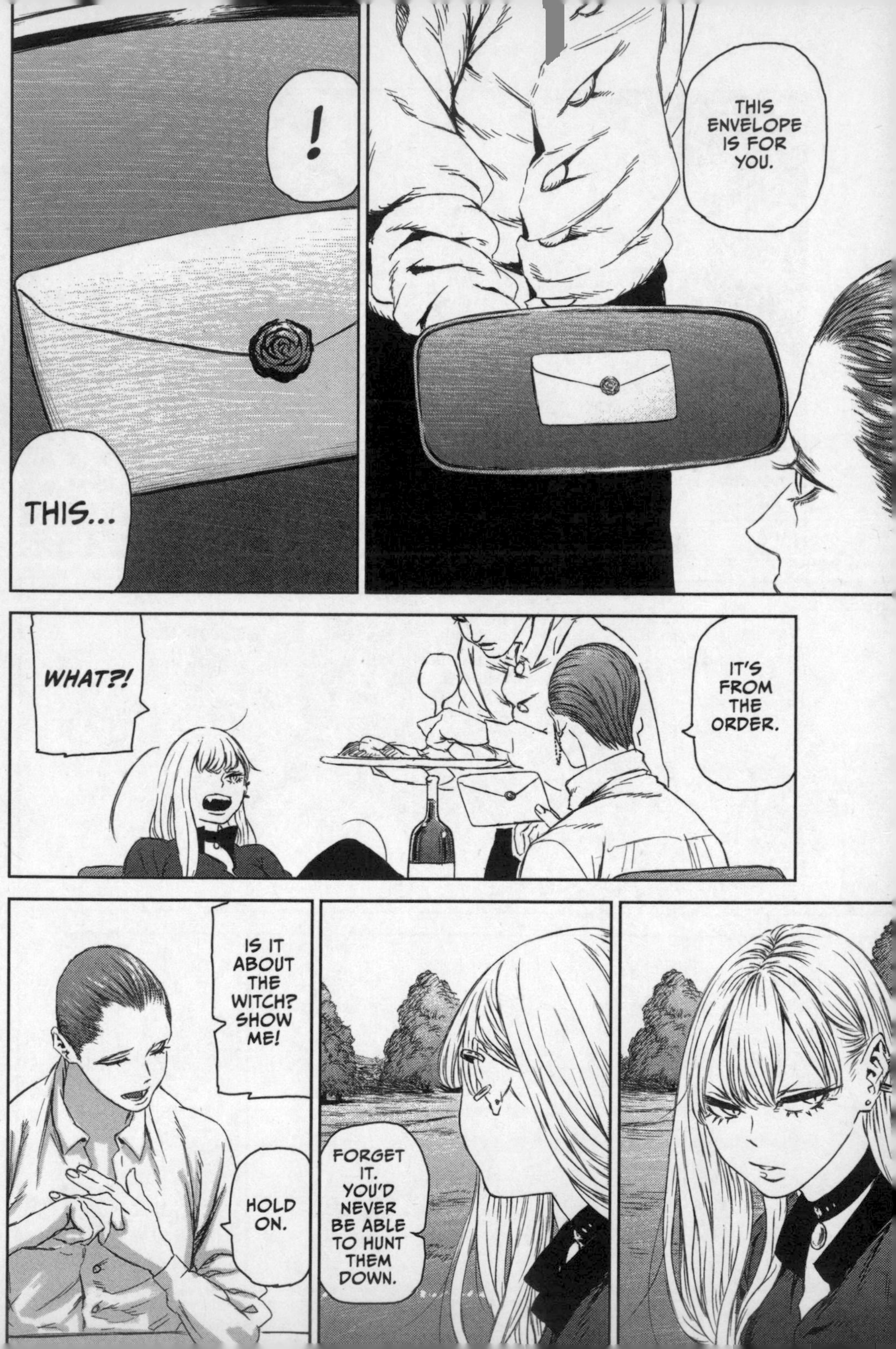
THIS ENVELOPE IS FOR YOU.
!
THIS...
IT'S FROM THE ORDER.
WHAT?!
FORGET IT. YOU'D NEVER BE ABLE TO HUNT THEM DOWN.
IS IT ABOUT THE WITCH? SHOW ME!
HOLD ON.

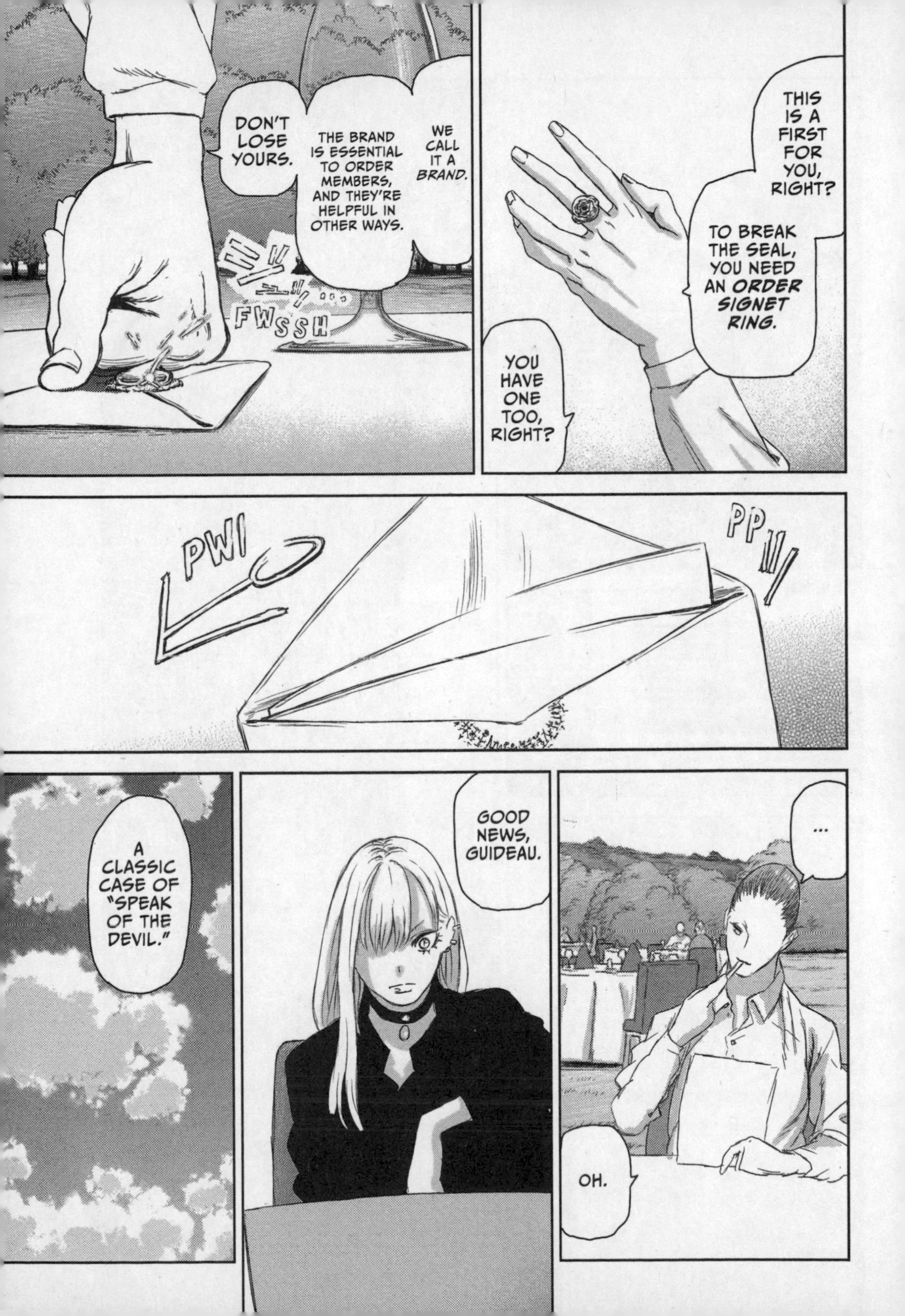
THIS IS A FIRST FOR YOU, RIGHT?
TO BREAK THE SEAL, YOU NEED AN *ORDER SIGNET RING.*
YOU HAVE ONE TOO, RIGHT?
WE CALL IT A *BRAND.*
THE BRAND IS ESSENTIAL TO ORDER MEMBERS, AND THEY'RE HELPFUL IN OTHER WAYS.
DON'T LOSE YOURS.
FWSSH
PP
PWI
...
OH.
GOOD NEWS, GUIDEAU.
A CLASSIC CASE OF "SPEAK OF THE DEVIL."

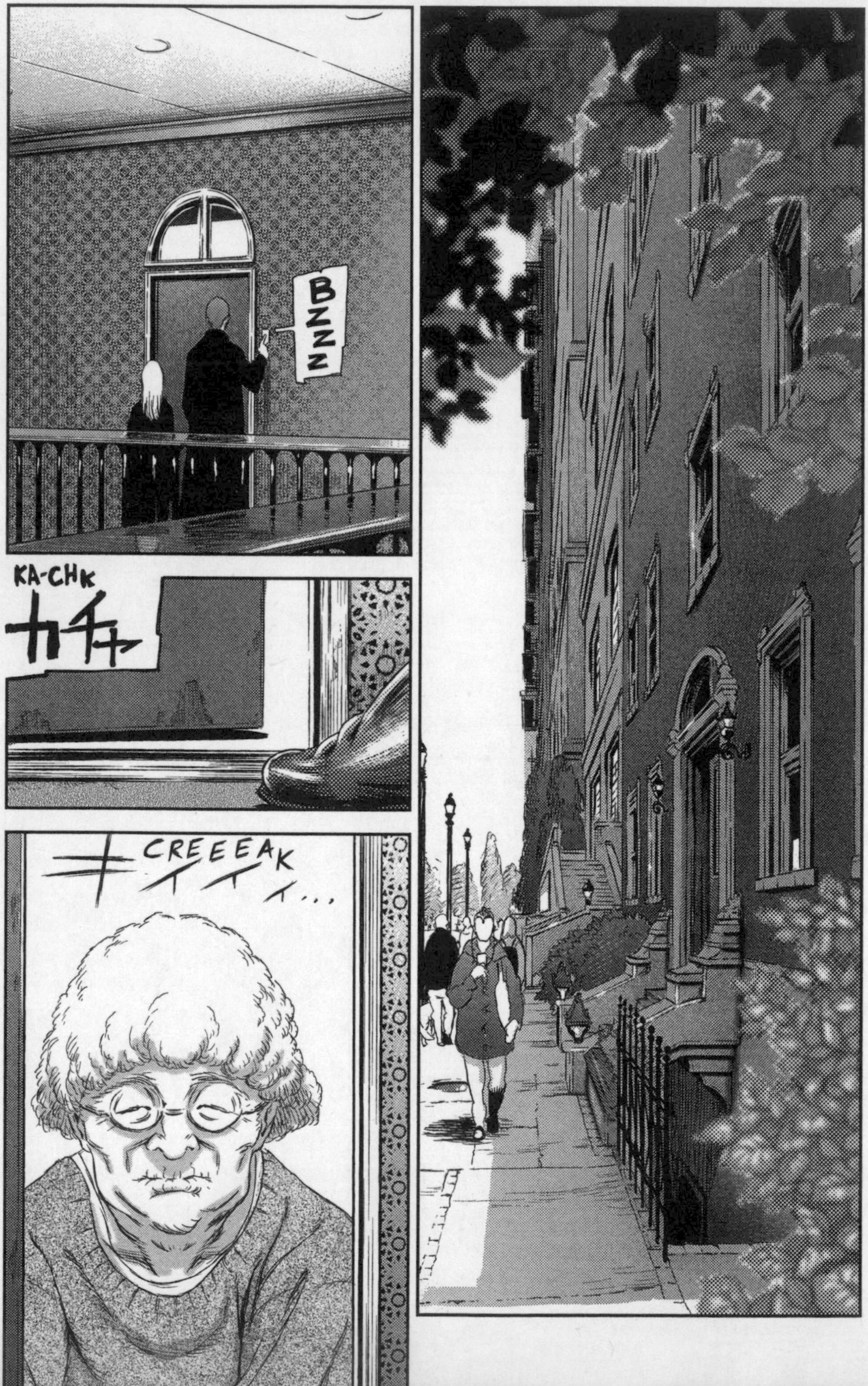
BZZZ
KA-CHK
カチャ
CREEEAK
キイイイ...

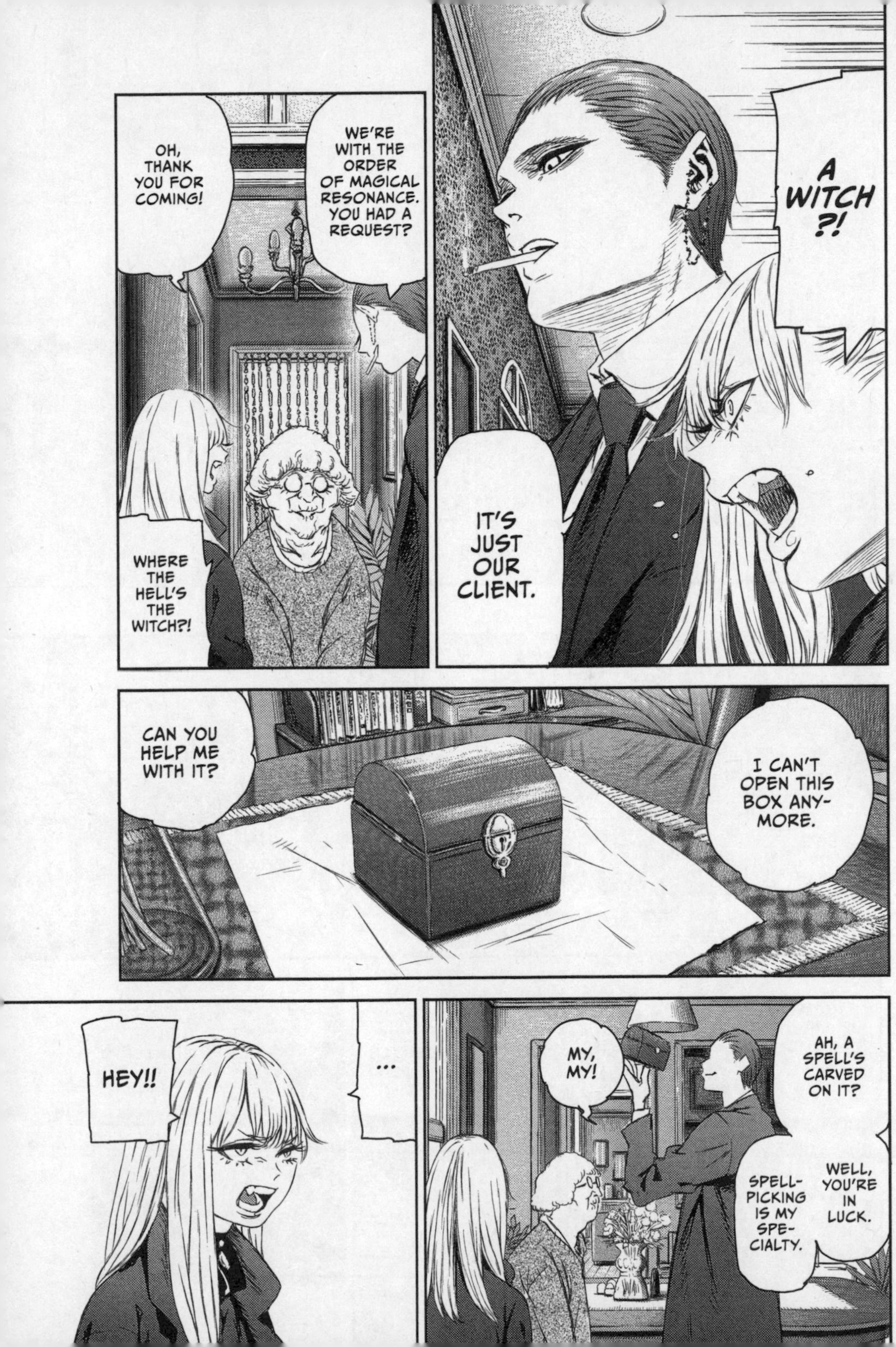
OH, THANK YOU FOR COMING!
WE'RE WITH THE ORDER OF MAGICAL RESONANCE. YOU HAD A REQUEST?
WHERE THE HELL'S THE WITCH?!
A WITCH ?!
IT'S JUST OUR CLIENT.
I CAN'T OPEN THIS BOX ANY-MORE.
CAN YOU HELP ME WITH IT?
HEY!!
...
MY, MY!
AH, A SPELL'S CARVED ON IT?
WELL, YOU'RE IN LUCK.
SPELL-PICKING IS MY SPE-CIALTY.

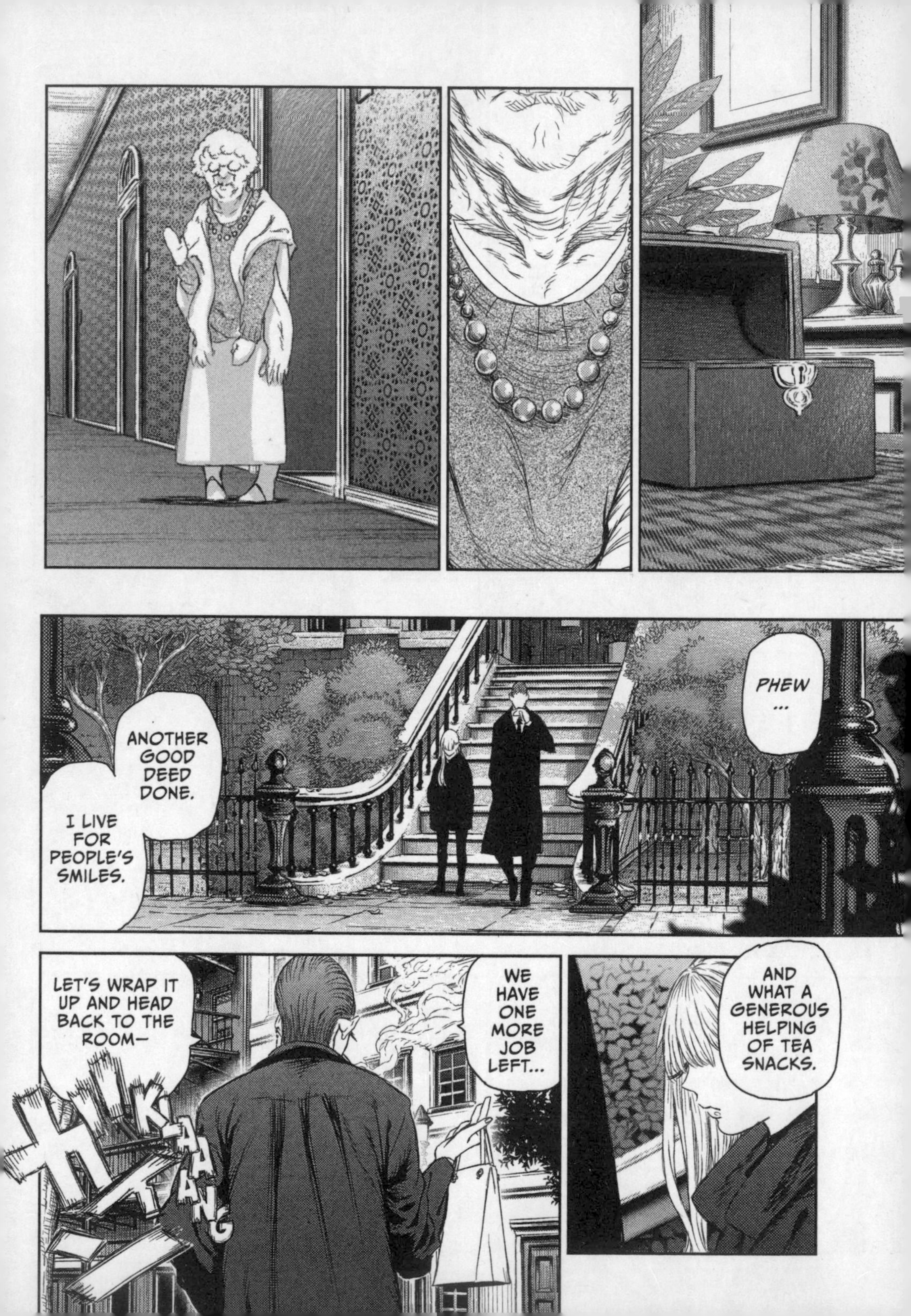
PHEW...
ANOTHER GOOD DEED DONE.
I LIVE FOR PEOPLE'S SMILES.
AND WHAT A GENEROUS HELPING OF TEA SNACKS.
WE HAVE ONE MORE JOB LEFT...
LET'S WRAP IT UP AND HEAD BACK TO THE ROOM—

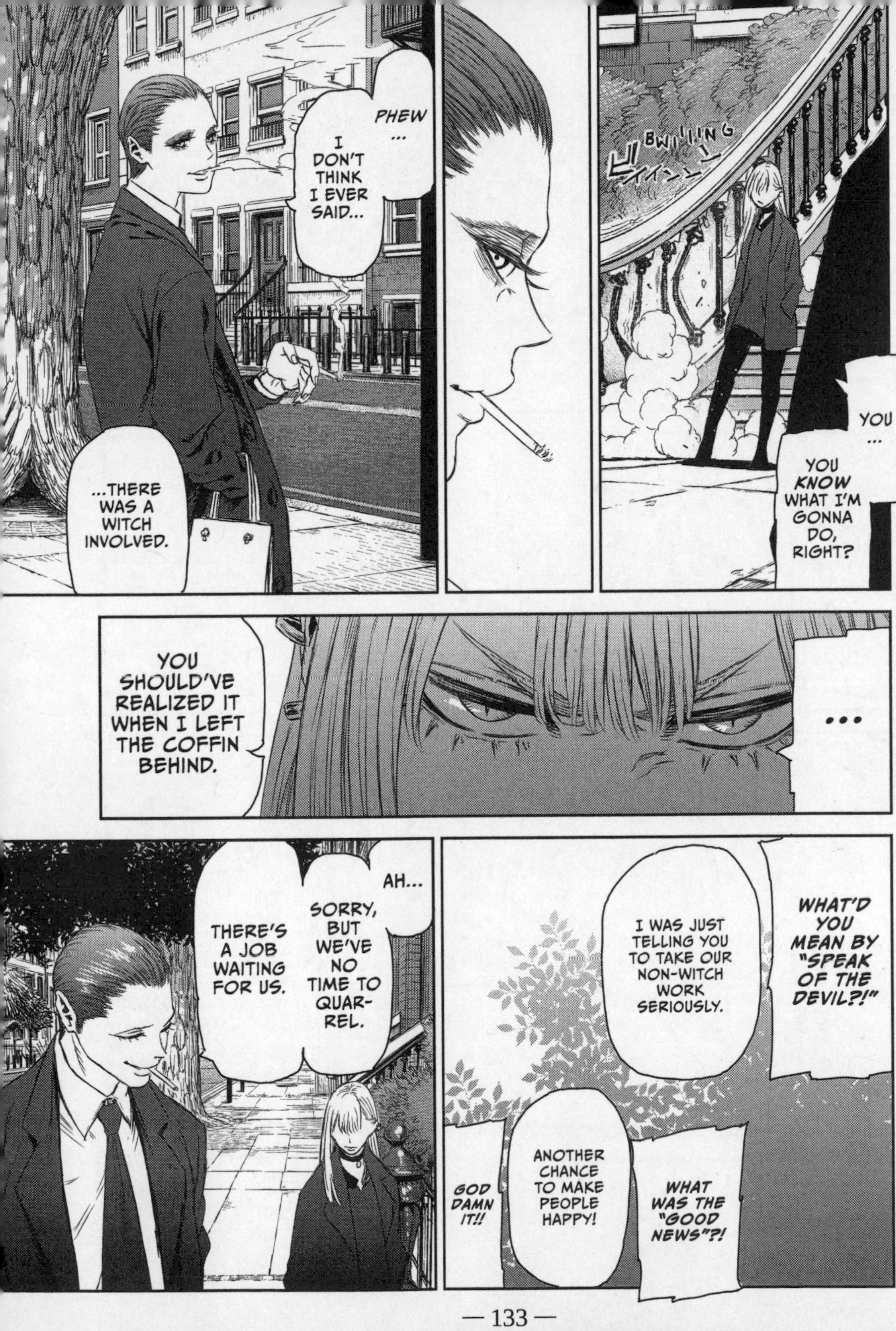
BWIIING
ビイイーン
YOU ...
YOU KNOW WHAT I'M GONNA DO, RIGHT?
PHEW ...
I DON'T THINK I EVER SAID...
...THERE WAS A WITCH INVOLVED.
...
YOU SHOULD'VE REALIZED IT WHEN I LEFT THE COFFIN BEHIND.
WHAT'D YOU MEAN BY "SPEAK OF THE DEVIL?!"
I WAS JUST TELLING YOU TO TAKE OUR NON-WITCH WORK SERIOUSLY.
WHAT WAS THE "GOOD NEWS"?!
ANOTHER CHANCE TO MAKE PEOPLE HAPPY!
GOD DAMN IT!!
AH...
SORRY, BUT WE'VE NO TIME TO QUAR-REL.
THERE'S A JOB WAITING FOR US.

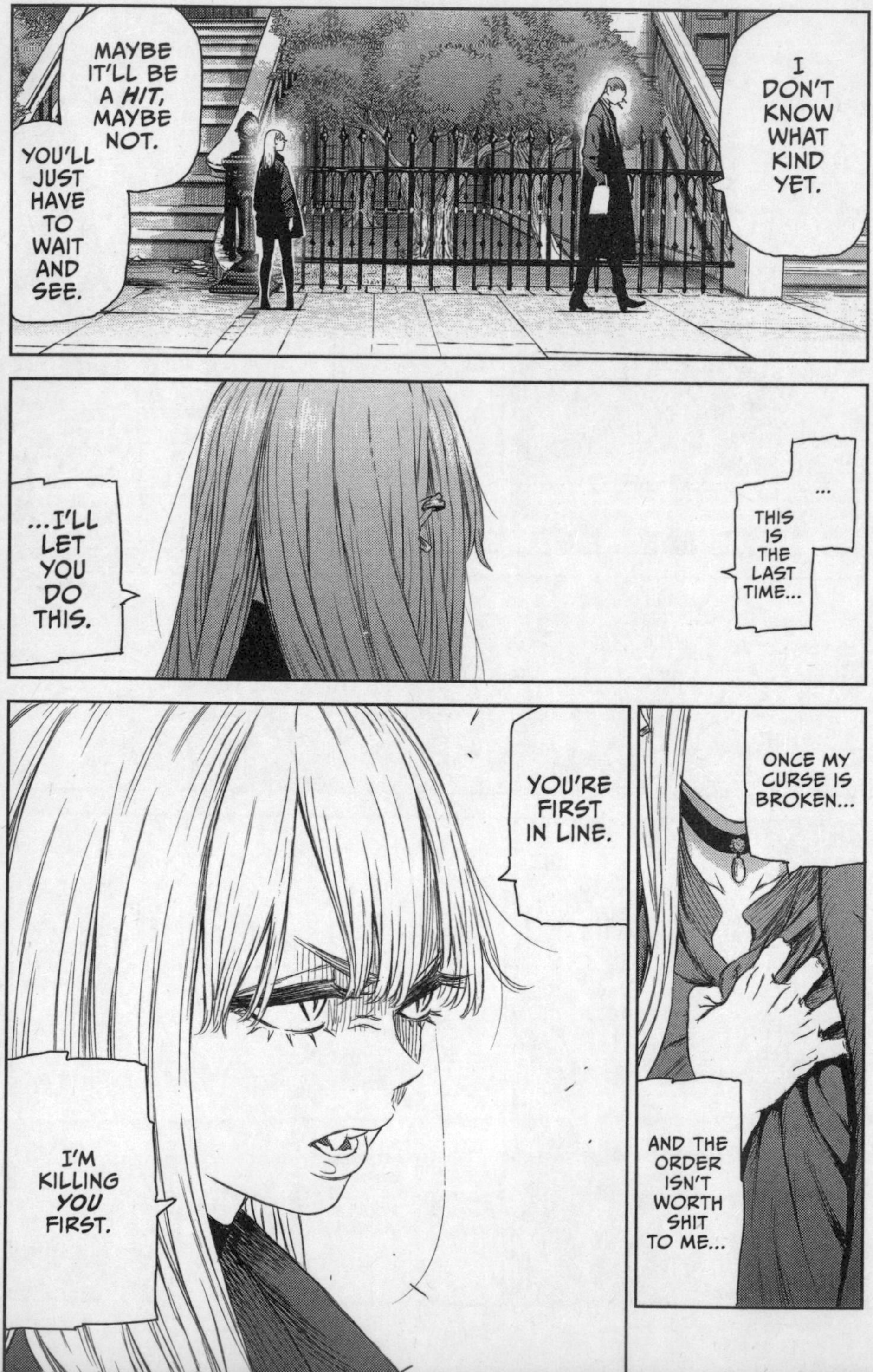
I DON'T KNOW WHAT KIND YET.
MAYBE IT'LL BE A *HIT*, MAYBE NOT.
YOU'LL JUST HAVE TO WAIT AND SEE.
... THIS IS THE LAST TIME...
...I'LL LET YOU DO THIS.
ONCE MY CURSE IS BROKEN...
AND THE ORDER ISN'T WORTH SHIT TO ME...
YOU'RE FIRST IN LINE.
I'M KILLING *YOU* FIRST.

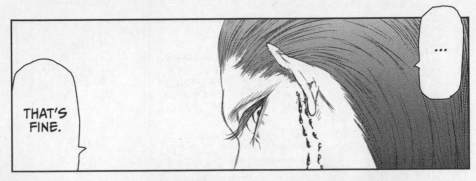

...
THAT'S FINE.
I'M LOOKING FOR-WARD...
...TO SEEING THAT DAY, TOO.

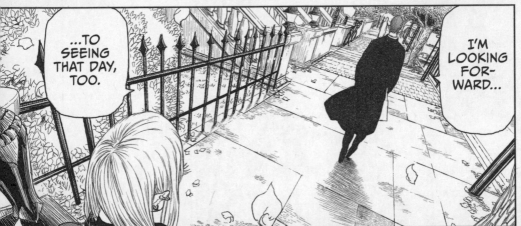

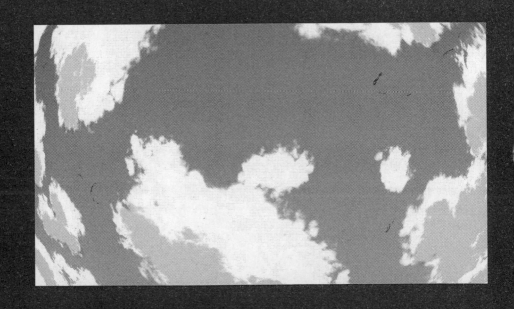

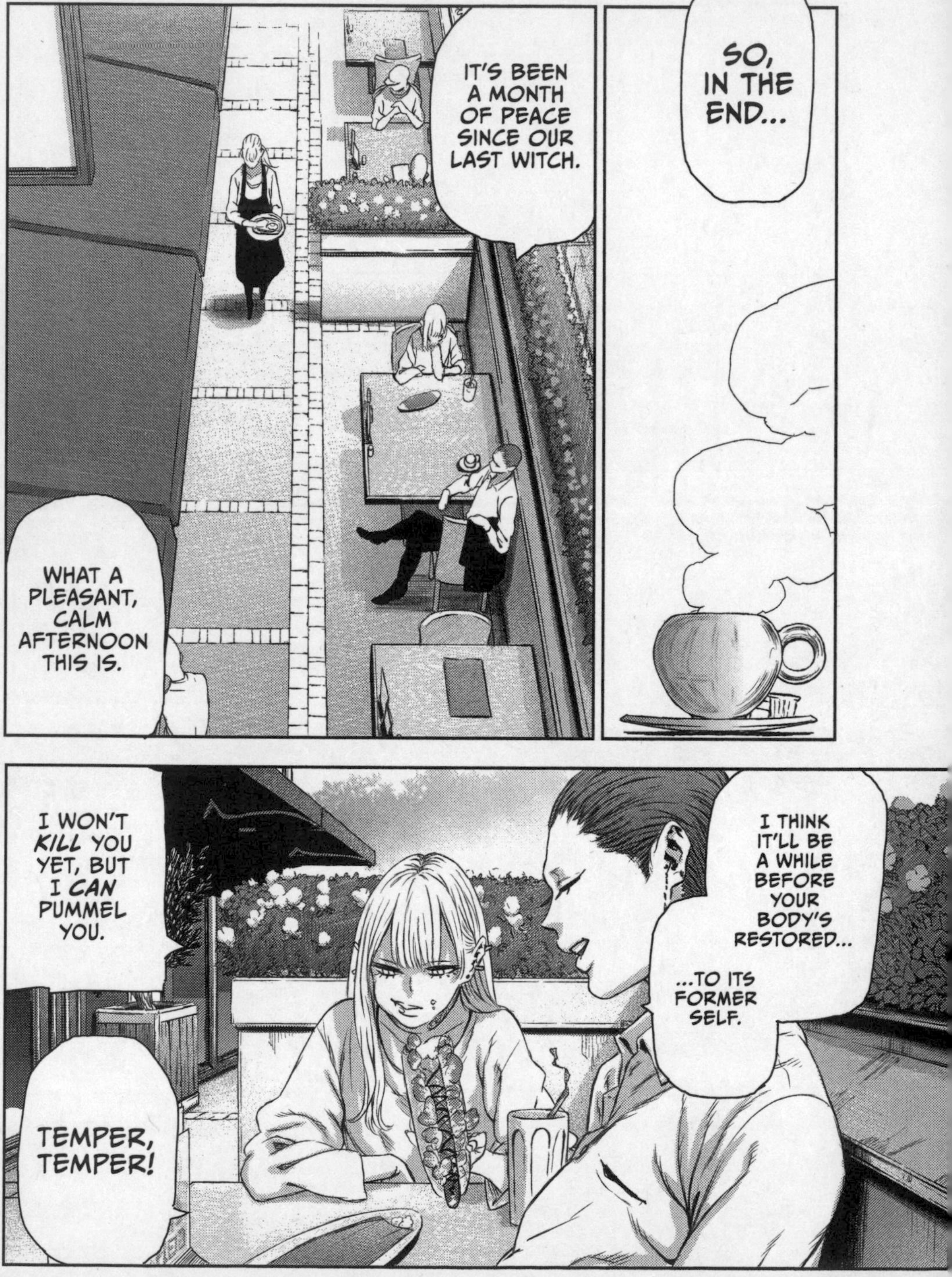
SO, IN THE END...
IT'S BEEN A MONTH OF PEACE SINCE OUR LAST WITCH.
WHAT A PLEASANT, CALM AFTERNOON THIS IS.
I THINK IT'LL BE A WHILE BEFORE YOUR BODY'S RESTORED...
...TO ITS FORMER SELF.
I WON'T *KILL* YOU YET, BUT I *CAN* PUMMEL YOU.
TEMPER, TEMPER!

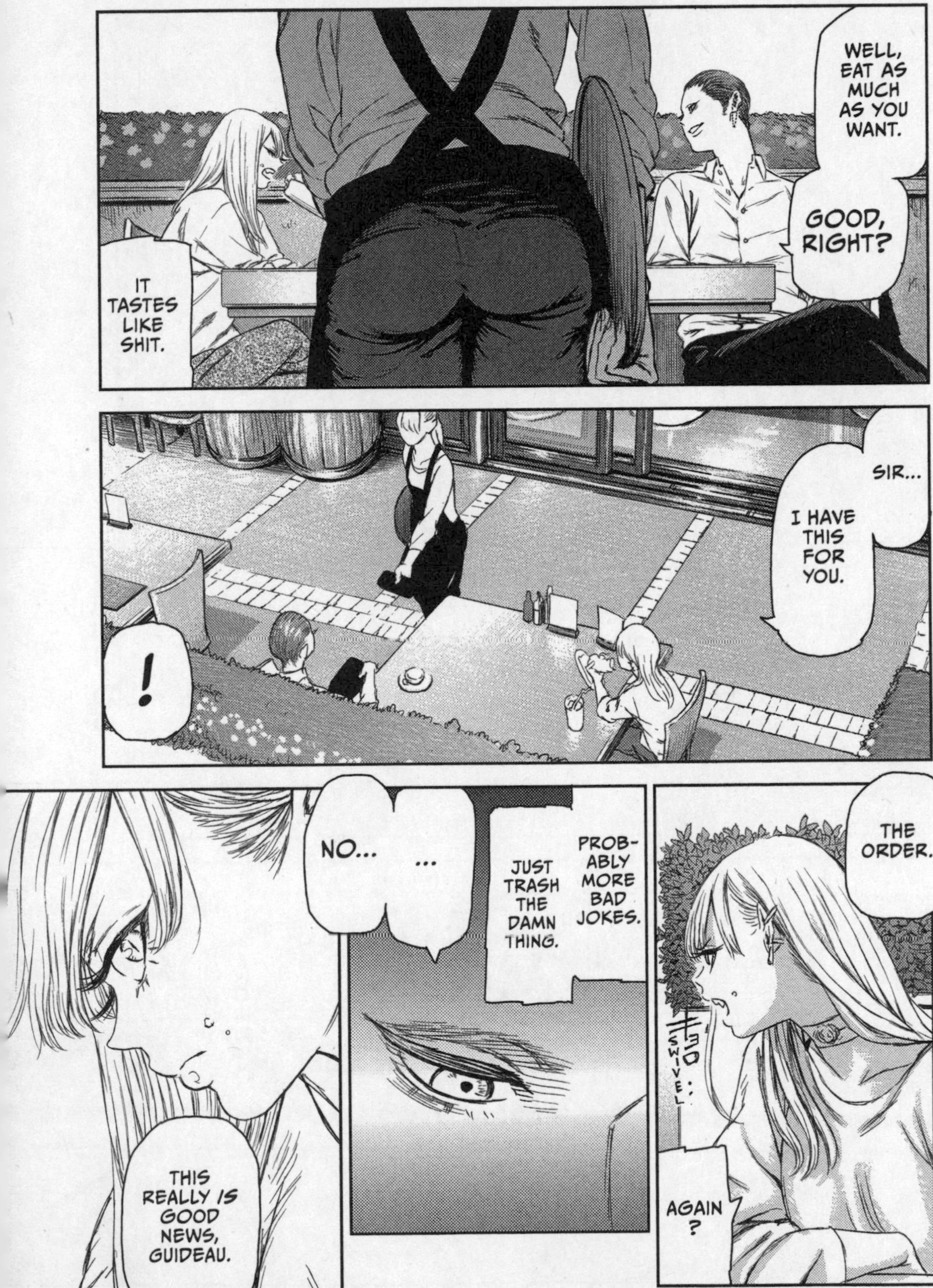
WELL, EAT AS MUCH AS YOU WANT.
GOOD, RIGHT?
IT TASTES LIKE SHIT.
SIR...
I HAVE THIS FOR YOU.
!
THE ORDER.
SWIVEL
AGAIN?
PROBABLY MORE BAD JOKES.
JUST TRASH THE DAMN THING.
NO... ...
THIS REALLY IS GOOD NEWS, GUIDEAU.

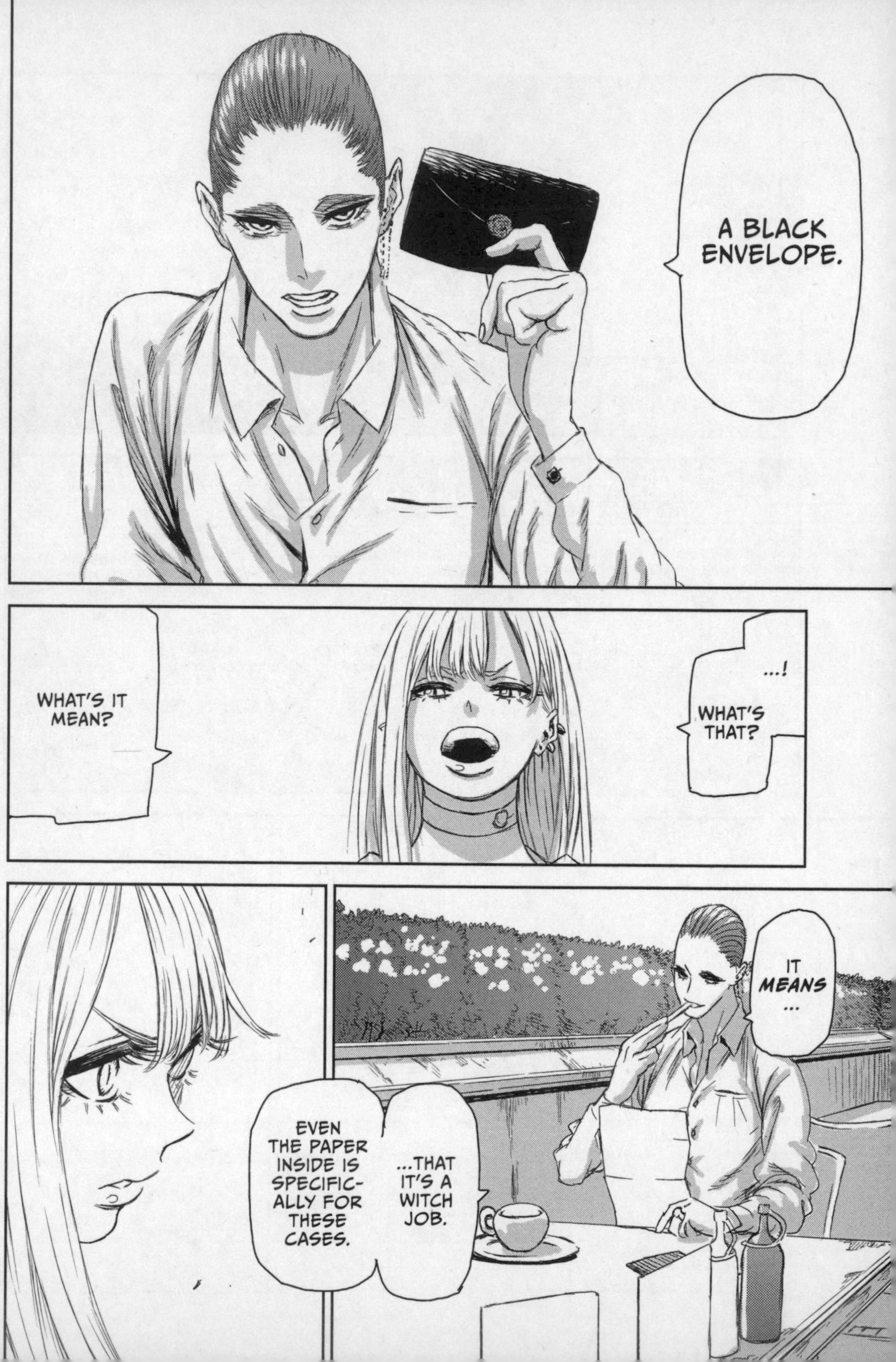
A BLACK ENVELOPE.
...! WHAT'S THAT?
WHAT'S IT MEAN?
IT MEANS ...
...THAT IT'S A WITCH JOB.
EVEN THE PAPER INSIDE IS SPECIFIC-ALLY FOR THESE CASES.

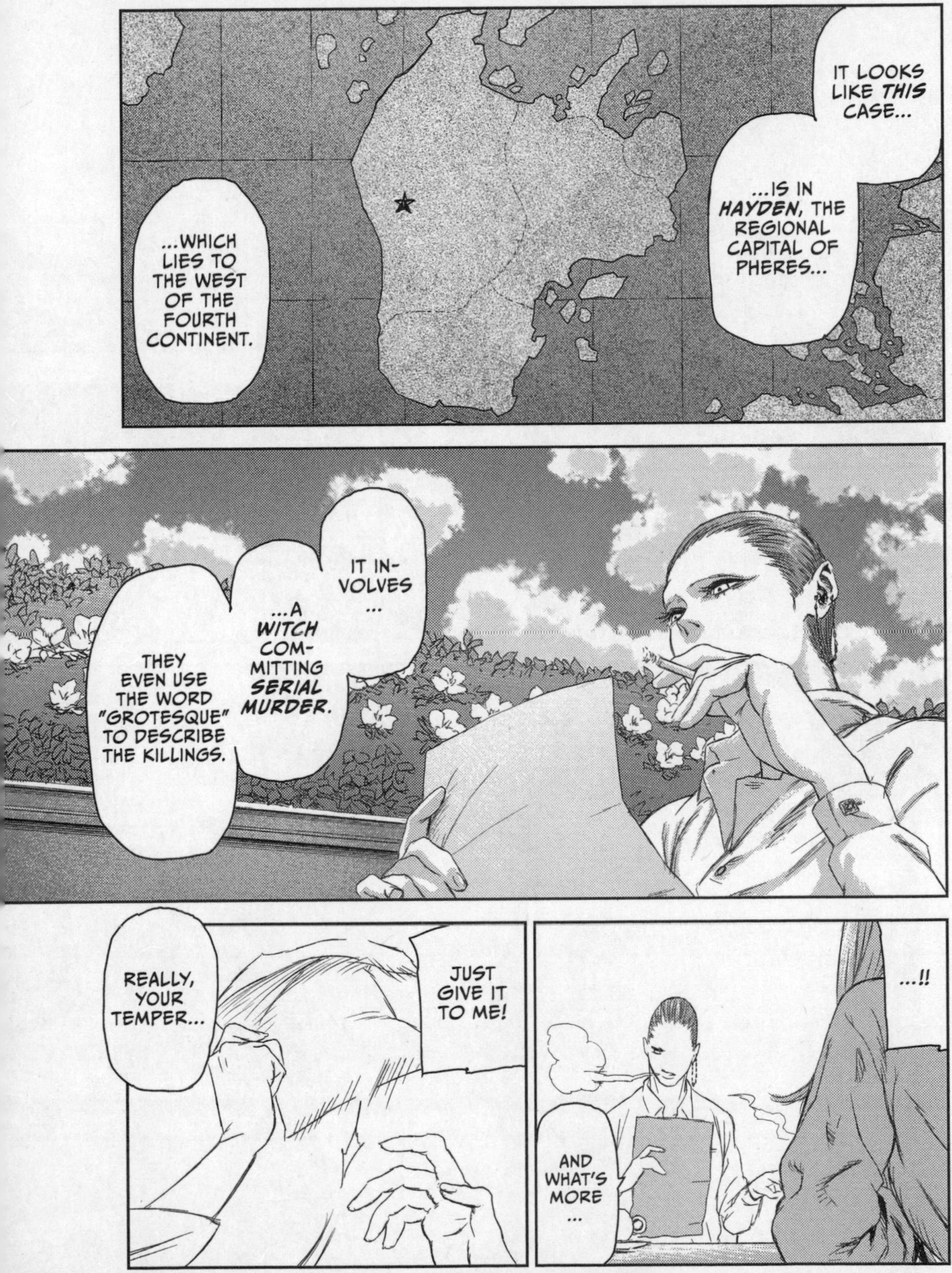
IT LOOKS LIKE *THIS* CASE...
...IS IN *HAYDEN*, THE REGIONAL CAPITAL OF PHERES...
...WHICH LIES TO THE WEST OF THE FOURTH CONTINENT.
IT IN-VOLVES ...
...A *WITCH* COM-MITTING *SERIAL MURDER*.
THEY EVEN USE THE WORD "GROTESQUE" TO DESCRIBE THE KILLINGS.
...!!
AND WHAT'S MORE ...
JUST GIVE IT TO ME!
REALLY, YOUR TEMPER...

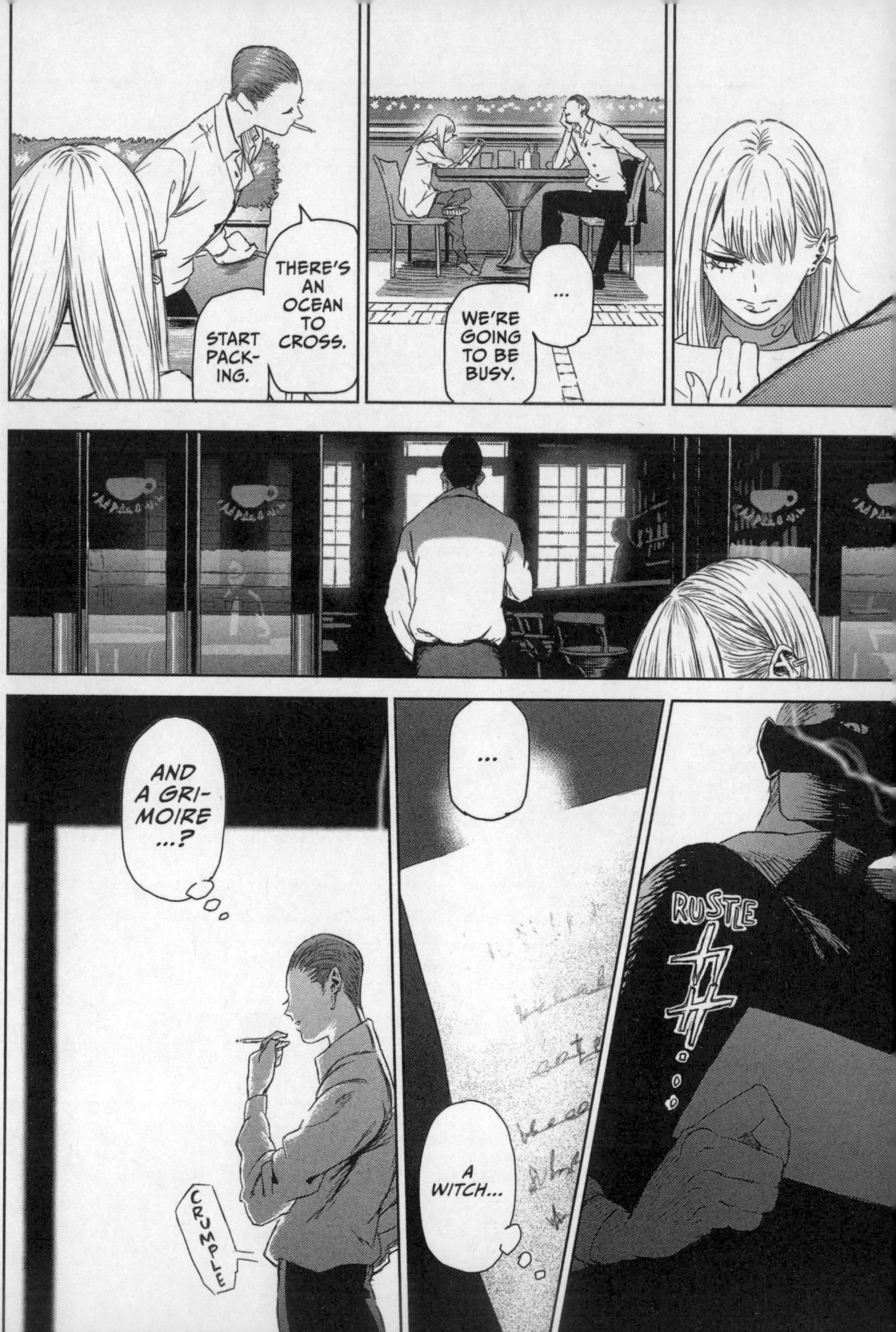
...
WE'RE GOING TO BE BUSY.
THERE'S AN OCEAN TO CROSS.
START PACK-ING.
RUSTLE
...
A WITCH...
AND A GRI-MOIRE ...?
CRUMPLE

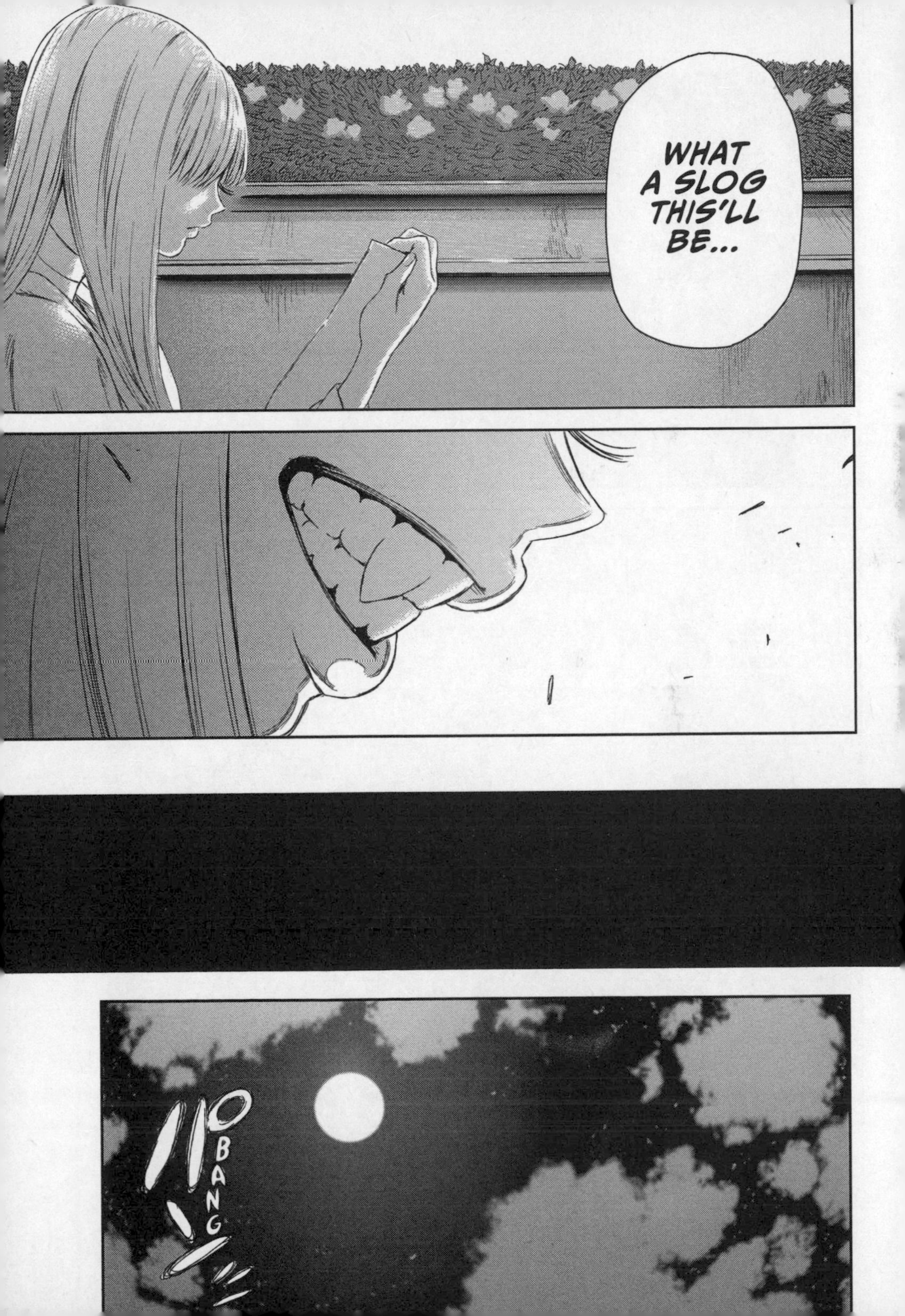
WHAT A SLOG THIS'LL BE...
BANG

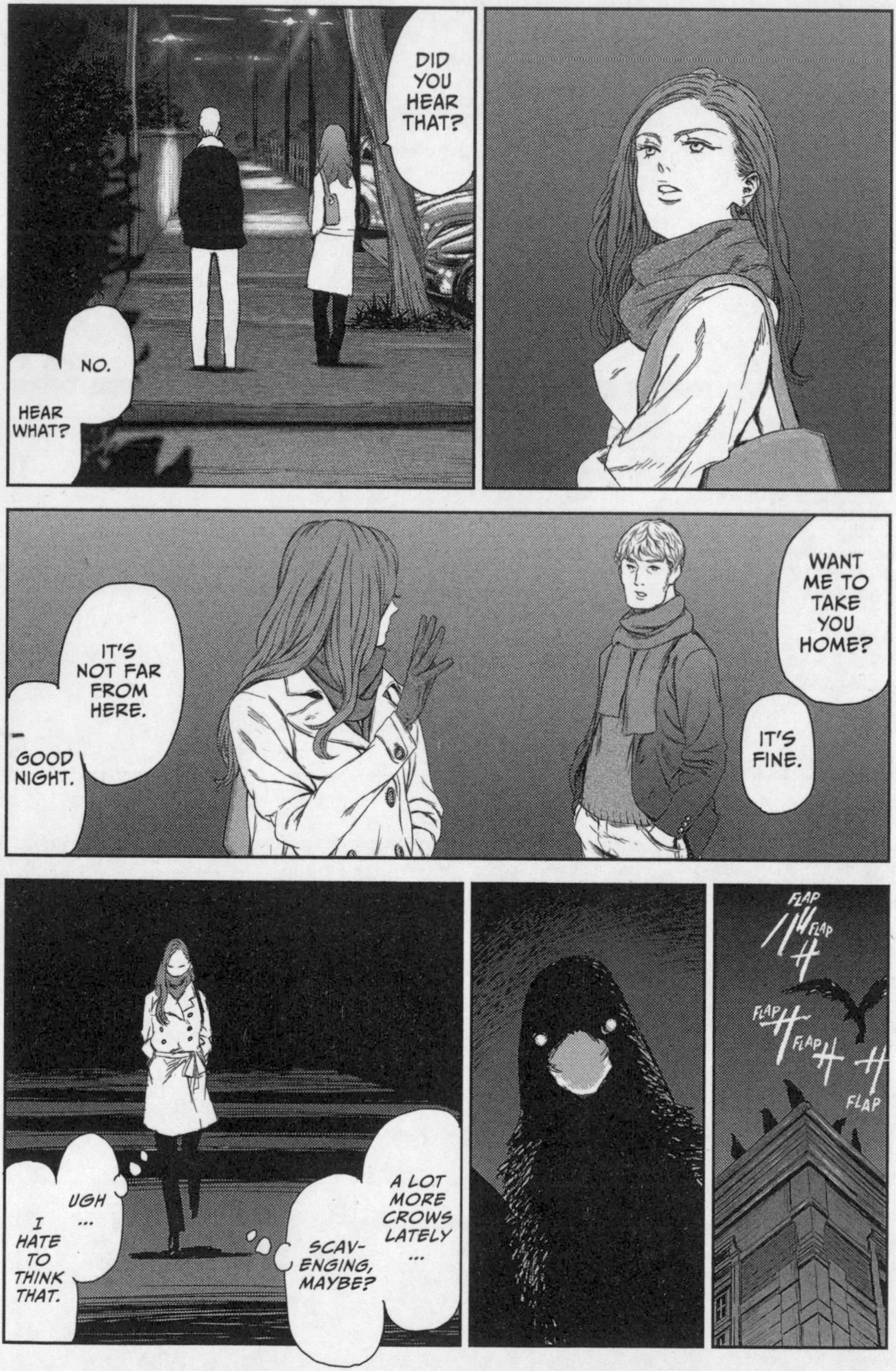
DID YOU HEAR THAT?
NO.
HEAR WHAT?
WANT ME TO TAKE YOU HOME?
IT'S FINE.
IT'S NOT FAR FROM HERE.
— GOOD NIGHT.
FLAP FLAP FLAP FLAP FLAP
A LOT MORE CROWS LATELY...
SCAV-ENGING, MAYBE?
UGH...
I HATE TO THINK THAT.

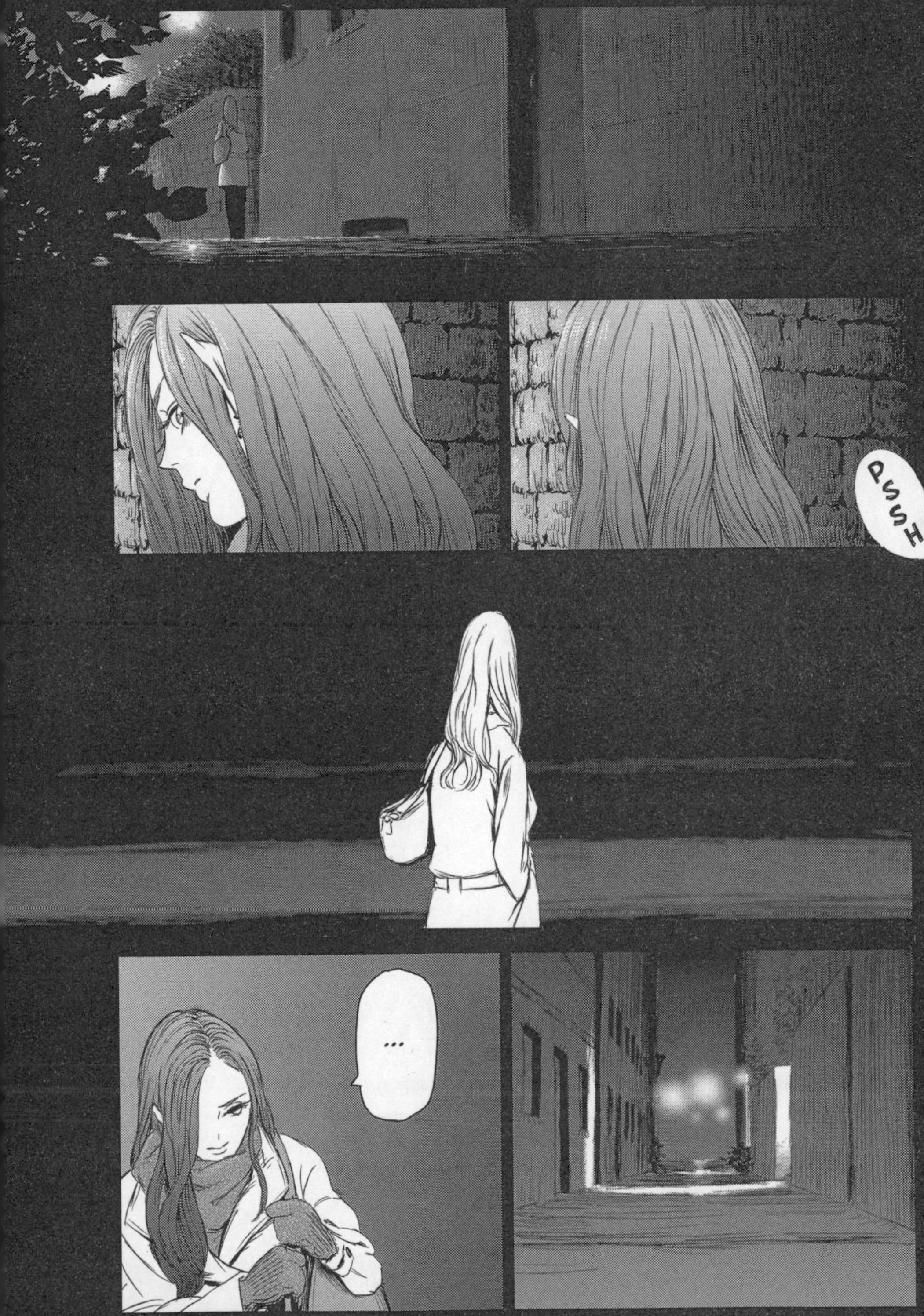
PSSH
...

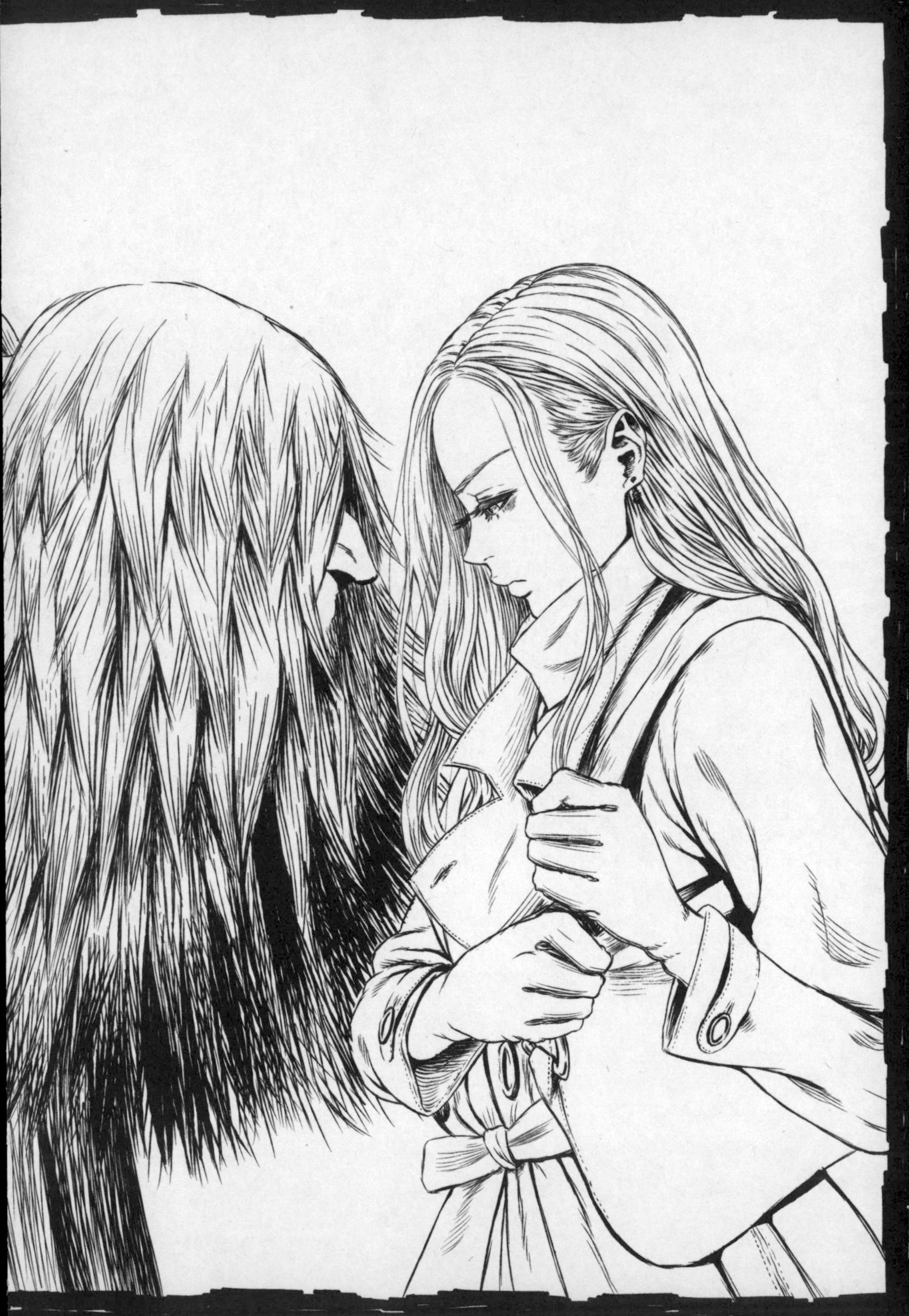

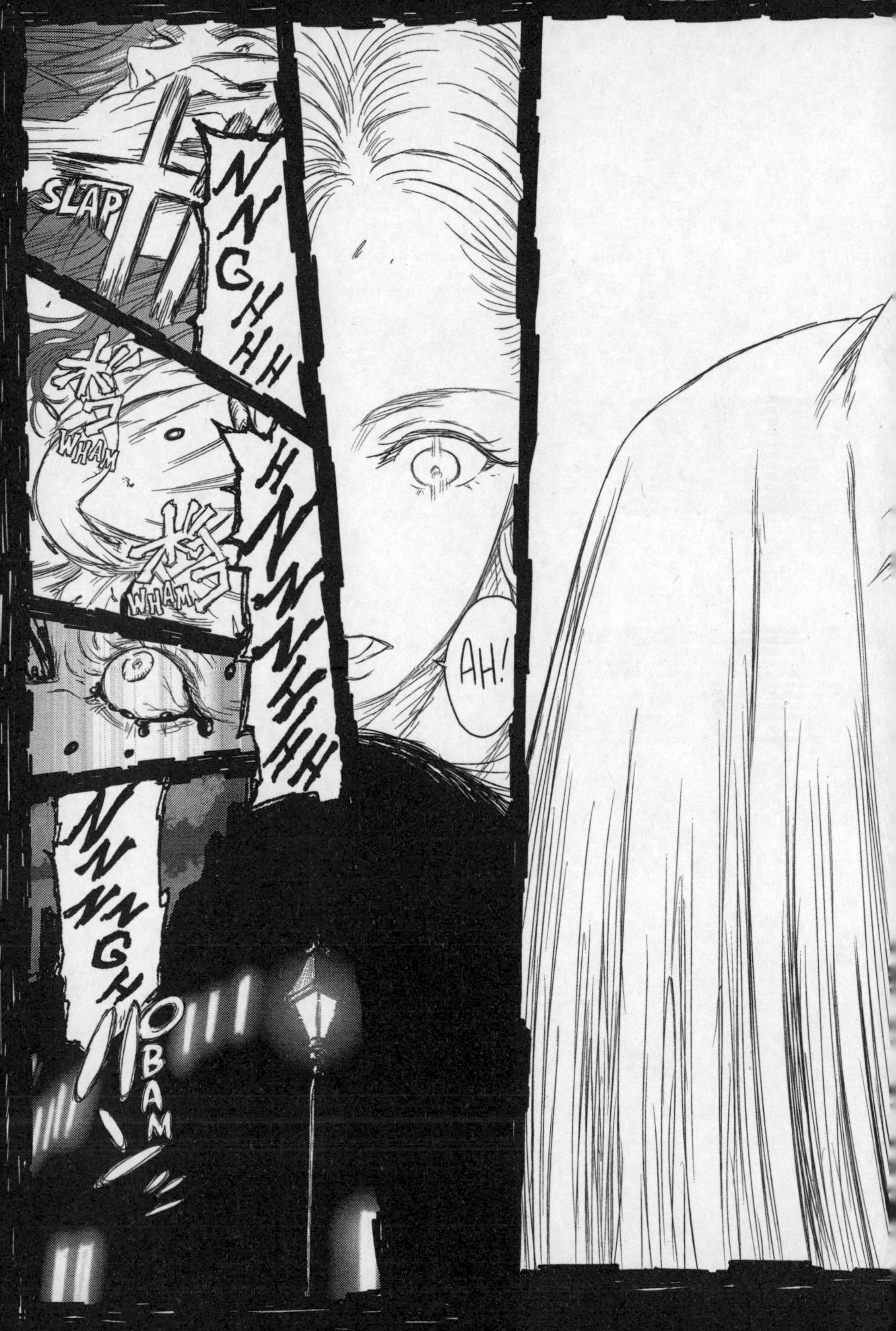
AH!
NNGHHH
HNNNNNHHHH
SLAP
WHAM
WHAM
NNNNGH
BAM

THE WITCH AND THE BEAST

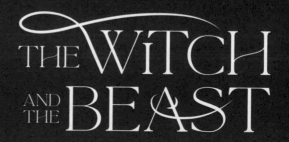

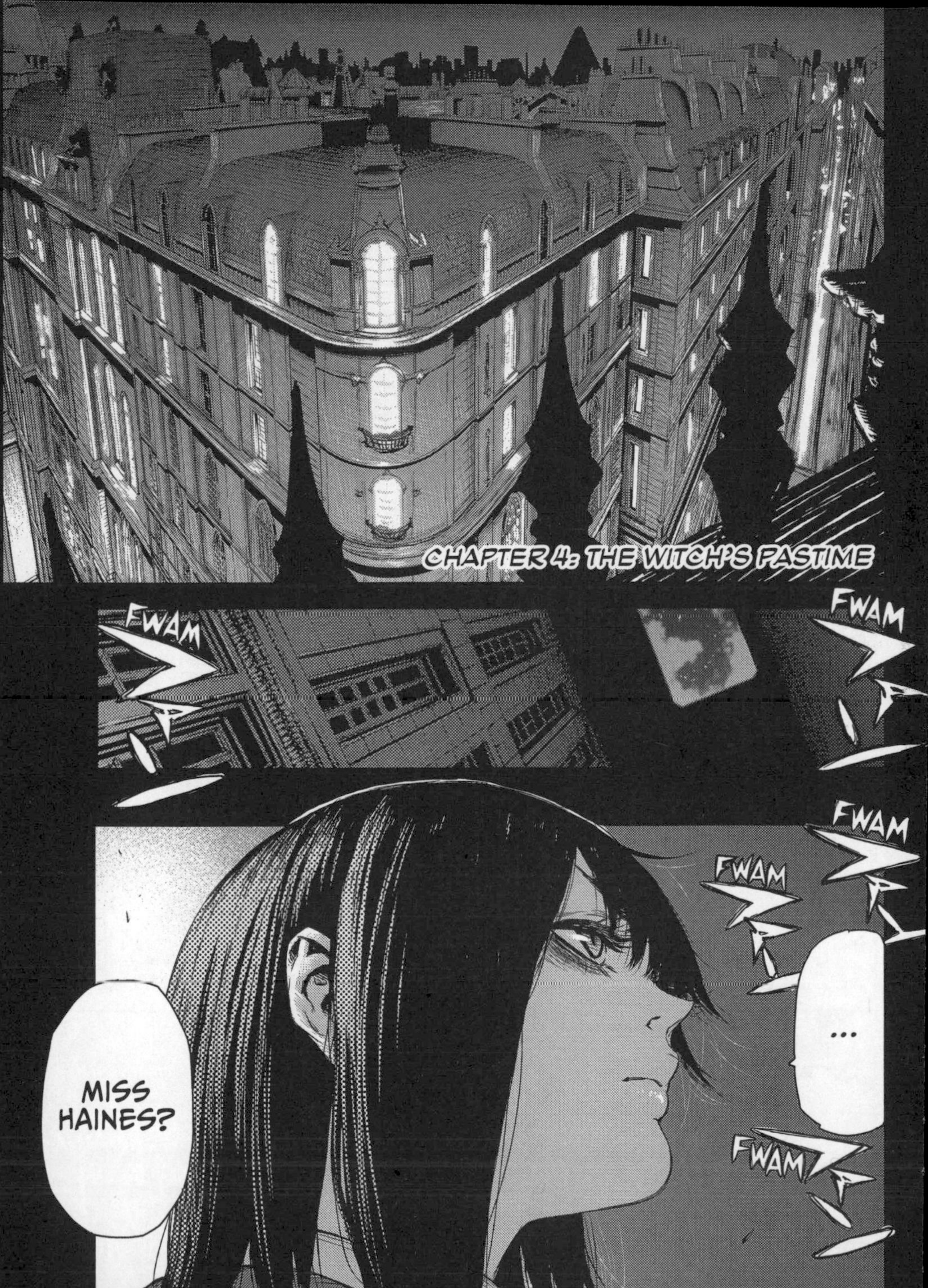
CHAPTER 4: THE WITCH'S PASTIME
FWAM
FWAM
FWAM
FWAM
...
FWAM
MISS HAINES?

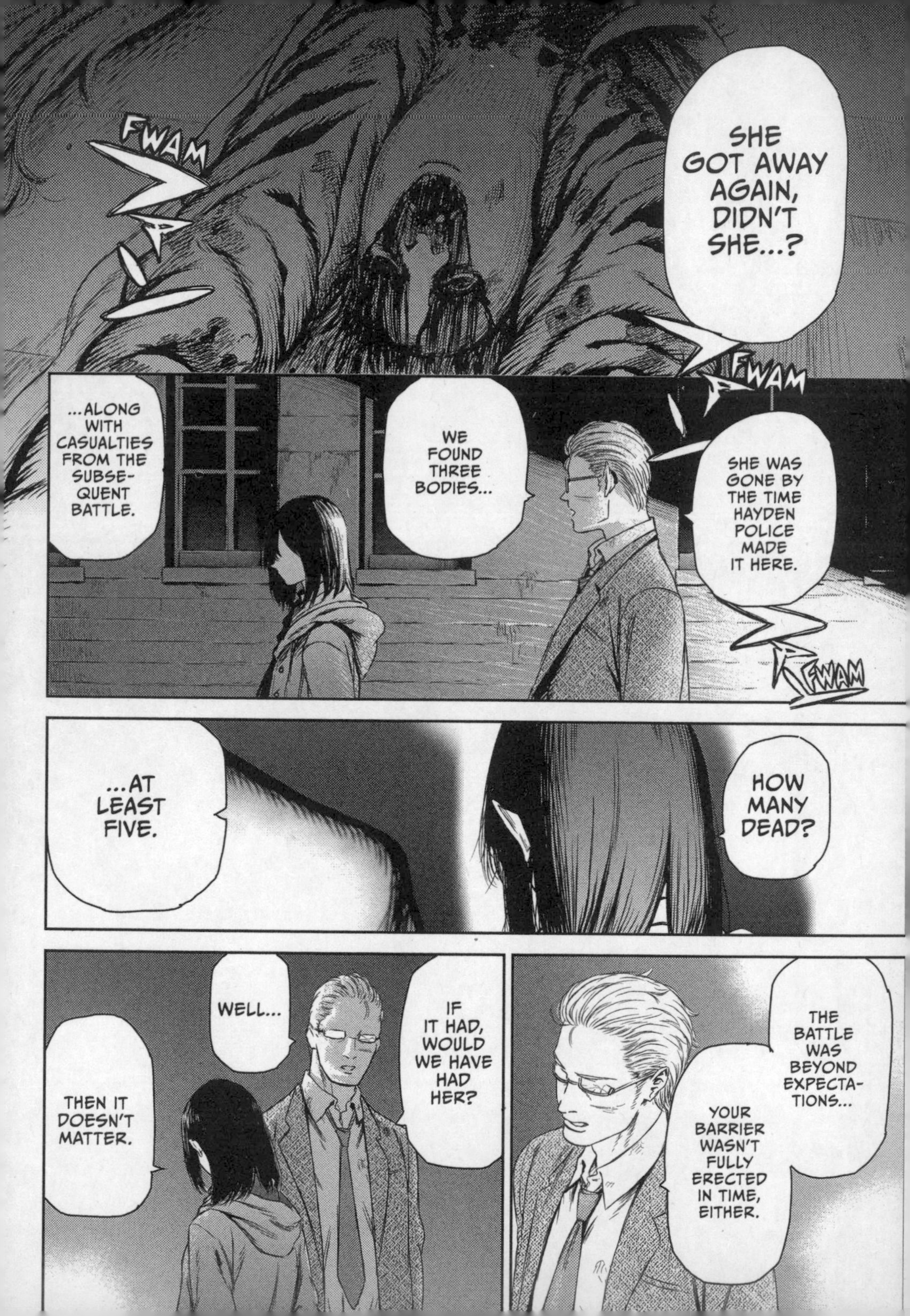
SHE GOT AWAY AGAIN, DIDN'T SHE...?
FWAM
FWAM
FWAM
SHE WAS GONE BY THE TIME HAYDEN POLICE MADE IT HERE.
WE FOUND THREE BODIES...
...ALONG WITH CASUALTIES FROM THE SUBSEQUENT BATTLE.
HOW MANY DEAD?
...AT LEAST FIVE.
THE BATTLE WAS BEYOND EXPECTATIONS...
YOUR BARRIER WASN'T FULLY ERECTED IN TIME, EITHER.
IF IT HAD, WOULD WE HAVE HAD HER?
WELL...
THEN IT DOESN'T MATTER.

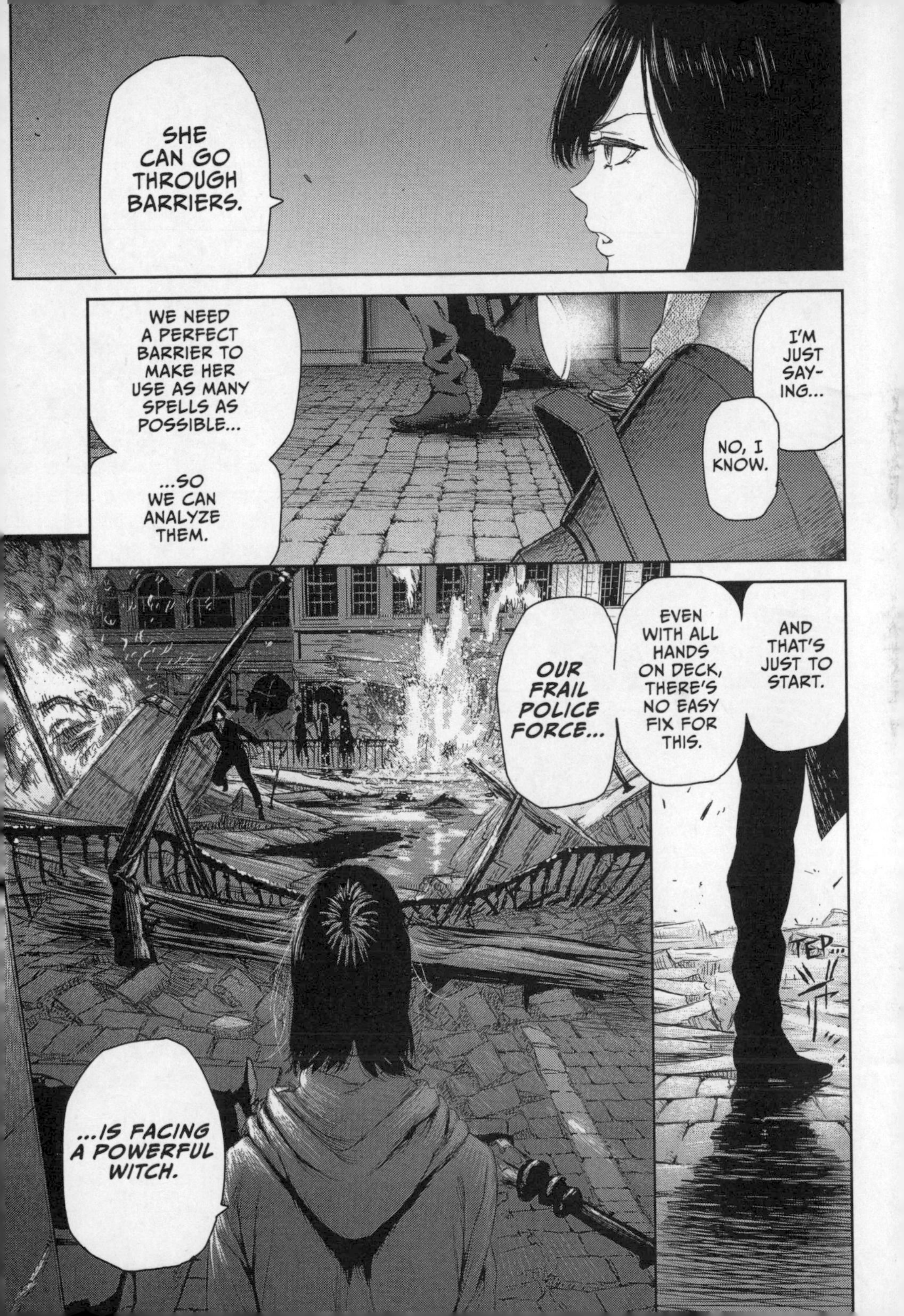
SHE CAN GO THROUGH BARRIERS.
I'M JUST SAYING...
NO, I KNOW.
WE NEED A PERFECT BARRIER TO MAKE HER USE AS MANY SPELLS AS POSSIBLE...
...SO WE CAN ANALYZE THEM.
AND THAT'S JUST TO START.
EVEN WITH ALL HANDS ON DECK, THERE'S NO EASY FIX FOR THIS.
OUR FRAIL POLICE FORCE...
TEP...
...IS FACING A POWERFUL WITCH.

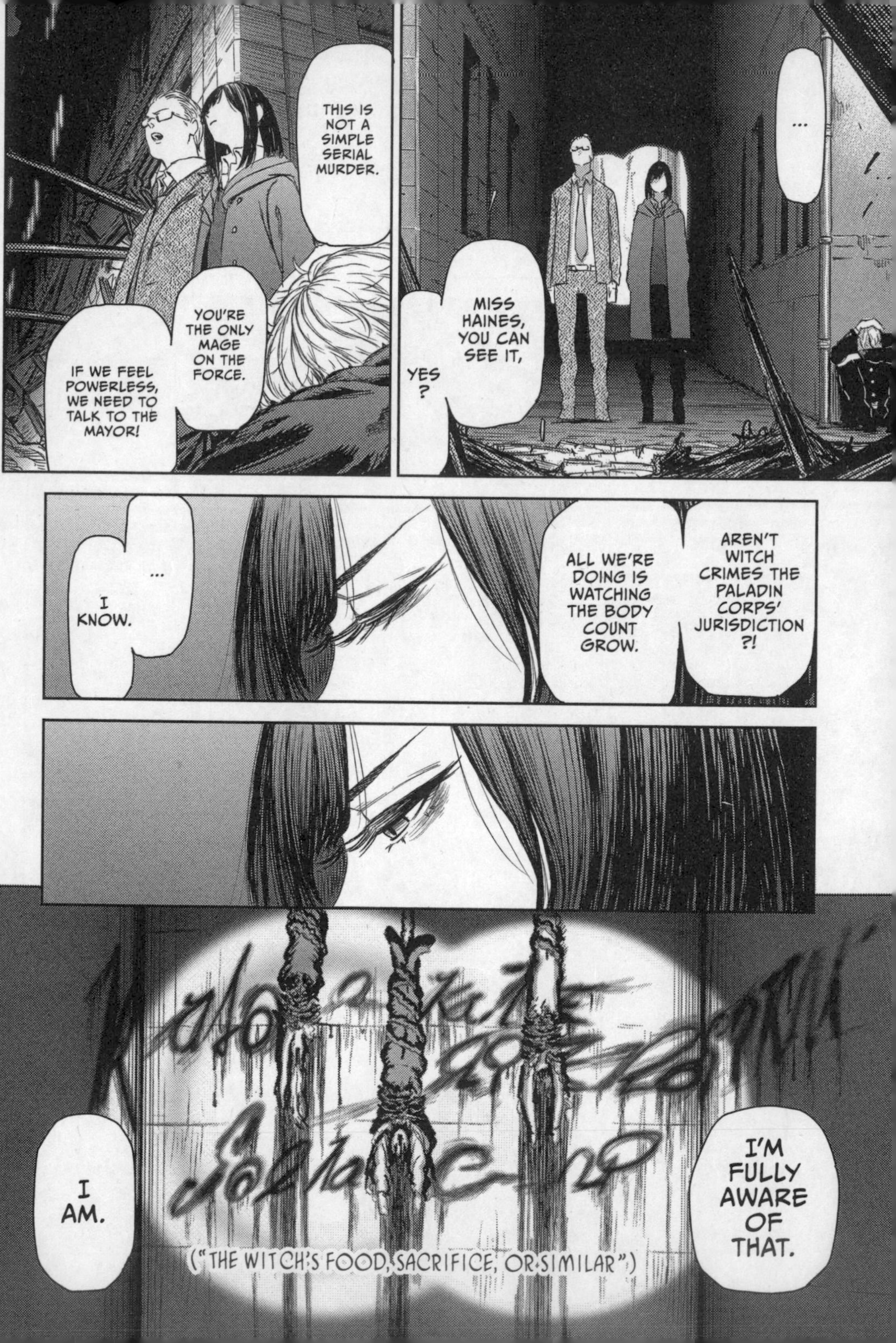
...
MISS HAINES, YOU CAN SEE IT,
YES?
THIS IS NOT A SIMPLE SERIAL MURDER.
YOU'RE THE ONLY MAGE ON THE FORCE.
IF WE FEEL POWERLESS, WE NEED TO TALK TO THE MAYOR!
AREN'T WITCH CRIMES THE PALADIN CORPS' JURISDICTION ?!
ALL WE'RE DOING IS WATCHING THE BODY COUNT GROW.
... I KNOW.
I'M FULLY AWARE OF THAT.
("THE WITCH'S FOOD, SACRIFICE, OR SIMILAR")
I AM.

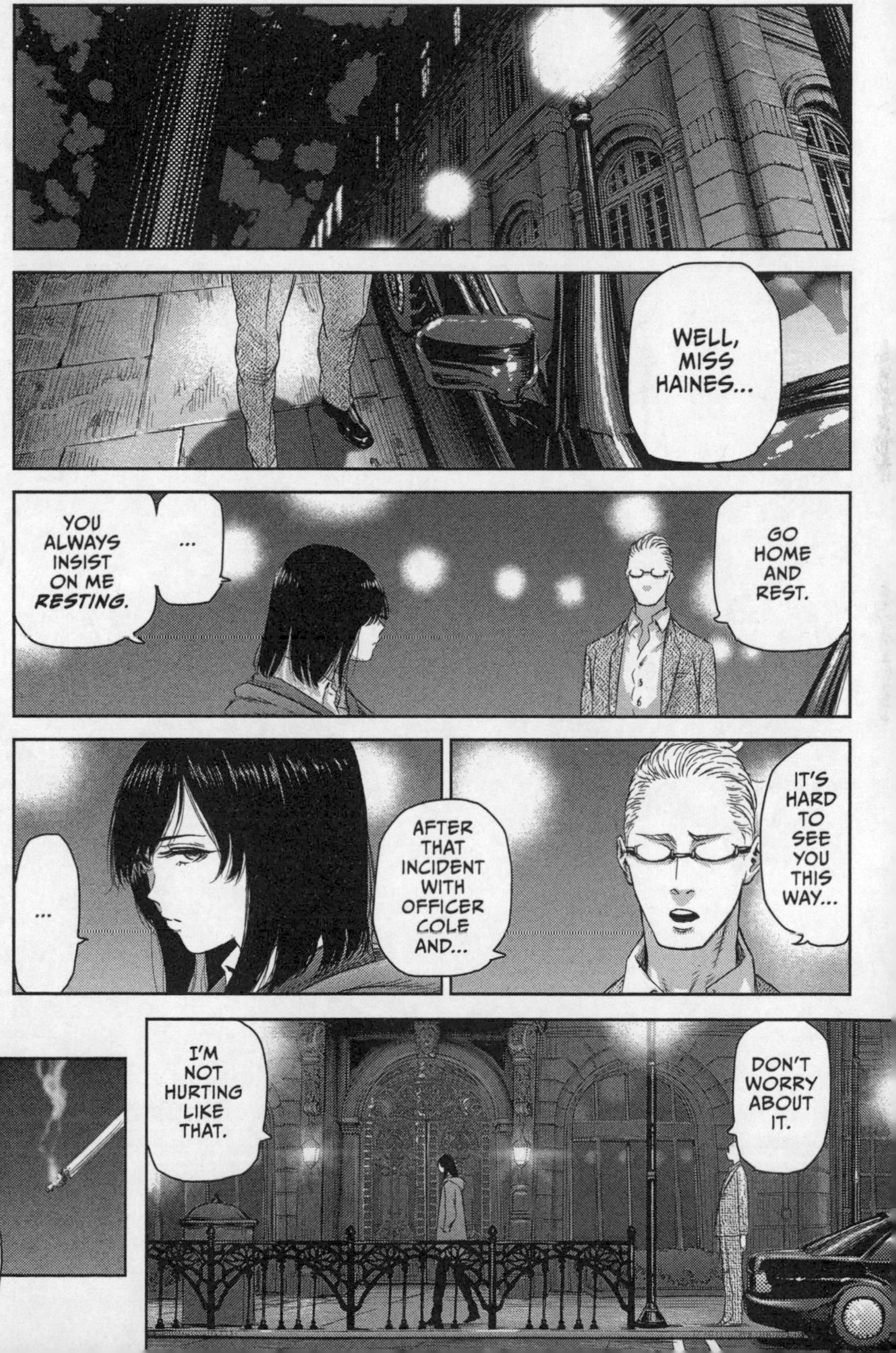
WELL, MISS HAINES...
GO HOME AND REST.
...
YOU ALWAYS INSIST ON ME *RESTING*.
IT'S HARD TO SEE YOU THIS WAY...
AFTER THAT INCIDENT WITH OFFICER COLE AND...
...
DON'T WORRY ABOUT IT.
I'M NOT HURTING LIKE THAT.
PHEW...

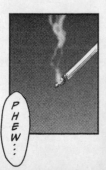

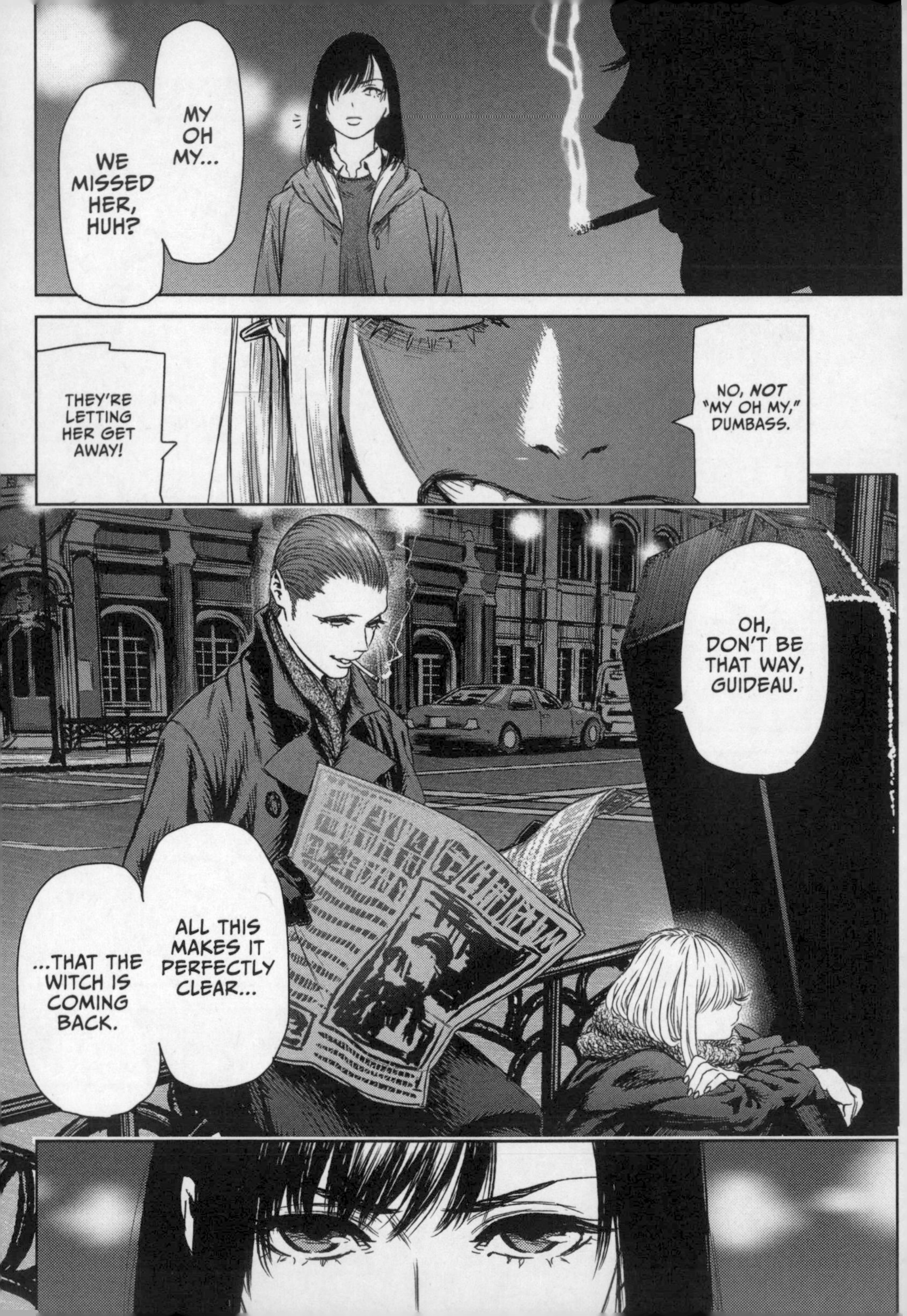
MY OH MY...
WE MISSED HER, HUH?
NO, NOT "MY OH MY," DUMBASS.
THEY'RE LETTING HER GET AWAY!
OH, DON'T BE THAT WAY, GUIDEAU.
ALL THIS MAKES IT PERFECTLY CLEAR...
...THAT THE WITCH IS COMING BACK.

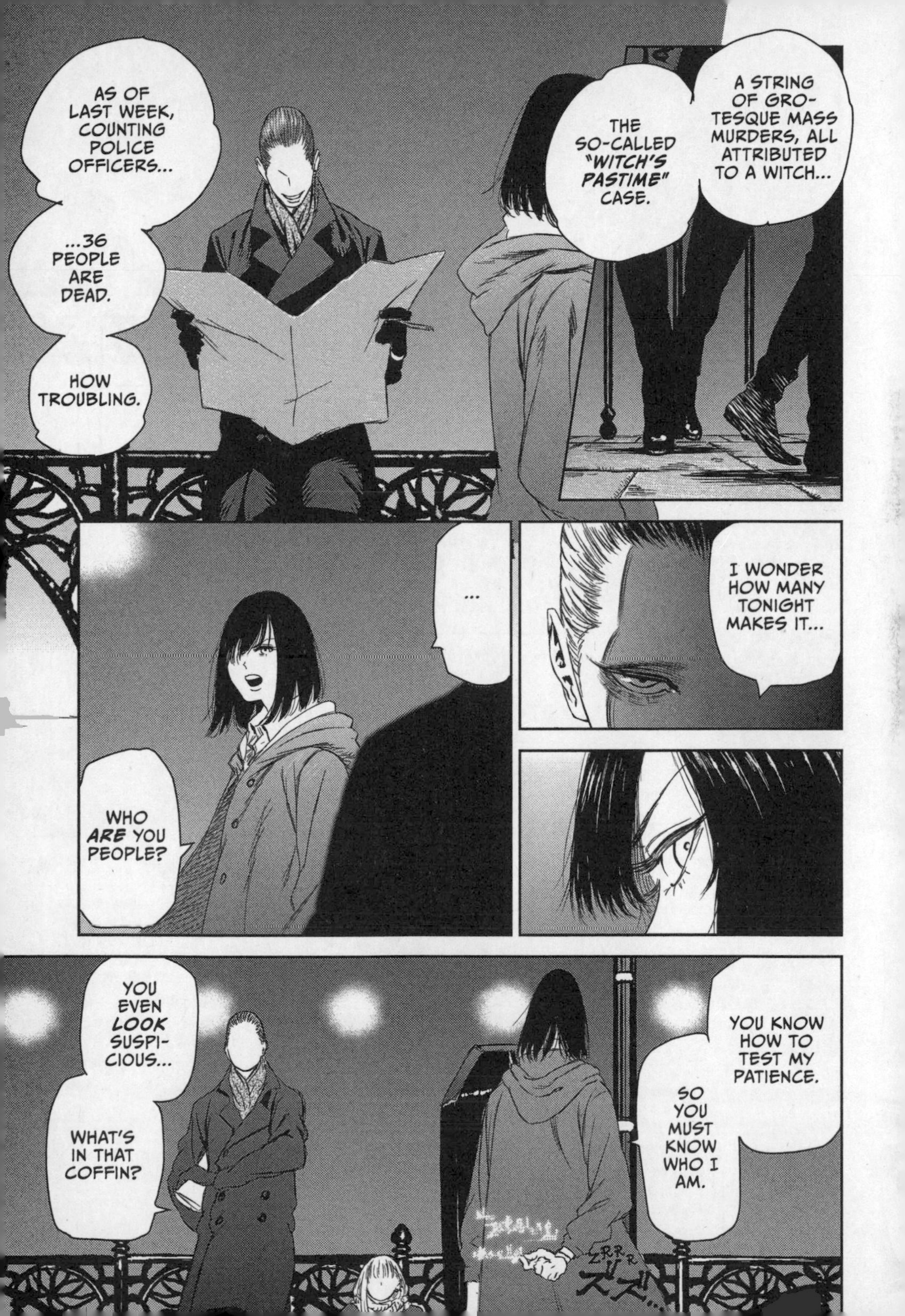
A STRING OF GRO-TESQUE MASS MURDERS, ALL ATTRIBUTED TO A WITCH...
THE SO-CALLED "WITCH'S PASTIME" CASE.
AS OF LAST WEEK, COUNTING POLICE OFFICERS...
...36 PEOPLE ARE DEAD.
HOW TROUBLING.
I WONDER HOW MANY TONIGHT MAKES IT...
...
WHO ARE YOU PEOPLE?
YOU KNOW HOW TO TEST MY PATIENCE.
SO YOU MUST KNOW WHO I AM.
YOU EVEN LOOK SUSPICIOUS...
WHAT'S IN THAT COFFIN?

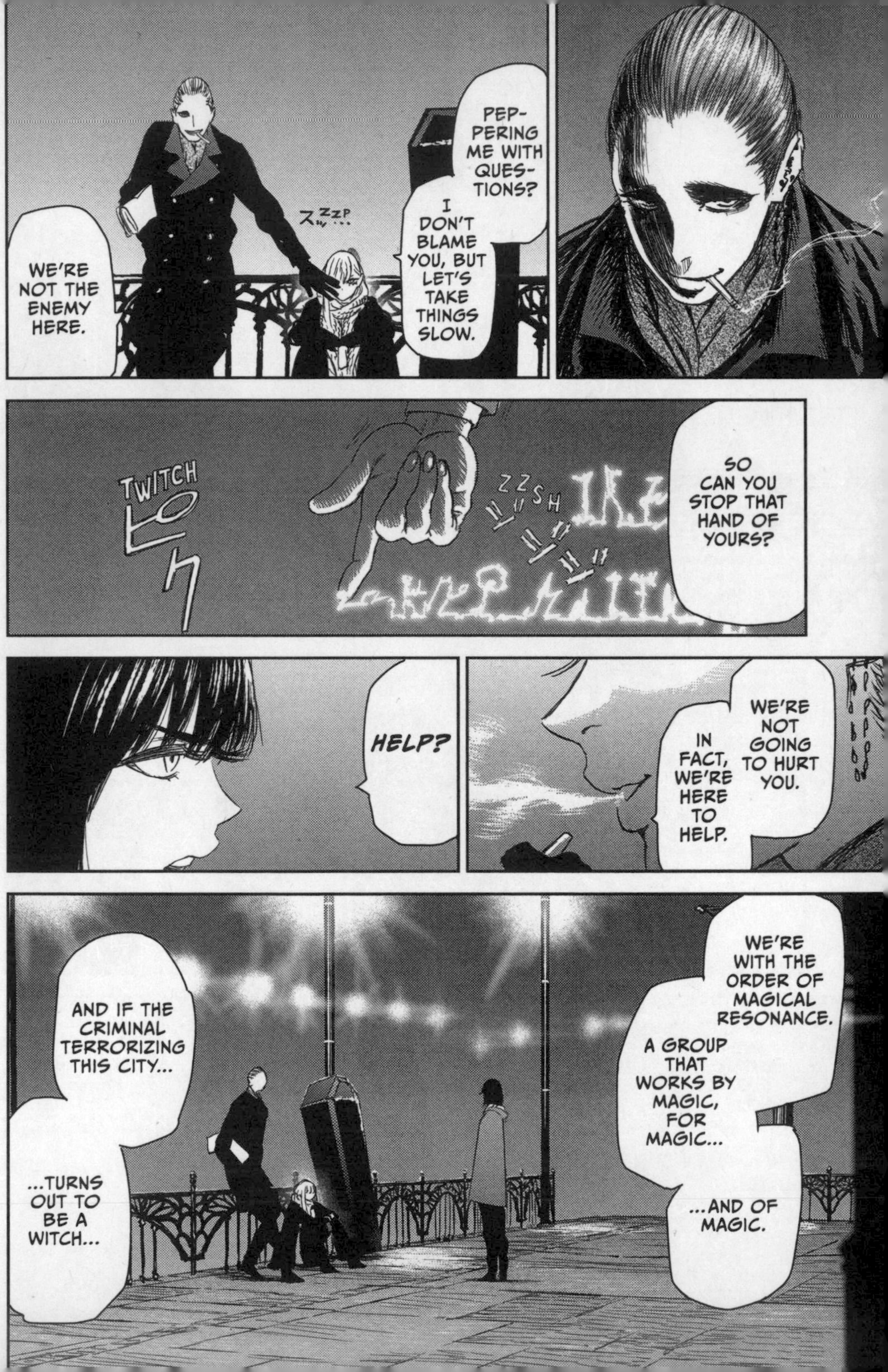
PEPPERING ME WITH QUESTIONS?
I DON'T BLAME YOU, BUT LET'S TAKE THINGS SLOW.
ZZZP
WE'RE NOT THE ENEMY HERE.
SO CAN YOU STOP THAT HAND OF YOURS?
ZZSH
TWITCH
WE'RE NOT GOING TO HURT YOU.
IN FACT, WE'RE HERE TO HELP.
HELP?
WE'RE WITH THE ORDER OF MAGICAL RESONANCE.
A GROUP THAT WORKS BY MAGIC, FOR MAGIC...
...AND OF MAGIC.
AND IF THE CRIMINAL TERRORIZING THIS CITY...
...TURNS OUT TO BE A WITCH...

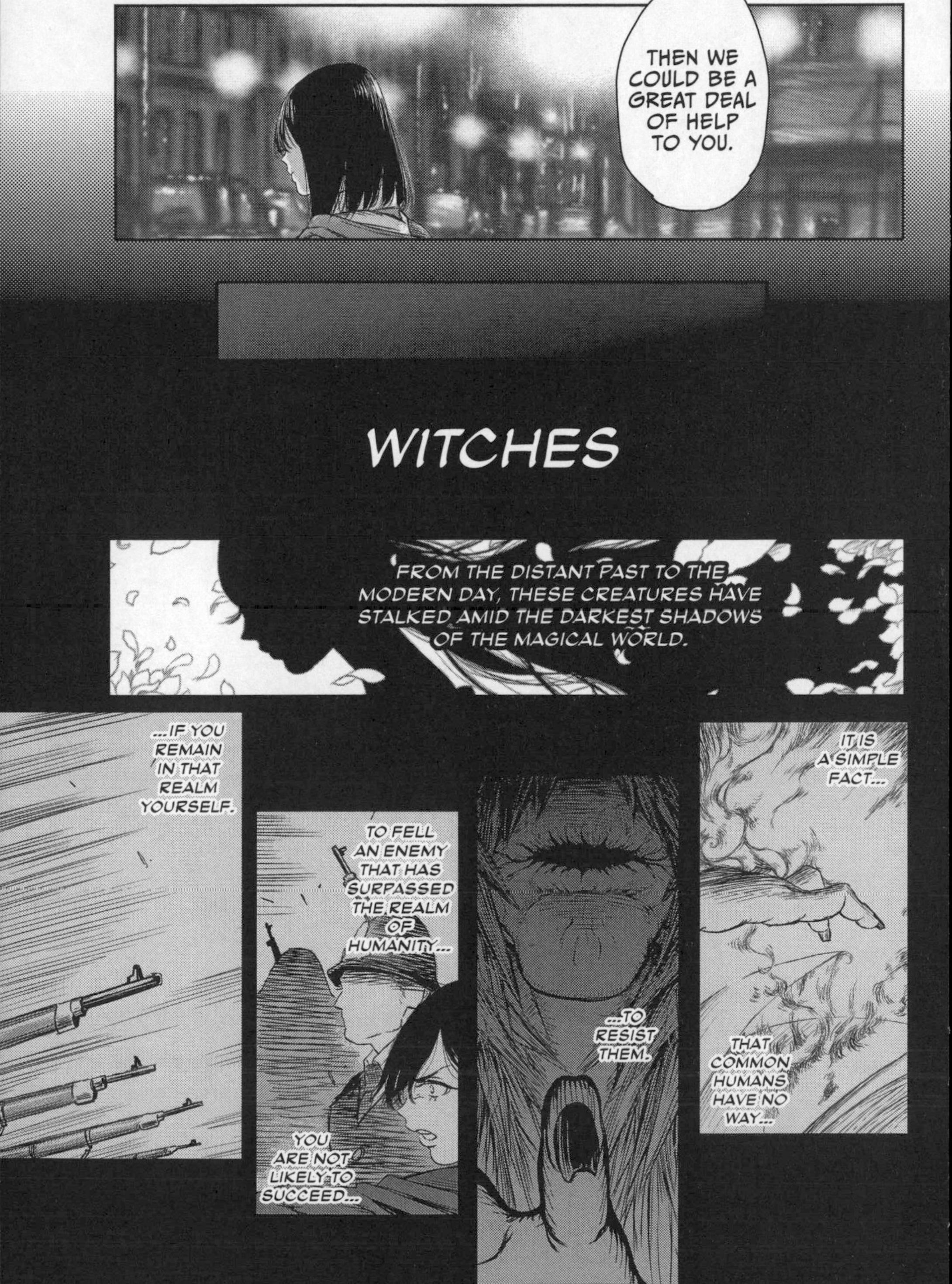
THEN WE COULD BE A GREAT DEAL OF HELP TO YOU.
WITCHES
FROM THE DISTANT PAST TO THE MODERN DAY, THESE CREATURES HAVE STALKED AMID THE DARKEST SHADOWS OF THE MAGICAL WORLD.
IT IS A SIMPLE FACT...
THAT COMMON HUMANS HAVE NO WAY...
...TO RESIST THEM.
TO FELL AN ENEMY THAT HAS SURPASSED THE REALM OF HUMANITY...
YOU ARE NOT LIKELY TO SUCCEED...
...IF YOU REMAIN IN THAT REALM YOURSELF.

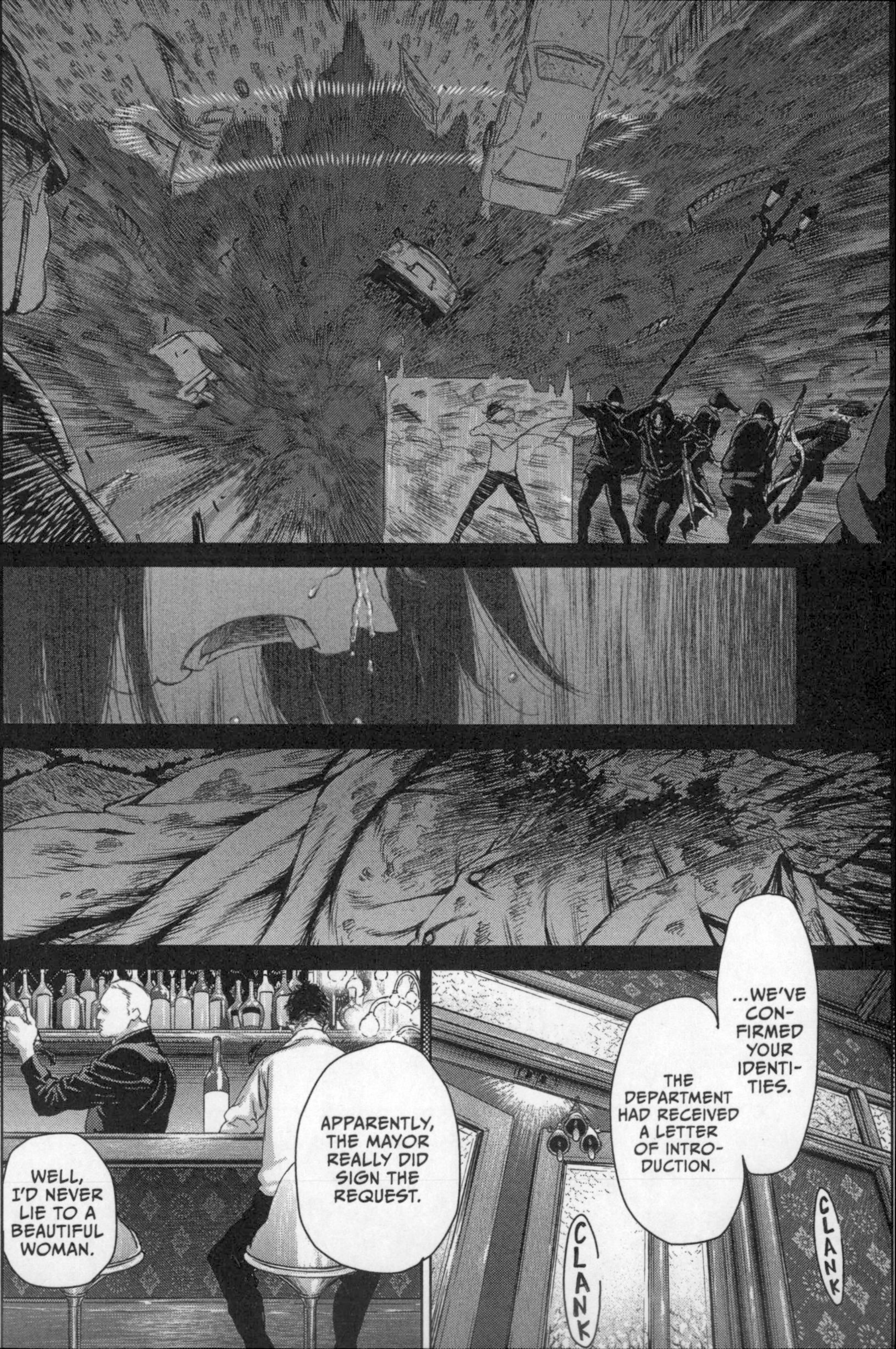
...WE'VE CONFIRMED YOUR IDENTITIES.
THE DEPARTMENT HAD RECEIVED A LETTER OF INTRODUCTION.
CLANK
CLANK
APPARENTLY, THE MAYOR REALLY DID SIGN THE REQUEST.
WELL, I'D NEVER LIE TO A BEAUTIFUL WOMAN.

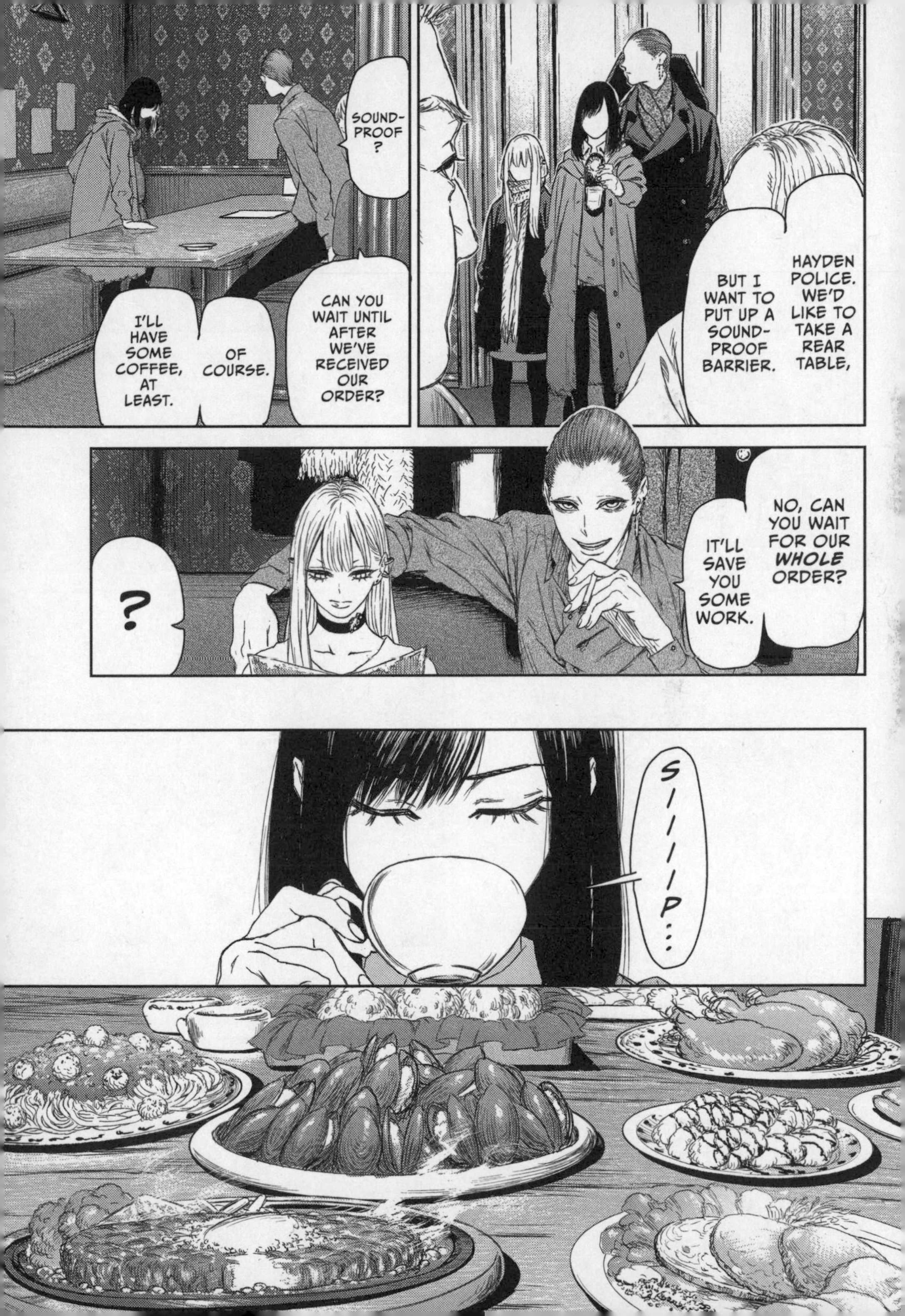
HAYDEN POLICE. WE'D LIKE TO TAKE A REAR TABLE,
BUT I WANT TO PUT UP A SOUND-PROOF BARRIER.
SOUND-PROOF?
CAN YOU WAIT UNTIL AFTER WE'VE RECEIVED OUR ORDER?
OF COURSE.
I'LL HAVE SOME COFFEE, AT LEAST.
NO, CAN YOU WAIT FOR OUR *WHOLE* ORDER?
IT'LL SAVE YOU SOME WORK.
?
SIIIIP...

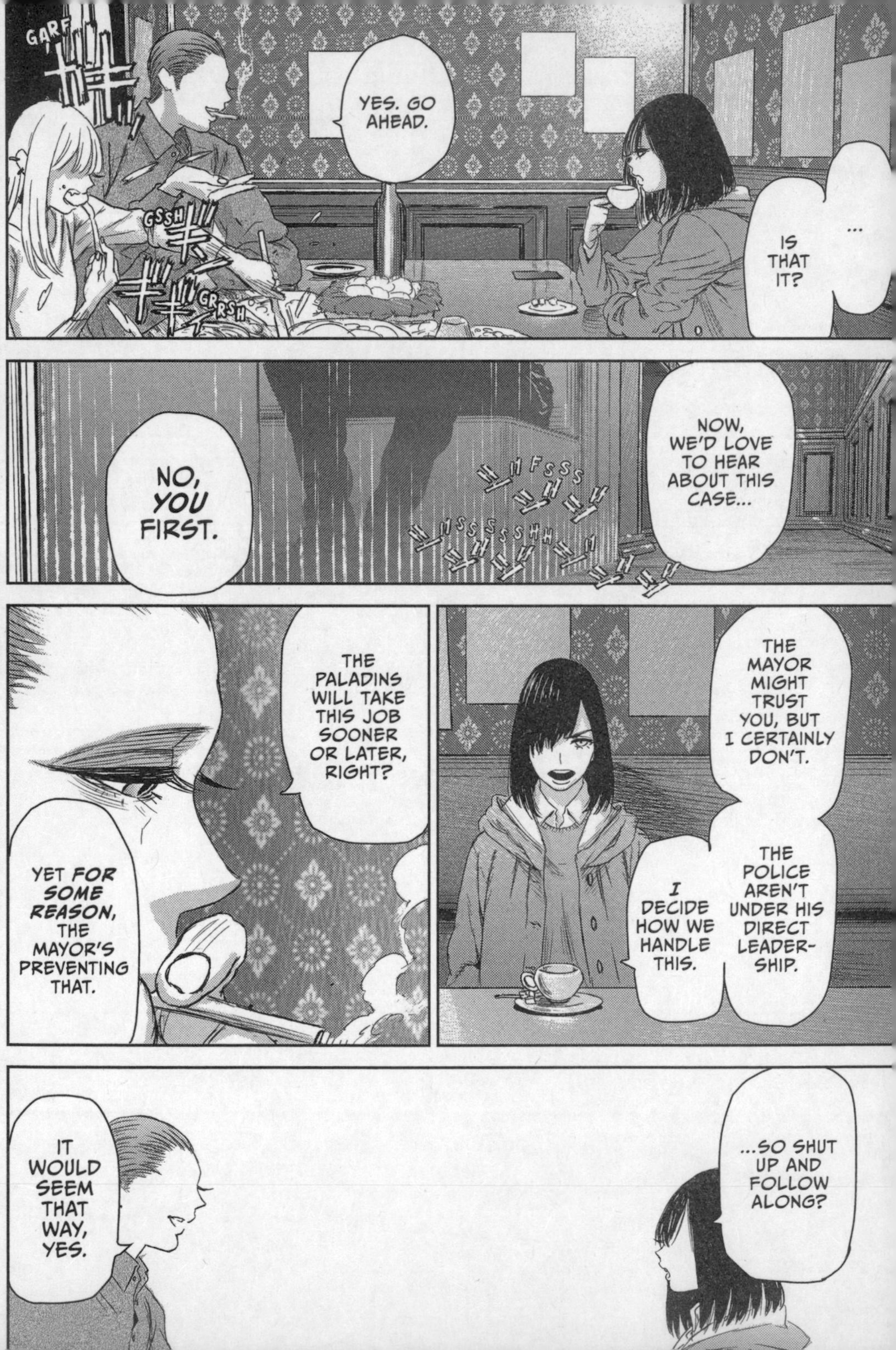
...
IS THAT IT?
YES. GO AHEAD.
GARF
GSSH
GRRSH
NOW, WE'D LOVE TO HEAR ABOUT THIS CASE...
HFSSS
MSSSSHH
NO, YOU FIRST.
THE MAYOR MIGHT TRUST YOU, BUT I CERTAINLY DON'T.
THE POLICE AREN'T UNDER HIS DIRECT LEADERSHIP.
I DECIDE HOW WE HANDLE THIS.
THE PALADINS WILL TAKE THIS JOB SOONER OR LATER, RIGHT?
YET FOR SOME REASON, THE MAYOR'S PREVENTING THAT.
...SO SHUT UP AND FOLLOW ALONG?
IT WOULD SEEM THAT WAY, YES.

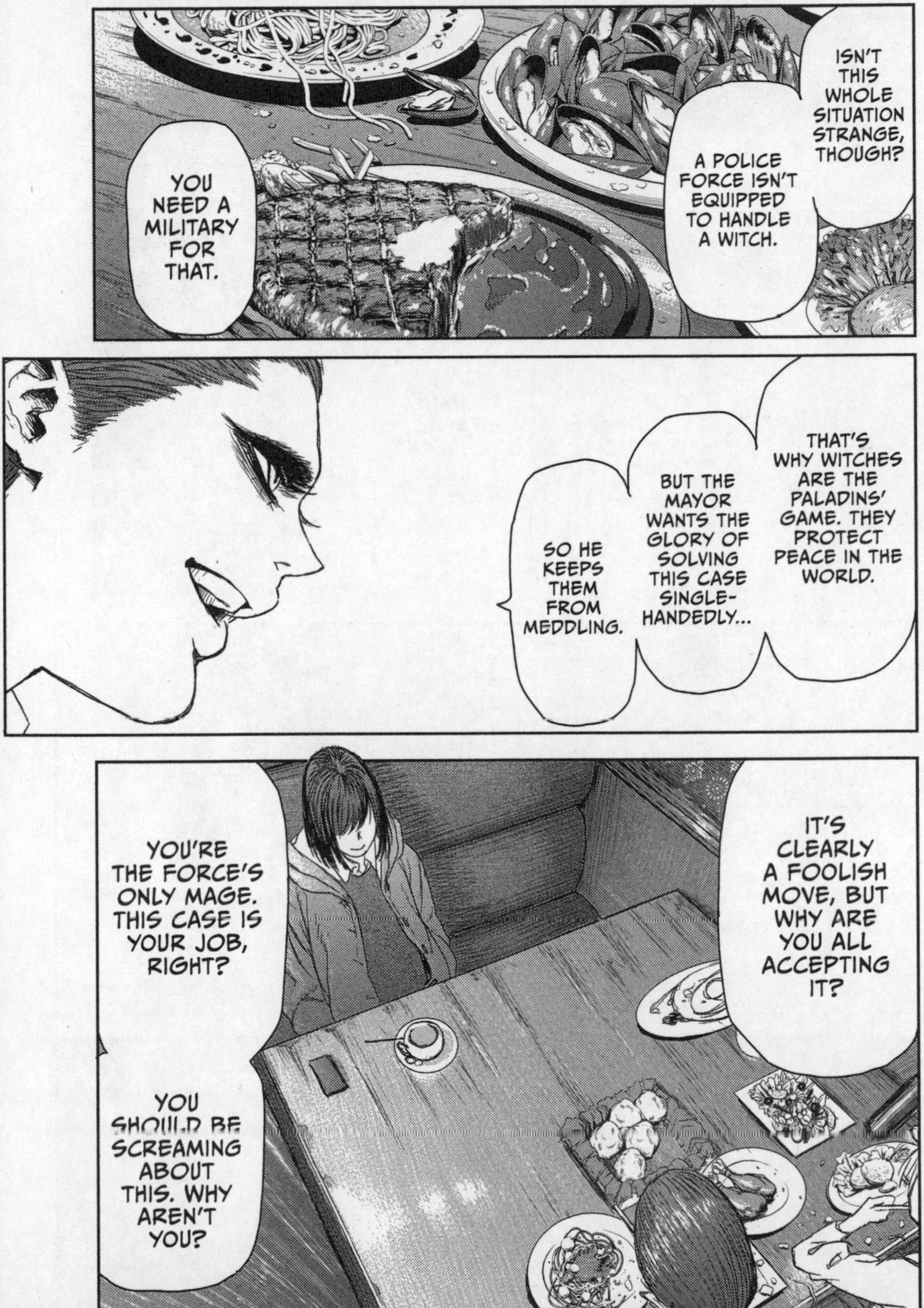
ISN'T THIS WHOLE SITUATION STRANGE, THOUGH?
A POLICE FORCE ISN'T EQUIPPED TO HANDLE A WITCH.
YOU NEED A MILITARY FOR THAT.
THAT'S WHY WITCHES ARE THE PALADINS' GAME. THEY PROTECT PEACE IN THE WORLD.
BUT THE MAYOR WANTS THE GLORY OF SOLVING THIS CASE SINGLE-HANDEDLY...
SO HE KEEPS THEM FROM MEDDLING.
IT'S CLEARLY A FOOLISH MOVE, BUT WHY ARE YOU ALL ACCEPTING IT?
YOU'RE THE FORCE'S ONLY MAGE. THIS CASE IS YOUR JOB, RIGHT?
YOU SHOULD BE SCREAMING ABOUT THIS. WHY AREN'T YOU?

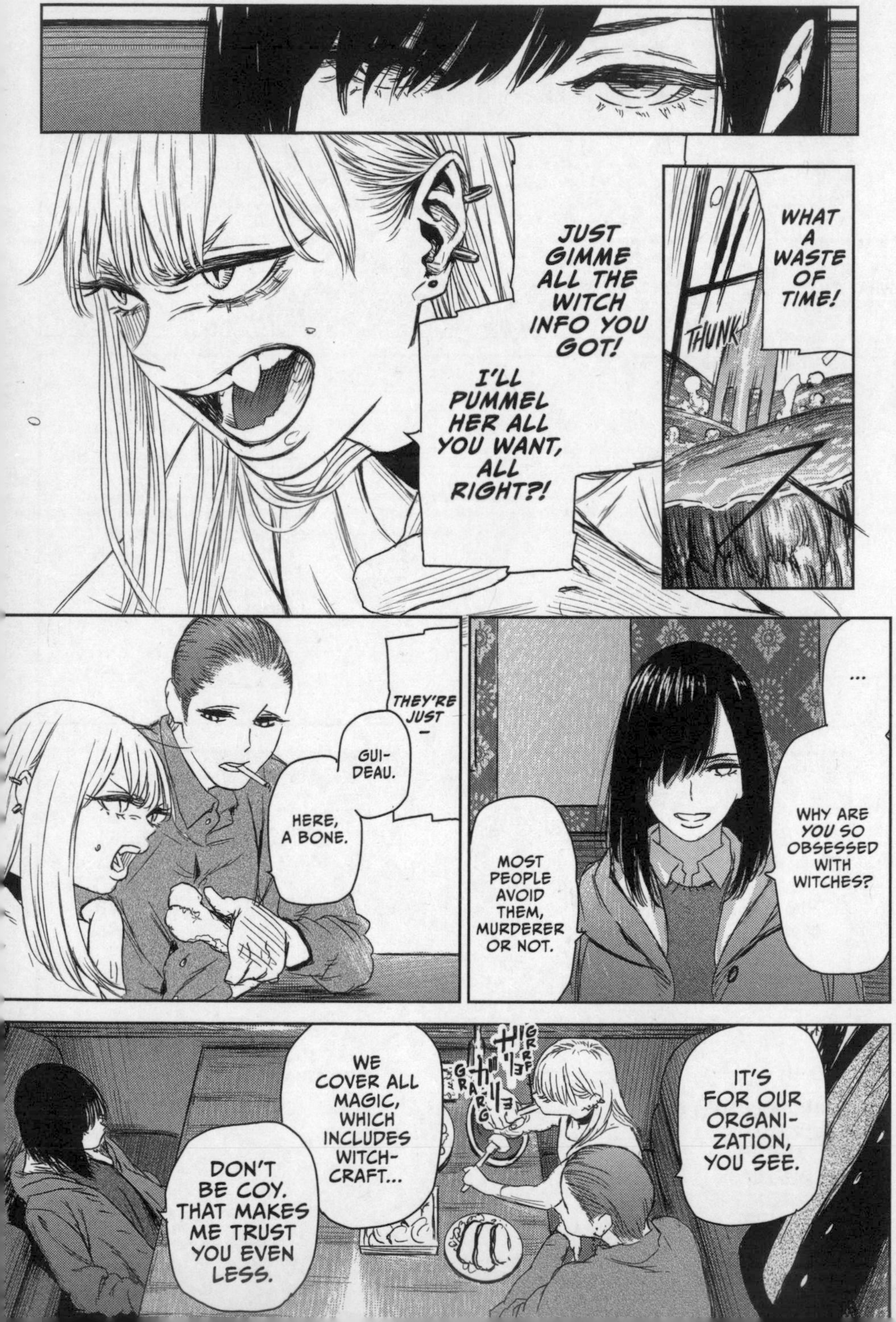
WHAT A WASTE OF TIME!
THUNK
JUST GIMME ALL THE WITCH INFO YOU GOT!
I'LL PUMMEL HER ALL YOU WANT, ALL RIGHT?!
...
WHY ARE YOU SO OBSESSED WITH WITCHES?
MOST PEOPLE AVOID THEM, MURDERER OR NOT.
THEY'RE JUST—
GUI-DEAU.
HERE, A BONE.
IT'S FOR OUR ORGANI-ZATION, YOU SEE.
WE COVER ALL MAGIC, WHICH INCLUDES WITCH-CRAFT...
DON'T BE COY. THAT MAKES ME TRUST YOU EVEN LESS.

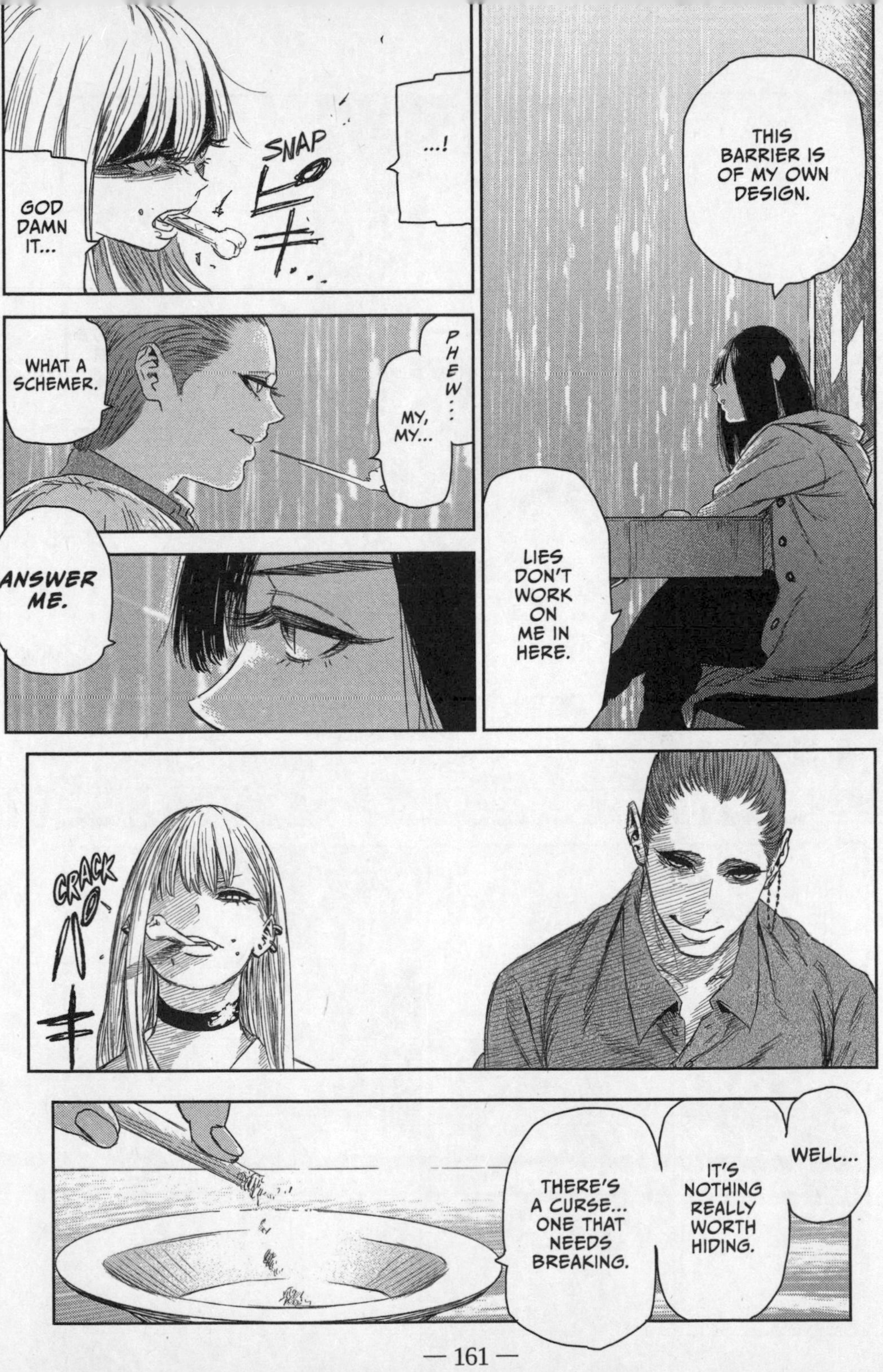
THIS BARRIER IS OF MY OWN DESIGN.
LIES DON'T WORK ON ME IN HERE.
...!
SNAP
GOD DAMN IT...
PHEW...
MY, MY...
WHAT A SCHEMER.
ANSWER ME.
CRACK
WELL...
IT'S NOTHING REALLY WORTH HIDING.
THERE'S A CURSE... ONE THAT NEEDS BREAKING.

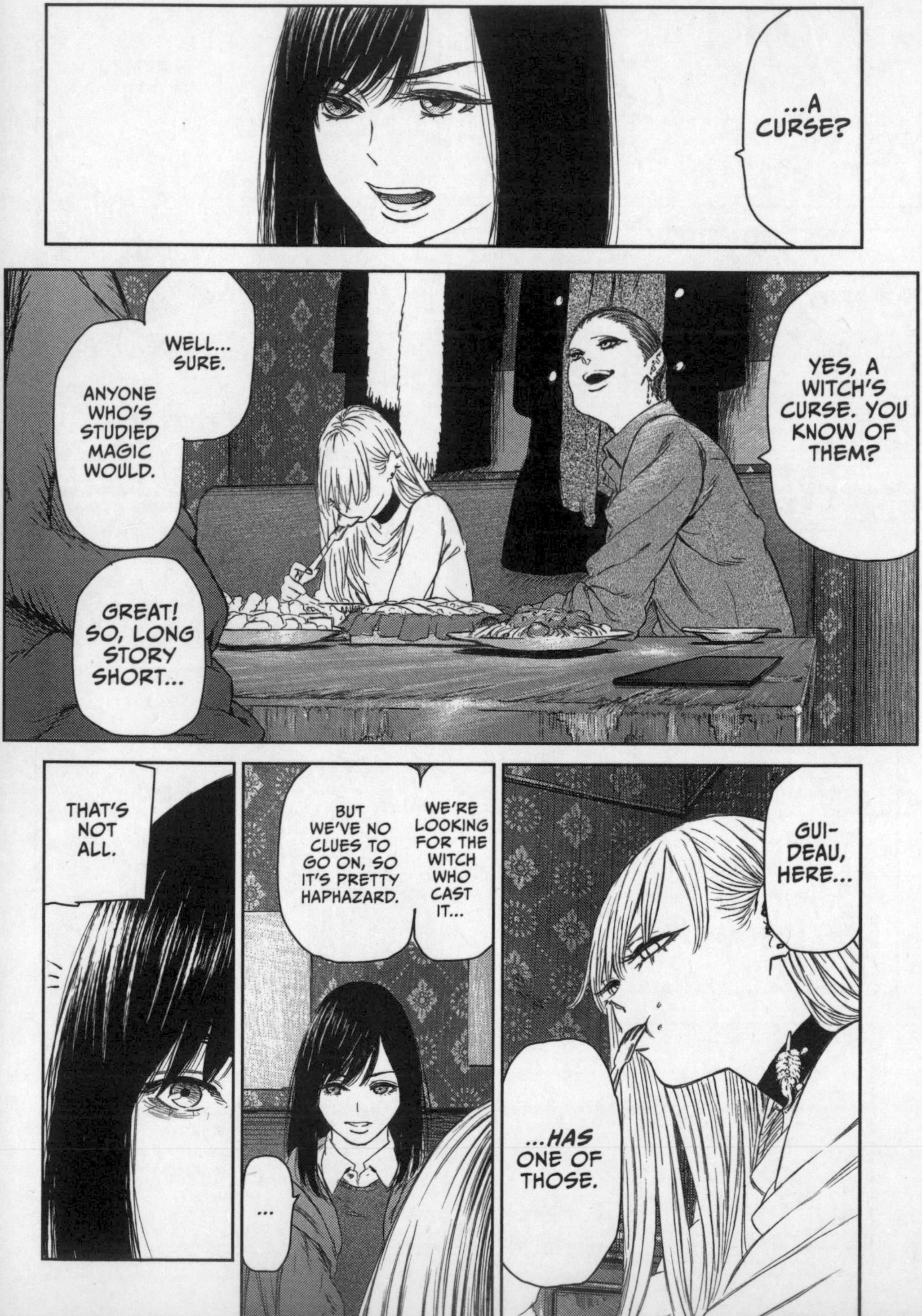
...A CURSE?
YES, A WITCH'S CURSE. YOU KNOW OF THEM?
WELL... SURE.
ANYONE WHO'S STUDIED MAGIC WOULD.
GREAT! SO, LONG STORY SHORT...
GUI-DEAU, HERE...
...HAS ONE OF THOSE.
WE'RE LOOKING FOR THE WITCH WHO CAST IT...
BUT WE'VE NO CLUES TO GO ON, SO IT'S PRETTY HAPHAZARD.
...
THAT'S NOT ALL.

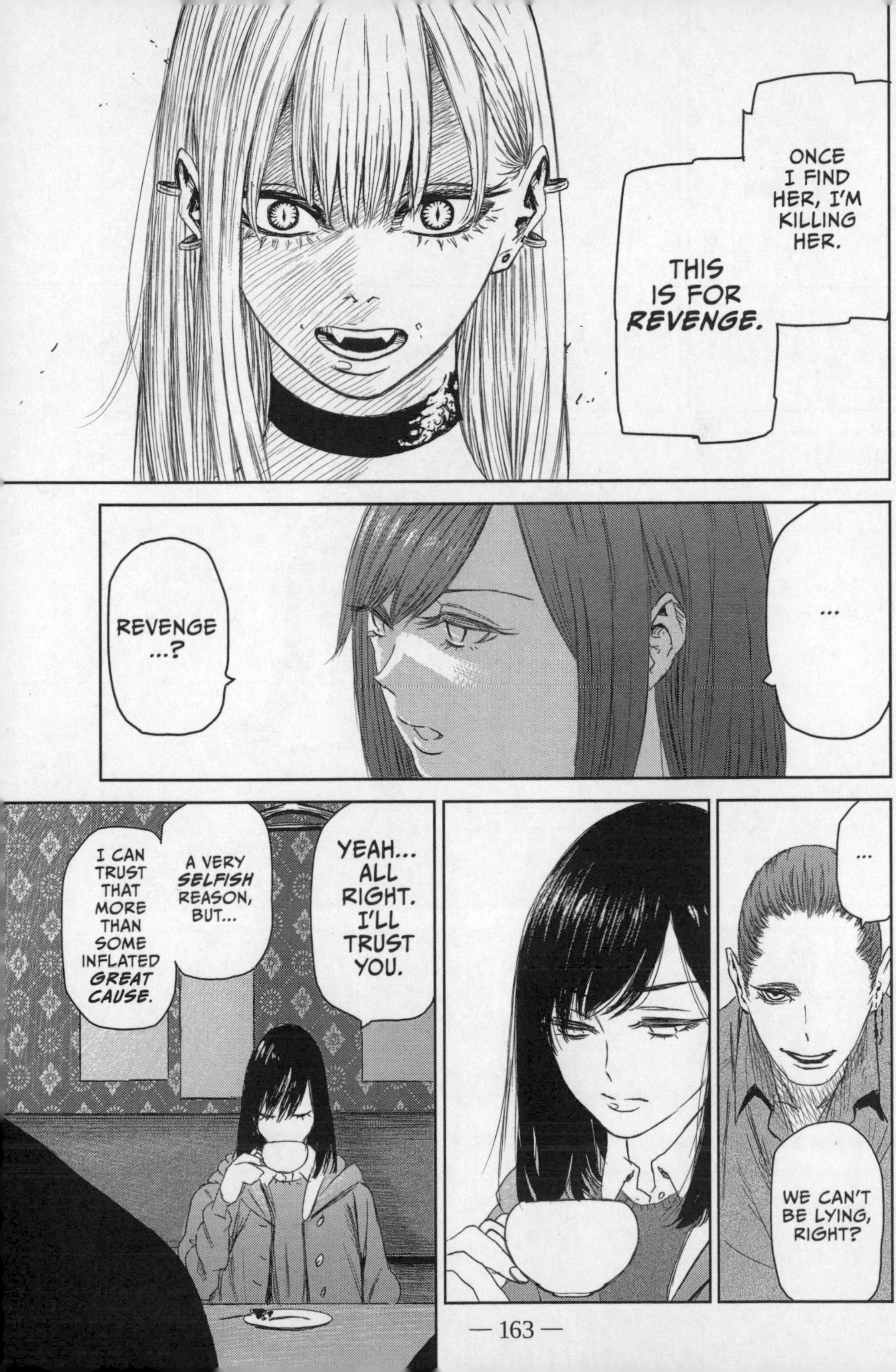
ONCE I FIND HER, I'M KILLING HER.
THIS IS FOR *REVENGE.*
...
REVENGE ...?
...
WE CAN'T BE LYING, RIGHT?
YEAH... ALL RIGHT. I'LL TRUST YOU.
A VERY *SELFISH* REASON, BUT...
I CAN TRUST THAT MORE THAN SOME INFLATED *GREAT CAUSE.*

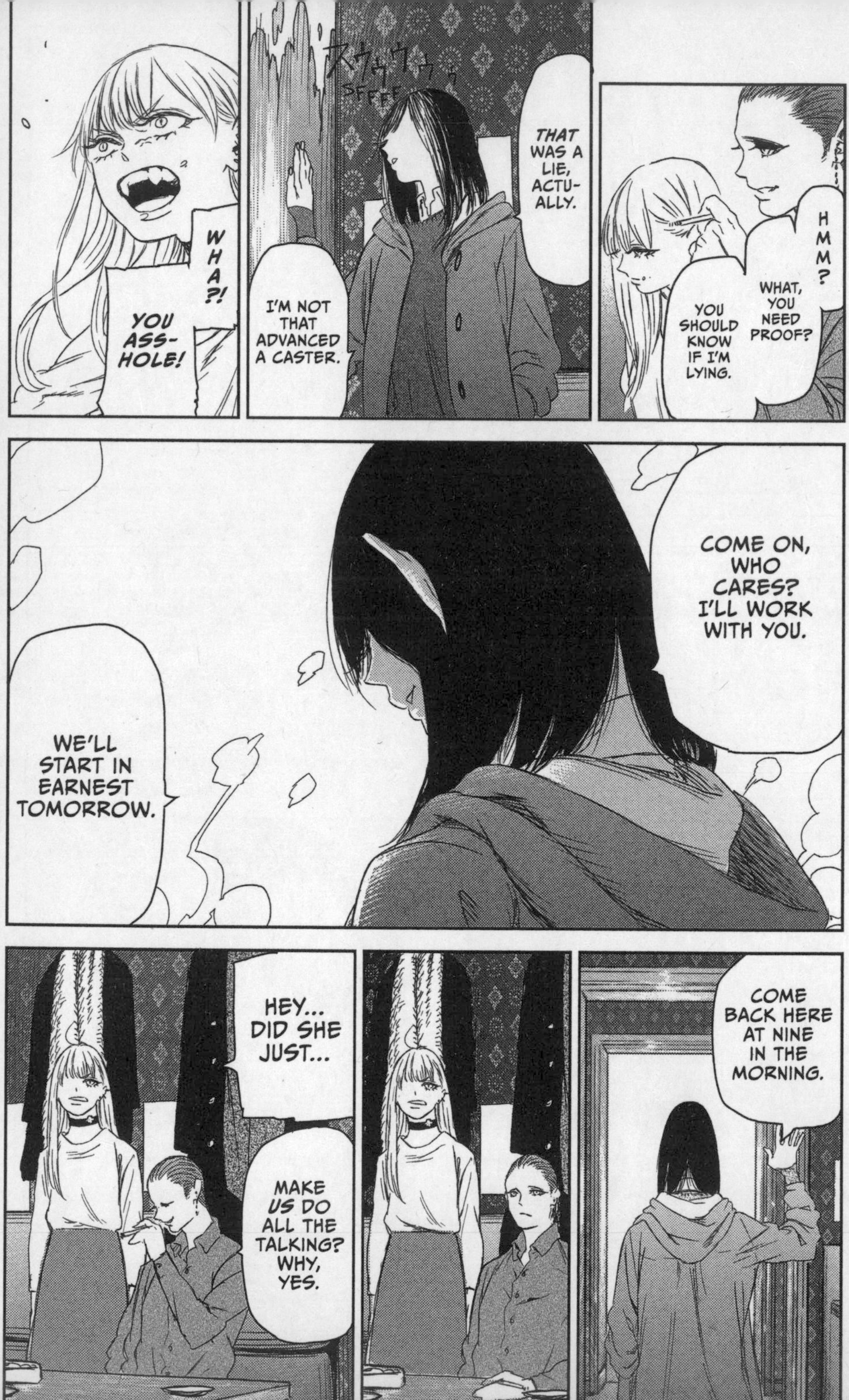
HMM?
WHAT, YOU NEED PROOF?
YOU SHOULD KNOW IF I'M LYING.
SFFFF
THAT WAS A LIE, ACTUALLY.
I'M NOT THAT ADVANCED A CASTER.
WHA?!
YOU ASS-HOLE!
COME ON, WHO CARES? I'LL WORK WITH YOU.
WE'LL START IN EARNEST TOMORROW.
COME BACK HERE AT NINE IN THE MORNING.
HEY... DID SHE JUST...
MAKE US DO ALL THE TALKING? WHY, YES.

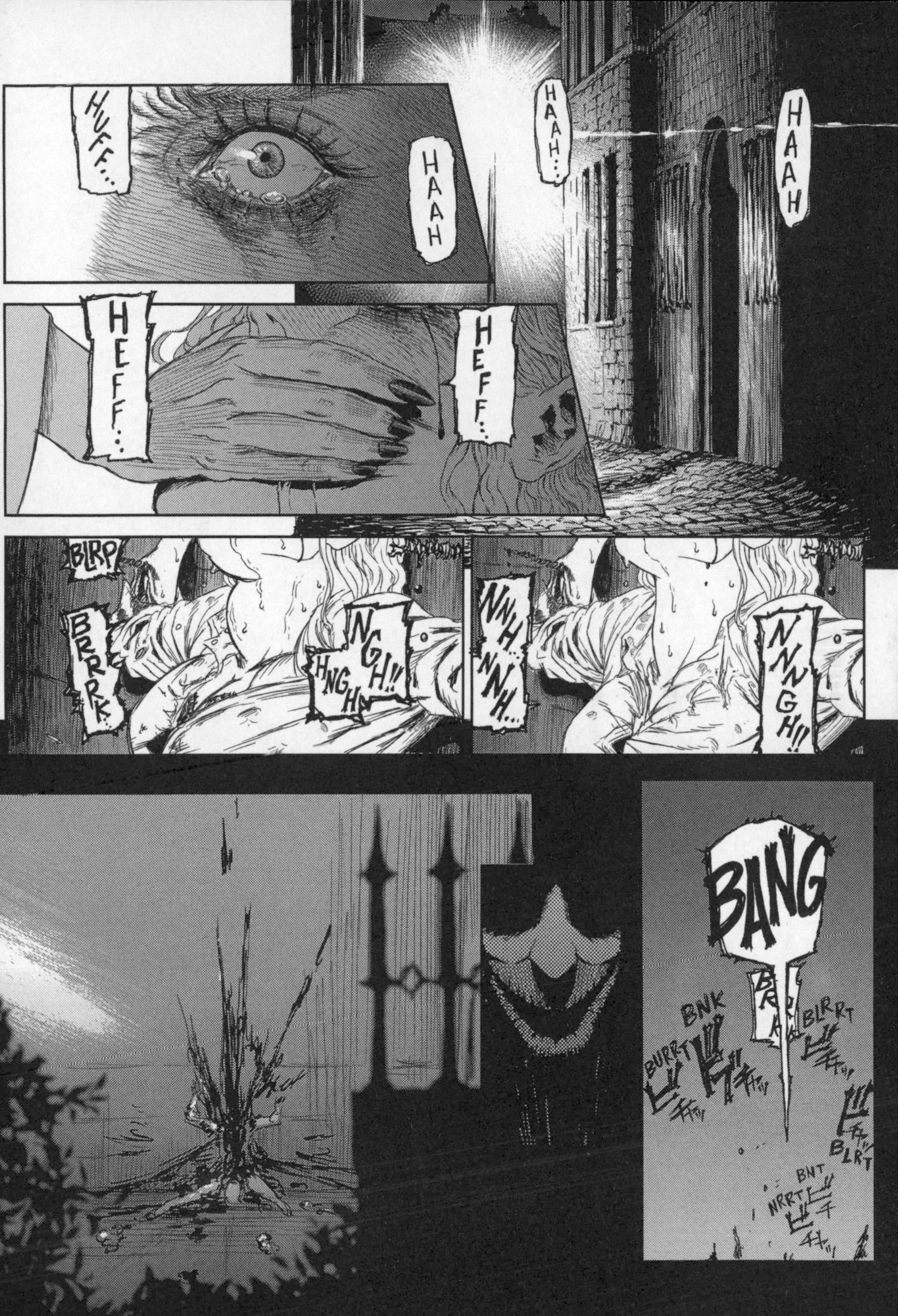
HAAAH
HAAH...
HAAH
HUFF...
HEFF...
HEFF...
NNNGH!!
NNH... NNNH...
NGH!!
HNGH!!
BRRRK...
BLRP
BANG
BRRR
BLRRT
BNK
BURRT
BLRT
BNT
NRRT

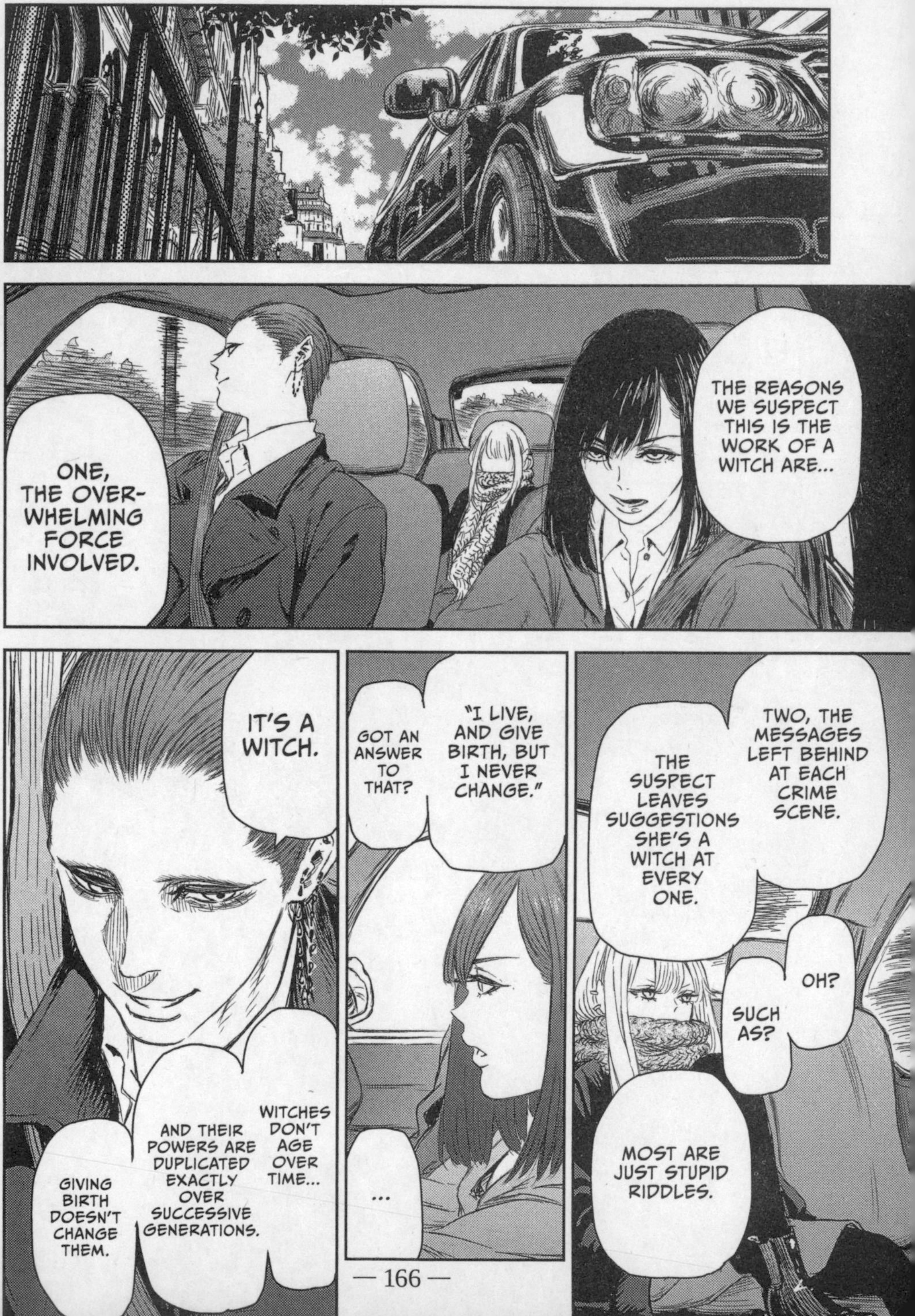
THE REASONS WE SUSPECT THIS IS THE WORK OF A WITCH ARE...
ONE, THE OVER-WHELMING FORCE INVOLVED.
TWO, THE MESSAGES LEFT BEHIND AT EACH CRIME SCENE.
THE SUSPECT LEAVES SUGGESTIONS SHE'S A WITCH AT EVERY ONE.
OH?
SUCH AS?
MOST ARE JUST STUPID RIDDLES.
"I LIVE, AND GIVE BIRTH, BUT I NEVER CHANGE."
GOT AN ANSWER TO THAT?
...
IT'S A WITCH.
WITCHES DON'T AGE OVER TIME...
AND THEIR POWERS ARE DUPLICATED EXACTLY OVER SUCCESSIVE GENERATIONS.
GIVING BIRTH DOESN'T CHANGE THEM.

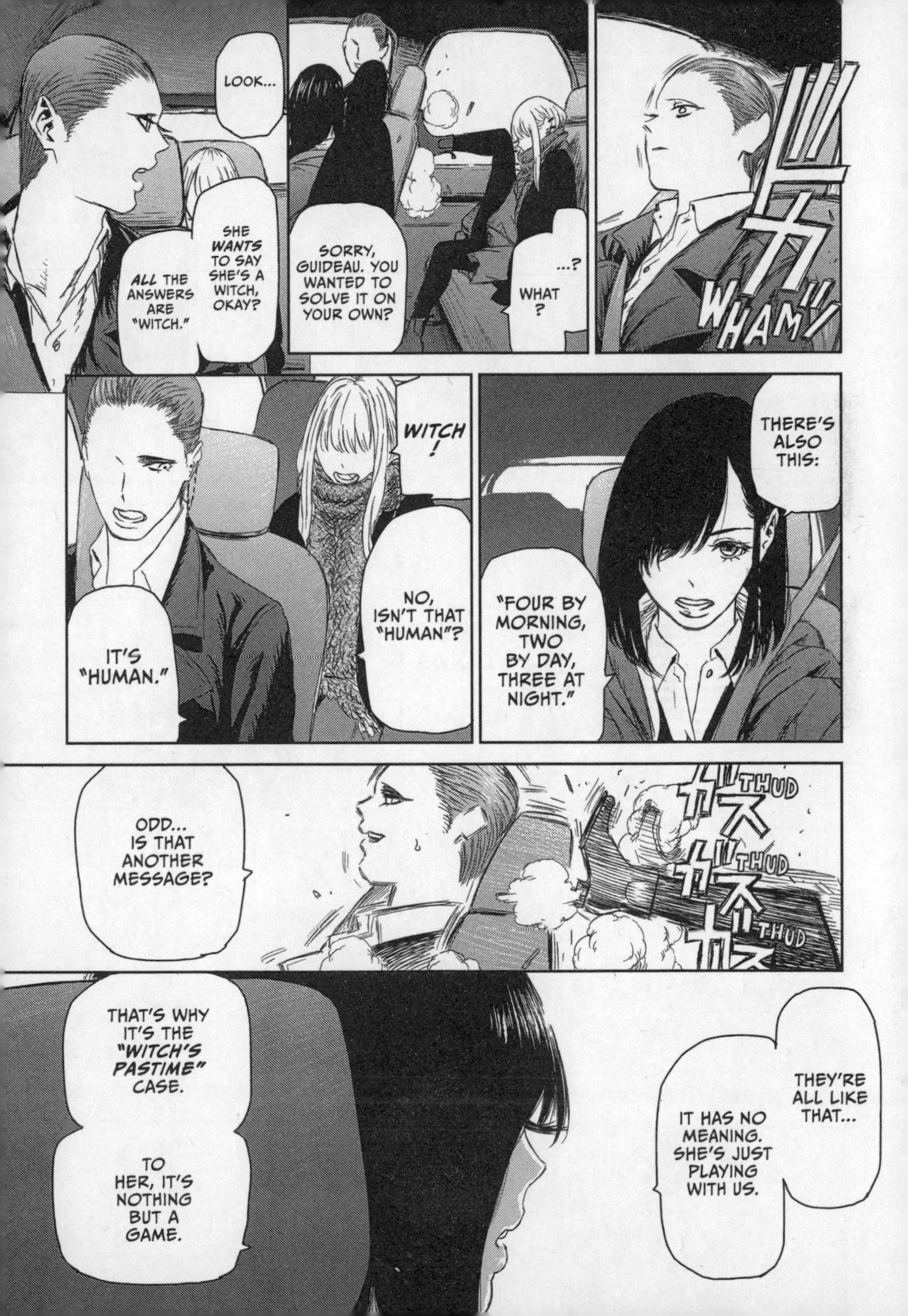
WHAM!!
...? WHAT?
SORRY, GUIDEAU. YOU WANTED TO SOLVE IT ON YOUR OWN?
LOOK...
SHE *WANTS* TO SAY SHE'S A WITCH, OKAY?
ALL THE ANSWERS ARE "WITCH."
THERE'S ALSO THIS:
"FOUR BY MORNING, TWO BY DAY, THREE AT NIGHT."
WITCH!
NO, ISN'T THAT "HUMAN"?
IT'S "HUMAN."
THUD
THUD
THUD
ODD... IS THAT ANOTHER MESSAGE?
THEY'RE ALL LIKE THAT...
IT HAS NO MEANING. SHE'S JUST PLAYING WITH US.
THAT'S WHY IT'S THE *"WITCH'S PASTIME"* CASE.
TO HER, IT'S NOTHING BUT A GAME.

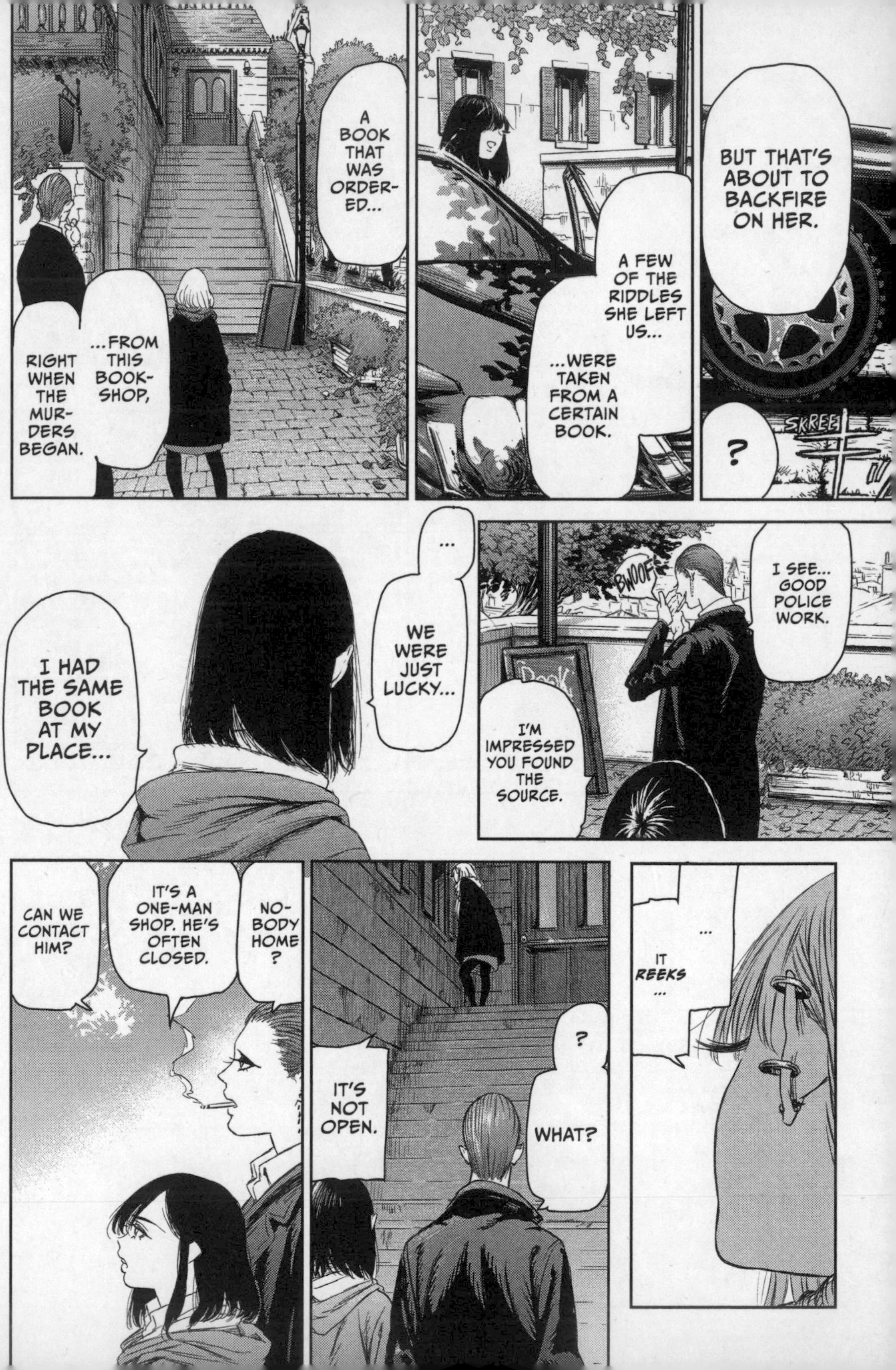
BUT THAT'S ABOUT TO BACKFIRE ON HER.
SKREE
?
A FEW OF THE RIDDLES SHE LEFT US...
...WERE TAKEN FROM A CERTAIN BOOK.
A BOOK THAT WAS ORDER-ED...
...FROM THIS BOOK-SHOP,
RIGHT WHEN THE MUR-DERS BEGAN.
I SEE... GOOD POLICE WORK.
BWOOF
I'M IMPRESSED YOU FOUND THE SOURCE.
...
WE WERE JUST LUCKY...
I HAD THE SAME BOOK AT MY PLACE...
...
IT REEKS ...
?
WHAT?
IT'S NOT OPEN.
NO-BODY HOME ?
IT'S A ONE-MAN SHOP. HE'S OFTEN CLOSED.
CAN WE CONTACT HIM?

!! SMASH WHAM

HE'S NOT ANSWER-ING—

...?!

YOU GUYS GO IN!

...

WHAT ARE YOU DOING?!

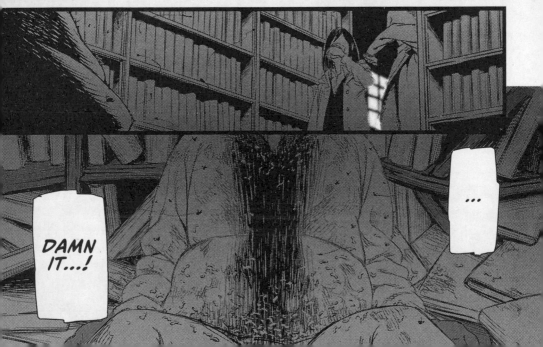

DAMN IT....!

...

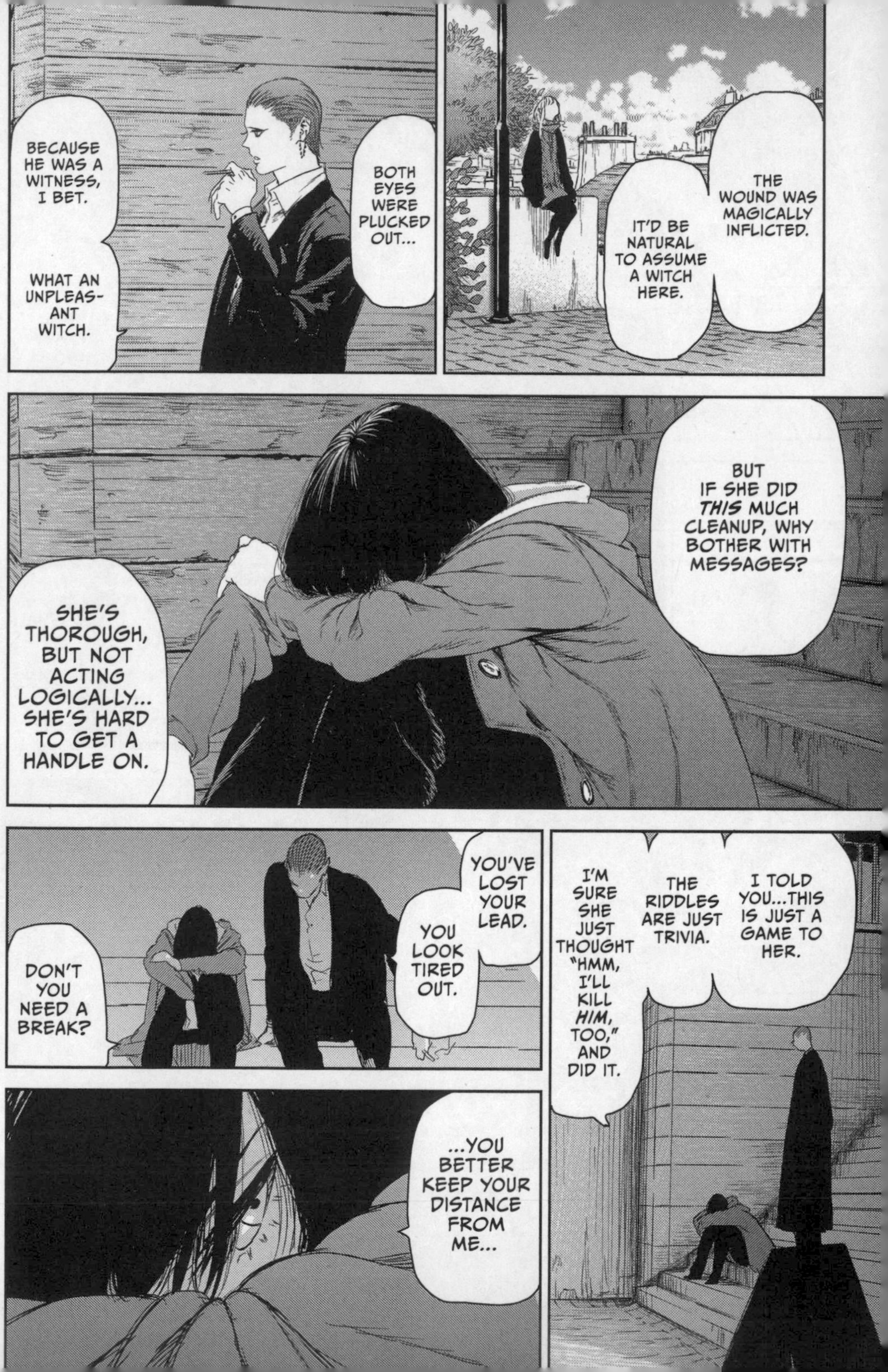
THE WOUND WAS MAGICALLY INFLICTED.
IT'D BE NATURAL TO ASSUME A WITCH HERE.
BOTH EYES WERE PLUCKED OUT...
BECAUSE HE WAS A WITNESS, I BET.
WHAT AN UNPLEAS-ANT WITCH.
BUT IF SHE DID *THIS* MUCH CLEANUP, WHY BOTHER WITH MESSAGES?
SHE'S THOROUGH, BUT NOT ACTING LOGICALLY... SHE'S HARD TO GET A HANDLE ON.
I TOLD YOU...THIS IS JUST A GAME TO HER.
THE RIDDLES ARE JUST TRIVIA.
I'M SURE SHE JUST THOUGHT "HMM, I'LL KILL *HIM*, TOO," AND DID IT.
YOU'VE LOST YOUR LEAD.
YOU LOOK TIRED OUT.
DON'T YOU NEED A BREAK?
...YOU BETTER KEEP YOUR DISTANCE FROM ME...

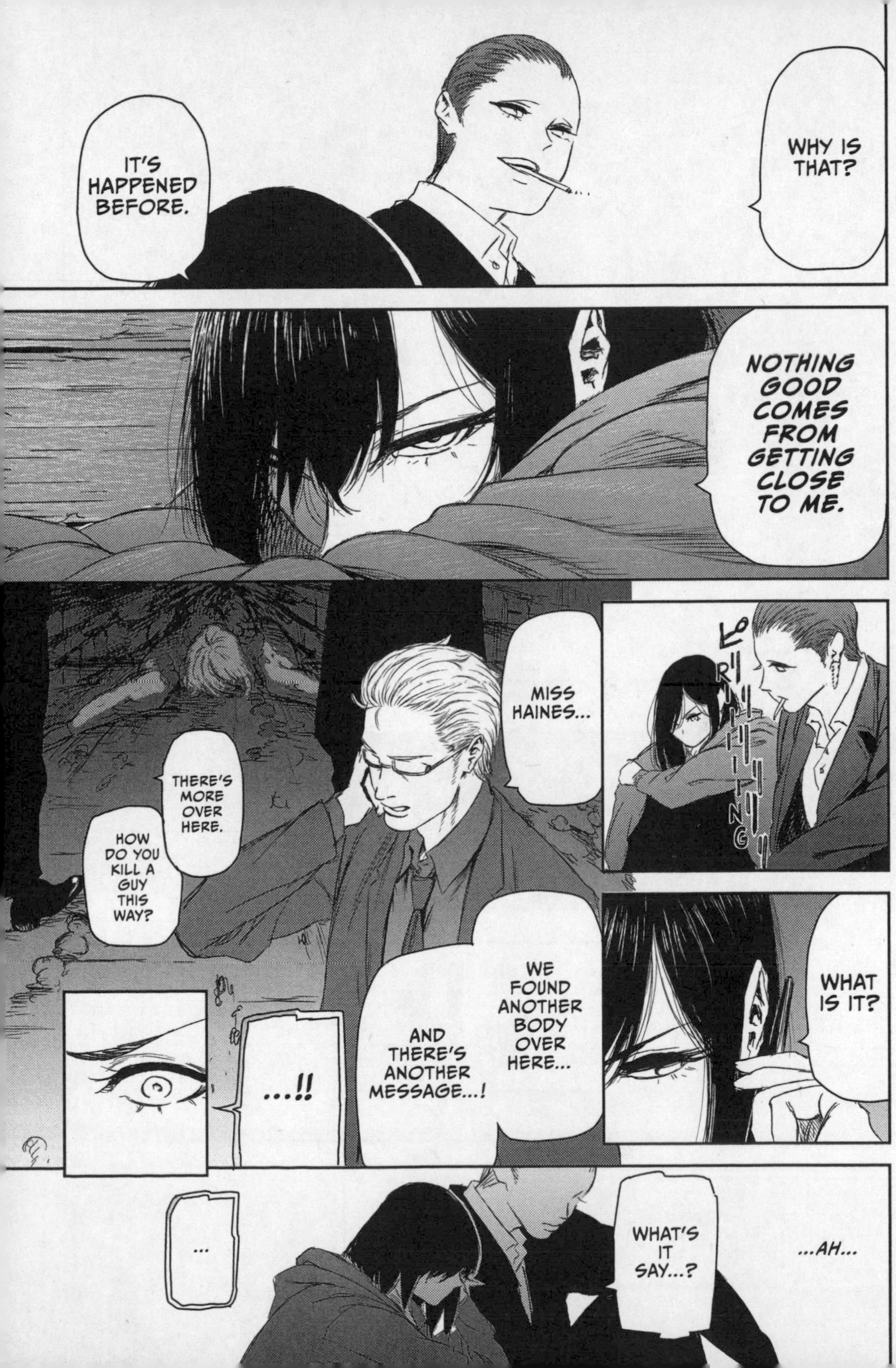
WHY IS THAT?
IT'S HAPPENED BEFORE.
NOTHING GOOD COMES FROM GETTING CLOSE TO ME.
ピ
RING
MISS HAINES...
THERE'S MORE OVER HERE.
HOW DO YOU KILL A GUY THIS WAY?
WHAT IS IT?
WE FOUND ANOTHER BODY OVER HERE...
AND THERE'S ANOTHER MESSAGE...!
...!!
...AH...
WHAT'S IT SAY...?
...

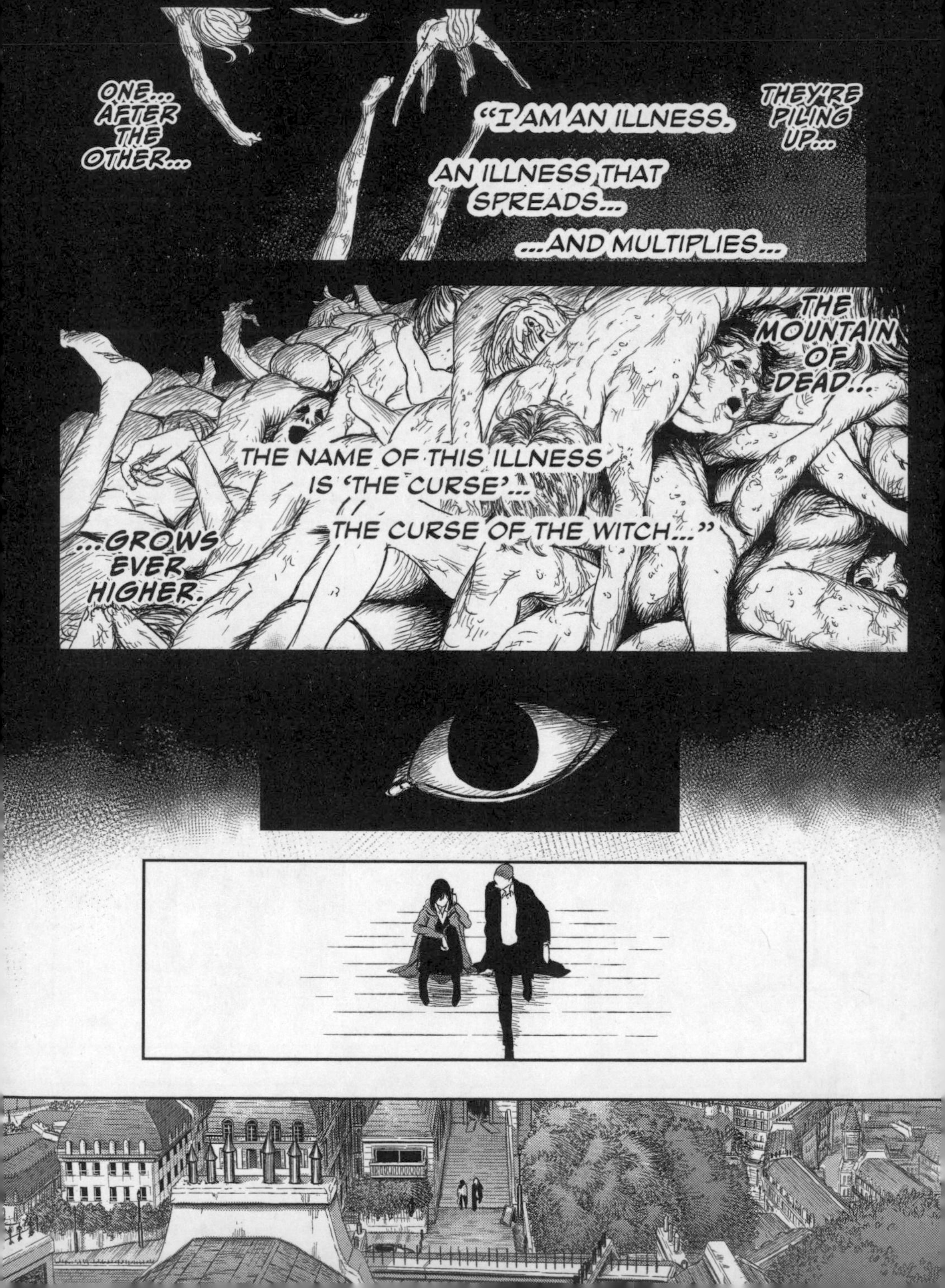
THEY'RE PILING UP...
"I AM AN ILLNESS.
AN ILLNESS THAT SPREADS...
...AND MULTIPLIES...
ONE... AFTER THE OTHER...
THE MOUNTAIN OF DEAD...
THE NAME OF THIS ILLNESS IS 'THE CURSE'...
THE CURSE OF THE WITCH..."
...GROWS EVER HIGHER.

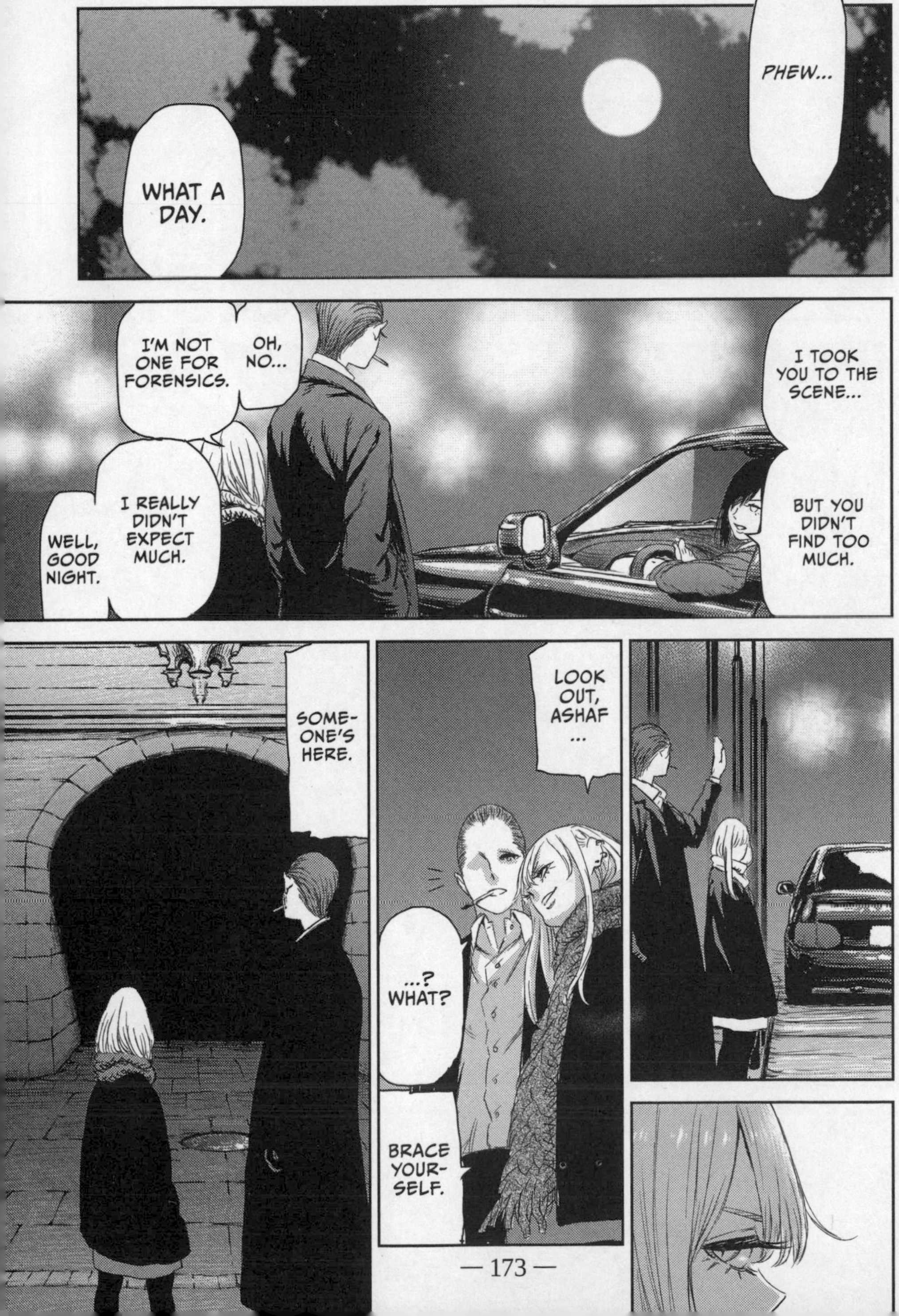
PHEW...
WHAT A DAY.
I TOOK YOU TO THE SCENE...
BUT YOU DIDN'T FIND TOO MUCH.
OH, NO...
I'M NOT ONE FOR FORENSICS.
I REALLY DIDN'T EXPECT MUCH.
WELL, GOOD NIGHT.
LOOK OUT, ASHAF ...
...? WHAT?
BRACE YOURSELF.
SOMEONE'S HERE.

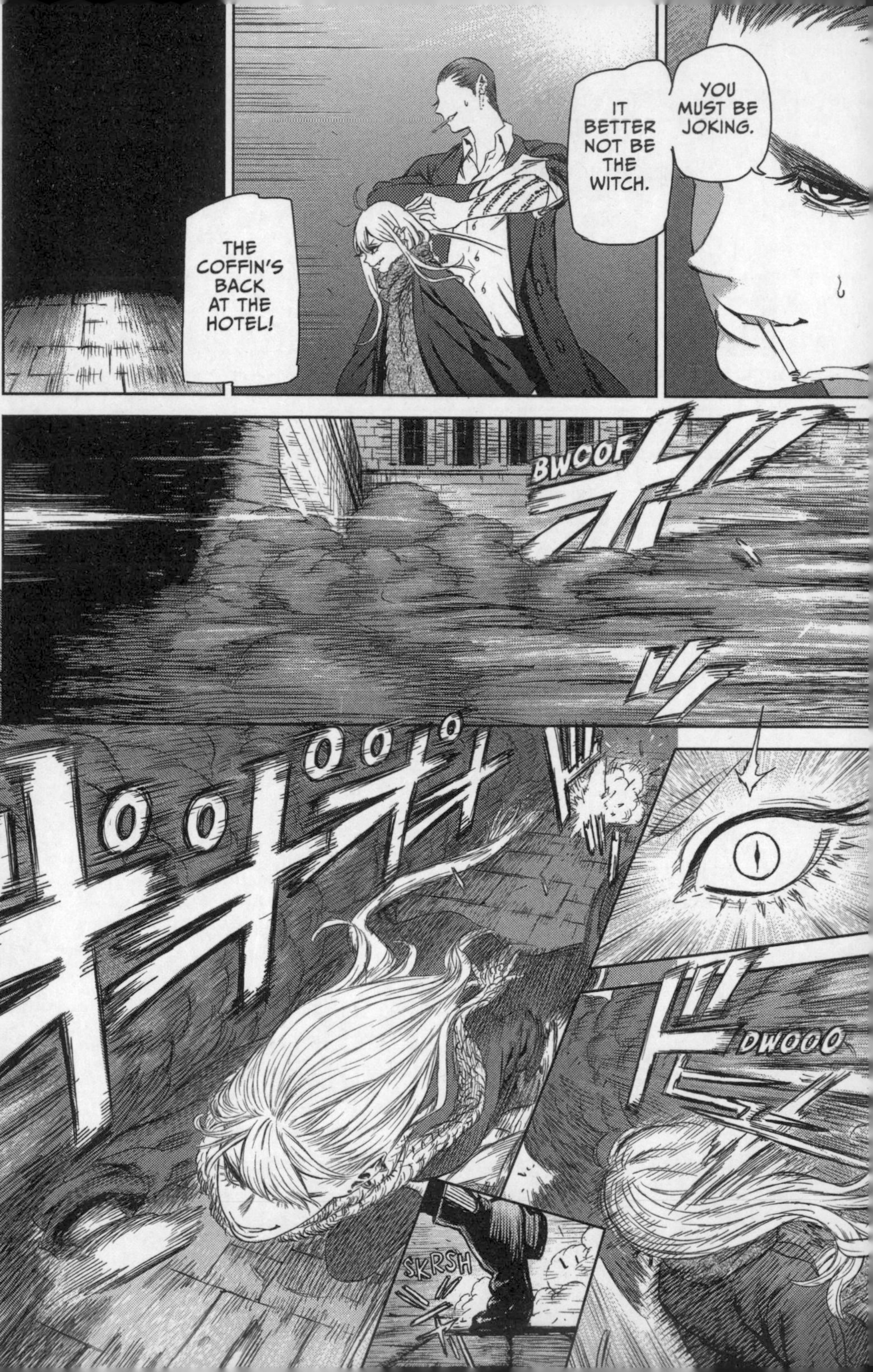
YOU MUST BE JOKING.
IT BETTER NOT BE THE WITCH.
THE COFFIN'S BACK AT THE HOTEL!
BWCOF
DWOOO
HOOOOOO
SKRSH

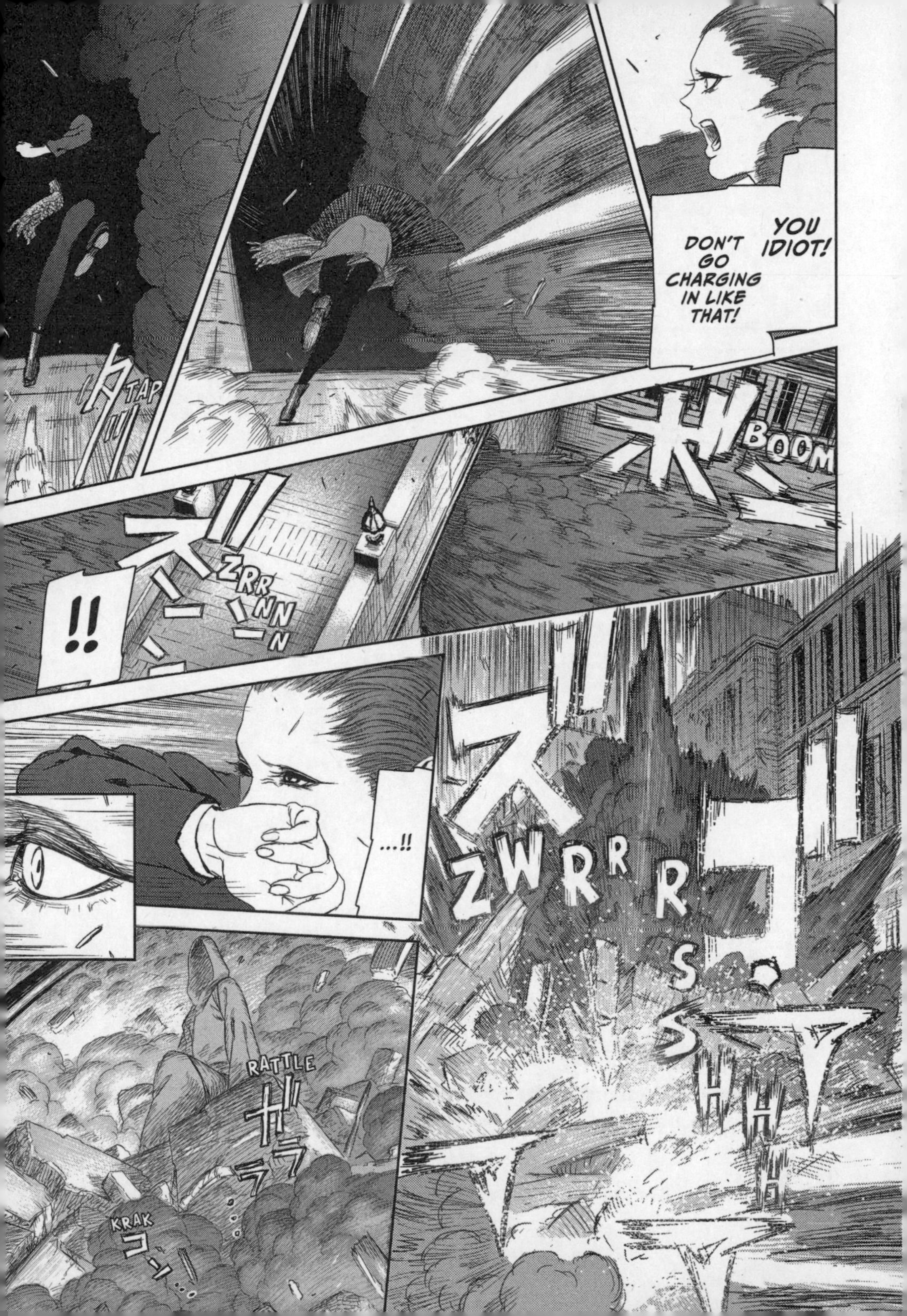

YOU IDIOT!
DON'T GO CHARGING IN LIKE THAT!
TAP
BOOM
ZRRNNN
!!
ZWRRRSSHHH
...!!
RATTLE
KRAK

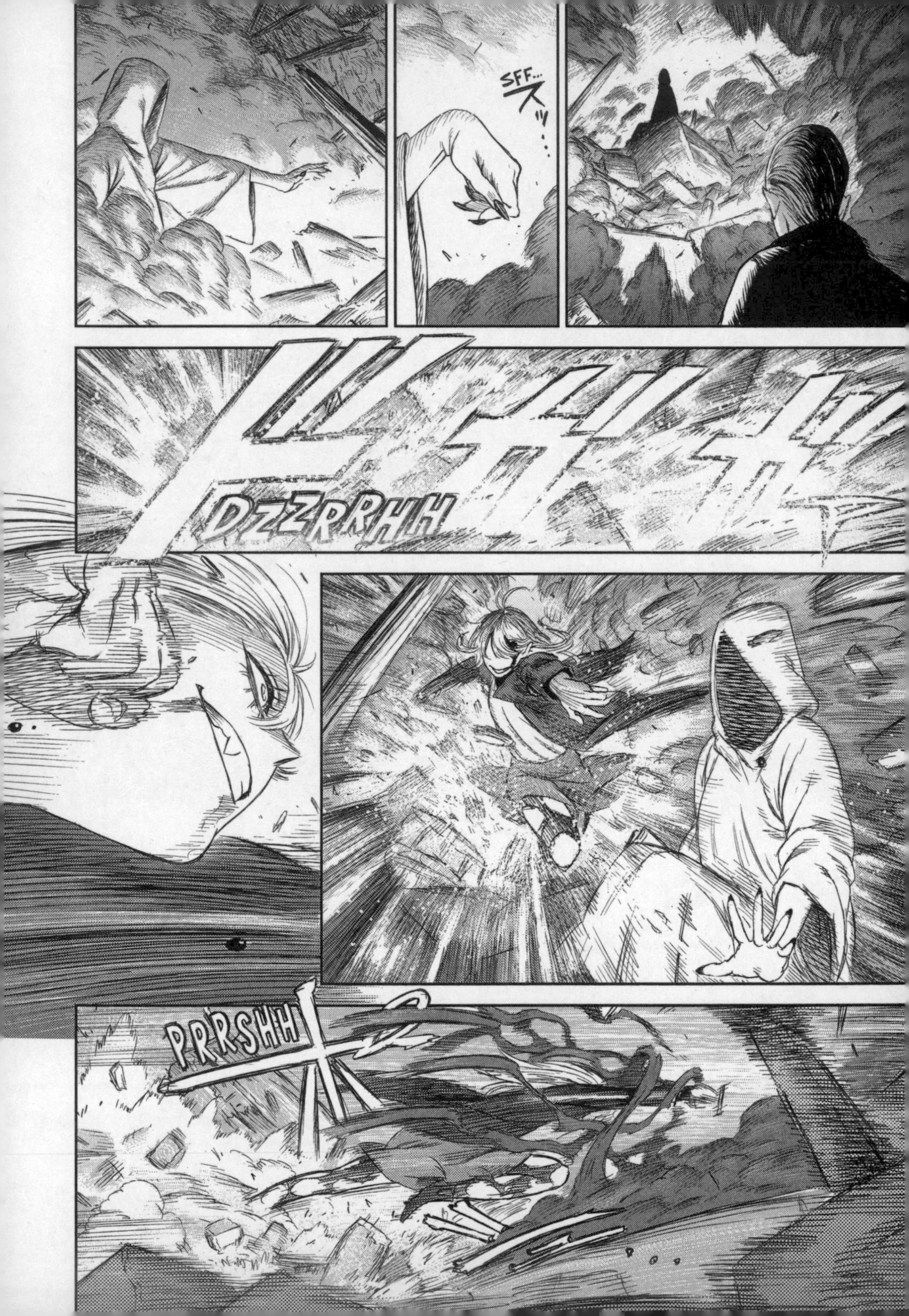
SFF...
DZZRRHH
PRRSHH

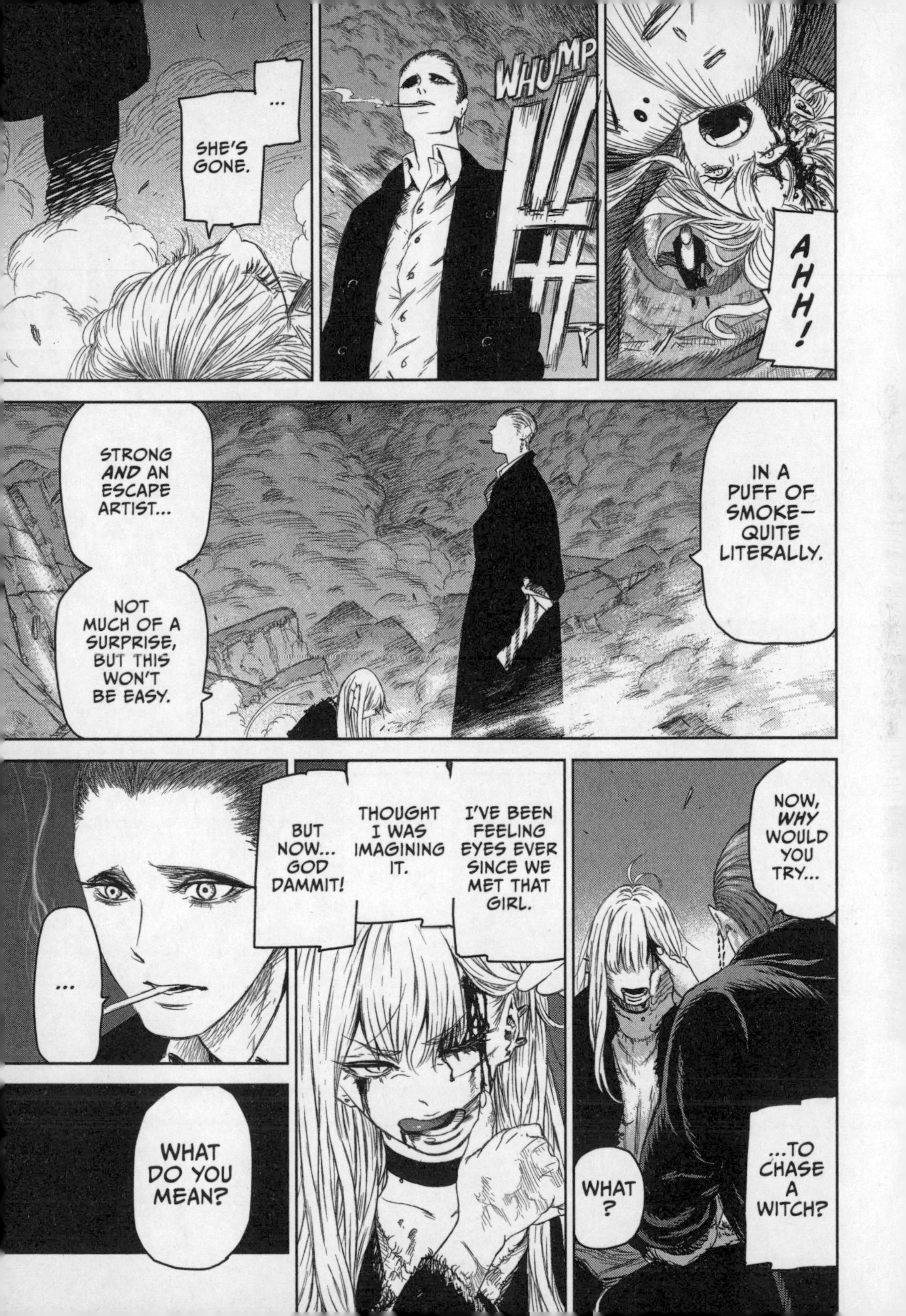
AHH!
WHUMP
...
SHE'S GONE.
IN A PUFF OF SMOKE—QUITE LITERALLY.
STRONG *AND* AN ESCAPE ARTIST...
NOT MUCH OF A SURPRISE, BUT THIS WON'T BE EASY.
NOW, *WHY* WOULD YOU TRY...
...TO CHASE A WITCH?
WHAT?
I'VE BEEN FEELING EYES EVER SINCE WE MET THAT GIRL.
THOUGHT I WAS IMAGINING IT.
BUT NOW... GOD DAMMIT!
...
WHAT DO YOU MEAN?

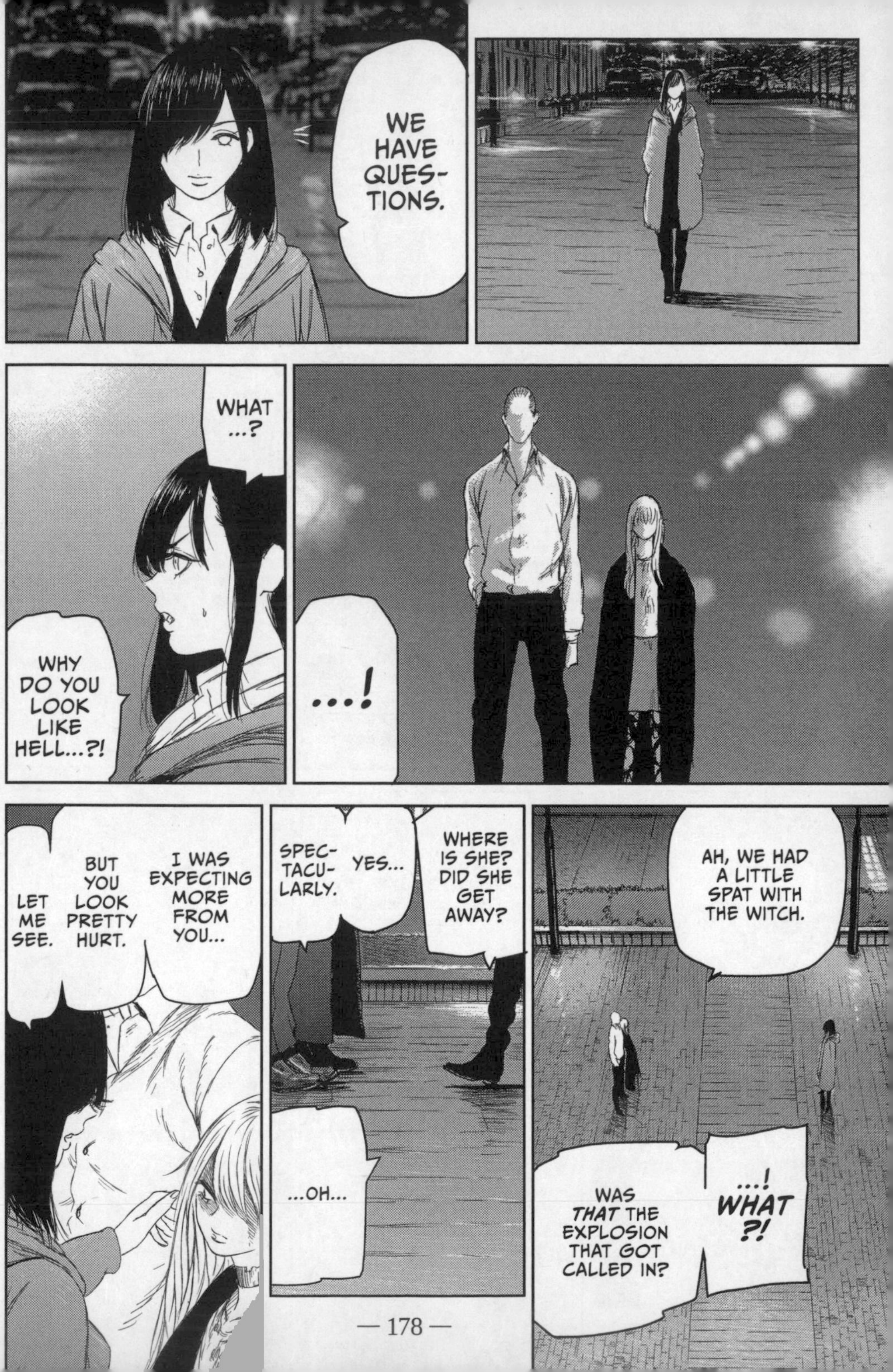
WE HAVE QUES-TIONS.
...!
WHAT ...?
WHY DO YOU LOOK LIKE HELL...?!
AH, WE HAD A LITTLE SPAT WITH THE WITCH.
...! WHAT ?!
WAS *THAT* THE EXPLOSION THAT GOT CALLED IN?
WHERE IS SHE? DID SHE GET AWAY?
YES...
SPEC-TACU-LARLY.
...OH...
I WAS EXPECTING MORE FROM YOU...
BUT YOU LOOK PRETTY HURT.
LET ME SEE.

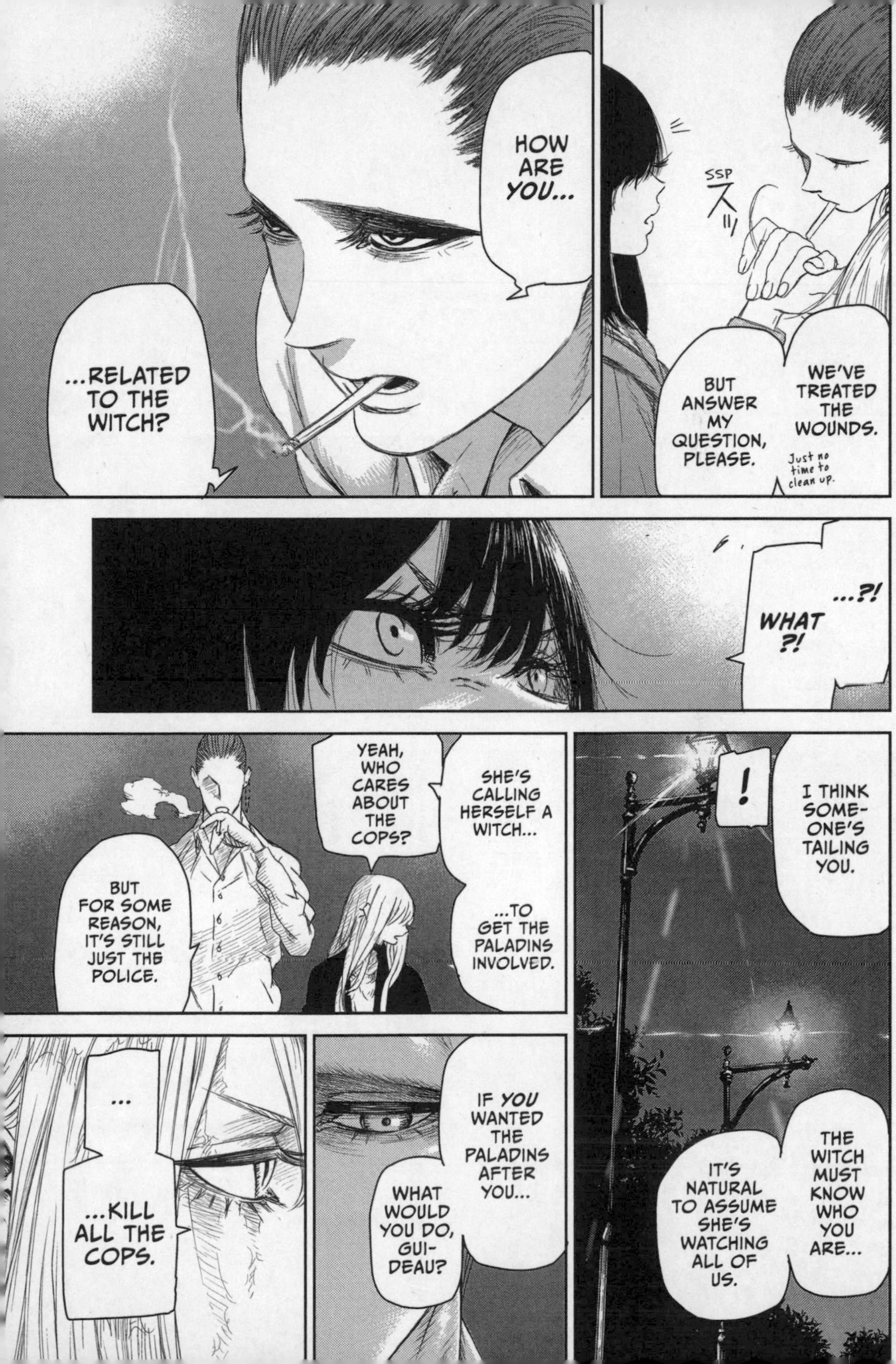
WE'VE TREATED THE WOUNDS.
Just no time to clean up.
SSP
BUT ANSWER MY QUESTION, PLEASE.
HOW ARE *YOU*...
...RELATED TO THE WITCH?
...?!
WHAT ?!
!
I THINK SOMEONE'S TAILING YOU.
THE WITCH MUST KNOW WHO YOU ARE...
IT'S NATURAL TO ASSUME SHE'S WATCHING ALL OF US.
SHE'S CALLING HERSELF A WITCH...
...TO GET THE PALADINS INVOLVED.
YEAH, WHO CARES ABOUT THE COPS?
BUT FOR SOME REASON, IT'S STILL JUST THE POLICE.
IF *YOU* WANTED THE PALADINS AFTER YOU...
WHAT WOULD YOU DO, GUIDEAU?
...
...KILL ALL THE COPS.

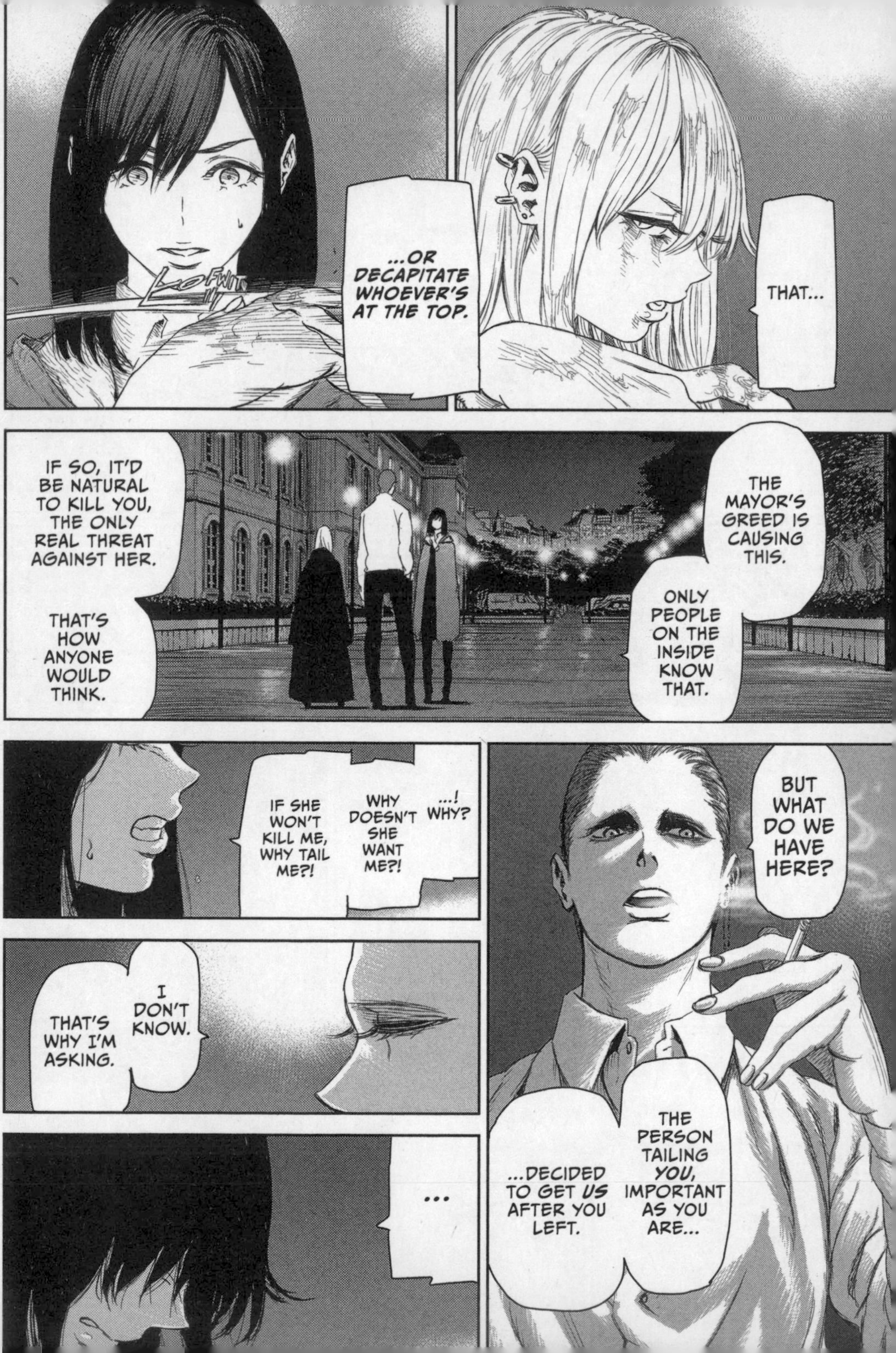
THAT...
...OR DECAPITATE WHOEVER'S AT THE TOP.
THE MAYOR'S GREED IS CAUSING THIS.
ONLY PEOPLE ON THE INSIDE KNOW THAT.
IF SO, IT'D BE NATURAL TO KILL YOU, THE ONLY REAL THREAT AGAINST HER.
THAT'S HOW ANYONE WOULD THINK.
BUT WHAT DO WE HAVE HERE?
THE PERSON TAILING *YOU*, IMPORTANT AS YOU ARE...
...DECIDED TO GET *US* AFTER YOU LEFT.
...! WHY?
WHY DOESN'T SHE WANT ME?!
IF SHE WON'T KILL ME, WHY TAIL ME?!
I DON'T KNOW.
THAT'S WHY I'M ASKING.
...

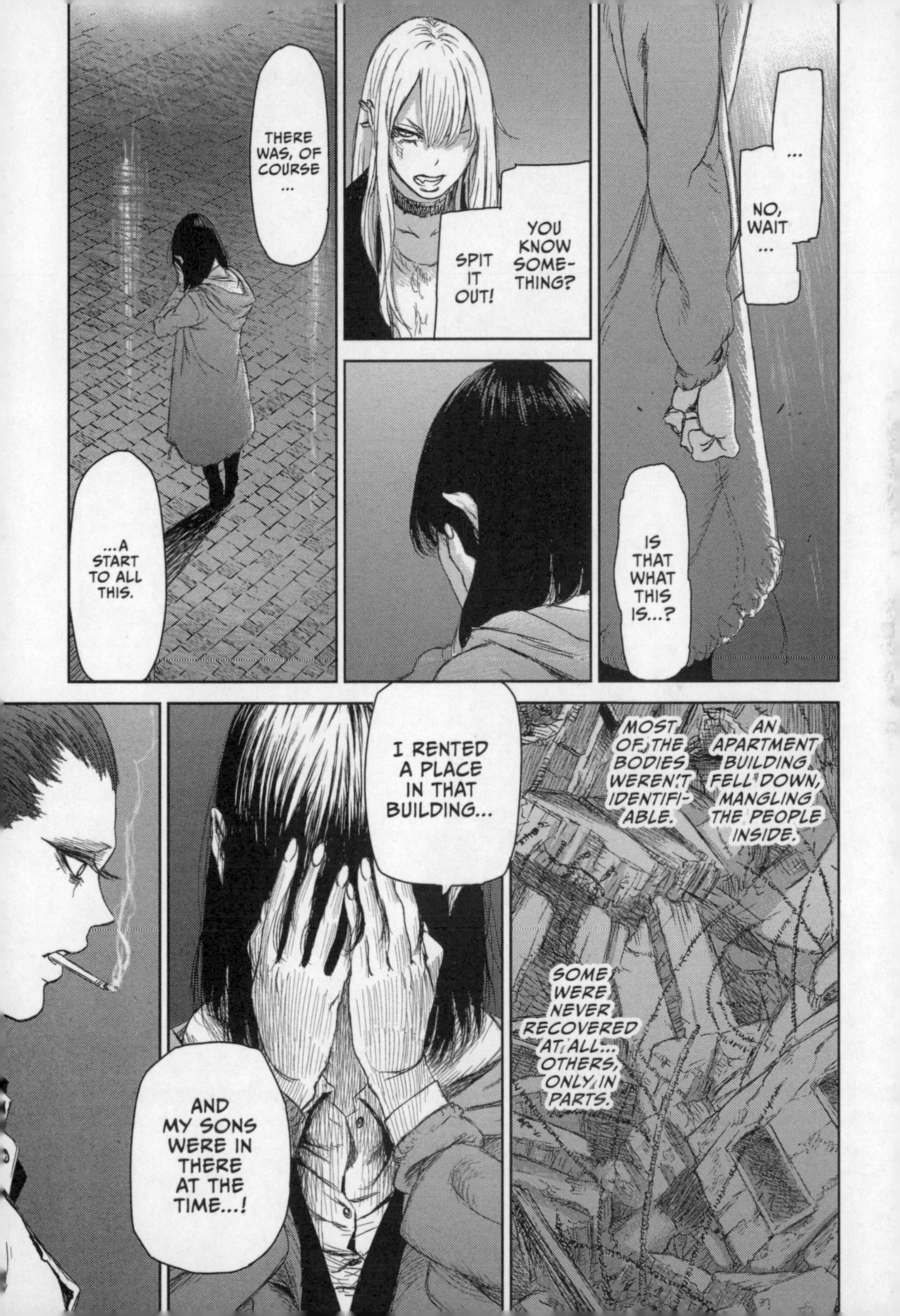
...
NO, WAIT ...
IS THAT WHAT THIS IS...?
YOU KNOW SOME-THING?
SPIT IT OUT!
THERE WAS, OF COURSE ...
...A START TO ALL THIS.
AN APARTMENT BUILDING FELL DOWN, MANGLING THE PEOPLE INSIDE.
MOST OF THE BODIES WEREN'T IDENTIFI-ABLE.
SOME WERE NEVER RECOVERED AT ALL... OTHERS, ONLY IN PARTS.
I RENTED A PLACE IN THAT BUILDING...
AND MY SONS WERE IN THERE AT THE TIME...!

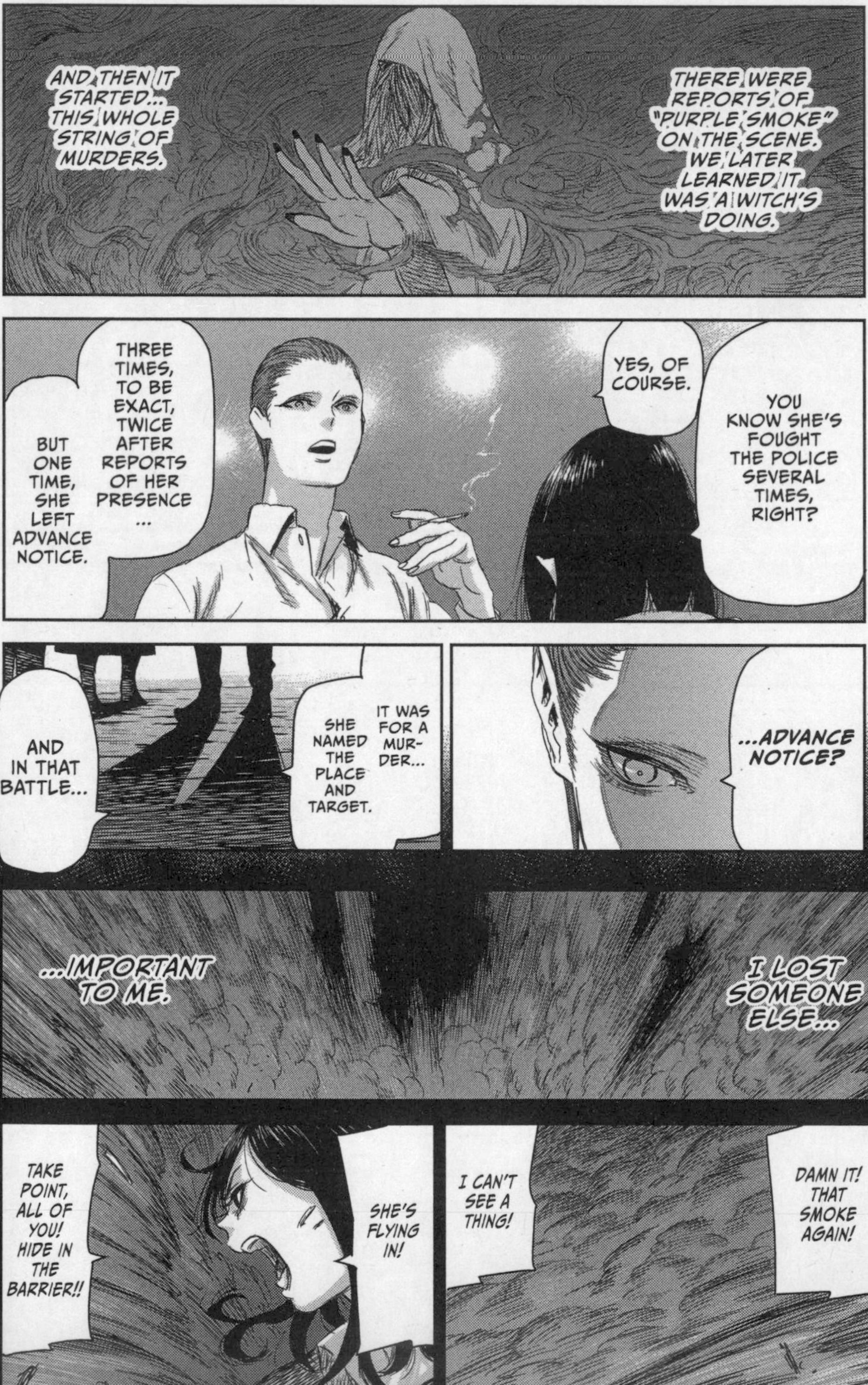
THERE WERE REPORTS OF "PURPLE SMOKE" ON THE SCENE. WE LATER LEARNED IT WAS A WITCH'S DOING.
AND THEN IT STARTED... THIS WHOLE STRING OF MURDERS.
YOU KNOW SHE'S FOUGHT THE POLICE SEVERAL TIMES, RIGHT?
YES, OF COURSE.
THREE TIMES, TO BE EXACT, TWICE AFTER REPORTS OF HER PRESENCE...
BUT ONE TIME, SHE LEFT ADVANCE NOTICE.
...ADVANCE NOTICE?
IT WAS FOR A MURDER...
SHE NAMED THE PLACE AND TARGET.
AND IN THAT BATTLE...
I LOST SOMEONE ELSE...
...IMPORTANT TO ME.
DAMN IT! THAT SMOKE AGAIN!
I CAN'T SEE A THING!
SHE'S FLYING IN!
TAKE POINT, ALL OF YOU! HIDE IN THE BARRIER!!

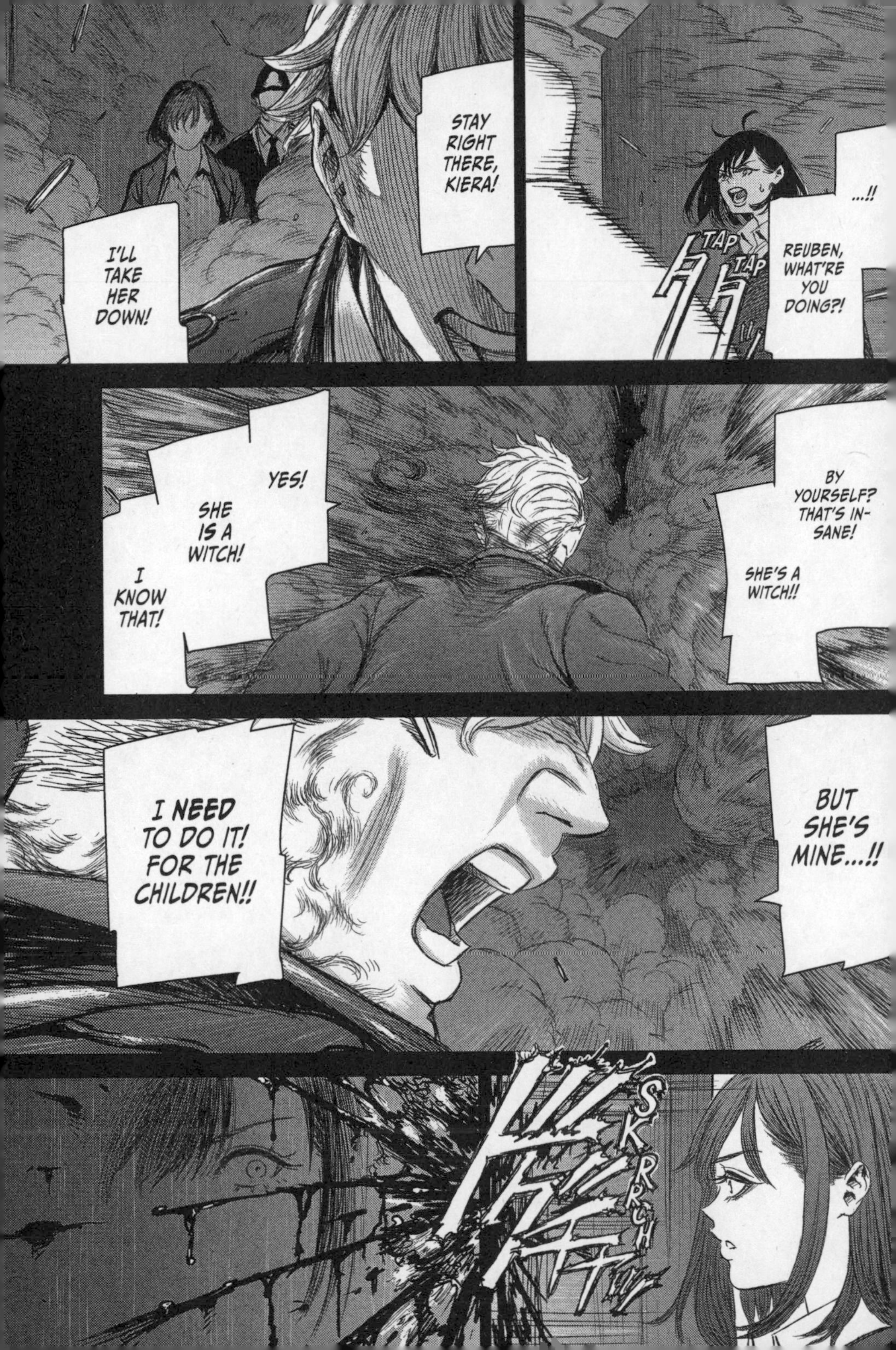
...!!
TAP TAP
REUBEN, WHAT'RE YOU DOING?!
STAY RIGHT THERE, KIERA!
I'LL TAKE HER DOWN!
BY YOURSELF? THAT'S IN-SANE!
SHE'S A WITCH!!
YES!
SHE IS A WITCH!
I KNOW THAT!
BUT SHE'S MINE...!!
I NEED TO DO IT! FOR THE CHILDREN!!
SKRRCH

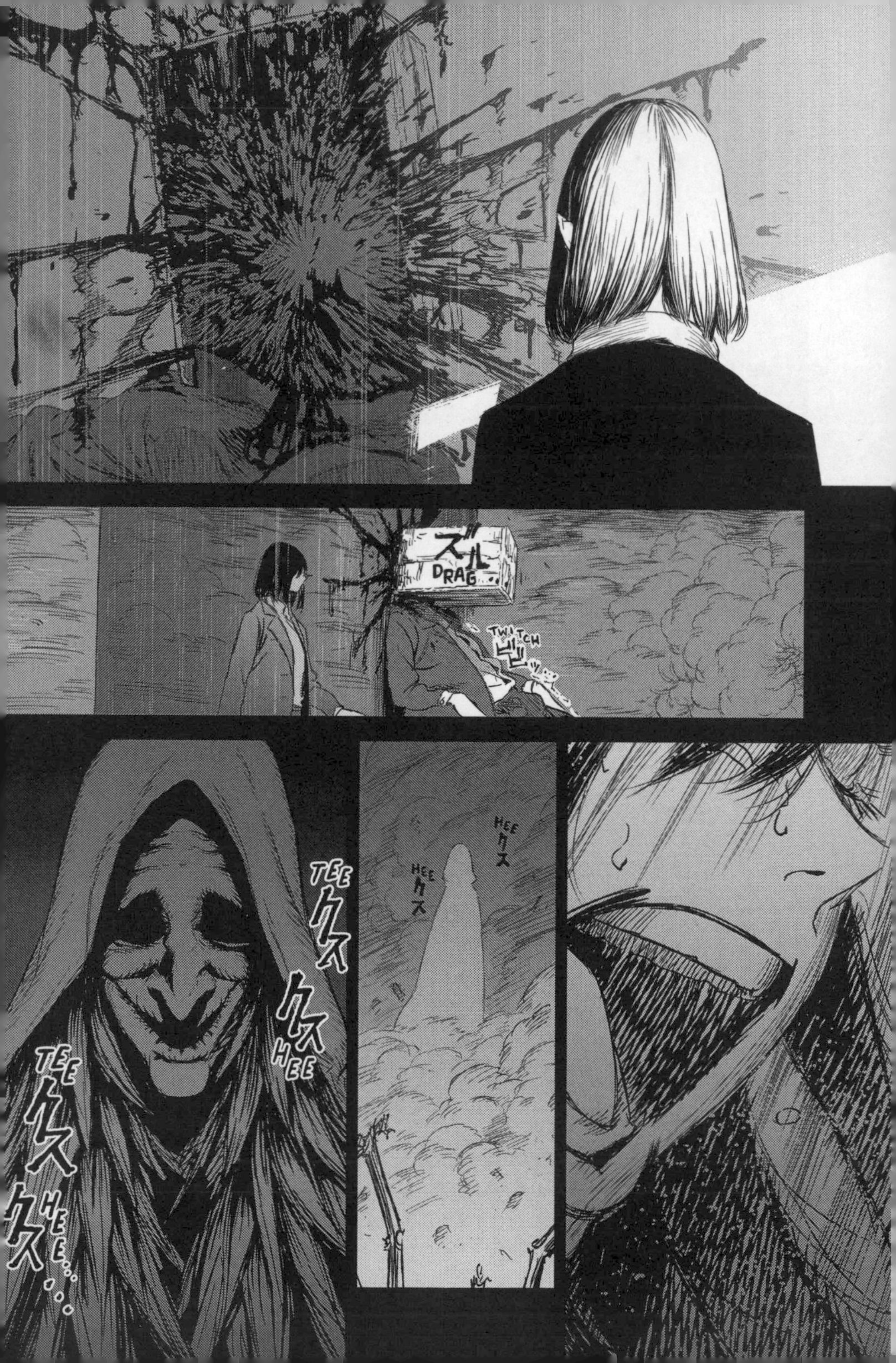

ズル
DRAG...
TWITCH
ビビッ...
HEE クス
HEE クス
TEE クス
クス HEE
TEE クス
クス HEE...

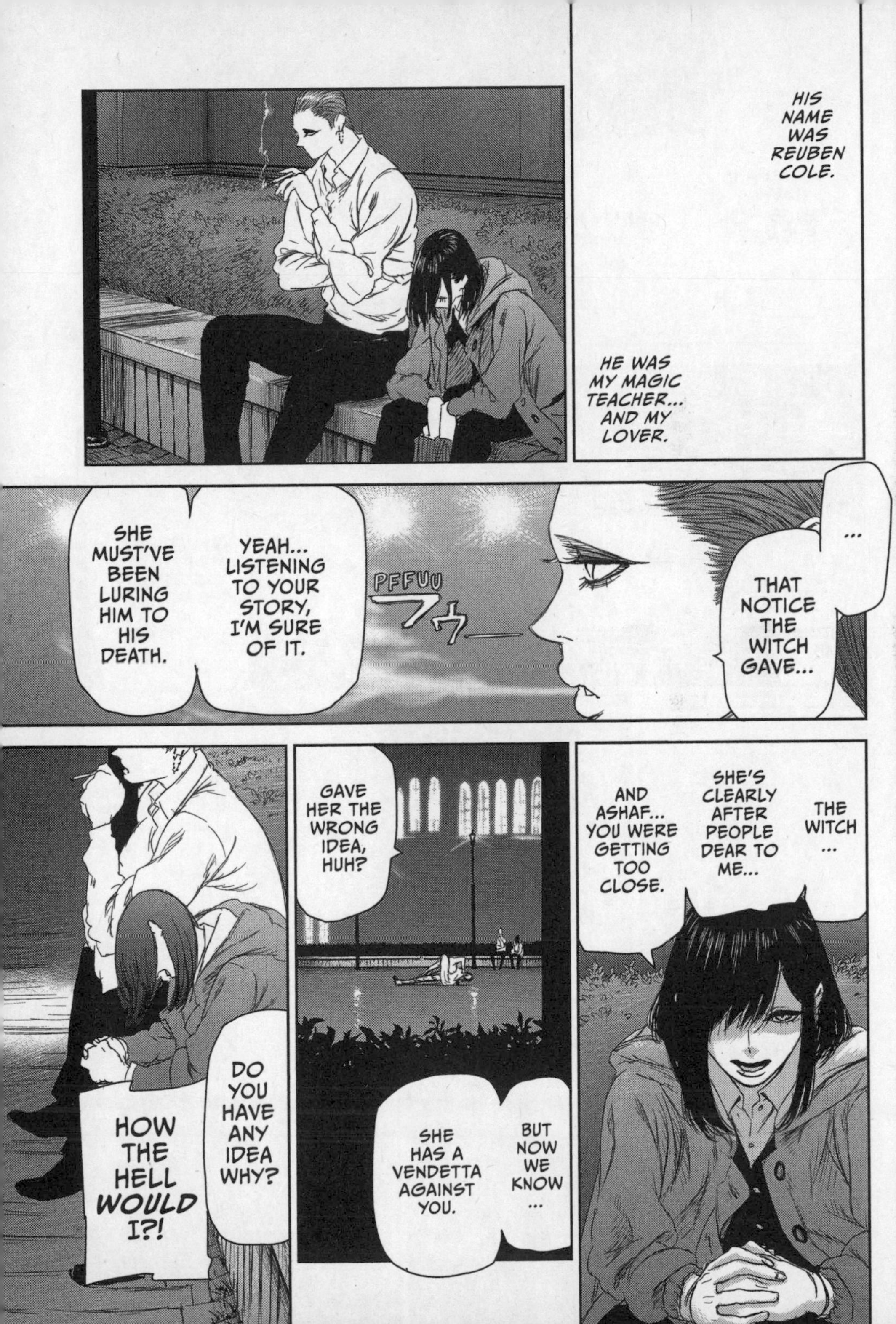
HIS NAME WAS REUBEN COLE.
HE WAS MY MAGIC TEACHER... AND MY LOVER.
... THAT NOTICE THE WITCH GAVE...
PFFUU
フゥー
YEAH... LISTENING TO YOUR STORY, I'M SURE OF IT.
SHE MUST'VE BEEN LURING HIM TO HIS DEATH.
THE WITCH ...
SHE'S CLEARLY AFTER PEOPLE DEAR TO ME...
AND ASHAF... YOU WERE GETTING TOO CLOSE.
GAVE HER THE WRONG IDEA, HUH?
BUT NOW WE KNOW ...
SHE HAS A VENDETTA AGAINST YOU.
DO YOU HAVE ANY IDEA WHY?
HOW THE HELL *WOULD* I?!

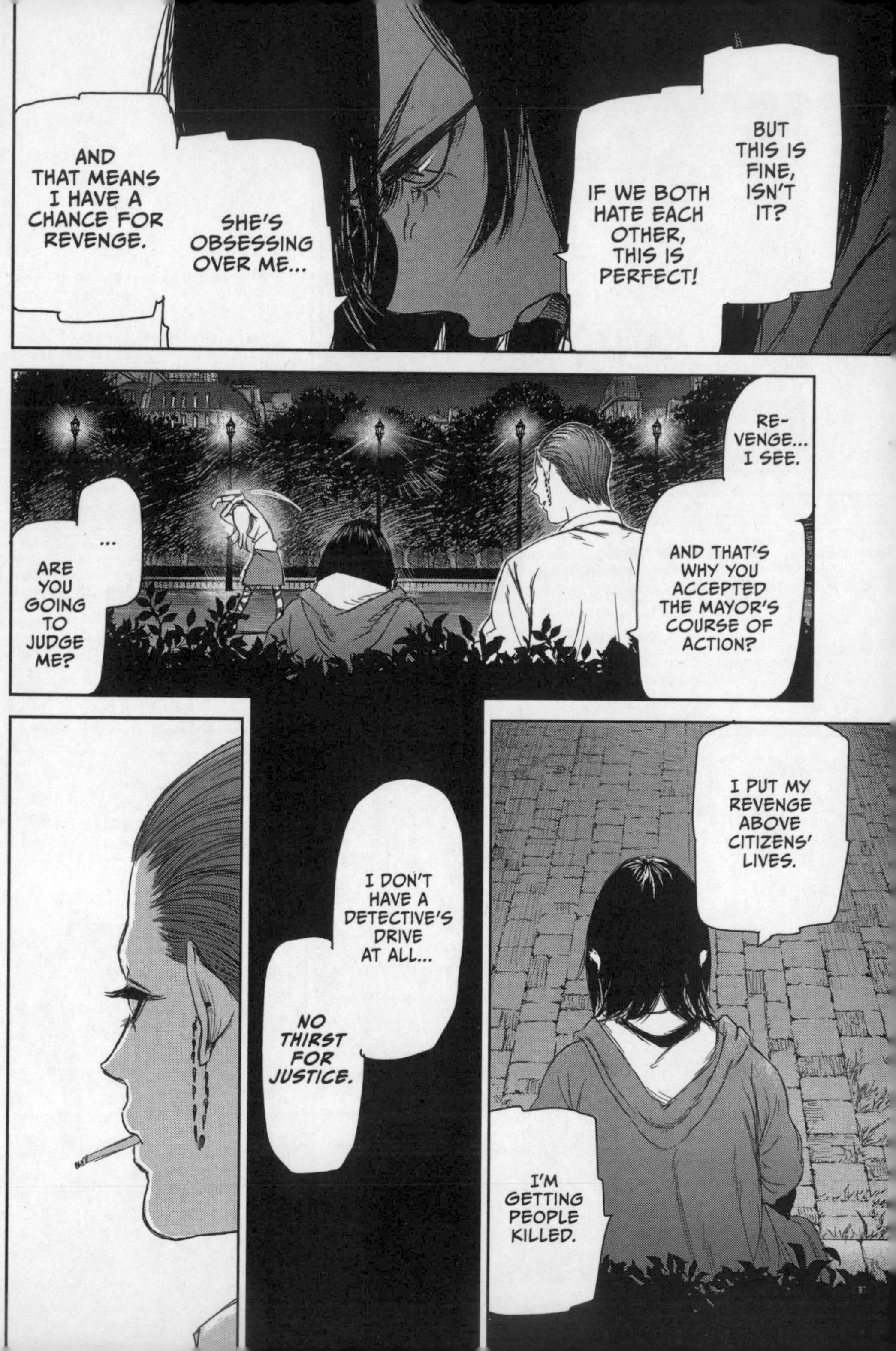
BUT THIS IS FINE, ISN'T IT?
IF WE BOTH HATE EACH OTHER, THIS IS PERFECT!
SHE'S OBSESSING OVER ME...
AND THAT MEANS I HAVE A CHANCE FOR REVENGE.
RE-VENGE... I SEE.
AND THAT'S WHY YOU ACCEPTED THE MAYOR'S COURSE OF ACTION?
...
ARE YOU GOING TO JUDGE ME?
I PUT MY REVENGE ABOVE CITIZENS' LIVES.
I'M GETTING PEOPLE KILLED.
I DON'T HAVE A DETECTIVE'S DRIVE AT ALL...
NO THIRST FOR JUSTICE.

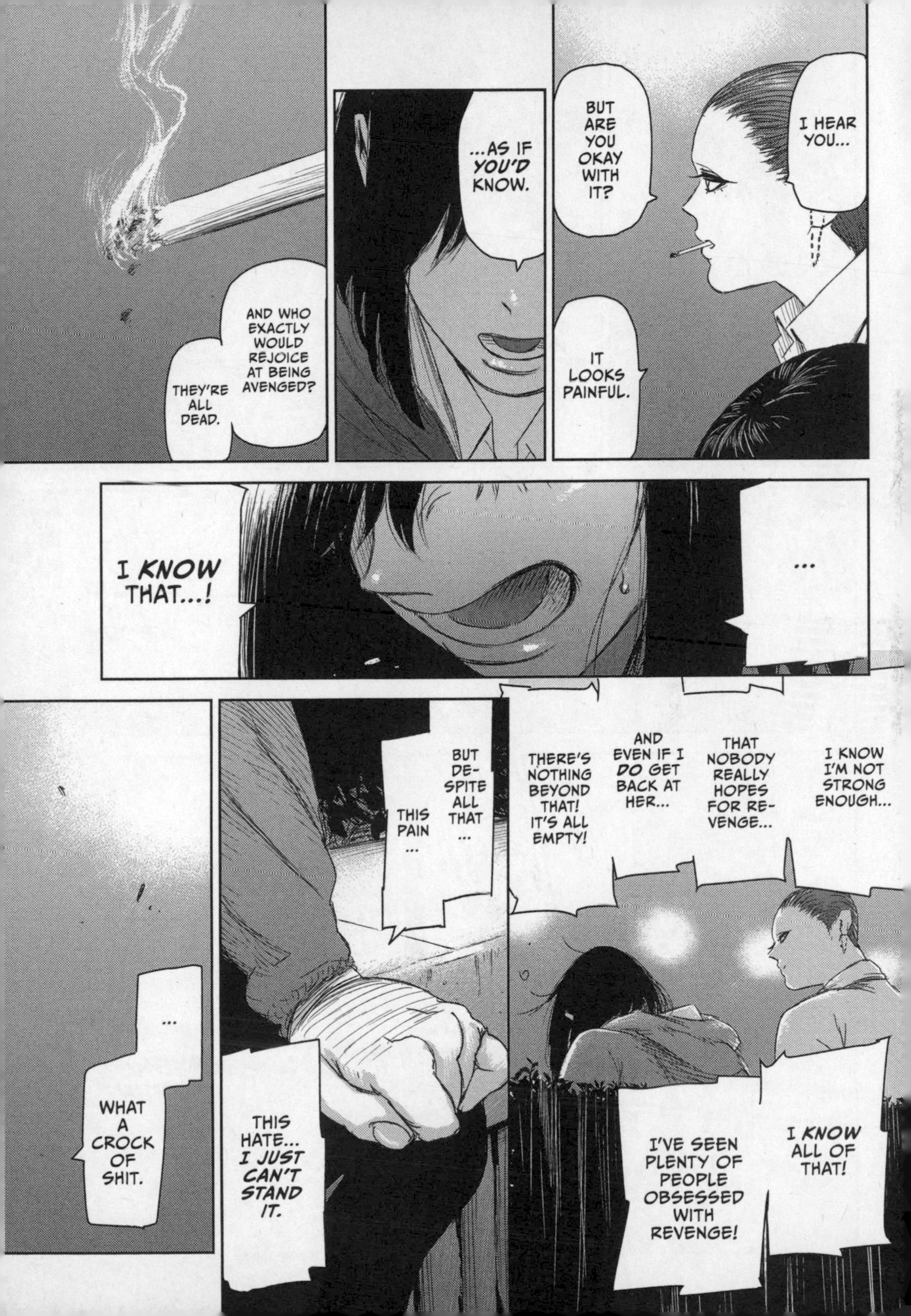
I HEAR YOU...
BUT ARE YOU OKAY WITH IT?
IT LOOKS PAINFUL.
...AS IF *YOU'D* KNOW.
AND WHO EXACTLY WOULD REJOICE AT BEING AVENGED?
THEY'RE ALL DEAD.
...
I *KNOW* THAT...!
I KNOW I'M NOT STRONG ENOUGH...
THAT NOBODY REALLY HOPES FOR RE-VENGE...
AND EVEN IF I *DO* GET BACK AT HER...
THERE'S NOTHING BEYOND THAT! IT'S ALL EMPTY!
I *KNOW* ALL OF THAT!
I'VE SEEN PLENTY OF PEOPLE OBSESSED WITH REVENGE!
BUT DE-SPITE ALL THAT...
THIS PAIN...
THIS HATE... *I JUST CAN'T STAND IT.*
...
WHAT A CROCK OF SHIT.

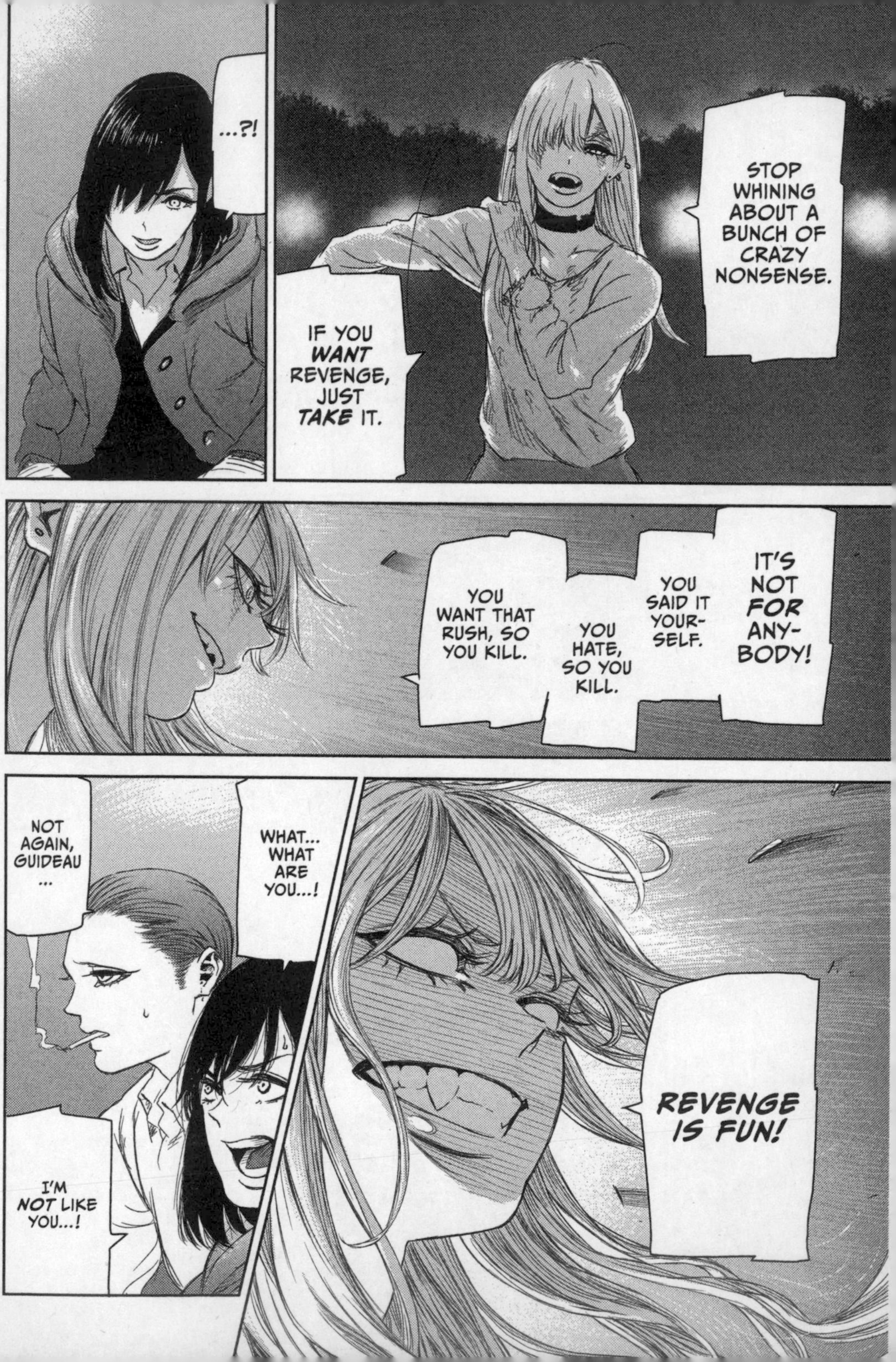
STOP WHINING ABOUT A BUNCH OF CRAZY NONSENSE.
IF YOU *WANT* REVENGE, JUST *TAKE* IT.
...?!
IT'S NOT *FOR* ANYBODY!
YOU SAID IT YOURSELF.
YOU HATE, SO YOU KILL.
YOU WANT THAT RUSH, SO YOU KILL.
REVENGE IS FUN!
WHAT... WHAT ARE YOU...!
NOT AGAIN, GUIDEAU ...
I'M *NOT* LIKE YOU...!

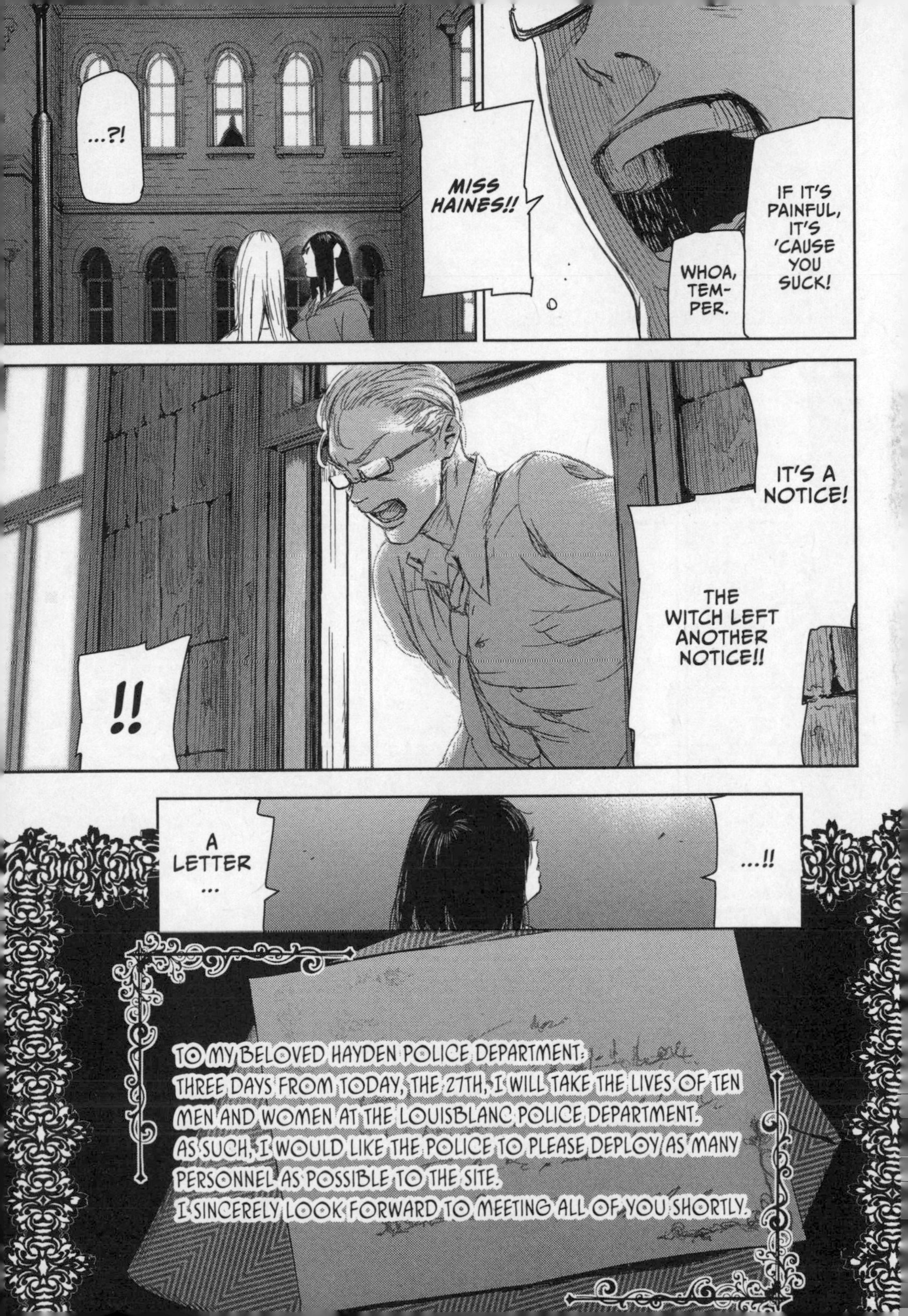
IF IT'S PAINFUL, IT'S 'CAUSE YOU SUCK!
WHOA, TEMPER.
MISS HAINES!!
...?!
IT'S A NOTICE!
THE WITCH LEFT ANOTHER NOTICE!!
!!
...!!
A LETTER ...
TO MY BELOVED HAYDEN POLICE DEPARTMENT:
THREE DAYS FROM TODAY, THE 27TH, I WILL TAKE THE LIVES OF TEN MEN AND WOMEN AT THE LOUISBLANC POLICE DEPARTMENT.
AS SUCH, I WOULD LIKE THE POLICE TO PLEASE DEPLOY AS MANY PERSONNEL AS POSSIBLE TO THE SITE.
I SINCERELY LOOK FORWARD TO MEETING ALL OF YOU SHORTLY.

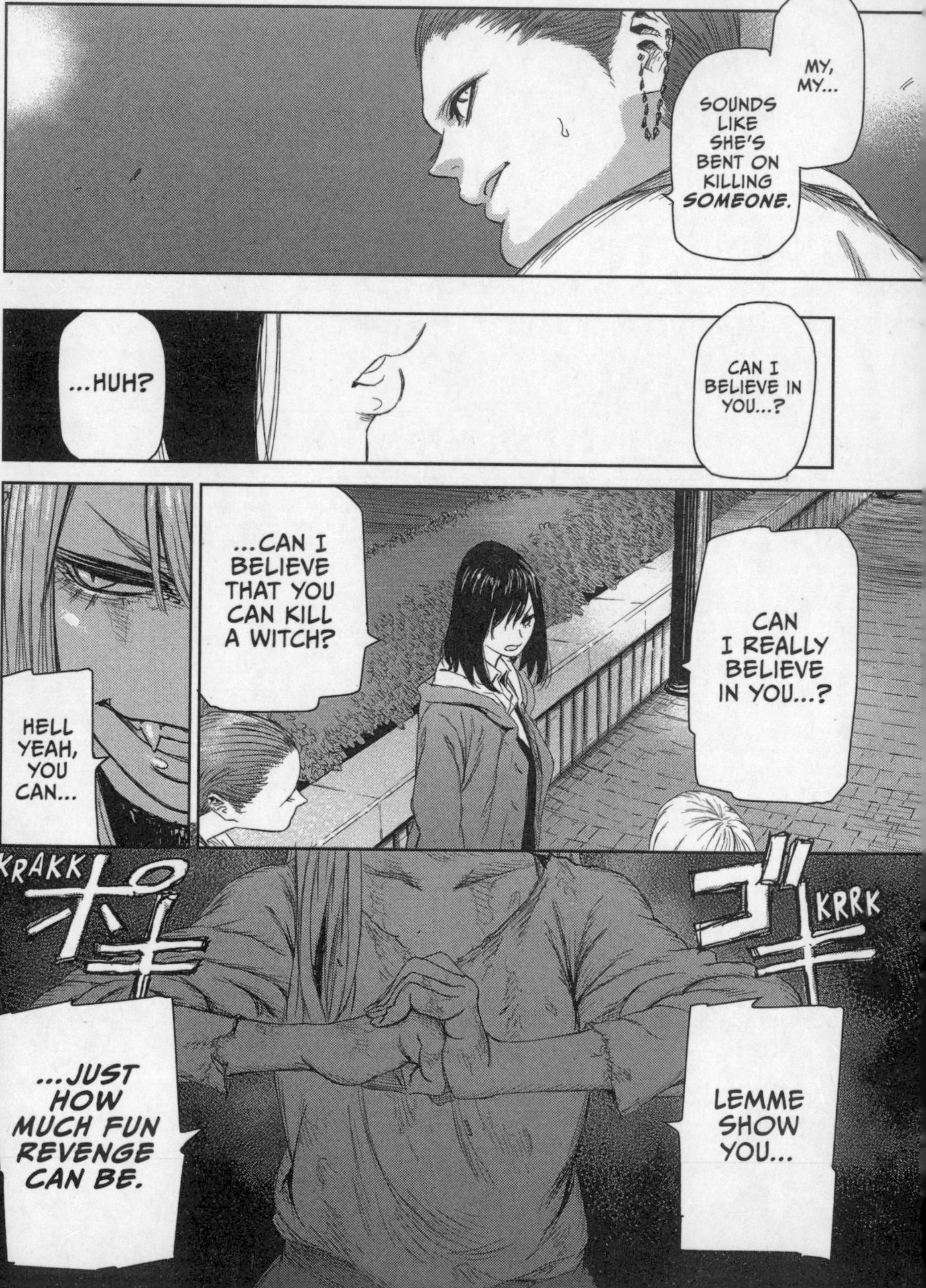
MY, MY... SOUNDS LIKE SHE'S BENT ON KILLING *SOMEONE.*
CAN I BELIEVE IN YOU...?
...HUH?
CAN I REALLY BELIEVE IN YOU...?
...CAN I BELIEVE THAT YOU CAN KILL A WITCH?
HELL YEAH, YOU CAN...
ゴキ
KRRK
LEMME SHOW YOU...
KRAKK
ポキ
...JUST HOW MUCH FUN REVENGE CAN BE.

THE WITCH AND THE BEAST

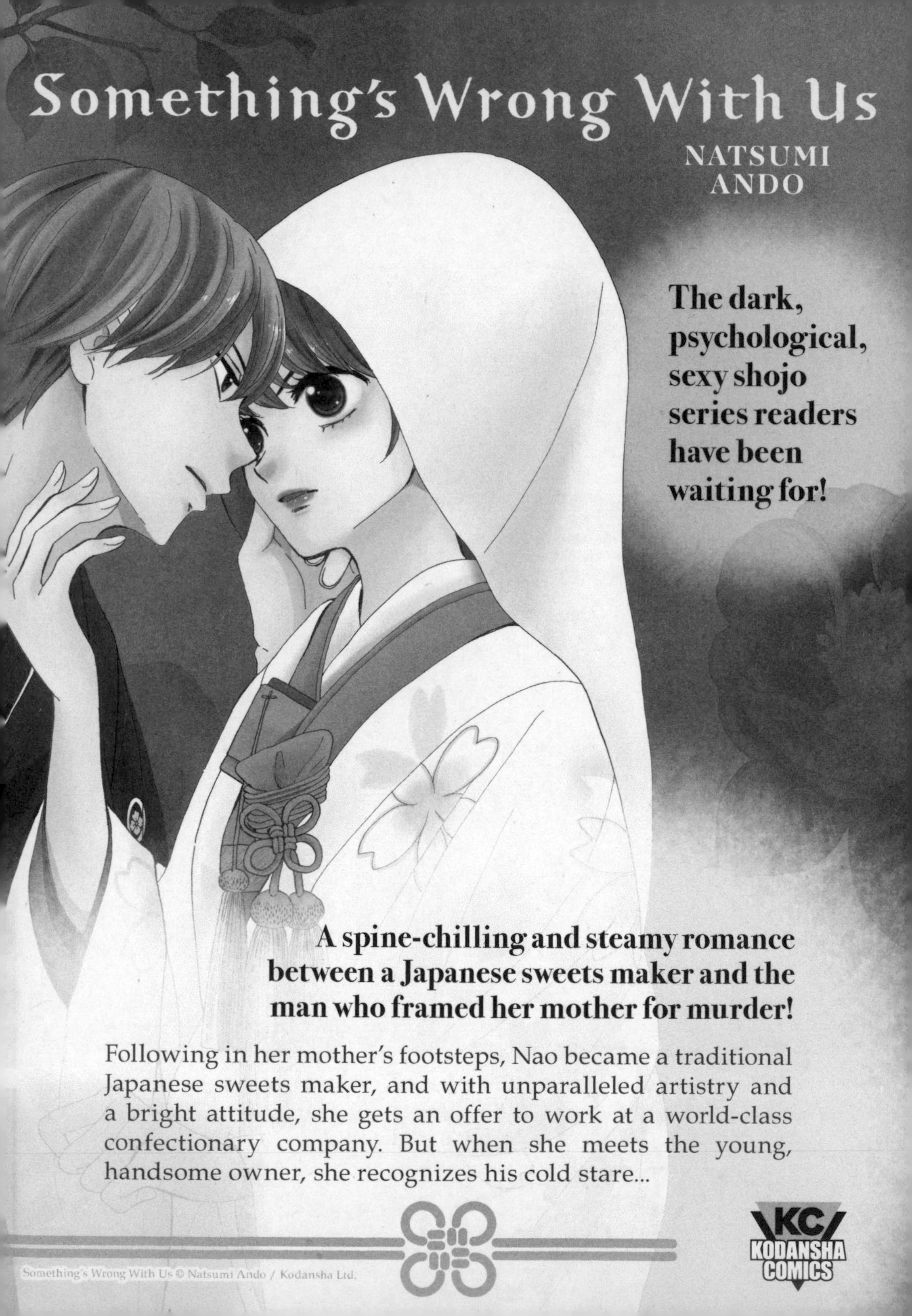
Something's Wrong With Us
NATSUMI ANDO
The dark, psychological, sexy shojo series readers have been waiting for!
A spine-chilling and steamy romance between a Japanese sweets maker and the man who framed her mother for murder!
Following in her mother's footsteps, Nao became a traditional Japanese sweets maker, and with unparalleled artistry and a bright attitude, she gets an offer to work at a world-class confectionary company. But when she meets the young, handsome owner, she recognizes his cold stare...
Something's Wrong With Us © Natsumi Ando / Kodansha Ltd.
KC KODANSHA COMICS

THE SWEET SCENT OF LOVE IS IN THE AIR! FOR FANS OF OFFBEAT ROMANCES LIKE *WOTAKOI*

Sweat and Soap © Kintetsu Yamada / Kodansha Ltd.

In an office romance, there's a fine line between sexy and awkward... and that line is where Asako — a woman who sweats copiously — meets Koutarou — a perfume developer who can't get enough of Asako's, er, scent. Don't miss a romcom manga like no other!

KC
KODANSHA
COMICS

A SMART, NEW ROMANTIC COMEDY FOR FANS OF *SHORTCAKE CAKE* AND *TERRACE HOUSE*!

A romance manga starring high school girl Meeko, who learns to live on her own in a boarding house whose living room is home to the odd (but handsome) Matsunaga-san. She begins to adjust to her new life away from her parents, but Meeko soon learns that no matter how far away from home she is, she's still a young girl at heart — especially when she finds herself falling for Matsunaga-san.

Knight of the ICE

Yayoi Ogawa

Knight of the Ice ©Yayoi Ogawa/Kodansha Ltd.

SKATING THRILLS AND ICY CHILLS WITH THIS NEW TINGLY ROMANCE SERIES!

A rom-com on ice, perfect for fans of *Princess Jellyfish* and *Wotakoi*. Kokoro is the talk of the figure-skating world, winning trophies and hearts. But little do they know... he's actually a huge nerd! From the beloved creator of *You're My Pet* (*Tramps Like Us*).

Chitose is a serious young woman, working for the health magazine *SASSO*. Or at least, she would be, if she wasn't constantly getting distracted by her childhood friend, international figure skating star Kokoro Kijinami! In the public eye and on the ice, Kokoro is a gallant, flawless knight, but behind his glittery costumes and breathtaking spins lies a secret: He's actually a hopelessly romantic otaku, who can only land his quad jumps when Chitose is on hand to recite a spell from his favorite magical girl anime!

KC
KODANSHA
COMICS

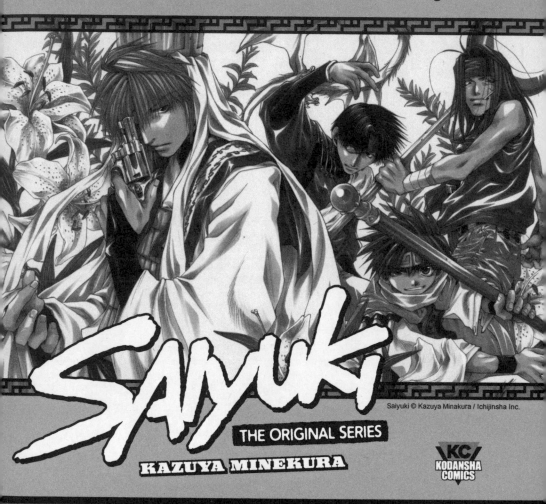

Young characters and steampunk setting, like *Howl's Moving Castle* and *Battle Angel Alita*

Beyond the Clouds © 2018 Nicke / Ki-oon

A boy with a talent for machines and a mysterious girl whose wings he's fixed will take you beyond the clouds! In the tradition of the high-flying, resonant adventure stories of Studio Ghibli comes a gorgeous tale about the longing of young hearts for adventure and friendship!

A Kodansha Comics Trade Paperback Original
The Witch and the Beast 1 copyright © 2017 Kousuke Satake
English translation copyright © 2020 Kousuke Satake

All rights reserved.

Published in the United States by Kodansha Comics, an imprint of Kodansha USA Publishing, LLC, New York.

Publication rights for this English edition arranged through Kodansha Ltd., Tokyo.

First published in Japan in 2017 by Kodansha Ltd., Tokyo as *Majo to yaju*, volume 1.

ISBN 978-1-64651-021-4

Original cover design by Yusuke Kurachi (Astrorb)

Printed in the United States of America.

www.kodansha.us

9 8 7 6 5 4 3
Translation: Kevin Gifford
Lettering: Phil Christie
Editing: Vanessa Tenazas
Kodansha Comics edition cover design by My Truong

Publisher: Kiichiro Sugawara

Director of publishing services: Ben Applegate
Associate director of operations: Stephen Pakula
Publishing services managing editor: Noelle Webster
Assistant production manager: Emi Lotto, Angela Zurlo
Logo and character art ©Kodansha USA Publishing, LLC